HITLER'S RELIGION

"Drawing on careful and thorough research, Prof. Weikart provides an overview of what we can know with a reasonable level of confidence about Hitler's religious beliefs and those of his inner circle. The picture that emerges reveals a public persona carefully crafted by Hitler that sought to avoid alienating his support base in Germany, which was to a great extent churchgoing. But in private Hitler led his top aids in developing a subtle strategy to gradually destroy any traces of religious faith that would dissent from his maniacal plans to redraw the map of Europe, eliminate all Jews, and extirpate from human consciousness the idea that all human beings have an equal dignity and value before God, and a call from God to love all people as neighbors, with particular care for the weak. This is an important book that deserves a wide audience beyond academia."

—Charles Bellinger, associate professor of theology and ethics, Brite Divinity School, Texas Christian University, and author of *The Genealogy of Violence* and *The Trinitarian Self*

"Just what was Hitler's religion? Based on a careful evaluation of a wide range of sources, Richard Weikart gives as good an answer as we are likely to get."

—Randall Bytwerk, professor of communications, emeritus, Calvin College, author of *Bending Spines: The Propagandas of Nazi Germany and the GDR*, and editor of the website *German Propaganda Archive*

"In this insightful work, Richard Weikart argues that Hitler's convoluted and often confusing religious ideas were, in the end, essentially pantheistic. Drawing together material from a wide variety of sources, Weikart is careful in his approach and, for the most part, judicious in his interpretations. While some of those interpretations may be open to debate, this book represents a major step forward in illuminating a murky, yet extremely significant, aspect of Hitler's mental universe. As such, it deserves a broad readership."

—Derek Hastings, associate professor of history, Oakland University, and author of *Catholicism and the Roots of Nazism: Religious Identity and National Socialism*

HITLER'S RELIGION

HITLER'S RELIGION

THE TWISTED BELIEFS THAT DROVE THE THIRD REICH

RICHARD WEIKART

REGNERY
HISTORY

Regnery History™ is a trademark of Salem Communications Holding Corporation;
Regnery® is a registered trademark of Salem Communications Holding Corporation

Cataloging-in-Publication Data on file with the Library of Congress

ISBN 978-1-62157-500-9

Published in the United States by
Regnery History
An imprint of Regnery Publishing
A Division of Salem Media Group
300 New Jersey Ave NW
Washington, DC 20001
www.RegneryHistory.com

Manufactured in the United States of America

10 9 8 7 6 5 4 3 2 1

Books are available in quantity for promotional or premium use. For information on discounts and terms, please visit our website: www.Regnery.com.

Distributed to the trade by
Perseus Distribution
250 West 57th Street
New York, NY 10107

CONTENTS

INTRODUCTION

THE DEBATE OVER HITLER'S RELIGION IS NOT A sterile academic controversy over the musty past, but a dispute that still arouses deep and intense passions. When Maurizio Cattelan's sculpture *Him* was placed in the Warsaw Ghetto Memorial in December 2012, it provoked considerable contention and even ire. In that exhibit, only the back of the kneeling supplicant is visible. In earlier displays of *Him* at art galleries around the world, visitors usually approached the praying figure from the back and received a jolt when they walked around to the front and recognized the face: a youthful rendition of Adolf Hitler. According to the notes accompanying one exhibition of *Him*, the "dictator is represented in the act of pleading for forgiveness." The Simon Wiesenthal Center, a Jewish organization, roundly criticized the statue's display at the Warsaw Ghetto Memorial as "a senseless provocation which insults the memory of the Nazis' Jewish victims."[1] When I first saw a photo of the sculpture, my gut reaction was negative, too, but the more I pondered it, the more I thought the sculptor might be imparting to us an important reminder: Evil often appears in the guise of piety.

It is hard for me to imagine Hitler kneeling in prayer, except perhaps during his childhood, and I rather doubt he ever indulged in such a spiritual exercise as an adult. There is certainly no evidence he ever sought forgiveness from God, for he was convinced to the end of his life that he was obeying his God. However, in his unreliable memoir, *Mein Kampf*, Hitler claimed he did kneel in prayer, at least on one occasion. When World War I broke out, he wrote, "Overpowered by stormy enthusiasm, I fell down on my knees and thanked Heaven from an overflowing heart for granting me the good fortune of being permitted to live at this time."[2] After Hitler came to power, he enjoined his fellow Germans in a 1936 speech, "Let us fall down upon our knees and beg the Almighty to grant us the strength to prevail in the struggle for freedom and the future and the honor and the peace of our Volk, so help us God!"[3] (*Volk*, a German term, is difficult to translate; it means people in the sense of an ethnic group and is sometimes translated as "nation," but this is not entirely satisfactory because, by the early twentieth century, it often had racial overtones.) Hitler intentionally cultivated an image of piety and righteousness that served him well in his climb to power and in maintaining popularity after achieving power. He wanted people to see him as a kneeling, devout supplicant.

Some people still believe in the image of Hitler the Pious and use it as a weapon against religion, while others recoil in horror at the thought that Hitler could have been religious. One of the most famous atheists in the world, Richard Dawkins, crossed swords intellectually with Pope Benedict XVI over the religious identity of Hitler and

Nazism. On his papal visit to Britain in September 2010, Benedict harshly criticized atheism and secularism while lauding Britain for having fought "against a Nazi tyranny that wished to eradicate God from society."[4] Dawkins was livid. In his article "Ratzinger [i.e., Benedict] Is an Enemy of Humanity," Dawkins reminded readers that Benedict was a former member of the Hitler Youth; thus, Dawkins maintained, Benedict should be more circumspect. Dawkins insisted that Hitler was not an atheist but a Catholic who sincerely believed in God. He even quoted a 1922 speech where Hitler called himself a Christian and referred to Jesus as "my Lord and Savior."[5] (This quotation is a favorite of atheists, appearing on dozens of atheist and secularist websites.)

This controversy over Hitler's religion—as well as the relationship between religion and Nazism in general—has raged since Hitler emerged as a significant political figure in Munich in the early 1920s. Otto Strasser, a leader in the early Nazi movement who broke away from Hitler in 1930, told his brother in the late 1920s why he was increasingly dissatisfied with Hitler: "We are Christians; without Christianity Europe is lost. Hitler is an atheist."[6] Despite the fact that Hitler never renounced his membership in the Catholic Church, before he seized power in 1933 and for about two months thereafter, the Catholic hierarchy forbade Catholics from joining the Nazi Party because they viewed Hitler's movement as fundamentally hostile to their faith. In 1937, Pope Pius XI condemned the Nazi regime, not only for persecuting the Catholic Church and harassing its clergy, but also for teaching ideology that conflicted with Catholic doctrines. The White Rose, a student resistance movement at the University of Munich that espoused Catholicism, wrote in a 1942 anti-Nazi pamphlet, "Every word that issues from Hitler's mouth is a lie. When he says peace he means war and when he most sinfully names the name of the Almighty, he means the force of evil, the fallen angel, Satan."[7] Hans and Sophie Scholl and other White Rose activists were guillotined after they were caught distributing leaflets denouncing the German atrocities in Eastern Europe and encouraging their fellow Germans to oppose the regime.

And yet, Hitler was incredibly popular during the Third Reich, almost to the very end. Most Germans who voted for Hitler or joined his party considered themselves good Christians, and many of them hailed Hitler as a protector of Christianity from the godless communists. Some Protestant pastors and Catholic priests joined the Nazi Party and cheered Hitler on, and some internationally respected Protestant theologians climbed aboard the Nazi juggernaut, too.[8] By the mid-1930s, about 600,000 German Protestants had joined the German Christian movement, which synthesized Nazi ideology and liberal Protestant theology.[9] In 1933, Hitler publicly promoted the German Christian candidates in the Protestant Church elections, giving encouragement to those who hoped for an amalgamation of Christianity and Nazism.

The conflicting views of Hitler as atheist or Hitler as devout Christian are further complicated by the widespread view of Hitler as a disciple of the occult. Hitler's evil was so intense and inexplicable that some suspect he must have had supernatural connections with the underworld that enabled him to sway the masses and rise to power in Germany. Myriads of books and films purport to prove Hitler was a follower of the black arts.

So what *was* Hitler—an atheist, a Christian, or an occultist? I demonstrate in the following pages that he was none of these three. He was not an atheist, because he sincerely believed in the existence of God. He was not a Christian, because the God he believed in was not Jesus Christ or the God of the Christian Bible. He was not an occultist, because he overtly rejected occult beliefs and mystical practices.

What, then, was his religion? After carefully sifting through Hitler's writings, speeches, and the testimony of his associates, as well as other historians' interpretations of Hitler, I have concluded that Hitler's religion was pantheism—or, if not pantheism, at least close to it. He believed that nature, or the entire cosmos, is God. My interpretation will not come as a complete shock to scholars, since I am by no means the first historian to suggest Hitler was a pantheist. However, there is still disagreement among scholars on the topic, and certainly the public remains divided on the issue. This book offers clarity to the debate through its detailed, sustained analysis of Hitler's religion—indeed, the most extensive to date in the English language.

At first glance, it might seem that Hitler's pantheistic worship of nature is incidental, a bit of trivia that does little or nothing to help us understand the man and the atrocities that he committed. But to suppose this would be a mistake. Hitler's devotion to nature as a divine being had a grim corollary: the laws of nature became his infallible guide to morality. Whatever conformed to the laws of nature was morally good, and whatever contravened nature and its ways was evil. When Hitler explained how he hoped to harmonize human society with the scientific laws of nature, he emphasized principles derived from Darwinian theory, especially the racist forms of Darwinism prominent among Darwin's German disciples. These laws included human biological inequality (especially racial inequality), the human struggle for existence, and natural selection. In the Darwinian struggle for existence, multitudes perish, and only a few of the fittest individuals survive and reproduce. If this is nature's way, Hitler thought, then he should emulate nature by destroying those destined for death. Thus, in his twisted vision of religion, Hitler believed he was serving his God by annihilating the allegedly inferior humans and promoting the welfare and prolific reproduction of the supposedly superior Aryans.[10]

Another debate that has exercised historians is whether the Nazi regime itself should be characterized as a "political religion." Most of those interpreting Nazism as such construe it as a secular substitute for the dominant religion in early twentieth-century Germany (i.e., Christianity).[11] There are some historians who interpret Nazism as a purely political movement and thus question the analytical helpfulness of the idea of political religion.[12] On the other extreme, historians insist that Nazism was not merely quasi-religious or pseudo-religious, but a full-blown religion.[13] Since the debate influences perceptions of Hitler's religion, I will address it briefly in this introduction.

There is no doubt Hitler and the Nazi Party appropriated religious symbols, terminology, and emotions in their speeches, mass rallies, and ceremonies. For instance, at the 1936 Nuremberg Party Congress, about 100,000 political leaders in the party gathered at the Zeppelin Field on Friday night. One hundred fifty powerful spotlights arranged in a rectangle around the crowd shined heavenward, creating pillars of light. The Nazis dubbed this spectacle a "cathedral of light," and before Hitler stepped up to the tribune to deliver his speech, the German Labor Front leader Robert Ley led the Nazi leadership in what he called a "confession of faith," stating, "In this hour of consecration, where an unending cathedral arches over us, proceeding into infinity, we vow: *We believe in a Lord God in heaven, who created us, who guides and protects us, and who has sent you, my Führer, to us, so that you may liberate Germany. That is what we believe, my Führer.*" According to the official Nazi report, this "confession of faith" was greeted with a roar of approval.[14] From the Nazi perspective, the beauty of this minimalist confession of faith in the outdoor cathedral was that it could potentially appeal to anyone who believed in any kind of God, whether Christian or anti-Christian, theist, deist, or pantheist. Indeed, the Nuremberg Party Rally continued through the weekend, and when it came time for the normal Sunday morning worship services for the Christian God, Hitler and the Nazi hierarchy conspicuously participated in Nazi Party festivities instead of going to church. Instead of celebrating the Lord's Day, Sunday at the

Nuremberg Party Rally was SA Day, a time to honor the SA, or Nazi stormtroopers.

The outdoor Cathedral of Light at the 1938 Nuremberg Party Rally, during which Robert Ley proclaimed that Germany had "One Volk, one Empire, one Führer."
Light Cathedral, 1938 Nuremberg Party Rally. From Der Parteitag Grossdeutschland vom 5. bis 12. September 1938: Offizieller Bericht über den Verlauf des Reichsparteitages mit sämtlichen Kongressreden (1938).

In his speech immediately after Ley's "confession of faith," Hitler gave this faith a slightly different twist, exhorting the party leaders to put their faith in the German Volk. He first rehearsed the way that Germany had risen up from its position of weakness and degradation since he had come to power four years earlier. This "miracle of renewal in our people (Volk)," Hitler suggested, came about not as a "gift from heaven for unworthy people" but because they had fanatically sacrificed for the "resurrection of a Volk." "It is the faith in our Volk that has made us small people (Menschen) great," Hitler pronounced. The future, he believed, was auspicious because the German Volk was *"born again."* The speech was saturated with religious terminology, most of it directed not toward God, but toward the German Volk. Nonetheless, Hitler closed his speech by promising the young people in Germany that if they would do their duty, "then God the Lord will never forsake our Volk."[15] This 1936 speech was not unusual, as Hitler often invoked religious themes to arouse consecration to the German Fatherland while simultaneously appealing to God as the providential creator and sustainer of the German Volk.

Apparently, Hitler liked the effects of the "cathedral of light," for the Nazis repeated it the following two years (the last party rallies held because of the advent of World War II). In his closing speech at the 1937 rally, Hitler reflected on the quasi-religious experience of that eventful week, stating, "What almost shook us several times this week was the confession of faith in a volkisch (nationalist-racist) worldview of a new generation, and more than once hundreds of thousands stood here, no longer under the impression of a political rally, but under the spell of deep prayer!"[16] At the "cathedral of light" at the 1938 Nuremberg Rally, Ley took matters a step further by almost deifying Hitler before the Führer came to the podium. During the Second German Empire (1871–1918), a common nationalist slogan had been "One Volk—one Empire—one God." Just about every German would have recognized this saying, since it was emblazoned on many postcards and even on a German postage stamp during the Second Empire. Ley used an altered version of that saying when he introduced Hitler to about 140,000 Nazi political leaders:

> One Volk—one Empire—one Führer! How often in the last decade and above all in the last years has this call of all Germans resounded upward again and again. This battle cry of all Germans is jubilation and joy for some, confession and faith for others, and pride and power for the entire German nation. Young and old, rich and poor, without distinction all Germans repeat it again and again, and so we also want to let this confession of Germans ring

out in this solemn hour in the cathedral of light: *One Empire—One Volk—One Führer!*[17]

Nazi poster proclaiming the new Nazi saying, "One Volk, one Empire, one Führer."
Nazi Poster: Ein Volk, ein Reich, ein Führer
– courtesy of Randy Bytwerk, Calvin College.

In this new slogan, which was widely disseminated in the Third Reich on posters and a postage stamp, the Führer had replaced God. Just two years earlier, Ley had led the gathered Nazi Party officials in confessing faith in a God who had sent the Führer. By 1938, the confession of faith did not even mention God and seemed to imply that Hitler was now filling His shoes.

To be sure, I doubt that Hitler ever thought he was God. But as many historians have suggested, he reveled in Messianism and often portrayed himself as the man chosen by Providence to liberate Germany and lead it to greatness. Derek Hastings concludes in his detailed examination of Hitler's early religious identity that by the time Hitler left prison in late 1924, he had come "to see his political mission in increasingly all-encompassing messianic terms."[18] In *The "Hitler Myth,"* Ian Kershaw does not use the term Messianism, as

Hastings and some other historians do, but he does note that a "pseudo-religious motivation...obviously lay for many behind the Hitler cult."[19] Indeed, plenty of Germans looked upon their Führer as a quasi-deity, elevating him high above mere mortals. After Goebbels finished reading Hitler's *Mein Kampf* in October 1925, he raved in his diary, "Who is this man? Half plebeian, half God! Actually the Christ or only John [the Baptist]?"[20] The messianic thrust of the Hitler cult manifested itself frequently, as in this Hitler Youth song at the 1934 Nuremberg Party Rally:

> We are the joyful Hitler Youth
> We need no Christian virtue
> For our Führer Adolf Hitler
> Is ever our Mediator.
> No pastor, no evil one, can hinder
> Us from feeling as Hitler's children.
> We follow not Christ but Horst Wessel,
> Away with incense and holy water.
> The church can be taken away from me,
> The swastika is redemption on the earth,
> It will I follow everywhere,
> Baldur von Schirach [leader of the Hitler Youth], take me
> along![21]

Not only was this a clear expression of a desire to replace Christianity with Nazism, but it also exalted Hitler to a position that the Christian churches gave Jesus, who is often called the Mediator in the Bible and Christian theology.

In the end, if all one means by "political religion" is the political appropriation of religious symbols, terminology, rites, ceremonies, and emotions, then clearly the Nazis excelled at this. However, is this enough for Nazism to qualify as a religion, a political religion, or a secular religion, all terms used at times to describe Nazism? I am hesitant to do so because definitions vary from one scholar to the next, making some of the debate look like shadow-boxing.

However, I want to pose a slightly different question: Did *Hitler* regard Nazism as a religion? This is easier to decipher, since he explicitly answered this question more than once. In *Mein Kampf*, he explicitly rejected the idea that he should become a religious reformer, insisting that Nazism was a political, not a religious movement.[22] In fact, throughout his career, Hitler urged neutrality on purely religious questions, and he tolerated a variety of views about religion within the Nazi Party. Some leading Nazis considered themselves Christians, while others were staunchly and forthrightly anti-Christian. Some Nazis embraced occultism, while others scoffed at it. Some promoted neo-paganism, while others considered pagan rites and ceremonies absurd. Hitler really did not care what they believed about the spiritual realm as long as it did not conflict with Nazi political and racial ideology. In October 1941, in the midst of a diatribe against the Christian churches, Hitler admitted that Nazism could never be a complete substitute for religion because it did not offer anyone a coherent position on metaphysics. Thus he counseled toleration for those who had a heartfelt desire for religion. He remarked that someone feeling a need for metaphysics cannot simply be handed the Party Program.[23]

Though Hitler dismissed the idea that Nazism was a religion, he did consider it more than just a political party or movement. He often presented Nazism as a fundamental worldview that provided a foundation for his political ideology and policies. The second volume of *Mein Kampf* contains two chapters on Weltanschauung, or worldview (rendered as "philosophy" in the standard English translation), in which Hitler argued that any successful political movement must be built on a coherent worldview. Hitler expressed the kernel of this worldview in one of these chapters:

The folkish worldview [i.e., Hitler's own position] finds the importance of mankind in its basic racial elements. In the state it sees in principle only a means to an end and construes its end as the preservation of the racial existence of man. Thus, it by no means believes in an equality of the races, but along with their difference it recognizes their higher or lesser value and feels itself obligated, through this knowledge, to promote the victory of the better and stronger, and demand the subordination of the inferior and weaker in accordance with the eternal will that dominates this universe. Thus, in principle, it serves the basic aristocratic idea of Nature and believes in the validity of this law down to the last individual. It sees not only the different value of the races, but also the different value of individuals.... But it cannot grant the right to existence even to an ethical idea if this idea represents a danger for the racial life of the bearers of a higher ethics.[24]

In this passage, Hitler hinted at his pantheism by equating the "eternal will that dominates the universe" with the "aristocratic idea of Nature." However, he clearly enunciated the central tenet of his worldview: the primacy of race. This racial worldview attempted to explain the essence of human existence and the meaning of history, while also providing moral guidance. Though this does not make Hitler's ideology a religion per se, his comprehensive philosophy of life inevitably came into conflict with many religions, because most religions also claim to provide answers to these fundamental questions. Hitler recognized this problem, maintaining in *Mein Kampf* that a worldview such as his own must be intolerant toward any other worldview that conflicts with it—and here he specifically mentioned Christianity as a rival.[25]

Hitler knew that converting Germans to his worldview would not leave the religious landscape unchanged. In an August 1933 speech, Hitler stated, "The unity of the Germans must be guaranteed by a new worldview, since Christianity in its present form is no longer equal to the demands being placed on the bearers of national unity."[26] Three years later, in his cultural speech to the Nuremberg Party Rally, he told the party faithful, "*A Christian era can only possess a Christian art, a National Socialist era only a National Socialist art.*" Hitler believed that the triumph of his worldview would transform the entire culture of Germany, whereupon it would no longer reflect previous religious concerns.[27]

Did Hitler's desire to supplant Christian culture with Nazi culture mean he was intent on secularizing German society? This is hotly debated. Already in 1947, the German theologian Walter Künneth argued that Nazism was the result of religious decay and secularization. The roots of Nazi ideology, he thought, were found in Darwin, Nietzsche, Houston Stewart Chamberlain, and Oswald Spengler, whose ideas he considered products of secularization.[28] Many scholars today agree with Künneth that Nazism is a manifestation of secularization. Detlev Peukert, for instance, argued in his seminal essay, "The Genesis of the 'Final Solution' from the Spirit of Science," for the importance of a secularized version of science in shaping Nazi ideology.[29] Claudia Koonz explicitly calls Nazis "modern secularists" and interprets the Nazi conscience as a "secular ethos."[30] Richard Steigmann-Gall, meanwhile, strenuously objects to this interpretation, arguing instead that "Nazism was not the result of a 'Death of God' in secularized society, but rather a radicalized and singularly horrific attempt to preserve God *against* secularized society."[31] And Todd Weir, while admitting that the Nazi stance toward secularism was ambiguous and even paradoxical, nevertheless argues that the Nazi's espousal of "positive Christianity" made them opponents of secularism.[32]

This question is closely linked to the debate over whether Nazism was a political religion, and it suffers from similar terminological imprecision. Part of the problem in defining secularization is that religion and secularism are often construed as polar opposites when they should be seen as two sides of a sliding scale. If by secularization we mean a process whereby any form of belief in God, the afterlife, and some kind of spiritual realm is completely discarded, then Hitler and his worldview were not secular. However, many would define secularism to include more than just atheism and agnosticism, though these are secularism's most radical expressions. In his study of the rise of organized secularism in late nineteenth and early twentieth-century Germany, Todd Weir explains that monism and pantheism were prominent forms of secularism at that time.[33] Owen Chadwick defines secularization as "a growing tendency in mankind to do without religion, or to try to do without religion." Chadwick links this decline in interest in religion with the vanishing belief in miracles and supernatural intervention in the natural world.[34] Thus, secularization does not necessarily mean that people completely abandon belief in God, but it means that God becomes irrelevant to one's practical life. Religion becomes restricted to the personal realm, having minimal impact on political, economic, or social life.

Using this definition of secular, it seems that despite Hitler's belief in God and his willingness to appeal to Divine Providence, his vision of National Socialism tilted more toward the secular than the religious side of the scale. Hitler was completely apathetic about religious practices in his personal life, and he did not really care what others believed about the nature of God or the afterlife. He consistently tried to separate politics from religion, insisting that Nazism as a political movement was neutral on religious questions. As long as the churches or other religious organizations allowed him to rule *this* world, they could say whatever they wanted about the spiritual realm. However, they were not allowed to make moral pronouncements because this impinged on the real world, where Nazism was supposed to hold sway. Hitler was clearly more focused on *this* world's concerns, which is a hallmark of a secular outlook.

I must stress, however, that even the most hardcore secularists often still retain religious influences (and Hitler was not as radically secular as most atheists or agnostics). Hitler still believed in some kind of God, and his thinking remained colored by religious elements, although in the end, earthly concerns dominated his political and racial ideology.[35] This is especially true if we consider the moral philosophy of Nazism, which centered on promoting the biological welfare and advancement of the Nordic race and often conflicted with Christian ethics. Hitler's Darwinian-inspired moral code called for the eradication of the weak, sick, and those deemed inferior, rather than universal love.[36]

Before exploring Hitler's religion in greater depth, we need to review the religious landscape in early twentieth-century Germany and Austria. This will ascertain what Hitler's religious options were. For the purposes of this book, I used the ecumenical definition of the World Council of Churches (WCC) regarding Christianity. The WCC will grant membership to any churches that "confess the Lord Jesus Christ as God and Saviour according to the scriptures, and therefore seek to fulfill together their common calling to the glory of the one God, Father, Son and Holy Spirit."[37] While not all Christian churches have joined the WCC, its definition includes the majority of Christian denominations worldwide: Roman Catholic, Lutheran, Eastern Orthodox, Anglican, Presbyterian, Methodist, Baptist, Church of Christ, United Church of Christ, Disciples of Christ, Assembly of God, Pentecostals, and many others. Two exclusions are the Jehovah's Witnesses, since they deny the deity of Jesus, and the Mormons, since they are polytheistic.

In the early twentieth century, Roman Catholicism was the dominant religion in Austria, where Hitler grew up, as well as in Bavaria, where he began his political career. Approximately one-third of the German population adhered to Catholicism, although this grew to 40 percent after Hitler annexed Austria. Almost two-thirds embraced Protestantism (54 percent after Austria was annexed). The Protestant Church was mostly Lutheran but did include a minority of Reformed (Calvinist) congregations.[38] Both the Protestant and Catholic churches were state churches, so the German government levied taxes to support them. The majority of Germans were baptized and confirmed into one of these two denominations and officially remained members until they went to city hall and petitioned to withdraw from the church. Since they were state-sponsored churches, public schools included religious instruction, often by clergy. Generally, this meant Catholic religious instruction in predominately Catholic regions and Protestant religion classes in Protestant areas. Both denominations were also allowed to establish parochial schools, though the Catholic Church took greater advantage of this right.

Catholicism in the early twentieth century adhered to traditional dogmas far more than the Protestant Church did. The Catholic Church upheld the ancient creeds, the reliability of the Bible (as interpreted by the Catholic Church), the virgin birth of Jesus, the historicity of biblical miracles, the death of Jesus for the forgiveness of sins, original sin, Jesus' bodily resurrection, and many other traditional doctrines. The Protestant Church in Germany, despite being predominately Lutheran, was more divided theologically. Beginning in the eighteenth century and increasing dramatically through the nineteenth century, German Protestantism had largely adopted theological liberalism, especially in the university theology faculties. Theological liberalism tended to dismiss many parts of the Bible as historically unreliable and rejected the miraculous. It opposed the idea of the inherent sinfulness of humanity and stressed the immanence rather than the transcendence of God. It also embraced Friedrich Schleiermacher's stress on individual religious experience or feeling, thus making religion impervious to scientific or historical criticism even while admitting such criticism's validity in the empirical realm.

Though theological liberalism dominated the German theological scene by the early twentieth century, some Protestants remained theologically conservative. Further, immediately after World War I, the Protestant theologian Karl Barth helped initiate a new movement—sometimes called neo-orthodoxy—which challenged liberal theology by emphasizing the authority of all of God's Word and stressing the sinfulness of humanity and the transcendence of God. Barth and neo-orthodox theologians did not reject biblical criticism, but they interpreted scripture in an existential sense, rather than as empirical historical claims.

Though the majority of Germans still identified as Christians, competing religious and secular philosophies had undermined the loyalty of a minority. During the eighteenth-century Enlightenment, some German intellectuals dispensed with the notion of a miracle-working God or a divine Jesus. Instead, they embraced deism, a rationalistic concept of a God who created the world to operate according to fixed scientific laws and then left it to run on its own accord. Many deists remained in the churches, especially in the Protestant Church, pushing it in a more liberal direction.

In the Romantic backlash against Enlightenment rationalism in the last decade of the eighteenth and opening decades of the nineteenth century, religion became more intellectually respectable. However, many Romantics were not entranced with traditional Christianity; they found pantheism more congenial to their mystical love of nature. Pantheism, the worship of nature or the cosmos as God, exerted a powerful influence on German intellectual life throughout the nineteenth century. In 1835, the poet Heinrich Heine asserted, "Nobody says it, but everyone knows it: pantheism is an open secret in Germany. We have in fact outgrown deism. We are free and want no thundering tyrant."[39] Sometimes known as monism, pantheism diverged into two main branches in the nineteenth century: a mystical or idealistic form and a scientific or naturalistic version. German idealism prevailed in German philosophy in the early nineteenth century, so idealistic pantheism was more pronounced then. Later in the nineteenth century, science and materialism became more significant forces in German intellectual life, giving impetus to naturalistic varieties of pantheism.[40] After World War I, pantheism experienced resurgence among German intellectuals, so it was still intellectually viable during Hitler's political career.[41]

In addition to pantheism, a position known as panentheism also emerged during the Romantic era. Panentheism is close to pantheism, but not quite the same, since it teaches that nature is a part of God, but God also transcends nature to some extent. In this view, nature is divine, but it is not *all* of God. In pantheism, God and nature are completely identical. Some scholars argue that panentheism, not pantheism, characterized the religious thought of German Romantic thinkers and artists. Nicholas Riasanovsky, however, makes this important point about both movements: "The supreme claim of pantheism or panentheism was to make men and women God. More precisely, they were parts of God; but because all divisions were ultimately unreal, they were, in effect, God himself."[42] During the Nazi period, the philosopher Kurt Hildebrandt argued that the pantheism or panentheism of German idealist philosophy—which he espoused— was the basis for any valid theory of biological evolution. He thus argued that pantheism and panentheism were the proper foundation for Nazi racial ideology.[43]

There were even more "isms" at work in Germany during this time. Materialism and positivism gained ground in the late nineteenth century, though primarily among scientists, physicians, and socialists. Materialism, the atheistic view that nothing exists but matter and energy, had achieved little traction in Germany until the 1850s, when several best-selling works on materialism created an intellectual sensation. It also received impetus in the mid- to late nineteenth century through Marxism, which dismissed all religion as the "opiate of the masses." Positivism declared that knowledge about God, the afterlife, and any other religious tenet is impossible. It opted for a thoroughgoing agnosticism, rejecting even materialism, because materialists claim to have knowledge about God (that He does not exist). Positivism had an obvious appeal to some scientists because it taught that the only path to knowledge was through scientific inquiry. Neither materialism nor positivism gained much traction in German academic philosophy, but they attracted many adherents nonetheless.

While deism, pantheism, panentheism, materialism, and positivism were more influential among the intellectual elites, other forms of religion percolated through the masses. Spiritualism and occultism increased in late nineteenth-century Germany and Austria as some people sought spiritual experiences outside the Christian churches. Rudolf Steiner's anthroposophy gained a following, as did many smaller spiritualist and occultist organizations. Various forms of occultism and neo-paganism were especially prominent in the radical nationalist scene that intersected with Hitler's early Nazi Party. Other Germans in the nineteenth and early twentieth centuries—but only small numbers compared to the whole population—were attracted to various Christian denominations, such as the Methodists, Baptists, Pentecostals, Salvation Army, and Quakers, or to other sects, such as the Jehovah's Witnesses and Mormons. However, all these remained small fringe groups compared to the two major Christian denominations. About 1 percent of the German population, meanwhile, was Jewish.

Interestingly, not all Germans who rejected the two major churches withdrew from them officially. A variety of considerations— such as family, social pressure, status, career advancement, or politics—hindered some from taking the decisive step to leave the church even after they had jettisoned its teachings and practices. (This pressure is still intense in Germany—I have talked with Germans who have no inward attachment to their church but maintain their official membership nonetheless.) One example illustrating this hesitancy is Max von Gruber, a famous professor of hygiene at the University of Munich. Gruber was promoting eugenics before and during the time Hitler was in Munich; Hitler may even have read some of Gruber's essays on eugenics in *Deutschlands Erneuerung*, a journal published by Hitler's friend Julius Friedrich Lehmann and edited by an early member of the Nazi Party. In a private letter in 1885 to his friend, Heinrich Friedjung, Gruber divulged that he was fed up with Catholicism, the faith of his upbringing, so in the next few weeks he was planning to withdraw from the church. However, even though he would prefer to register as a non-Christian, he had resolved to join the Protestant Church. Why? He did not want to put such a large cleft between his children and the rest of society, he explained. Thus, he concluded, he would go "the way of gradual transition, from Catholicism through Protestantism to Prometheanism!"[44] This reticence about leaving the church was common. Even the rabidly anticlerical biologist Ernst Haeckel remained a member of the Protestant Church until 1910, even though he had rejected Christianity already in the 1860s. It may strike modern-day Americans as bizarre, but Haeckel attacked Christianity publicly for decades even while he was still paying church taxes.

Haeckel's situation, however, highlights a conundrum: Should Haeckel be considered a Christian before 1910, despite his public attacks against the religion, just because he was baptized and confirmed in the Protestant Church, raised in a pious family, and remained an official member of the church? I do not know of anyone who has made such a nonsensical claim regarding Haeckel. Yet in Hitler's case, some seem to think these same considerations are important evidence verifying that Hitler was a Christian. And what about the positive statements that Haeckel made about Jesus and Christian ethics? Was that enough to make him a Christian? Undoubtedly not, for then Muhammed, Mahatma Gandhi, and multitudes of Buddhists, Hindus, and Muslims would be Christians, too, which is absurd. Even some atheists and agnostics have a high regard for Jesus. Does that make them Christians? Why should we treat Hitler, knowing his full body of work, differently?

Scholars and especially popular works on Hitler, in fact, have identified him with just about every major expression of religion present in early twentieth-century Germany: Catholic Christianity, non-Catholic Christianity, non-Christian monotheism, deism, pantheism, occultism, agnosticism, and atheism. One reason for this confusion is that Hitler consciously obfuscated his position whenever he thought he could gain political capital needed to secure power or retain popularity. While many of his long-term goals were fixed, he was flexible about short-term policies, and he was not averse to concealing his goals if he knew they would not be popular. I discuss this methodological problem in chapter 1 to help clear away some of the misconceptions about Hitler's religion that he himself propagated. It still amazes me that some people actually believe the public religious image that Hitler created for himself, as if Hitler would never have stooped to deceiving anyone about such important matters.[45]

Another problem creating confusion about Hitler's religion is that some people (though usually not historians, who know better) think the Nazis had a coherent religious position. Some wrongly assume that because Rosenberg or Himmler embraced neo-paganism, this must have been the official Nazi position. However, there was no official Nazi position on religion, except perhaps for the rather vague and minimalist position that some kind of God existed. Thus, looking at the views of other leading Nazis will not give us a definitive answer about Hitler's own religious perspective. To understand

Hitler's religion, we have to examine Hitler's own statements and actions, as I do in the body of this book.

ONE

WAS HITLER A RELIGIOUS HYPOCRITE?

ON APRIL 12, 1922, HITLER PROCLAIMED TO A crowd in Munich that he was a Christian: "My Christian feeling directs me to my Lord and Savior as a fighter.... As a Christian I do not have the duty to allow the wool to be pulled over my eyes, but I have the duty to be a fighter for the truth and for what is right.... As a Christian I also have a duty toward my own people."[1] Those who want to prove Hitler was a bona fide Christian frequently reference this passage. Strangely, their attitude seems to be *Hitler said it, I believe it, and that settles it*. Of course, they conveniently ignore the many other things Hitler said about God and religion.

Joseph Goebbels, based on his frequent and extensive conversations with Hitler, recorded numerous times in his diary that Hitler was anti-Christian and wanted to destroy the churches. A few days after Christmas in 1939, he conversed with Hitler and reported, "The Führer is deeply religious, but entirely anti-Christian. He sees in Christianity a symptom of decay. Rightly so. It is a strata deposited by the Jewish race."[2] In fact, Goebbels often claimed that Hitler spurned Christianity and wanted to undermine it.

Which image of Hitler is true? Were his public professions of Christianity merely the hypocritical rhetoric of a deceptive politician wooing voters, while his private anti-Christian utterances reflected his true feelings? Or did Hitler change his religious views between 1922 and 1939, so that both images reflected his genuine position at the time? Another option is to doubt *both* images. As a consummate and shrewd politician seeking supporters, was Hitler simply telling different constituencies what they wanted to hear? Maybe in 1922, he was pandering to the religious sensibilities of the Munich crowds, but in conversations with Goebbels he preyed on Goebbels' anti-Christian sympathies. Which was the authentic Hitler?

We have many reasons to be skeptical about anything Hitler professed. In general, he lied whenever he thought it would benefit him. While building up his military in the mid-1930s, he assured everyone that he was a man dedicated to peace—how dare anyone think that he harbored aggressive intentions! Though he made no secret of his contempt for the humiliating Versailles Treaty, he repeatedly asserted that he would only use peaceful means to throw off its shackles. He merely wanted Germany restored to a position of equality with other nations. When he annexed Austria in 1938, he assured the world that he had no other designs; simultaneously, he was encouraging German leaders in Czechoslovakia's Sudetenland region to foment unrest in their country so that he would have a pretext to launch a military invasion. Later in 1938, Hitler ordered his generals to prepare to invade Czechoslovakia. Fearing a devastating war, British Prime Minister Neville Chamberlain intervened, met with Hitler at the Munich Conference, and gave Hitler the Sudetenland in exchange for Hitler's pledge to be a good chap and respect the new borders of Czechoslovakia.

Today, most people shake their heads in dismay at the naïvité of Chamberlain and the British public, who largely agreed with him. His appeasement policy assumed that Hitler was an honorable man of his word who would uphold the peace settlement he signed in Munich. When he stepped off the plane from the Munich Conference, Chamberlain triumphantly held up a piece of paper, rejoicing that Hitler had signed it. Six months later, Chamberlain discovered to his dismay how much Hitler's word was worth: Hitler took over the rest of Czechoslovakia, which flagrantly violated his promise. The British prime minister finally woke up to the reality that Hitler could not be trusted. Later, the Poles, the Danes, and the Soviets also faced Hitler's aggression, despite non-aggression pacts he had signed with each of them.

It was not just Hitler's actions that proved he was not a man of his word. In private talks with like-minded Nazi officials, Hitler made it clear that he would not be bound by promises and agreements. During a November 1938 secret speech to press leaders in Munich, Hitler told them that for years he had been compelled to pose as a man of peace, but now the press needed to prepare the German people psychologically for violence to attain their foreign policy goals.[3] Over a year earlier in a private speech to Nazi leaders, he revealed the duplicitous nature of his rearmament program and his Four-Year Plan, both of which aimed at offensive warfare. He told his Nazi colleagues:

> We all know that there are some things about which we should never speak.... We know certainly, that we are building our army up, in order to keep the peace. And we are running the Four-Year Plan in order, we say, to be able

to exist economically. Only *thus* can we speak of these matters. Each of us knows that. Other thoughts will never be uttered, and that is true in very many areas. This must be an iron principle. Each one [of us] can look the other in the eye, and he can from the eyes perceive, that the other thinks exactly the same way that he thinks, and knows exactly the same as he also knows.[4]

Hitler understood that some policies must be camouflaged, since they would stir up opposition to his regime, either from other countries or within Germany. Thus he urged his followers to lie to cover up policies that might offend or antagonize others. Interestingly, he admitted this was "true in very many areas." Was religion also one of the areas where a smokescreen was required?

Plenty of evidence suggests Hitler was concerned lest he offend the religious sensibilities of the German public. In a lengthy passage in *Mein Kampf,* he warned against repeating the disastrous course that caused Georg von Schönerer's Pan-German Party to nose dive. Schönerer was an Austrian politician in the late nineteenth and early twentieth centuries who wanted to unite all Germans in a common empire. His fervent German nationalism brought him into conflict with the multi-ethnic Austro-Hungarian Empire, which would dissolve if Schönerer had his way. He also promoted a biological form of anti-Semitism, wanting to purify the German people by getting rid of this allegedly foreign race. In 1941, Hitler told his colleagues that when he arrived in Vienna in 1907, he was already a follower of Schönerer.[5] By the time he wrote *Mein Kampf,* he agreed fully with Schönerer's Pan-German ideals, affirming, "Theoretically speaking, all the Pan-German's [Schönerer's] thoughts were correct."[6] However, he blamed Schönerer for not recognizing the importance of winning the masses over to Pan-Germanism and harshly criticized him for launching the Los-von-Rom (Away-from-Rome) Movement, which

called on Austrians to abandon the Roman Catholic Church. Schönerer opposed Catholicism because he considered it an international-
ist organization that undermined nationalism. He believed it posed
a danger to the German people since it included many different
nationalities, including his enemies: the Slavic groups in the Austro-
Hungarian Empire. Schönerer himself personally left the Catholic
Church in January 1900 and joined the Lutheran denomination.
Though he occasionally lauded Luther and Protestantism, his concern
was purely political. According to Andrew G. Whiteside, a leading
expert on Schönerer, he remained a pagan at heart and was indifferent to Christianity; though sometimes he claimed to be a Christian,
at other times he admitted, "I am and remain a pagan." Another
time, he stated, "Where Germandom and Christendom are in conflict, we are Germans first.... If it is un-Christian to prefer the scent
of flowers in God's own free nature to the smoke of incense...then I
am not a Christian." According to Whiteside, "none of the Pan-
German leaders was in the least religious."[7]

Hitler viewed the Los-von-Rom Movement as an unmitigated
disaster because it unnecessarily alienated the masses from the Pan-
German Party, precipitating its decline. Hitler suggested the proper
political course would be to imbue ethnically German Catholics (and
Protestants) with nationalist sentiments so they would support a "single holy German nation," just as they had done during World War I.[8]
Hitler also rejected Schönerer's anti-Catholic crusade because he
insisted that a successful political movement must concentrate all its
fury on a single enemy. A struggle against Catholicism would dissipate
the Nazi movement's power and sense of conviction it needed to carry
on its fight against the Jews.[9] In the second volume of *Mein Kampf,*
Hitler even accused the Jews of conspiring to divide Germans from
each other by arousing religious sectarianism. By stirring up German
Catholics to fight against German Protestants, Jews were diverting
them from confronting their real threat: the Jews themselves. Hitler

insisted that his political movement should unite all Germans to oppose the Jews, becoming a party where *"the most devout Protestant could sit beside the most devout Catholic,* without coming into the slightest conflict with his religious convictions."[10] He did not care whether his fellow Germans were Protestant or Catholic (or of some other religious persuasion). However, he wanted to ensure that religion did not create divisions and thereby weaken the German Volk.

While Hitler faulted Schönerer for alienating the masses through his anti-Catholic campaign, he was not thereby endorsing Catholicism. Overall, he supported Schönerer's ideological goals and only objected to his inopportune tactics: "[The Pan-German movement's] goal had been correct, its will pure, but the road it chose was wrong."[11] What Hitler learned from Schönerer's tactical mistake was that political parties should steer clear of interfering with people's religious beliefs or attacking religious organizations: *"For the political leader the religious doctrines and institutions of his people must always remain inviolable; or else he has no right to be in politics, but should become a reformer, if he has what it takes!* Especially in Germany any other attitude would lead to a catastrophe."[12] Hitler thus warned any anticlerical members of his party to keep their antireligious inclinations private, lest they alienate the masses.

However, despite his use of the superlative, Hitler did not really think religious beliefs and institutions must *"always remain inviolable."* Just two paragraphs earlier, he had already qualified this statement by declaring, "Political parties have nothing to do with religious problems, as long as these are not alien to the nation [Volk], undermining the morals and ethics of the race." Thus, Hitler recognized there could be some cases of conflict with religious institutions, and, in these cases, the needs of the Volk would take precedence over religious beliefs or organizations. However, he clearly hoped religious conflict could be kept to a minimum. This position in *Mein Kampf* accorded fully with Point Twenty-Four of the Nazi Party's Twenty-Five Point Program, where the Nazi Party guaranteed religious freedom, but with this qualification: "We insist upon freedom for all religious confessions in the state, providing they do not endanger its existence or offend the German race's sense of decency and morality."[13] Hitler only believed in religious liberty insofar as it did not conflict with his own ideology.

In 1924, when Hitler was interned in Landsberg Prison after his failed Beer Hall Putsch, his fellow prisoner and confidante Rudolf Hess talked with other Nazis about religion. Hitler did not join the conversation; afterward, he told Hess that he dared not divulge his true feelings about religion publicly. Hitler confessed that, even though he found it distasteful, "for reasons of political expediency he had to play the hypocrite toward his church."[14] From the early days of his political activity, Hitler recognized that being a religious hypocrite had its political advantages.

In his diaries, Goebbels confirmed that Hitler camouflaged his religious position to placate the masses. Based on his conversations with Hitler more than a year before the Nazis came to power, Goebbels wrote that Hitler not only wanted to withdraw officially from the Catholic Church but even wanted to "wage war against it" later. However, Hitler knew withdrawing from Catholicism at that moment would be scandalous and undermine his chances of gaining power. Rather than commit political suicide, he would bide his time, waiting for a more opportune moment to strike against the churches. Goebbels, meanwhile, was convinced the day of reckoning would eventually come when he, Hitler, and other Nazi leaders would all leave the Church together.[15] If Hitler was being frank with Goebbels, then his public religious image was indeed a façade to avoid offending his supporters. If, on the other hand, Hitler was simply telling Goebbels what he wanted to hear, then Hitler was still masking his true religious thoughts and feelings.

Even those in Hitler's inner circle admitted that they were not sure what Hitler's religious beliefs were. After the demise of the Third Reich, Alfred Rosenberg, a close friend of Hitler from the early days of the Nazi movement, explained in his memoirs that Hitler strictly separated politics from religious beliefs and wanted to keep his own religious views hidden. Hitler told Rosenberg that one time he had been asked directly what his religious beliefs were but had refused to answer. Rosenberg confessed that even he was not sure what Hitler believed: "What his own beliefs were he never told me in so many words." Rosenberg noted that Hitler often mentioned Providence and the Almighty in his speeches, but ultimately his vision of God was vague and amorphous.[16]

In a diary entry from June 1934, Rosenberg also explained how Hitler masked his true religious feelings for political purposes. At that time, Rosenberg himself was under assault by the churches because of his anticlerical writings and speeches. Hitler told Rosenberg he should not reply to these attacks because the Saar referendum was coming up, when the people of the Saarland would decide whether to join Germany or not. Hitler did not want to alienate the Christians of the Saarland. Despite this, according to Rosenberg, Hitler divulged his anti-Christian stance and "more than once emphasized, laughing, that he had been a heathen from time immemorial," and that "the Christian poison" was approaching its demise. Rosenberg explained, however, that Hitler kept these views top secret.[17]

When one of Hitler's secretaries, Johanna Wolf, was interrogated in 1948 about Hitler's religious inclinations, she had just as much difficulty as Rosenberg in figuring out what Hitler believed. When asked if Hitler had some kind of mystic faith, she replied, "It is difficult to say. I am sure that he had some sense of something behind and beyond the daily life and that he acted in spite of that—inspired by that sense." Then she was asked, "You would not say that he was religious, would you?" She replied, "No, I wouldn't call him religious, but that sense might inspire people who are not religious in the ordinary sense of the word." Like Rosenberg, she was not able to provide any specifics of Hitler's religion.[18]

No wonder, then, that so many people today are confused about Hitler's religion. *He wanted it that way.* He was a notorious liar and made conflicting statements about his religious commitments to suit different audiences. Even his friends and associates were not always sure what his religious beliefs were. It also requires us to exercise a great deal of methodological caution in reaching our own conclusion on the extent of his religious hypocrisy. Since we know that Hitler's own statements are not trustworthy, we need to examine them carefully in context. What audience was he addressing, and why was he staking out a particular religious position at a particular time? We must also identify consistencies or inconsistencies in his statements to help discern whether they reflect his desire to placate different audiences, or if they reflect genuine changes in his personal views. Further, we should compare his statements with his actions: what were his private religious activities, and how did he treat religious leaders and organizations? By doing all this, we will gain traction toward understanding Hitler's religious beliefs.

Whatever his private religious convictions, Hitler tried to build his movement and later maintain power and popular support by pledging to respect religious liberty. The Nazi Twenty-Five Point Program of 1920 had already promised this, and after coming to power in 1933, Hitler persistently stressed his commitment to allow everyone to worship however they wanted. In a speech in Munich in November 1941, Hitler confronted the recurring accusation that his regime was antireligious. It is a complete fabrication, he assured them, that the Nazi regime wants to destroy religion. He did not care what religion anyone professed. "In the German Reich—and according to our view," Hitler stated, "everyone can be saved in his own fashion!" This last phrase—"everyone can be saved in his own fashion"—was a famous quotation from the eighteenth-century Prussian King Frederick the Great that emphasized his religious toleration. Hitler piously maintained that he had never persecuted anyone for his or her religion; the only religious leaders his regime had arrested were those who had crossed over the red line by meddling in politics.[19]

There, however, was the rub. Hitler wanted to maintain a strict division of labor with religious institutions. He really did not care what they taught people about the spiritual world or the afterlife, or what religious rites and ceremonies they conducted. But he insisted—with all the power of the state behind him—that they refrain from politics.

This might have been a workable division of labor, except that Hitler had a slightly different definition of politics than most people. For him, politics included just about everything in this life. He admitted this to a crowd in Koblenz in August 1934. He told them not to heed those negative voices proclaiming Nazism was contrary to Christianity. He also promised to protect religious institutions and not to interfere with their doctrines. But he also said, "We have only carried through a clear division between politics, which have to do with terrestrial things, and religion, which must concern itself with the celestial sphere."[20] The two spheres that Hitler envisaged for politics and religion were rather lopsided. Politics dealt with everything in this world, so religion had no say over earthly matters. Religious leaders could tell people anything they wanted about God and the afterlife, but they were meddling in politics if they taught that God issues commands valid in the here and now. After all, this would interfere with "the German race's sense of decency and morality," as Point 24 of the Nazi Party Program put it. Since most forms of religion include moral imperatives that affect behavior in the present world, Hitler's offer of religious freedom was not very robust. It only encompassed those willing to eviscerate their religion of any morality not in line with Nazi ethics.

In November 1937, Hitler explained to fellow Nazi officials his willingness to cooperate with the churches. He pledged to allow the churches complete freedom in doctrine. However, while willingly granting them complete control over the German people in relation to the other world (*Jenseits*), he reserved for the government complete control in this world (*Diesseits*). He argued that this division of responsibility was the only one tolerable. Hitler's claim that this gave the churches an "immeasurably broad field" of activity ignored the fact that the freedom of doctrine is meaningless if the state can stipulate that some doctrines—such as the Ten Commandments or any other moral teachings—are off limits.[21]

In a major speech on the sixth anniversary of the Nazi regime (the same speech where he threatened to destroy the Jews if a world war broke out), Hitler remonstrated against the "so-called democracies" for accusing his government of being antireligious. He reminded them that the German government continued to support the churches financially through taxes and pointed out that thousands of church leaders were exercising their offices unrestrained. But what about the hundreds of pastors and priests who had been arrested and thrown into prison or concentration camps? Hitler defended his regime by once again trotting out his distinction between politics and religion. Religion, according to Hitler, had complete liberty in Germany. The government had never intervened in doctrinal matters or in the conduct of church services. The only religious leaders persecuted by his regime, he smugly said, were those who criticized the government or committed egregious moral transgressions, such as sexually abusing children. He stated, "We will protect the German priest who is a servant of God, but we will destroy the priest who is a political enemy of the German Reich." Once again, Hitler's offer of religious liberty did not include the right to contradict anything the government did, even if the regime was violating basic Christian morality.[22]

Indeed, Hitler told the German churches point-blank that they had no business trying to teach the state about morality. In May 1937, he adjured the churches not to stray from their own realm of responsibility, which is religion, by meddling with the affairs of the state. "Nor is it acceptable," Hitler told the churches, "to criticize the morality of a state," when they should be policing their own morals (the Nazi regime was at this time conducting trials of Catholic clergy for sexual abuse). He continued, "The German leadership of state will take care of the morality of the German state and Volk." In Hitler's view, morality was the purview of the state and its political leaders, not religious institutions and religious leaders. Any pastor or priest teaching his congregation morality contrary to Nazi policy or ideology could be labeled a political oppositionist, even if he was simply teaching moral precepts that Christians had been teaching for centuries.[23]

In private conversations, he never seemed as friendly toward religion as in his public speeches. In one of his private monologues in December 1941, Hitler reiterated his opposition to religious leaders dabbling in politics. On this occasion, he told his entourage, "I don't concern myself about articles of faith, but I will not tolerate it, if a cleric (*Pfaffe*) concerns himself with earthly matters. The organized lie must somehow be broken, so that the state is absolute lord."[24] As in his earlier public statements, he still claimed to allow religious toleration in matters of doctrine. However, calling churches "the organized lie" is not exactly religiously neutral. Unlike in his public statements, where he feigned a little more respect for religion, this time he used the contemptuous term *Pfaffe* for priests and pastors. Most importantly, however, he revealed his primary concern: he wanted to clear away any obstacles to the state becoming "absolute lord." Churches and other religious organizations could continue to operate, but only if they recognized the state as the final arbiter of all political, social, and moral behavior.

In sum, Hitler was a savvy politician who recognized the negative repercussions of offending the German people's religious feelings. He tried to curry favor by portraying himself as a coreligionist both to

Christian audiences in public speeches and to anti-Christian Nazi Party leaders. In order to avoid schisms within his party, he usually emphasized religious neutrality. However, in his inner circle he often criticized specific religious positions. Even though he rather frequently attacked Christianity, he rarely if ever explained clearly what he believed about religion. He was a religious chameleon, a quintessential religious hypocrite.

TWO

WHO INFLUENCED HITLER'S RELIGION?

EVEN AS ALLIED BOMBERS REDUCED GERMAN cities to rubble in 1944, Hitler fantasized about his post-war architectural exploits. One of his most grandiose schemes was to transform his hometown of Linz, Austria, into the cultural capital of the Third Reich. A secretary of his remembered this as one of Hitler's favorite topics of conversation.[1] On May 19, 1944, Hitler regaled his entourage with his plans for Linz, which included a huge library. Inside a large hall of the library, he planned to display the busts of "our greatest thinkers," whom he considered vastly superior to any English, French, or Americans intellectuals.

Whom did Hitler want to honor as the greatest German thinkers? Immanuel Kant, Arthur Schopenhauer, and Friedrich Nietzsche.

Kant, Hitler said, performed the tremendous service of overcoming the church's dogmatic scholasticism. Schopenhauer built on Kant's epistemology and buried Hegel's misguided idealistic philosophy. Schopenhauer was especially dear to Hitler as is indicated by the fact that he carried a five-volume set of Schopenhauer's works with him during World War I and learned a great deal from reading them—or so he claimed. However, he was not impressed by Schopenhauer's pessimism, and this is where Nietzsche came in. Nietzsche's notable contribution was to overturn Schopenhauer's pessimism.[2]

A year earlier, Goebbels had recounted an "interesting and profound conversation" with Hitler about Kant, Schopenhauer, Nietzsche, and Hegel. Kant was still "dynastically bound," according to Hitler, and Hegel deserved the drubbing that Schopenhauer gave him. Despite his rich mind and wit, however, Schopenhauer was too pessimistic. Hitler suggested that if Schopenhauer really believed the world was so horrible, he should have ended his own misery (Hitler apparently forgot that Schopenhauer staunchly opposed suicide.) Hitler enthused about Nietzsche, however, asserting: "Nietzsche is the more realistic and more consistent one. He certainly sees the grief of the world and the human race, but he deduces from it the demand of the Superman (*Übermensch*), the demand for an elevated and intensified life. Thus Nietzsche is naturally much closer to our viewpoint than Schopenhauer, even though we may appreciate Schopenhauer in some matters." Hitler also mentioned yet another reason to reject Schopenhauer's pessimism: it does not correspond to the struggle for existence. He explained, "Human life is the occasion of a constant selective struggle (*Auslesekampf*). Whoever does not struggle, will perish."[3] The term "selective struggle" blended Darwin's two terms, the struggle for existence and natural selection. Both concepts featured prominently in Hitler's worldview, though he used a variety of terms to express them: struggle, struggle for life (usually *Lebenskampf*), struggle for existence (either *Kampf ums Dasein, Existenzkampf*, or even more frequently *Daseinskampf*), selection, or natural selection. Social Darwinism thus played a prominent role in Hitler's worldview, too.[4]

I am by no means trying to imply that any of these three philosophers (or social Darwinism) were *the* decisive influences on Hitler's intellectual development. This would be impossible anyway, for there are fundamental disagreements among them, and not just between Schopenhauer's will-denying pessimism and Nietzsche's life-affirming optimism. Kant was an Enlightenment rationalist, while Nietzsche was an anti-Enlightenment irrationalist. They also disagreed about religion. Kant was a deist who purported to prove the existence of God via "practical reason," i.e., he argued that the existence of morality points toward the existence of God (or to be more precise, he really only demonstrated that we as rational beings must believe in the existence of God; he did not prove that God actually exists). The atheist Schopenhauer rejected Kantian ethics, as did Nietzsche, who was renowned for his dictum, "God is dead." Kant's religious and ethical perspectives were fundamentally contradictory to Schopenhauer's and Nietzsche's.

In fact, no single person, philosophy, or movement inspired Hitler's thought or his religious beliefs. He imbibed a wide variety of influences, some from the German academic mainstream, and others from the lunatic fringe. It is almost impossible to track the myriad of influences on Hitler, because he read widely, consciously obscured the influences on him, and probably derived many of his ideas secondhand from newspapers, journals, and conversations. Further, many elements of his ideology were circulating so widely in Vienna, Munich, and elsewhere in Austria and Germany that they are not easily traceable to one particular individual or movement.[5] In this chapter, I highlight several of the most important thinkers who impacted his perspective: Schopenhauer, Nietzsche, Richard Wagner, Houston Stewart Chamberlain, and Julius Friedrich Lehmann. In subsequent chapters, I discuss some other influential figures, such as

Paul de Lagarde, Theodor Fritsch, Dietrich Eckart, Alfred Rosenberg, Jörg Lanz von Liebenfels, Hans F. K. Günther, and Ernst Haeckel. Examining the religious views of these men gives us the context in which Hitler's ideas took shape.

While examining the religious perspectives of these thinkers, however, we should not forget the obvious: Hitler was baptized and confirmed in the Catholic faith and raised in a largely Catholic society. Even though his father seems to have had a freethinking bent, and Hitler rebelled against his Catholic upbringing, it would not be surprising if many vestiges of Christianity remained with him. Nonetheless, as we examine the religious perspectives of these men who contributed to Hitler's ideology, we find that most of them were either completely anti-religious or at least sharply opposed to the extant Christian churches. Even those who claimed to be sympathetic to Christianity wanted to overthrow what most people considered Christianity and hoped to introduce a radically stripped-down, mystical version that had little in common with Catholicism or Protestantism.

While Hitler rejected the pessimistic thrust of Schopenhauer's philosophy, Schopenhauer still seems to have been one of his favorites. His roommate for awhile in Vienna, August Kubizek, claimed that Hitler had "Schopenhauer constantly with him," and Hitler testified repeatedly that he had read Schopenhauer assiduously during World War I.[6] In a May 1944 speech to army officers, he confessed that while some soldiers had Bibles in their knapsacks, he carried around Schopenhauer during the entire war.[7] Hitler's publicity man, Otto Dietrich, testified that the only philosopher he heard Hitler mention aside from Nietzsche was Schopenhauer. Dietrich remembered Hitler saying that as a soldier he had carried the Reclam paperback edition of Schopenhauer in his backpack. Perceptively, Dietrich noted that Hitler was not interested in Schopenhauer's pessimism, nor his epistemology or ethics, but only in his brilliant use of language, his ruthless criticism, and his polemical style.[8] Once, in the midst of dictating a discourse, Hitler's secretary recognized a passage from Schopenhauer that he either quoted or paraphrased without attributing his source.[9] Two of the most important early Nazi ideologists—Dietrich Eckart and Alfred Rosenberg—were also enthusiastic about Schopenhauer.

After World War I, Hitler's infatuation with Schopenhauer continued. In his speeches prior to the Beer Hall Putsch in November 1923, Hitler quoted from and referred to Schopenhauer more than any other German philosopher. In March 1922, he named Schopenhauer one of three great German thinkers, next to Kant and Goethe.[10] Almost a year later he advised that all German young people should read the works of Goethe, Schiller, and Schopenhauer.[11] On multiple occasions he quoted Schopenhauer's opinion that the Jews are the "great masters of lying."[12] Hitler reiterated this anti-Semitic saying of Schopenhauer twice in *Mein Kampf*. The first of these does not refer to Schopenhauer by name but credits the aphorism to "one of the greatest minds of humanity," showing again Hitler's immense respect for the philosopher.[13] In October 1941, Hitler placed Schopenhauer at the pinnacle of humanity, stating, "The ape is distinguished from the lowest human less than such a human is from a thinker like, for example, Schopenhauer."[14]

So what did Hitler derive from Schopenhauer's philosophy, and what implications did this have for Hitler's religion? Schopenhauer's philosophy—especially as expressed in his major work, *The World as Will and Representation* (1819)—built on Kant's epistemology by dividing the world into two distinct realms: a phenomenal realm that is mere "representation," and a realm of the "things-in-themselves," i.e., the fundamental essence behind the phenomenal world of appearances. The rationalist Kant had included God, immortality, and free will in the realm of the "things-in-themselves," but here Schopenhauer diverged from Kant. Schopenhauer took an atheistic turn, positing the existence of an unconscious, non-rational will as the essence behind the cosmos. Schopenhauer stated, "Will is the thing-in-itself, the inner content, the essence of the world. Life, the visible world, the phenomenon, is only the mirror of the will."[15] In Schopenhauer the will is a blind, purposeless striving, not part of some conscious design.[16]

Schopenhauer's emphasis on the primacy of will appealed to Hitler, who also stressed its importance. Hitler not only spoke incessantly about the importance of the *human* will, but he also often referred to the "will of nature" in his writings and speeches. His notion of the "will of nature" may have derived from Schopenhauer's insistence that will "appears in every blind force of nature."[17] However, Hitler ultimately seemed to equate the "will of nature" with the laws of nature, thus eliding the two realms that Schopenhauer kept compartmentalized. Hitler's notion of the "will of nature" also seemed to carry with it a pantheistic and purposive tendency that would not have suited Schopenhauer, who dismissed pantheism as just another name for atheism.[18]

Another element in Schopenhauer's philosophy that finds expression in Hitler's ruminations was his vision of the "will to life" (Wille zum Leben, sometimes translated as "will to live") and humanity's place in nature. Schopenhauer claimed that the will to life is the blind striving to preserve one's own life, as well as the urge to engender new life.[19] Hitler opened his *Second Book* by claiming that though humans do not know their purpose in life, they recognize that they have two main drives or instincts that dominate their existence: self-preservation and reproduction. Further, Schopenhauer stated, "Everywhere in nature we see contest, struggle, and the fluctuation of victory.... Every grade of the will's objectification fights for the matter, the space, and the time of another."[20] Hitler, of course, likewise stressed the supreme importance of struggle in nature.[21] Schopenhauer also accepted the validity of biological evolution, an idea that was gaining popularity in the nineteenth century (even before Darwin).[22]

Since Schopenhauer believed in biological evolution, saw nature as a field of struggle, and considered humans an integral part of nature, perhaps it is not remarkable that some of his ideas presaged later concepts prominent among social Darwinist thinkers. According to Christopher Janaway, Schopenhaur's "notion of the will to life has the effect of demoting humanity from any special status separate from the rest of nature."[23] In *The World as Will and Idea*, published forty years before Darwin's *Origin*, Schopenhauer wrote that the death of an individual was not all that tragic, because

> it is not the individual, but only the species that Nature cares for, and for the preservation of which she so earnestly strives, providing for it with the utmost prodigality through the vast surplus of the seed and the great strength of the fructifying impulse. The individual, on the contrary, neither has nor can have any value for Nature, for her kingdom is infinite time and infinite space, and in these infinite multiplicity of possible individuals. Therefore she is always ready to let the individual fall, and hence it is not only exposed to destruction in a thousand ways by the most insignificant accident, but originally destined for it, and conducted towards it by Nature herself from the moment it has served its end of maintaining the species.[24]

Many social Darwinists in late nineteenth- and early twentieth-century Germany agreed with Schopenhauer that individuals are ultimately insignificant, and Hitler certainly concurred.[25]

What, meanwhile, could Hitler have derived from Schopenhauer's *religious* conceptions? According to Janaway—and other Schopenhauer scholars agree—Schopenhauer's "philosophical system is atheist through and through."[26] Pessimist that he was, the problem of evil convinced him that no all-benevolent, omniscient being could possibly exist.[27] He rejected religions as a "pack of lies" and harshly criticized the three major monotheistic faiths for their intolerance, cruelty, religious wars, and inquisitions.[28] Schopenhauer also rejected any personal afterlife, believing instead that only the will underlying individual existence would continue after the individual's death.[29] Any influence he exerted on Hitler's religious beliefs would have pushed him in an anti-monotheistic direction. Indeed, Rosenberg jotted down in his diary that Hitler once cited Schopenhauer as the source of the saying that "antiquity did not know two evils: Christianity and syphilis." (Rosenberg, a Schopenhauer adept, apparently was not sure if this was really a Schopenhauer quote, for he placed a question mark by it.)[30] Goebbels recorded the same conversation in his diary, but he remembered Hitler saying, "According to Schopenhauer, Christianity and syphilis made humanity unhappy and unfree."[31] Either way, Hitler saw Schopenhauer as an opponent of Christianity and was agreeing with his anti-Christian outlook.

Then there was Nietzsche. Although Hitler regarded him as one of the greatest German thinkers (indeed, as more congenial to Nazi ideology than Schopenhauer), it does not automatically follow that Hitler was a Nietzschean. Many philosophers and historians have emphasized multiple points of tension and outright contradiction between Nietzsche and Nazism. In *Nietzsche, Godfather of Fascism?: On the Uses and Abuses of a Philosophy*, for instance, the editors Jacob Golomb and Robert Wistrich argue that Nazis "could only use Nietzsche by fundamentally twisting his philosophy."[32] Many of these scholars point out that Nietzsche was neither anti-Semitic nor nationalistic, and his stress on individual freedom was incompatible with the biological determinism in Nazi ideology. The very core of Hitler's ideology—biological racism—is absent from Nietzsche's philosophy. How, then, could Nietzsche be considered a forerunner of Nazi ideology?

Other scholars are not so sure Nietzsche should be let off the hook. In addition to Nietzsche's anti-Christian, anti-Enlightenment, anti-egalitarian, and anti-democratic ideas, which were shared by many non-Nietzscheans in late nineteenth- and early twentieth-century Germany, Martin Schwab identifies three distinctively Nietzschean positions that were manifested in Nazi ideology: (1) the primacy of the will to power, (2) the naturalism of values, and (3) the stress on hierarchy and rank.[33] Renowned scholar Steven Aschheim, while admitting the road was not direct, also insists there are important lines of influence running from Nietzsche to Nazism.[34] Simon May argues that even if Nietzsche was personally opposed to anti-Semitism and nationalism, and even if he were a non-violent, kindly, gentle scholar, his "war on morality" still bears some responsibility for Nazi misdeeds, because "his philosophy licenses the atrocities of a Hitler." May claims that "the supreme value he [Nietzsche] places on individual life-enhancement and self-legislation leaves room for, and in some cases explicitly justifies, unfettered brutality."[35] Some elements of Nietzschean philosophy, above all his rejection of Judeo-Christian morality and compassion for the weak and sickly, did resonate with many Nazis.

The debate over the affinities and discontinuities between Nietzsche and Nazism began in earnest already during the Third Reich. Many idealist philosophers at German universities were ill-disposed toward Nietzsche and tried instead to exalt Johann Gottlieb Fichte as the quintessential Nazi philosopher. However, other philosophers sympathetic to Nietzsche, such as Martin Heidegger and Alfred Bäumler, tried to synthesize Nietzsche and Nazism.[36] The Nazi regime signaled their support for Nietzschean philosophy by appointing Bäumler to a prestigious professorship at the University of Berlin in May 1933, and Bäumler worked closely with the regime in trying to Nazify the German universities. According to Max Whyte, "For many intellectuals in the Third Reich, Nietzsche provided not merely the decorative furnishing of National Socialism, but its core ideology."[37] The official Nazi newspaper published articles honoring Nietzsche, and they "applauded

Nietzsche's 'battle against Christianity.'"[38] In his 1936 speech to the Nazi Party Congress, the party ideologist, Rosenberg, identified Nietzsche as one of three major forerunners of Nazism.[39] The following year, Heinrich Härtle published *Nietzsche und der Nationalsozialismus* (*Nietzsche and National Socialism*) with the official Nazi publishing house. He admitted that some of Nietzsche's political perspectives were problematic from a Nazi standpoint, but his final verdict was that Nietzsche was an important forerunner of Nazism.[40] When the Nazis placed three books in the Tannenberg Memorial, they chose Hitler's *Mein Kampf*, Rosenberg's *Myth of the Twentieth Century*, and Nietzsche's *Thus Spake Zarathustra*.[41] Clearly, the view from inside the Third Reich was that Nietzsche and Nazism were largely compatible.

Hitler contributed mightily to the positive perception of Nietzsche within the Nazi Party. He conversed for an hour with Bäumler at the Brown House in Munich in 1931.[42] In January 1932, Hitler personally presented a bouquet of roses to Nietzsche's sister, Elisabeth Förster-Nietzsche, who administered the Nietzsche Archive in Weimar. He visited her again at the Nietzsche Archive at least three times in 1933–34, and in November 1935 he attended her funeral, where Gauleiter Fritz Sauckel spoke. Over a year before she died, Hitler granted her a monthly stipend of 300 marks from his personal funds. On his visit to the Nietzsche Archive in October 1934, he brought along his architect friend, Albert Speer, and commissioned the building of a memorial hall, where conferences and workshops could be held to promote Nietzschean philosophy. The project cost Hitler 50,000 marks from his private funds and was almost completed by the end of World War II. During that same visit, Hitler's personal photographer, Heinrich Hoffmann, took a photo that circulated widely of Hitler gazing on the bust of Nietzsche.[43] The caption under the photo read, "In the Nietzsche Archive in Weimar. The Führer with the bust of the German philosopher, whose ideas spawned two great people's movements (*Volksbewegungen*): the National Socialist one in Germany and the

Fascist one in Italy."[44] On Mussolini's sixtieth birthday in 1943, Hitler presented him a special edition of Nietzsche's works.[45] Hitler was too busy directing the war effort in October 1944 to attend the festivities surrounding Nietzsche's hundredth birthday, but he sent Rosenberg as his emissary.[46]

Hitler looking at Nietzsche's bust at the Nietzsche Archive in Weimar, 1934. Hitler not only visited the Nietzsche Archive multiple times, but provided funding for it from his personal funds.
Hitler with Nietzsche's bust. From Heinrich Hoffmann, Hitler wie ihn keiner kennt (1938).

Hitler clearly reveled in Nietzsche's philosophy and publicly sought to connect National Socialism with Nietzscheanism. However, tracing the influence of Nietzsche on Hitler is more complicated, because Nietzsche was heavily indebted to Schopenhauer. Thus it is not always clear when Hitler's stress on the importance of will derived from Schopenhauer or when it came from Nietzsche. It also seems likely that the influence of Nietzsche may not have been as strong on Hitler in the 1920s as it was later. Hitler's friend, Ernst Hanfstaengl, claimed that when he heard Hitler give his March 21, 1933, speech in Potsdam, he detected a shift in Hitler's thought. Hanfstaengl wrote,

> I pulled myself together with a start. What was this? Where had I read that before? This was not Schopenhauer, who had been Hitler's philosophical god in the old Dietrich Eckart days. No, this was new. It was Nietzsche.... From that day at Potsdam the Nietzschean catch-phrases began to appear more frequently—the will to power of the Herrenvolk [master people], slave morality, the fight for the heroic life, against reactionary education, Christian philosophy and ethics based on compassion.[47]

Hanfstaengl's testimony is probably somewhat self-serving, since he was trying to distance himself from the "later Hitler," but the ideas that he thinks Hitler imbibed from Nietzsche seem to be on target. Also, my own analysis of Hitler's writings and speeches confirms his impression to some extent: Schopenhauer was more important to Hitler in the early 1920s, and Nietzsche became more important to him as time went on.

So what did Hitler derive from Nietzsche? Otto Dietrich claimed that the only two elements of Nietzsche's philosophy that interested Hitler were the "cult of personality and the doctrine of the superman."[48] Certainly these two elements were important to Hitler, but unless one interprets these two points broadly, surely other Nietzschean ideas found favor with Hitler, too, such as the will to power and his aristocratic morality. Hitler did not use Nietzschean terms very often in the 1920s, but in an article he published in April 1924, he wrote that what Germany needed in that time of crisis was the "will to power."[49] At the 1933 Nuremberg Party Congress, Hitler endorsed the Nietzschean transvaluation of values, i.e., Nietzsche's rejection and inversion of traditional Judeo-Christian morality. Then, alluding to the Nazi ascent to power, Hitler stated, "Nietzsche's word that a blow which does not fell a strong man only strengthens him found its verification a thousandfold."[50]

Nazi slogan with a Nietzschen overtone at the 1938 Nuremberg Party Congress: "One Volk, one Empire, one Will."
"Ein Volk, Ein Reich, Ein Wille." From Heinrich Hoffmann, Parteitag Grossdeutschland (1938).

Hitler was convinced that willpower was sufficient to overcome any obstacle, and he found comfort in Nietzsche's teachings about this. In January 1942, the winter in the East was wreaking havoc with Hitler's plan for a rapid triumph over the Soviet "subhumans" (Nazis referred to the Slavs in the East as *Untermenschen* or subhumans, which would be the direct opposite of the Nietzschean *Übermensch* or Superman). During his annual speech on January 30 commemorating his seizure of power, Hitler appealed to Nietzsche to inspire his fellow Germans to press on toward victory:

> But I have preserved this boundless faith, in my person as well, that nothing, no matter what, would ever be able to

throw me out of the saddle, would shake me up anymore. Whoever thinks he can frighten me somehow or surprise me is wrong. I have always taken to heart the words of a great German philosopher: 'A blow that does not knock a strong man over, only makes him stronger!'[51]

That "great German philosopher" was, of course, Nietzsche. Hitler's fanatical optimism until very late in the war may have owed something to his faith in the Nietzschean will to power and his faith in himself as a Nietzschean Superman.

How did Hitler's embrace of several Nietzschean tenets influence his religion? It certainly does not mean that he endorsed Nietzsche's "death of God," a term Hitler did not use. However, he did not shrink from associating with this famous, outspoken atheist. While never endorsing the "death of God," Hitler expressed agreement with Nietzsche's rejection of Christianity. In January 1941, Goebbels recorded in his diary that Hitler was riled up against scholars, including philosophers, but he made an exception for Nietzsche, who, he asserted, "proved in detail the absurdity of Christianity. In two hundred years it [i.e., Christianity] will only remain a grotesque memory."[52] Thus, Hitler approved of Nietzsche's anti-Christian stance and predicted the ultimate demise of Christianity.

Schopenhauer and Nietzsche were also potent influences on Richard Wagner, Hitler's favorite composer. In fact, Hitler's enthusiasm for Wagner was well known. The Führer regularly attended the Bayreuth Festival and forged personal connections with the Wagner family and the Bayreuth Circle, who were powerful influences on the racist and anti-Semitic scene in early twentieth-century Germany. However, the possible influence of Wagner on Hitler's religion (and anti-Semitism) is not all that straightforward. Leon Stein explains the problem with analyzing Wagner's religion: "On the surface, the attitude of Wagner toward Christianity may seem to be contradictory and full of paradoxes. To term Wagner anti-Christian is to disregard the affirmative references to Christianity which appear throughout his works; yet, these references are neither as numerous nor as intense as his anti-Christian utterances." Not only does Stein portray Wagner as more anti-Christian than Christian, but he clarifies that the kind of Christianity Wagner embraced was an idiosyncratic version that would not have been recognizable to most Christians.[53] However, some scholars have wrongly taken Wagner's scattered pro-Christian comments as an indication that Wagner was essentially a Christian.[54]

Wagner's rendition of Christianity was to return to the teachings of Jesus before the Jews allegedly corrupted them. Wagner portrayed Jesus as the son of God, but not the *unique* son of God. He thought all people had divinity within them, and Jesus had exemplified this, especially by teaching people to negate their will to live. This emphasis on denial of the will was a theme that Wagner shared with Schopenhauer, and like Schopenhauer, Wagner was enthralled with Eastern religion. He once asserted that "pure and unadulterated Christianity is nothing more or less than a branch of that venerable Buddhism." Wagner doubted that Jesus was a Jew, because he was killed by the Jews for heroically opposing their materialistic lifestyle. Wagner especially appreciated the story of Jesus driving the greedy Jews out of the temple, a story that was dear to Hitler later, as well. Wagner even suggested that vengeance against the Jews for killing Jesus was still in order, recapitulating a common theme of Christian anti-Semitism. However, unlike most Christians, Wagner did not believe that Jesus rose from the dead.[55] Joachim Köhler speculates that both Wagner and Hitler believed Jesus had been martyred because he lacked the necessary ruthlessness to prevail against the Jews.[56]

Despite venerating Jesus, Wagner had intense antipathy for the Christian churches. He befriended Nietzsche for a time, and, according to Stein, "One of the ties that most closely bound Nietzsche and

Hitler attending a Wagner opera at the Nuremberg Party Congress in 1938.
Hitler at Wagner opera. From Heinrich Hoffmann, Parteitag Grossdeutschland (1938).

Wagner was their deep-seated opposition to Christianity." Wagner thought Christianity had corrupted the spiritual message of Jesus by introducing dogmas, rites, and ceremonies, and by adopting the Jewish Bible as their Old Testament. Christianity went off the rails of pure religion, as far as Wagner was concerned, immediately after Jesus died.[57] He was especially contemptuous of the Catholic Church, which he called "a universal pestilence" and "the most terrible thing that had ever happened in history."[58]

Wagner's hatred for Jews was an odd blend of Christian and racial anti-Semitism (and he consorted with Jewish friends and colleagues, so he was not consistent with his own anti-Semitic feelings). He waffled about whether Jews could assimilate into German society.[59] However, in 1881 he read Gobineau and adopted his racist theory at once, calling him "one of the cleverest men of our day." He embraced Gobineau's view that race was the guiding factor behind historical development. Further, the key problem with humanity—the primary sin—was that the white race, the Aryans, had mixed with other races, contaminating their blood.[60] Gobineau's theory would have a powerful impact on German racial thought by the early twentieth century and would help shape Hitler's worldview, possibly through Wagner or the Bayreuth Circle, but likely also through other racist writers.

Another Schopenhauer devotee and Wagner's son-in-law, Houston Stewart Chamberlain, was an important precursor of Nazi racial ideology. When Hitler was in Bayreuth for a speaking engagement, he requested an appointment with Chamberlain, so they met for the first time on September 30 and October 1, 1923. A few days after that first meeting, Chamberlain wrote excitedly to his new acquaintance, expressing his great admiration for Hitler.[61] Until his death in January 1927, Chamberlain remained his devoted supporter. A few days after attending Chamberlain's funeral, Hitler told a Nazi Party assembly that Chamberlain was a "great thinker."[62] Many Nazi speakers and publications, including the *Völkischer Beobachter*, feted Chamberlain as the preeminent racial thinker.[63]

Chamberlain was an extremely influential racist ideologue in early twentieth-century Austria and Germany, and he undoubtedly influenced many members and supporters of the Nazi Party. However, as Chamberlain's biographer Geoffrey Field explains, it is almost impossible to determine how much Hitler or other Nazis were impacted by Chamberlain. Field states,

But for all this it is exceedingly difficult with Chamberlain, as with other so-called ideological mentors of Nazism, to define his influence with any precision. The evidence is ambiguous and it is rarely possible to separate his impact from that of other cultural critics, journalists, and popularizers of similar views who together played a major role in molding the consciousness and self-image of Germans.[64]

The parallels between some of Chamberlain's and Hitler's ideas are patently obvious, such as Germanic racial supremacy, anti-Semitism, and the constant struggle between races. Both men believed that Indo-Germanic people were the sole creators of higher culture. However, these ideas were circulating widely in Germany independently of Chamberlain. Indeed, before Chamberlain wrote his major works, he had studied Gobineau and corresponded with Ludwig Schemann, founder of the Gobineau Society and translator of Gobineau's works.[65] Hitler could have imbibed his racist ideology from a wide variety of Gobineau enthusiasts, and Chamberlain was only one of these.

As with Wagner, Chamberlain's racial ideology was an odd synthesis of Christian and anti-Christian elements.[66] Though he wove religious themes into his anti-Semitism, biological racism was a central feature of his thought. He portrayed world history as a constant struggle for existence between different races. For Germans, this racial struggle was primarily against the Jews, who were using any economic or political tools in their power to subjugate and destroy the Germanic people.[67] Many of these ideas would find their way—one way or another—into the mind of Hitler. However, this did not make Hitler a subservient acolyte of Chamberlain's racist ideology, even though he agreed with many elements of it. In fact, in his history of European racism, the historian George Mosse claimed that Hitler was not influenced much by Chamberlain.[68]

Religion was central to Chamberlain's enterprise of racial rejuve-
nation. He was devoted to creating a Germanic form of Christianity
by purging present forms of Christianity of their allegedly Jewish
elements. Indeed, in his quest to return to the original teaching of
Jesus of Nazareth, Chamberlain wanted to sweep away all of historic
Christianity.[69] He rejected both Catholicism and Protestantism as
perversions of Jesus' message. Chamberlain favored a kind of Christianity without any official dogmas, without any sacraments, and
without any hierarchy. He favored a religion characterized by loving
and mystically seeking after an unknowable God. He believed that
Indo-Germanic peoples had always embraced such a religion, not
only in various forms of Christian mysticism, but also in the Hindu
Upanishads. Chamberlain considered the Jews, on the other hand,
the antithesis of true religion. Their focus on the law, sin, and the fear
of God, as well as their conception of God as a powerful ruler, were
materialistic and degraded.[70]

Chamberlain claimed to be a devoted disciple of Jesus' original
teachings, but he was rather selective about what parts of the gospels
to include in his religion. In his most influential book, the two-volume
Foundations of the Nineteenth Century (1899), he devoted an entire
chapter to Jesus. He assured his readers that Jesus almost certainly
had no Jewish blood. In a section entitled "Christ No Jew," he portrayed Jesus as the antithesis of the Jewish faith. He argued that the
Jews persecuted Jesus because they recognized the real opposition
between their own legalistic religion of fear and the inward religion
of love that Jesus was teaching.[71]

However, despite his admiration for Jesus and his contempt for
the Jews, Chamberlain admitted that because of Jesus' upbringing in
a society saturated with Judaism, he was in some ways still too Jewish. In a section on "Christ a Jew," Chamberlain mentioned several
errors of the Jews that Jesus had perpetuated: divine omnipotence,
divine providence, freedom of the divine and human will, human

equality, and a historical conception of religion.[72] Chamberlain also
followed liberal Protestant biblical scholarship in rejecting most of
Jesus' miracles.[73] According to Field, Chamberlain took an ambiguous
position on some of the central tenets of Christianity: "The Resurrection, Virgin Birth, and Last Supper, Chamberlain refused either to
explain away or to accept literally—they were impenetrable mysteries.
Was Christ God? For Chamberlain the question was unanswerable:
all that could be said was that God was knowable through Christ."[74]
Chamberlain's vision of Christianity was poles apart from most
people's understanding of Christianity, which is why he opposed all
extant expressions of it.

Some of these religious ideas could easily have influenced Hitler,
and in subsequent chapters I demonstrate a number of religious beliefs
that he shared with Chamberlain, such as Jesus being Aryan, rejecting
historic Christianity as a corruption of Jesus' teachings, and dismissing Judaism and the Old Testament as materialistic. Further, Chamberlain embraced a deterministic worldview, claiming that nature is
ruled by lawfulness that even God cannot contravene. He denied that
God could arbitrarily act in nature, and he drew the logical conclusion: prayer is useless, because it cannot change anything. Chamberlain also denied that God is a "world creator" as Genesis portrays
him.[75] These religious ideas appeared to resonate with Hitler.

However, before we jump to the false conclusion that Hitler was
a disciple of Chamberlain's Germanic Christianity, we should examine two accounts from December 1941 (probably of the same conversation) where Hitler explicitly criticized Chamberlain's views.
According to Rosenberg's diary entry, Hitler agreed with Rosenberg
that Chamberlain was mistaken to defend Paul's teachings.[76] To be
sure, Chamberlain thought Paul's writings were riddled with contradictions, and he spurned Paul's Epistle to the Romans because he
viewed it as a continuation of the Jewish conception of a God who
"creates, commands, forbids, becomes angry, punishes, and rewards."

Nonetheless, Chamberlain insisted that many passages in Paul evince a more refreshing, mystical approach to God.[77] Hitler, on the other hand, rejected Paul altogether, as the account of the same conversation recorded in Hitler's monologues made clear. Further, in the midst of this long discourse rejecting the Christian conception of the afterlife as too materialistic, he asserted, "H. St. Chamberlain's mistake was to believe in Christianity as in a spiritual world."[78] The context suggests that Hitler considered Chamberlain's conception of religion too otherworldly. Since Hitler directly criticized some aspects of Chamberlain's religion, it would be misguided to see Hitler as a slavish disciple of Chamberlain's religious philosophy.

Chamberlain's religious ideas resonated with Julius Friedrich Lehmann, a Munich publisher specializing in medical texts, as well as works disseminating scientific racism and eugenics. Lehmann befriended Hitler in the early 1920s and sent him inscribed copies of many of the racist books churned out by his publishing house, including those by Hans F. K. Günther, whom Lehmann had recruited and subsidized to popularize racist anthropology. Lehmann also published the journal *Deutschlands Erneuerung* (*Germany's Renewal*), which was filled with articles promoting racism and eugenics. In a March 1922 circular, Hitler recommended that Nazi Party members read this journal, and in 1924 he published an article in it himself (in part because the Nazi press had been banned in the wake of the Beer Hall Putsch).[79] Many of the ideas Hitler embraced about scientific racism and eugenics can be found in the pages of *Deutschlands Erneuerung*, Günther's *Rassenkunde des deutschen Volkes* (*Racial Science of the German People*), and other works from Lehmann's press.[80]

When Lehmann read Chamberlain's *Foundations* in 1904, he was so excited by Chamberlain's discussions about religion that he tried to recruit him to write a book about comparative religion. Lehmann was an active member of the Evangelical League, an organization that promoted the conversion of Catholics to the Protestant Church, though Lehmann was driven more by anti-Catholicism and the desire for greater German unity than he was by his zeal for the Protestant faith. Indeed, he wanted to see Protestantism move in an even more theologically liberal direction. To this end he began publishing theological works by liberal Protestant voices. In 1904 he wrote to Chamberlain that the Father in heaven was his God and Jesus was his example. However, he explicitly denied that Jesus was God, so he fell outside the boundaries of Christianity.[81] Since Lehmann never wrote about religion and since we have little or no information about his conversations with Hitler, it is impossible to know if Lehmann's theology could have influenced Hitler. However, it helps show the range of religious persuasions that could synthesize with Nazi views, including its racism and eugenics ideology.

From examining the intellectual influences on Hitler, we find a range of religious beliefs. Schopenhauer and Nietzsche were atheists, Wagner and Chamberlain wanted to return to some pristine form of Christianity (which only existed in their imaginations), and Lehmann believed in some kind of God but denied the deity of Jesus. In subsequent chapters, I examine the religious ideologies of other men who influenced Hitler. These include occultists, such as Lanz von Liebenfels and Guido von List; pantheists, such as Ernst Haeckel and Hans F. K. Günther; and various anti-Semitic thinkers. In the final analysis, Hitler's intellectual antecedents embraced a variety of religious viewpoints, and it remains unclear which individuals helped shape his religious beliefs (or if any of them did). However, two points *are* clear. First, Hitler was willing to honor as great thinkers atheists like Nietzsche, as well as proponents of a Germanic form of "Christianity," like Chamberlain. Second, despite the variety of religious views among these thinkers influencing Hitler, the spectrum was not as broad as it might first appear. It included atheism, occultism, pantheism, and theism, but it did not include Christianity, at least as most people would define it. Knowing this, we can now examine Hitler's own religious views in greater depth.

THREE

WAS HITLER AN ATHEIST?

ERNST HANFSTAENGL, A FRIEND OF HITLER during his early political career who later turned against him, claimed Hitler "was to all intents and purposes an atheist by the time I got to know him, although he still paid lip-service to religious beliefs and certainly acknowledged them as the basis for the thinking of others."[1] One of Hitler's most influential biographers, Alan Bullock, seems to think Hanfstaengl's conclusion was slightly off. Bullock explains, "The truth is that, in matters of religion at least, Hitler was a rationalist and a materialist." It is not entirely clear what Bullock means by materialism, because he quickly clarifies that "Hitler's belief in his own destiny held him back from a thorough-going atheism."[2] In his subsequent dual biography of Hitler and Stalin, he outlines essentially the same position, stating, "Stalin and Hitler were materialists not only in their dismissal of religion but also in their insensitivity to humanity as well." Bullock admits Hitler was not a complete atheist, but he depicts him as very close to atheism, not only because Hitler rejected Christianity but also because of his inhumane worldview and policies.[3]

Even though Hitler was not an atheist, it's understandable why some people would see him that way. Since he was a cunning, unscrupulous politician, his public professions of religious faith do not carry much weight. Why would anyone be naïve enough to believe Hitler's sincerity about his religious faith, when he lied so often about so many other matters? His numerous private statements bashing the Christian churches, together with the Nazi persecution of church leaders, also make him seem antireligious, and his exaltation of the atheistic philosophers, Nietzsche and Schopenhauer, contribute to his atheist credentials. Furthermore, in one speech during November 1941, Hitler seemed to indicate that he was a materialist. That month, as the war against the Soviet Union entered its first winter, Hitler explained Germany was trying to remove Jewish-dominated Bolshevism from the earth. He then stated, "This is a gigantic task posed to us. However, I am so much a materialist that I regard it as far more important than worrying about what religions are predominant in what countries."[4]

While this statement clearly suggests that Hitler did not have much appreciation for religion, I doubt, however, that Hitler was intending it as a profession of faith in atheism. The remark is rather cryptic and may have been facetious. It certainly does not comport with his clearer statements opposing atheism and his many affirmations of belief in some kind of deity, many originating from this same time period.

Nonetheless, when we look carefully at Hitler's position, we notice some other affinities between Hitler's religious views and atheism. In many of his private conversations and monologues, as well as in some of his public speeches, Hitler sounded like a rationalist, using science to undermine religion. Also, he denied a personal afterlife. Though these positions do not entail atheism, they are positions that many atheists hold, and they certainly comport better with atheism than with traditional forms of Christianity.

Hitler's freethinking bent seems to go back to his youth and may have come from his father, who was also disgruntled with the church. When reflecting back on his childhood religion classes in a January 1942 monologue, Hitler claimed that he "was the eternal questioner." He read a lot of freethinking literature, and he challenged his religion teacher with his findings, allegedly driving his teacher to despair. He would continually ask his teacher about doubtful themes in the Bible, but the teacher's answers were always evasive. One day Hitler's teacher asked him if he prayed, and he responded, "No, Sir, I do not pray; I do not believe that the dear God has an interest if a pupil prays!" Hitler also reported that he hated the mendacity of his religion instructor, who once told Hitler's mother in front of him that Hitler's soul was lost. Hitler responded by telling his teacher that some scholars doubt there is an afterlife.[5] In February 1942, Hitler confessed that he had not believed in Christianity since he was about thirteen to fifteen years old. According to Hitler, "None of my [school] comrades believed in the so-called communion any longer."[6] Hitler regaled his secretaries with accounts of his youthful exploits, including stories about embarrassing his religion teacher, whom he considered unkempt and filthy. He told his secretaries that he developed an aversion to clergymen from his earliest youth.[7] These two depictions by Hitler of his youthful penchant toward religious unbelief and freethinking agree with each other and seem to accord with what we know from other sources, too. However, even if they were not entirely accurate, they certainly show us that later in life Hitler wanted to appear as a freethinker who broke away from religion at an early age.

Historians are divided about the influence of Enlightenment rationalism on Hitler's ideology. In the early aftermath of the Nazi period, many scholars portrayed Hitler as an irrationalist—completely anti-scientific and anti-intellectual (I am not using the term irrationalist here to mean crazy or insane; rather it means those who believe that knowledge comes through non-rational means, such as the will, emotions, or intuition.) George Mosse, for instance, argued that Nazi racism was built entirely on irrationalist strains of racial thought. He even denied that scientific racism exerted any significant influence on Hitler's ideology.[8] Other historians, such as Jeffrey Herf, largely agree with Mosse, arguing that Nazism suffered from a rejection of Enlightenment rationalism.[9] However, many historians have taken the opposite view, noting the influence of the Enlightenment on Hitler and Nazism.[10] Stanley Payne even claimed, "All of Hitler's political ideas had their origin in the Enlightenment."[11] Detlev Peukert's influential essay, "The Genesis of the 'Final Solution' from the Spirit of Science" (1993), has caused many historians to reconsider the importance of science and rationalism in Nazi ideology and policies.[12] In the past couple of decades, historians of science have explored the largely friendly relationship between the German scientific establishment (excluding the Jews, of course) and the Nazi regime.

I am not quite sure why some historians think we need to choose between Hitler the rationalist and Hitler the irrationalist.[13] After all, the most prominent German Enlightenment philosopher, Kant, profoundly influenced subsequent European thought by positing a strict dichotomy between the phenomenal realm, which was deterministic and thus subject to scientific investigation, and the noumenal realm, where the inscrutable things-in-themselves, such as God, immortality, and freedom existed. In the *Critique of Pure Reason*, Kant asserted, "I had to abolish knowledge to make room for faith."[14] Some rationalist thinkers after Kant, such as positivists, followed Kant by giving up on knowledge about the noumenal realm, but unlike Kant, they abandoned faith, too. They claimed the only way to gain knowledge is through empirical, scientific investigation; for them, God was unknowable. Other thinkers, such as poets and artists in the Romantic movement, pursued irrationalist forms of knowledge through the will, intuition, or art. However, during the nineteenth and especially by the early twentieth century, many post-Kantian German scholars and intellectuals drew on both rationalist and irrationalist strains of thought. Robert Richards has explored the way that German scientists integrated Romanticism into their scientific thought in the nineteenth century.[15] As H. Stuart Hughes so powerfully demonstrated, European social thought in the period 1890–1930 was both an heir of the Enlightenment and a revolt against positivism. Many intellectuals, such as Sigmund Freud and Max Weber, were fascinated by the irrational side of the human psyche, though ultimately they remained committed to rational explanations for it.[16]

Among non-intellectuals—and Hitler was, of course, not an intellectual—blending rationalism and irrationalism was not uncommon in early twentieth-century Germany or Austria. Occultists like Lanz von Liebenfels would cite scientific sources just as readily as they cited biblical passages (usually mystically interpreted) or the Kabbala or esoteric writings to buttress their Aryan racial theories. One of the most prominent racial thinkers in the Third Reich, Hans F. K. Günther, usually accentuated the scientific character of his Nordic racism, posing as a rationalist. In one of his most popular books, he claimed, "Race is a concept of natural science."[17] However, at times he manifested an irrationalist side, especially in his book on Nordic religiosity.[18] In the early twentieth century, especially in Hitler's milieu in Vienna and Munich, rationalism and irrationalism were not neatly compartmentalized, but rather intertwined, especially among those influenced by Kant and Schopenhauer.

With his stress on will and instinct, Hitler did indeed have an irrationalist bent, and I explore this theme in greater depth elsewhere in this book. However, many of his comments in both public and private about the Enlightenment, religious toleration, and the science-religion nexus seem consistent with rationalism. On the few occasions that Hitler forthrightly discussed his attitude toward Enlightenment thinkers, he uniformly expressed appreciation and admiration for them. Kant, whose bust he wanted to place in his magnificent library in Linz, was one of the leading philosophers of the Enlightenment.[19]

This was not the only time Hitler praised Enlightenment philosophers. During a monologue in October 1941, he lamented that current discussions about religion were in a miserable state compared to the writings of the French Enlightenment or to Frederick the Great's discussions with Voltaire.[20] Nine months later, he told Bormann that of the books that Bormann had given him to look at, he was especially interested in Frederick the Great's books, *Briefe über die Religion* (*Letters on Religion*) and *Theologische Streitschriften* (*Theological Polemics*). Hitler commented that it would be valuable if all Germans, especially leaders and military officers, could read these works by Frederick, because then they would see that Hitler was not alone in his "heretical thoughts."[21] Hitler obviously thought highly of Frederick, not only for his military exploits and tenacity but also for his Enlightened religious views. Hans Frank noticed this tendency, too, testifying that Hitler increasingly identified with Frederick the Great's Enlightened rationalism, which completely suppressed his childhood faith.[22] The theologian Paul Hinlicky claims that Hitler's conception of God was shaped by Enlightenment thought, asserting, "Hitler embraced the rationalist, watch-maker God typical of deistic (not 'theistic') thought whose stern and ruthless law he discovered anew in Darwinian natural selection. In this way, Hitler renounced the God identified by biblical narrative."[23]

One feature of Frederick's Enlightened religious policy that appealed to Hitler was his religious toleration. Hitler repeatedly remonstrated against the churches for their religious intolerance. Like many atheists and freethinkers, he often associated the Christian churches with the Inquisition and witch hunts. According to August Kubizek, Hitler got riled up even as a youth by reading books about witch trials and the Inquisition.[24] In 1927, Hitler corresponded with a Catholic priest who had previously supported Nazism but by this time had some misgivings. Hitler contradicted the priest's claim that Christianity had brought an end to Roman barbarism. Instead, Hitler insisted that Christianity was even more barbaric than the Romans had been, killing hundreds of thousands for their heretical beliefs. He then rattled off a list of Christian atrocities: killing the Aztecs and Incas, slave hunts during medieval times, and enslaving millions of black Africans.[25] Otto Wagener reported that Hitler made similar comments several years later. Hitler attacked those in the churches who opposed his regime, indignantly claiming that their resistance was "nothing more than the continuation of the crime of the Inquisition and the burning of witches, by which the Jewish-Roman world exterminated whatever offered resistance to that shameful parasitism."[26] In a February 1942 monologue, Hitler mocked the Christian story of God sending His Son to die for humanity. Then, after Christianity became established, Hitler complained, Christians used violence to force everyone to believe. Hitler wondered why the thumbscrews of the Inquisition were necessary if the Christian faith was based on knowledge.[27] Overall, when he thought of Christianity, he tended to focus on its dark side.

Another way that Hitler paralleled Enlightenment rationalism was by stressing the variety of religions in the world. Hitler saw the presence of numerous religions in the world as a major hurdle to believing in any particular one. The basic idea was that since there were so many different religions, each claiming to be the sole and exclusive truth, most religions were necessarily wrong. Why, then, believe in one particular religion, just because by accident you happened to be raised in the society that embraced it? In a monologue in

October 1941, Hitler expressed this point clearly. Where he got his statistics from is uncertain, but he claimed that there were 170 large religions in the world, so at least 169 must be wrong. The implication, however, was that *all* 170 were probably wrong. Then he claimed that no religion still being practiced was older than 2,500 years, while humans have existed for at least 300,000 years (having evolved from primates).[28] This implied that religions were temporary phenomena of questionable validity. A few months later, he made similar remarks, claiming that human conceptions of Providence are constantly shifting. Only about 10 percent of people in the world believed in Catholicism, he claimed, and the rest of humanity had many different beliefs. This time, he gave the figure of 500,000 years for the existence of the human species, noting that Christianity only existed during an "extremely short epoch of humanity."[29]

In his 1935 speech to the Nuremberg Party Rally, he argued that religious ideas and institutions are inseparably linked to the continued existence of its practitioners and thus are not eternal truths. Religions, according to Hitler, are only valid to the extent that they contribute to the survival of the people (Volk) practicing them. If the people perish—and he specifically mentioned the Aztecs and Incas—then their religion will die out, too. In this speech, he expressed that ideas, including religious doctrines, must be evaluated according to their value in helping preserve the people (Volk).[30] Hitler took an instrumental view of religion, judging it according to whether it helped a people survive and thrive, not whether it was objectively true.

He also shared with many rationalists the view that science was an obstacle to faith in religion, or at least any religion that contradicted the tenets of science. The tendency of some historians to depict Hitler as anti-scientific or pseudo-scientific is completely understandable in light of the outrageous nature of some of his beliefs, especially with our current knowledge. However, we need to recognize that Hitler saw his own worldview as completely consistent with science.

He told his party faithful at the Nuremberg Party Rally in September 1938, "National Socialism is a cool-headed doctrine of realities; it mirrors clearly scientific knowledge and its expression in thought." It rejected all mysticism, he continued.[31] Five years earlier, he had given his first Nuremberg Party Rally speech after taking power and at the time presented his racial ideology as scientific. "In nature," he explained, "there are no inexplicable accidents.... Every development proceeds according to cause and effect." Therefore, in order to triumph as a Volk, Germans needed to discover the "eternal laws of life" and conform to them. Some of the most important laws of nature, Hitler explained, are that races are unequal and culture depends on the biological quality of the people, not on their environment.[32] These two ideas—racial inequality and biological determinism—were prominent among German biologists and anthropologists, so in this case Hitler's views *were* consistent with the science of his day.

In fact, throughout his career, Hitler exalted science above religion and criticized any religion that collided with science.[33] He insisted many times that his own worldview was in complete accord with the latest findings of modern science.[34] In May 1943, after a monologue sharply denouncing the arrogance of the Christian clergy, Hitler contrasted the sure path of scientific knowledge with the faulty basis of religious knowledge. Goebbels then commented that the "Führer is an enthusiastic adherent of pure science" and has high regard for scientists.[35] Hitler had taken a similar position in *Mein Kampf* while lamenting that religious unbelief was increasing in Germany. One cause he identified for the pitiful condition of religion was its "totally unnecessary conflict with so-called exact science." The conflict between science and religion will almost always result in the victory of science, according to Hitler, leading to a decline in religion. Hitler was not arguing that science demolishes every kind of religious belief, but he was warning against religions taking positions on "things of a purely earthly nature," thus opening themselves up to conflict with science.[36] A couple of years later, Hitler expressed the same basic point in private correspondence, telling a Catholic priest that he considered it a disaster for religion to get involved with matters that put it in conflict with the exact sciences.[37]

After coming to power, Hitler continued to prioritize science over religion. When meeting with Cardinal Michael von Faulhaber, Hitler reminded him that the world was changing, and he thought the Catholic Church should change with it. He reminded the cardinal of the Church's past conflicts with science over its belief in a six-day creation and the geocentric theory of the solar system. Then he told Faulhaber that the Church must abandon its opposition to Nazi racial and eugenics legislation, because such policies "rest on absolute scientific research." Strange as it may seem to us today, Hitler saw his racial and eugenics agenda as scientific and all opposition to it as the product of benighted, outmoded religion.[38] In April 1940, Goebbels reported that, in Hitler's view, Catholicism was "setting itself in ever sharper contrast to the exact sciences. Its [Catholicism's] end will be accelerated by this."[39] In November 1941, Hitler overtly dismissed the teachings of Catholicism and any other religion that contradicted the findings of science. He stated, "Today no one who is familiar with natural science can any longer take seriously the teaching of the church. What stands in contradiction to natural laws cannot be from God."[40] Again, Hitler was not discounting all religion, but he clearly thought science had a superior claim to knowledge. As Michael Burleigh argues, Hitler "subscribed to the view that science had largely supplanted Christianity, without rationalism eradicating the need for belief, or undermining the existence of a creator God in whom he continued to believe."[41]

Hitler's view of the primacy of science over religion colored his understanding of God as creator; however, in October 1941, Hitler remarked that the Christian churches were in constant conflict with scientific research. Evolutionary theory in particular conflicts with Christian teachings, he thought. When he was a boy, his religion teachers would teach the creation story from the Bible, while his science teachers would teach the theory of evolution. As a pupil, he recognized that these teachings were completely contradictory. He admitted that the churches in recent times had saved face somewhat by retreating to the position that biblical stories could be interpreted symbolically. However, he took the side of science and evolutionary theory against religion and the churches' doctrines.[42]

Another reason that some people might mistake Hitler for an atheist was his aforementioned rejection of a personal afterlife. Based on his interaction with Hitler, Walter Schellenberg, one of the most influential SS officers during World War II, testified the following:

> Hitler did not believe in a personal god. He believed only in the bond of blood between succeeding generations and in a vague conception of fate or providence. Nor did he believe in a life after death. In this connection he often quoted a sentence from the *Edda*, that remarkable collection of ancient Icelandic literature, which to him represented the profoundest Nordic wisdom: "All things will pass away, nothing will remain but death and the glory of deeds."[43]

In his New Year's Proclamation in 1943, Hitler publicly insinuated that he did not believe in an individual afterlife, telling his fellow Germans, "The individual must and will pass away, as in all times, but the Volk must live on."[44] According to Albert Speer, one of Hitler's closest friends who met with him not long before he committed suicide, Hitler faced his own death without any hope of an afterlife. Hitler told him, "Believe me, Speer, it is easy for me to end my life.

A brief moment and I'm free of everything, liberated from this painful existence."[45] Hitler clearly did not think there was any kind of personal afterlife and certainly had no inkling of any divine judgment after death.

In fact, in his Table Talks, he ridiculed Christian teachings about the afterlife. In April 1942, he called the Catholic Church's doctrine of hell "great stupidity," because people's bodies decompose and cannot be resurrected. He disparaged the Christian heaven as an undesirable place occupied by dim-witted people and "unattractive and boring women."[46] Apparently he found an afterlife surrounded by beautiful young virgins more appealing, as four months earlier he told his colleagues that he preferred the Muslim version of paradise to the boring Christian conception of heaven with its constant hallelujahs and palm leaves. In that monologue, however, he dismissed both Christian and Muslim teachings about the afterlife because he did not believe in any physical life after death.[47] In February 1942, in the midst of a screed accusing Christianity of destroying the noble, ancient world, Hitler blamed the Jews for introducing the "beastly idea" that one's life continues in a future world. The Jews used this promise of life after death as an excuse, according to Hitler, to exterminate life in the present world. Hitler contradicted this allegedly Jewish view, asserting that persons cease to exist at death.[48] About a week later, Hitler lambasted the church's idea of the afterlife again. He would rather have it good in this life than to endure poverty in this world and then sing hallelujah in heaven.[49]

However, despite rejecting a personal afterlife, Hitler did retain a vague notion of an impersonal life after death. He once wrote that those who are not strong or healthy enough to survive the ruthless process of natural selection were "forced back into the womb of the eternal unknown."[50] He also thought the German people's continued existence after the death of an individual gave meaning to that individual's life and death. In *Mein Kampf*, Hitler claimed that true Aryan religion must uphold "the conviction of survival after death in some form."[51] This, however, still underscores the fuzziness of his conception of the afterlife, since "in some form" is rather vague and open-ended. It could mean a personal afterlife, but it could also simply mean continuing to exist in one's descendants or in matter rearranged. The latter seems closer to the position Hitler stated elsewhere. In a November 1941 monologue, Hitler professed a level of agnosticism about the afterlife, stating, "I know nothing about the next world (*Jenseits*) and I am honest enough to confess that."[52] Hitler never claimed to understand the spiritual world, which he often represented as mysterious and unfathomable, yet he certainly knew enough about it to reject the Christian teachings about heaven and hell. He also thought he knew that individuals do not continue to exist as individuals after death, because their bodies cannot rise from the dead.

In a monologue in December 1941, Hitler tried to describe briefly his view of the afterlife. He admitted his view was murky, because it was impossible to comprehend such matters completely. He stated, "The idea of eternity is in a way well-grounded. Spirit and soul certainly go back again into the general reservoir, just as the body does. As basic matter we thus fertilize the stock out of which new life arises. I do not need to rack my brains about the whys and wherefores! We will not fathom the essence of the soul!"[53] Fuzzy as it is, this is the clearest expression of Hitler's view of the afterlife. Rather than the continued existence of an individual person, he saw the afterlife as the dissolution of individuals, whose matter—but also their soul and spirit—somehow contribute to spawning new life. A few months earlier, he had made similar remarks, claiming that one who committed suicide could not completely leave the world, because the matter from his physical body would "remain in the household of nature." Further, Hitler stated that we do not know if the soul flows back into a "reservoir" and might return again in some form. He also suggested that it was preferable to teach people to live their lives in a worthy manner in this life by conforming to natural laws than to seduce people with visions of the afterlife, as the churches do.[54]

What was this "reservoir" Hitler referred to in both monologues? One can make an educated guess based on the general contours of his worldview and the religious context in which he lived. There are two strong possibilities, and they overlap. Hitler could have been referring to nature as a whole, or he might have been referring to the *Volk*. Both would make sense in light of his discussions about the afterlife and the world to come. But they also are consistent with the preponderance of evidence that Hitler was a pantheist. Pantheists and many social Darwinists in the early twentieth century (plenty of whom were atheists or agnostics) embraced the view that the individual was not so important, because its life was short, but the species or race were far more significant, because it endured much longer. Detlev Peukert explains that many versions of the secularized scientific worldview circulating in early twentieth-century Germany gave the Volk priority over individuals, because individuals die. Peukert states, "Science therefore sought its salvation in the specious immortality of the racial *Volkskörper* [body politic], for the sake of which mere real, and hence imperfect, life could be sacrificed."[55] Hitler certainly embraced this view of the relationship between the individual and the Volk, and it had dire consequences for those whose "life could be sacrificed" for the well-being of the race.

Indeed, in July 1926, Hitler articulated the idea that the afterlife is simply the continuation of one's posterity and one's entire species. He believed that the desire and longing people feel for immortality should be channeled toward striving for the well-being of their children and of future humanity.[56] He reiterated this point in a January 1928 speech, where he posed the question crucial to all religions, *"Why is the individual in the world at all?"* He answered that we do not know why we are living, but we do know that we have an instinct not only to live, but also to continue our existence in to the future. This is "the yearning to immortalize oneself in the body of a child." The highest humans—and Hitler clearly thought the Aryans were the highest—extend this desire to preserving the entire species, not just one's own children.[57]

The view that Hitler saw the afterlife as an impersonal return to nature or the Volk is reinforced by an entry in Goebbels' diary during December 1941. The entry is especially intriguing because it was one of the only times that Goebbels noted a point of disagreement between Hitler and himself about religion. Goebbels claimed that in his view—but not in Hitler's—the average German needs to regard the afterlife as a continuation of the individual. "One cannot make do by saying, he goes again into his Volk (people) or into his native soil (*Mutterboden*)."[58] In this discussion, Goebbels states that Hitler did not believe in an individual afterlife, and he implies that Hitler took the position that afterlife simply means returning to the blood and soil from which one came.

The view that the afterlife is simply a continuation of life in future generations was reflected in an SS pamphlet on funerals. It quoted Himmler, who stated that death held no terror, because it found meaning in the continuation of life. He explained, "The individual dies, but in his children his people (Volk) grow beyond him even during his life. Because we love the future of the life of our people (Volk) more than ourselves, we freely and bravely consent to go to the death, wherever it must be."[59] This notion of an impersonal afterlife was not uncommon in Nazi circles. It was so widespread that Pope Pius XI criticized the Nazi view of the afterlife in his 1937 encyclical, "Mit brennender Sorge." Pius complained, "'Immortality' in a Christian sense means the survival of man after his terrestrial death, for the purpose of eternal reward or punishment. Whoever only means by the term, the collective survival here on earth of his people for an indefinite length of time, distorts one of the fundamental notions of the Christian Faith and tampers with the very foundations of the religious concept of the universe, which requires a moral order."[60] The vision of the afterlife that Pius is criticizing seems to reflect Hitler's position. His rejection of a personal afterlife was likely part of a pantheistic view that saw humans upon their death as being absorbed back into nature, somehow mysteriously reemerging in the lives of future generations.

In fact, despite some affinities with rationalism and his rejection of a personal afterlife, Hitler never embraced an atheistic worldview. Every time he discussed atheism overtly, both publicly and privately, he rejected it, associating it with the Marxist Social Democrats, the Communist Party, or the Bolsheviks. In the electioneering phase of his career, he regularly slammed the Catholic Center Party for cooperating with the Social Democrats, who—he often asserted—were atheists.[61] Several times in 1933, when he was trying to woo the churches to support his anti-Marxist policies, he portrayed his regime as a Christian regime combating the atheistic tendencies of the Marxist parties. He was trying to counter criticism, especially from the Catholic Center Party, that warned about the danger Hitler posed to Christianity. Just two weeks after coming to power he tried to reassure his critics, proclaiming, "For the time being, Christians and not international atheists are now standing at Germany's fore." He reminded his audience that the Center Party had cooperated with the atheistic Social Democrats during the Weimar Republic, resulting in cultural degradation.[62] A month later, while celebrating his election victory, he enjoined the churches to join him in "the fight against a materialistic Weltanschauung."[63] In an October 1933 radio address, he pledged to restore order, work, loyalty, and morality to the German people and to fight against corruption and deceit. He continued, "We have been waging a heroic battle against the Communist threat to our Volk, the decomposition of our culture, the subversion of our art, and the poisoning of our public morality. We have put an end to the denial of God and abuse of religion."[64] Hypocritically ignoring his own pact with Stalin that ended less than a year earlier, Hitler openly railed at England's archbishops in April 1942 for embracing "the bloody beasts of Bolshevik atheism."[65]

It's true that Hitler's *public* statements opposing atheism should not be given too much weight, since they obviously served Hitler's political purposes to tar political opponents. However, in his private monologues, he likewise rejected atheism, providing further evidence that this was indeed his personal conviction. In July 1941, he told his colleagues that humans do not really know where the laws of nature come from. He continued, "Thus people discovered the wonderful concept of the Almighty, whose rule they venerate. We do not want to train people in atheism." He then maintained that every person has a consciousness of what we call God. This God was apparently not the Christian God preached in the churches, however, since Hitler continued, "In the long run National Socialism and the church cannot continue to exist together." The monologue confirms that Hitler rejected atheism, but it also underscores the vagueness of his conception of God.[66]

A few months later, Hitler again insisted that atheism was not reasonable. He commented that the Soviet regime had fought against their religious leaders, "but they may not convert that into a struggle against the higher power (*Gewalt*). The fact is, that we are creatures lacking willpower, but the fact is also that there is a creative power (*Kraft*). To deny that is stupidity."[67] The "higher power" and "creative power" are clearly allusions to some kind of God. Hitler thought it was self-evident that some kind of God existed, even though he did not have a well-defined conception of it. In an extremely sarcastic and caustic discourse about Christian beliefs in February 1942, he dismissed Catholic beliefs as idolatry yet nevertheless insisted that belief in some kind of God was valid. He asserted, "What gives humans an advantage over animals, perhaps the most wonderful proof for the superiority of humans, is that he has comprehended that there must be a creative power!" Belief in God, for Hitler, was part of what it means to be human.[68]

In his speeches, writings, and monologues, he often expressed faith in some kind of God, generously sprinkling his rhetoric with thanks to Providence and pleas for the blessing of the Almighty. As to who this Providence or God was, Hitler stayed studiously vague. In a secret speech at the Adolf Hitler School in Sonthofen, an institution training the up-and-coming Nazi Party elite, Hitler told his party cadres that good Nazis are religious, but they should not allow religious differences to undermine the unity of the German people. He promised to give the churches complete freedom to teach their conceptions of God, not because he thought their teachings were accurate, but because he did not think humans could understand the real essence of God anyway. He stated,

> At the bottom of our hearts, we National Socialists are religious. For the space of many millenniums, a uniform concept of God did not exist. Yet it is the most brilliant and most sublime notion of mankind, that which distinguishes him most from animals, that he not only views a phenomenon from without, but always poses the question of why and how. This entire world, a world so clear-cut in its external manifestation, is just as unclear to us in its purpose. And here mankind has bowed down in humility before the conviction that it is confronted by an incredible power, an Omnipotence, which is so incredible and so deep that we men are unable to fathom it. That is a good thing! For it can serve to comfort people in bad times; it avoids that superficiality and sense of superiority that misleads man to believe that he—but a tiny bacillus on this earth, in this universe—rules the world, and that he lays down

the laws of Nature which he can at best but study. It is, therefore, our desire that our Volk remains humble and truly believes in a God.[69]

While confessing faith in an omnipotent being of some sort, however, Hitler denied we could know anything about it. No wonder Michael Rissmann argues that Hitler's religion was indeterminate and "void of content."[70] Of the latter description, however, I am not convinced. Despite his suggestion that God is inscrutable and unfathomable, Hitler did sometimes claim to know something about the workings of Providence. But his agnosticism about the fundamental essence and nature of God was probably not feigned, for other testimony confirms it. Rosenberg noted that Hitler often referred to Providence and the Almighty in his speeches, but he thought Hitler probably only meant an impersonal fate.[71] Hans Frank agreed with Rosenberg, claiming that Hitler adopted an ancient Greek notion of a fate that is superior even to divine beings.[72]

Could such vague religious beliefs have a significant impact on Hitler's life, career, or policies? The answer is unequivocally yes. Despite the inability of humans to probe the mysteries of God's essence, Hitler claimed to know the path to find the blessings of Providence. Perhaps even more significantly, he had complete faith that Providence had chosen him to lead the German people to greatness. His faith in Providence motivated him to persevere in times of distress and defeat. Indeed, as Hitler's secretary Johanna Wolf explained when she was interrogated in 1948, Hitler believed that Providence had saved him from the July 20, 1944 assassination attempt, giving him renewed confidence in his mission. Almost until the end, Hitler had complete confidence that Providence would somehow rescue the Germans from their impending defeat.

Hitler's vague notion of God inspired him because he considered God the creator and sustainer of the German Volk. When Hitler used the term Volk, he was referring to the Germanic people as a racial entity, so Volk was synonymous with the Aryan or Nordic race (terms also used interchangeably). But it was also conveniently ambiguous, making it a great propaganda tool appealing to Germans who might differ in their interpretations of it. It could mean all the German people belonging to the unified German nation, or it could mean all those who were ethnically German, or it could even mean all those having Nordic racial characteristics, even if they were ethnically Danish or Dutch or Norwegian or Polish. Hitler preferred this last definition and tried during World War II to construct a Greater Germanic Reich that incorporated all those identified as members of the Nordic race, no matter their nationality. However, most Germans opted for one of the first two definitions.

Hitler often correlated his faith in God with his faith in the German Volk. In a speech a few days after coming to power, he proclaimed that he wanted to lead the Volk "back to the eternal sources of its strength; we want, by means of an education starting in the cradle, to implant in young minds a belief in a God and the belief in our Volk."[73] Hitler made the connection between God and the German Volk so often that Max Domarus, who edited a massive four-volume collection of Hitler's speeches, claimed Hitler's God was a "peculiarly German God," not the God worshipped by most other people throughout the ages.[74]

In July 1937, Hitler explained the significance of God in the life of the German Volk. First, he extolled faith in the Volk that resonated in the German national anthem, *Deutschland, Deutschland über alles* ("Germany, Germany above all"). Then he remarked, "Hence this song also constitutes a pledge to the Almighty, to His will and to His work: for man has not created this Volk, but God, that God who stands above us all. He formed this Volk, and it has become what it should according to God's will, and according to our will, it shall remain, nevermore to fade!" He then assured them that anyone who promoted the interests of the German Volk "has acted in accordance with the will of his Creator."[75] Domarus added this insightful footnote to the passage: "In this context as well it is evident that Hitler understood the term 'Almighty' to refer to a god that existed exclusively for the German people."[76] Of course, Hitler believed that God existed everywhere, but he also believed the Volk was God's special people with a special mission, and he tried to instill this faith in his fellow Germans. Rather frequently Hitler encouraged his fellow Germans to believe that their work and struggle on behalf of their people was assured of success, because God was with them. In June 1937, while boasting of his achievements and preparing for future conquest, Hitler exhorted his compatriots to expect that God would bless them if they tenaciously worked for Germany.[77]

Hitler's faith in the German people and his confidence that they had a God-ordained destiny to rise to prominence as a "master race" sustained him in times of distress; it contributed to his determination to wage a bitter, fruitless struggle long after the war was obviously lost. On New Years' Day 1945, as Germany was facing disaster after the last-ditch Battle of the Bulge had failed, Hitler tried to inspire his German comrades to continue the struggle by appealing to their special divine calling. The Volk, he affirmed, owed its origin to "the inscrutable will of the Almighty. The insight into the moral value of our conviction and the resulting objectives of our struggle for life give us, and above all, give me the strength to continue to wage this fight in the most difficult hours with the strongest faith and with an unshakable confidence."[78] All the evidence suggests that this was not mere rhetoric but that Hitler sincerely believed Germany would triumph against all adversity. His faith in Providence sustained him.

But Hitler's faith was not just in the German people. He believed that he was specially chosen by God to lead the German people. In the early days of his political career, Hitler often referred to himself as a forerunner of a coming leader who would bring Germany to greatness. However, by 1924 his self-image had shifted, as he became convinced that *he* was the coming leader—*der Führer*—chosen by destiny to lead Germany to glory.[79] He regularly invoked Providence or God as the source of his calling. Several months before coming to power, Hitler explained why he had confidence that he would ultimately prevail in his political struggle, stating, "I also have the conviction and the certain feeling that nothing can happen to me, for I know that Providence has chosen me to fulfill my task. My will is tough, unrestrained, and unshakable."[80] Whenever he experienced success, he interpreted it as a sign that Providence was blessing him. It reinforced his faith that his plans for the future would likewise be crowned with success.

And so Hitler insisted that he was a tool in the hands of God, fulfilling the purposes of the Almighty. He told a Munich crowd in March 1936, "I follow the path assigned to me by Providence with the instinctive sureness of a sleepwalker."[81] In June 1937, he explained his providential vision of history, claiming that only through divine guidance had he been able to reach "these dizzy paths." He then encouraged his audience to put their faith in the workings of divine Providence. Without the blessings of Providence, no one can achieve anything in history, he claimed.[82]

When Hitler celebrated his historical achievements, he regularly ascribed his success to the blessings of God. After annexing Austria without firing a shot, he addressed the new members of his expanded German Empire in Vienna, claiming divine sanction for his action. Much earlier in his career, in the opening sentence of *Mein Kampf*, he had only given credit to "Fate" (*Schicksal*) and a "lucky arrangement" ("*glückliche Bestimmung*," which Manheim mistranslates as "providential" in the English edition) for his birth on the border of Austria and Germany. In this speech in April 1938, however, he interpreted it as the will of God that he had been born in Austria and risen to power in Germany to incorporate Austria into the German

Empire. Hitler told these Austrians, "There is a divine will, and all we are is its instruments."[83] He posed as a humble worker in the Lord's vineyard, with God smiling on his efforts.

Was this just a pose for public consumption? Not likely. Hitler not only appealed to Providence as his guide in many public speeches and in both his books, but he also did the same in his private monologues. His closest colleagues also testified that he believed Providence had anointed him for a special task. Schellenberg, for example, asserted, "But his one dominant and dominating characteristic was that he felt himself appointed by providence to do great things for the German people. This was his historic 'mission,' in which he believed completely."[84] The sense of being chosen to fulfill a world-historical purpose had a profound influence on Hitler's psychology.[85]

Interestingly, even though Hitler always interpreted success as an indication of God's favor, he never allowed failures, troubles, or problems to sway him. Positive events confirmed his faith; negative events were sent by God to steel his will and make him stronger. He was so confident that he was following the will and purposes of Providence that he just *knew* success was on the way. Hitler's close friend and confidante, the architect Albert Speer, claimed that Hitler "was by nature a religious man, but his capacity for belief had been perverted into belief in himself." Speer explained Hitler had complete faith that Providence would eventually bring him to victory, no matter how bleak the circumstances looked at the time.[86] In his January 30, 1945 address, Hitler renewed his claim that Providence spared him from the July 20, 1944 assassination attempt. This sign from the Almighty gave him strength and a "holy conviction" to continue, despite the trouble facing Germany. He insisted that God would not leave them in the lurch, but would rescue them, because their cause was righteous.[87]

Though at times he enjoined the German people to pray, he often reminded them that God or Providence would not give his blessing to them or lead them to victory in the war as a free gift. They would have to work for their salvation. In a 1928 speech, Hitler stated that everything comes through struggle. "There is no gift," he said, "nothing that is given to humans through a higher Providence."[88] Ten years later at the Nuremberg Party Rally, he told an assembly of German workers, "You represent the most noble of slogans known to us: 'God helps those who help themselves!'"[89] Hitler repeated this common proverb in a Table Talk in February 1942, when he also stated, "Providence always grants the victory to the one who properly uses the brain given to him." Shortly thereafter he asked, "Why fight at all, if it can be accomplished with prayer?"[90] Several months later, he repeated the same thought in different words: "The saying that the dear God is with the stronger battalion has its significance."[91] Hitler often disparaged those who used prayer as a substitute for action and at times claimed that labor and activity in harmony with the divine will was a form of prayer.[92] Even when he *did* urge the German people to pray, he often exhorted them to work diligently so they could become worthy of divine favor.[93] In his New Years' address in 1944, he encouraged his fellow Germans, "Let us pray to the Lord for the victory not as a gift, but let us ask Him to weigh justly our bravery, our diligence, and our sacrifices."[94]

On the first celebration of Labor Day (May 1) after he came to power, Hitler told the German workers that it was no use to pray to the Almighty unless the German people changed their lives. They needed to become strong, brave, and willing to sacrifice for the German people. Only then could they ask the Lord to bless their efforts.[95] At the 1935 Nuremberg Party Congress he stated, "In the long run God's grace will only be granted to those who earn it."[96] When he discussed the role of Providence in shaping past events, he always interpreted both victories and defeats as Providence blessing or withholding blessing based on the character and actions of the people. He did not complain to God about Germany's defeat in World War I, because Providence had simply given them what they deserved. However, Hitler had reversed the decline of Germany. He had come to power, he claimed, "not unearned as a gift from heaven, but rather as the reward for a unique tenacious struggle, a brave enduring in the struggle for power."[97] In Hitler's view, Germany under the Nazi regime had proven its worthiness and would thus enjoy God's favor.

During World War II, Hitler continued to cling to the hope that Providence would rescue Germany from impending doom, but only if Germans would fight bravely and refuse to back down. He told a group of economic leaders in July 1944 that he was not a sanctimonious churchman, but "deep in my heart I am a religious man; that is, I believe that the man who, in accordance with the natural laws created by God, bravely fights and never capitulates in this world— *that this man will not be abandoned by the Lawgiver.* Instead, he will in the end receive the blessings of Providence."[98]

Some think that because Hitler spoke so often about praying to God that he believed in a God that intervened in history. That, however, would be to ignore the times he disparaged prayer and suggested that humans only receive from God what they earn by their own efforts. In *Mein Kampf*, he denied that Germany's lost territories could be restored through *"solemn appeals to the Lord."* A nation, he insisted, *"cannot be made free by prayers."* On the contrary, Germany could only regain its freedom and lost territory through the *"force of arms."*[99] Indeed, on several occasions Hitler clarified that his kind of prayer is not a matter of words, but of deeds. It was not asking God for divine intervention but rather man taking action to bring about the desired results. In September 1938 at the Nuremberg Party Congress, he stated that "our prayer is this: brave fulfillment of the duties entailed [by the laws of nature]."[100] In his New Year appeal to the German people in 1940, he urged the German people to ask for God's blessing, but then he explained what he meant: The German people were supposed to pray by helping themselves and by dint of their own power, not by saying words to God.[101] Hitler did not construe prayer as talking to a personal God. Rather, he thought that knowing and following the laws of nature paved the true path to success.

Nonetheless, in his typically confusing manner, Hitler at times did seem to think his deity intervened in historical events. In January 1942, he remarked that if the frost had not come at just the right time, German troops would have lost more ground in the Soviet Union. Hitler rejoiced, "Providence intervened and preserved us from a catastrophe."[102] When Hitler survived multiple assassination attempts, he generally credited his good fortune to the solicitude of divine Providence. Thus, even though he usually stressed the need to work for divine assistance, and sometimes the inviolability of natural law, he seemed occasionally to think God really could work in the laws of nature to accomplish His divine purposes.

Hitler sometimes portrayed God or Providence as a righteous Judge, but once again, this God usually seemed to be an impersonal force in the universe. In keeping with his denial of a personal afterlife, God's judgment always pertained to the nation and world-historical events. Unlike the Protestant teaching that salvation comes by unearned grace through faith, Hitler's God dispensed judgment solely on the basis of works. During the war he assured his fellow Germans that Providence would be a just judge by leading them to victory, if only they would persevere and continue to sacrifice in the face of mounting adversity. In March 1940, while the war was still going well for Germany, he appealed to Providence to "bestow His blessings on our struggle for existence." He stirred his soldiers to increase bravery and endurance by telling them that Providence is ever weighing the nations to determine if they are worthy. Hitler had complete confidence that Germany's soldiers would rise to the occasion and gain the favor of Providence.[103]

Three years later, when the war was turning against Germany, Hitler still relied on the righteous judgment of Providence. Germans would have to prove themselves worthy of his divine help. "In this mightiest struggle of all time," Hitler explained, "We cannot expect that Providence give us victory as a present. Each and every people will be weighed, and what is judged too light will fall.... The Almighty will be a just judge. It is our task to fulfill our duty in such a manner that we prove ourselves to Him as the Creator of the world, in accordance with His law on the struggle for existence."[104] Hitler promised that if they would just persist in fighting, they would triumph. Their efforts would result in new life and a glorious future for the German people. God's judgment was not the decision of a personal God, but simply people getting the results of their own efforts.

All told, this is enough to show that he was no atheist. While Hitler admitted that he did not have a clear idea about the nature of God—and he implied that in some respects the nature of God was unknowable—he nonetheless believed that some kind of God existed. His faith in God gave him confidence that he could lead Germany to triumph, despite all the adversities and setbacks. He continually exhorted his people to trust in the righteous judgment of Providence, who would bestow blessing and victory to those with determination, willpower, diligence, and the willingness to sacrifice for the sake of their racial comrades. Hitler's faith did not falter, even to the very end. Indeed, when he finally despaired of victory—long after he should have known the war was lost—he did not blame God. Rather, he bitterly accused the German people of having shown themselves unworthy. It never occurred to him that both he and his God had failed.

FOUR

WAS HITLER A CHRISTIAN?

DURING HITLER'S LIFETIME, SOME OBSERVERS warned that he was the Antichrist. In 1942, Arthur Szyk, a Polish Jew living in the United States, drew a caricature of Hitler as the Antichrist bringing death and destruction to humanity. Many Christian leaders in the 1930s and 1940s, both within and outside Germany, recognized Hitler was no friend to their religion. In 1936, Karl Spiecker, a German Catholic living in exile in France, detailed the Nazi fight against Christianity in his book *Hitler gegen Christus* (*Hitler against Christ*). The Swedish Lutheran bishop Nathan Soderblom, a leading figure in the early twentieth-century ecumenical movement, was not so ecumenical that he included Hitler in the ranks of Christianity. After meeting with Hitler sometime in the mid-1930s, he stated, "As far as Christianity is concerned, this man is chemically pure from it."[1]

Many Germans, however, had quite a different image of their Führer. Aside from those who saw him as a Messiah worthy of veneration and maybe even worship, many regarded him as a faithful Christian. Rumors circulated widely in Nazi Germany that Hitler carried a New Testament in his vest pocket, or that he read daily a Protestant devotional booklet. Though these rumors were false, at the time many Germans believed them.[2]

Indeed, savvy politician that he was, Hitler often cultivated the image of being a Christian. One of the more spectacular examples was the striking photograph that Heinrich Hoffmann captured on April 23, 1932, as Hitler was exiting the Marienkirche (Mary's Church) in Bremerhaven. In that photo, a bright cross is hovering directly over Hitler's head, giving him a halo effect. This photo was included in Hoffmann's popular book of Hitler photographs, *Hitler wie ihn keiner kennt (Hitler as no one knows him)*. The caption reinforced the image: "A photographic chance event becomes a symbol: Adolf Hitler, the supposed 'heretic,' leaving the Marinekirche [sic] in Wilhelmshaven." Hoffmann's claim that this was a "chance event" is rather suspicious, as the photo looks too good to be true. The caption, meanwhile, implied that Hitler was not a heretic, as some presumed, because here he was at church. The photo was such brilliant propaganda that the historian Richard Steigmann-Gall used it on the dust jacket of his 2003 book, *The Holy Reich: Nazi Conceptions of Christianity, 1919–1945*, in which he tries to show the affinities of Nazism and Christianity. Apparently, it still convinces some that Hitler is a Christian.

In any case, sometime between 1935 and 1938, Hitler apparently decided that he no longer needed to pander to the Christian sensibilities of the German public. In the 1938 edition of *Hitler wie ihn keiner kennt*, Hoffmann altered the photo by removing the cross

Original photo of Hitler leaving the Marienkirche in Bremerhaven, from
Hoffmann's 1935 edition of Hitler wie ihn keiner kennt.
*Hitler leaving Marienkirche, Bremerhaven (1935 edition). From Heinrich
Hoffmann, Hitler wie ihn keiner kennt (1935).*

(apparently, Hitler no longer wanted to be associated with this symbol). Hoffmann also changed the caption: "Adolf Hitler after sightsee-
ing at the historic Marinekirche [sic] in Wilhelmshaven." While
Germans viewing the version with the cross would likely think Hitler
was leaving a church service, the later caption made clear Hitler was
not attending a worship service, but merely visiting a historic site.[3]

Most historians today agree that Hitler was not a Christian in
any meaningful sense. Neil Gregor, for instance, warns that Hitler's

Doctored photo of Hitler leaving the Marienkirche in Bremerhaven, from Hoffmann's 1938 edition of Hitler wie ihn keiner kennt.
Hitler leaving Marienkirche, Bremerhaven (1938 edition). From Heinrich Hoffmann, Hitler wie ihn keiner kennt (1938).

"superficial deployment of elements of Christian discourse" should not mislead people to think that Hitler shared the views of "established religion."[4] Michael Burleigh argues that Nazism was anticlerical and despised Christianity. He recognizes that Hitler was not an atheist, but "Hitler's God was not the Christian God, as conventionally understood."[5] In his withering but sober analysis of the complicity of the Christian churches in Nazi Germany, Robert Ericksen depicts Hitler as duplicitous when he presented himself publicly as a Christian.[6]

And yet, in *The Holy Reich*, Richard Steigmann-Gall insists that Hitler's religious position was closer to Christianity than many have suspected. He does not explicitly claim Nazism was a completely Christian movement and correctly notes some Nazi leaders were explicitly anti-Christian. However, the main thrust of his work is to "demonstrate with abundant empirical evidence that a wide swath of the party believed themselves and their movement to be Christian," and he tries to detect Christian influences on even some of the most anti-Christian figures in the Nazi regime, such as Goebbels.[7] He portrays Hitler as a sincere Christian, at least until 1937. Unfortunately, Steigmann-Gall never defines the word Christian or Christianity (and he confuses theism with deism). Often while correctly demonstrating ways that Christianity influenced Nazi officials or resembled Nazi ideology, or while convincingly proving that Hitler or other leading Nazis spoke highly about Jesus, he ignores the ways those same individuals interpreted Jesus differently from the majority of Christians. Steigmann-Gall's implicit definition of Christianity seems so expansive that even Muhammad or Nietzsche would probably fit, since they also spoke highly about Jesus, claiming—as Hitler did—that Christians coming after Jesus had distorted his original message.[8]

Why do some people, even today, insist that Hitler was a Christian? Primarily because he said so himself. Hitler publicly professed Christianity on numerous occasions during his political career. In public speeches, he claimed to be upholding a "positive Christianity." He once called Jesus his Lord and Savior and often praised Jesus as a great Aryan. Far more frequently, he invoked God, Providence, and the Lord. Since he had already identified himself as an adherent to "positive Christianity," many assumed—and some still assume—that whenever he mentioned God, he must have had the Christian one in mind.

One of his earliest public statements about Christianity came in the Twenty-Five Point Program of the fledgling National Socialist German Workers' Party. Hitler had only been a member of the party for five months when he unveiled the program to a Munich audience in February 1920. Anton Drexler was still officially the leader of the party, and both he and Hitler authored the program. Thus it is not entirely clear who contributed Point 24, which set forth the party's position on religion. The article proclaimed,

> We insist upon freedom for all religious confessions in the state, providing they do not endanger its existence or offend the German race's sense of decency and morality. The Party as such stands for a positive Christianity, without binding itself denominationally to a particular confession. It fights against the Jewish-materialistic spirit at home and abroad and believes that any lasting recovery of our people must be based on the spiritual principle: the welfare of the community comes before that of the individual.[9]

The first sentence offers religious freedom, but then immediately makes exceptions that cast doubt on the Nazi Party's real commitment to religious liberty. For Hitler and the party, the preservation of the German state and race took clear precedence over religious freedom. Other planks in the party program emphasized the importance of race, which always trumped religion. Additionally, once they were in power, the Nazi rulers would, of course, be the ones to determine whether a religious leader or organization was violating "the German race's sense of decency and morality," thereby forfeiting its right to freedom.

What was this "positive Christianity" that the Nazi Party claimed to be supporting? Samuel Koehne has demonstrated that the term

normally meant traditional, orthodox forms of Christianity. However, he concludes that the Nazis were most likely using the term as
a political ploy, since most Nazis who considered themselves Christians were theologically liberal and thus did not ascribe to this kind
of "positive Christianity."[10] Koehne also argues that religion and
"positive Christianity" were peripheral to Nazi concerns, since they
considered religion an expression of racial character.[11]

In examining what content the Nazis seemed to give to the term
"positive Christianity," Steigmann-Gall correctly identifies three key
elements mentioned in the program: "the spiritual struggle against
the Jews, the promulgation of a social ethic, and a new syncretism
that would bridge Germany's confessional divide."[12] Hitler and the
Nazis were trying to enlist Germans from both major Christian
denominations—Roman Catholic and Protestant—into their ranks,
so they did not want to identify with either denomination. The Nazis
already had to contend with major Catholic political parties, such as
the national Center Party and the Bavarian People's Party. They
hoped to draw Catholics away from these parties while also winning
adherents from the smaller Protestant milieu in Munich and Bavaria.[13]
As we shall see, Hitler regularly connected his vision of "positive
Christianity" and his Aryan Jesus with fighting against Jewish materialism and helping the poor and needy (but only the poor who happened to be of the right racial stock).

Samuel Koehne, however, argues that Steigmann-Gall's analysis
is misleading because all three of these points—anti-Semitism, a
social ethic, and German unity across the confessional divide—were
usually construed by Hitler and other leading Nazis as part of their
"racial-nationalist ideology." More often than not, these three features were not identified with "positive Christianity." While Koehne
is undoubtedly correct that the "racial-nationalist ideology" was
paramount in Nazi ideology, with "positive Christianity" peripheral
at best, he underestimates the zeal of Hitler and other Nazis to

smooth the way for Christians to join their ranks. Hitler often tried to find points in common—and enemies in common—between Nazi ideology and Christianity.[14]

In fact, Hitler declared the Twenty-Five Points inviolable, and Steigmann-Gall reminds us that they were never revoked.[15] But does that mean we should regard the Twenty-Five Points as the infallible word of Hitler, expressing his unshakable and unchangeable will? If we do so, we ignore what Hitler told his loyal followers about them. In *Mein Kampf*, Hitler explained why he thought the Twenty-Five Point Program should be honored as immutable, *even if it really was not*: "With a doctrine that is really sound in its broad outlines, it is less harmful to retain a formulation, even if it should not entirely correspond to reality, than by improving it to expose what hitherto seemed a granite principle of the movement to general discussion with all its evil consequences."[16] He thereby admitted that he did not think everything in the program was absolutely valid, but he did not want to open it up for criticism. It should appear as solid as granite to the public. In reality, however, it *was* flexible, subject to Hitler's own interpretation. This becomes even clearer when we examine the way that Hitler and his regime played fast and loose with the Twenty-Five Points once they came to power. While implementing some points, such as the expansionist and anti-Semitic ones, he completely ignored the anti-capitalist planks, such as dismantling large industries and large department stores. After the Nazis came to power, Point Twenty-Four did not seem terribly important to many of them, Hitler included.

Despite this, Hitler fully supported "positive Christianity" in his public speeches. Several months after promulgating the party program, Hitler defended the program at a Nazi Party meeting in Rosenheim and specifically mentioned Point Twenty-Four: "The Party stands on the basis of a positive Christianity and supports every Christian endeavor as the foundation of authority."[17] A couple of years later, he reiterated his support for "positive Christianity," but this time, he offered a qualification. He was not promoting *all* forms of Christianity. The kind of religion he favored was a Christianity of the sword, not the kind of Christianity that teaches people who have already been struck to allow themselves to be struck again.[18] Hitler made essentially the same point in April 1923, when he stressed the importance of Christianity to the Nazi movement:

> *Third we must bring Christianity to the fore again, but the fighting Christianity (Kampfchristentum).* Christianity is not the doctrine of mute acceptance and suffering, but rather a doctrine of struggle. As Christians we have the duty to fight against injustice with all means that Christ has given us; and now is the time to fight with fist and sword.[19]

The Christianity that Hitler was preaching was a religion of violence. This is highly ironic, since Hitler often harshly criticized the Christian churches for their intolerance in killing heretics and witches. During this same speech, Hitler also mentioned that the kind of Christianity he was promoting did not recognize any difference between Catholics and Protestants.[20]

A few months later, Hitler again appealed to Germans to put aside their confessional loyalties so they could unite together as Germans. Those who foster unity and mutual respect among Germans, he said, are "all the more Christians" than those who maintain religious divisions.[21] Hitler clearly hoped his positive Christianity would heal the religious divisions and forge greater German unity—although positive Christianity was not a universal religion, but only for Aryans, Hitler explained to a Munich crowd in December of 1922: "The Christian religion is created only for the Aryans; for other people it is absurd."[22] Hitler's positive Christianity was subordinated to his racial ideology, because it was supposed to forge unity among the

Aryan elements of Germany while combating non-Aryans. It was a political tool, not an integral part of his worldview.[23]

After 1923, Hitler still used the term "positive Christianity," but not very often. In February 1939, he proclaimed that Nazi social concern was the essence of positive Christianity: "If positive Christianity means love of one's neighbor, i.e. the tending of the sick, the clothing of the poor, the feeding of the hungry, the giving of drink to those who are thirsty, then it is we who are the more positive Christians."[24] Other times, Hitler equated Nazi social programs with Christianity, but usually he did not call it "positive Christianity." When he opened the 1937 Winter Aid Campaign, which collected supposedly voluntary contributions to help needy Germans get through the winter, he called this campaign a true manifestation of Christianity.[25]

In a private conversation with Goebbels just a few days after Christmas in 1939, Hitler referred to positive Christianity more cynically than in his pious public pronouncements. This does not tell us what Hitler thought about positive Christianity in the 1920s, when he used the term more freely, but it still provides insight into his perspective in 1939 (only ten months after publicly equating positive Christianity with Nazi social programs). In this conversation, Goebbels had complained to Hitler about the churches. Hitler expressed his sympathy for Goebbels' antichurch attitude but told Goebbels he would not take any action during the war. He then suggested another approach: "The best way to finish off the churches is to pretend to be a more positive Christian."[26] Apparently, at least by this time, "positive Christianity" was a ploy to undermine the Christian churches, not a way to advance the cause of Christianity.

In addition to promoting "positive Christianity" in the party program, Hitler proclaimed his own commitment to Christianity in a number of public speeches in the 1920s. He delivered his most powerful affirmation of Christian faith on April 12, 1922. This speech is widely cited today as proof positive that Hitler was a sincere Christian, because he stated, *"My Christian feeling directs me to my Lord and Savior as a fighter."* In this brief passage of his speech, Hitler repeatedly called himself a Christian and expressed love and appreciation for Jesus. His main point, however, was to enlist Jesus's legacy in the cause of anti-Semitism. The context of Hitler's remarks offers insight into his use of Christian themes in his propaganda. In this speech, Hitler was responding to a comment by one of his political opponents, a leader in the Catholic Bavarian People's Party. This man had claimed that his Christian feeling kept him from embracing anti-Semitism. Indignantly, Hitler retorted that Jesus was a pugnacious anti-Semite, so Christians should join Hitler and his party in combating the Jewish threat.[27] Hitler's comments supporting Christianity, therefore, were intended to counter his political rivals, who were telling Christians that they should line up behind a Catholic political party rather than the Nazi Party. Hitler knew he needed votes from Catholics, since they comprised the majority of Bavarians. Thus, given this context, it seems likely that Hitler, a savvy politician, was playing the Christian card to score political points.

Between 1924 and 1932, Hitler professed Christianity publicly on several occasions, especially around Christmas, when he frequently compared Jesus's struggle against the materialistic Jews with the Nazi political struggle. Shortly before Christmas in 1925, Hitler encouraged his followers to emulate the fanatical faith of Jesus in fighting against materialism. Hitler told them to carry on this struggle "not only as Germans, but also as Christians."[28] The following year at Christmas, he reminded his fellow Nazis about Jesus taking up a whip to clear the temple of the greedy Jews.[29] In the late 1920s, Hitler also continued to challenge widespread accusations that his party was un-Christian or even anti-Christian. In May 1927, Hitler replied to those accusing Nazis of being bad Christians:

If one understands Christianity as only [commitment to] a denomination, then we are indeed bad Christians. *However, if the Word of the Lord is authoritative, then we are the best ones.* We National Socialists refuse to bring denominational strife into our ranks. In that today we condemn the denominational struggle from our ranks, we believe that we are behaving the best way in the spirit of our most high Lord. We serve Christ more than those who conclude electoral alliances with Marxists, atheists, and Jews.[30]

The following year, Hitler responded yet again to those berating his party for its anti-Christian stance. He admitted that he opposed political Catholicism but denied he or his party was anti-Christian. They simply wanted to end denominational squabbling by promoting "positive Christianity."[31]

Once he came to power in January 1933, Hitler continued grooming this appearance of piety. In order to become chancellor, Hitler had to negotiate with Franz von Papen, a member of the Catholic Center Party who became Hitler's vice-chancellor. In the original coalition cabinet, conservatives outnumbered Nazis and Papen naively thought he could control Hitler. In the early days of his regime, Hitler had to placate the other conservatives on his cabinet, many of whom considered themselves Christians, as well as President Hindenburg, a Protestant, who as president could have declared an emergency and unseated Hitler. If Hindenburg had ousted Hitler, the army would undoubtedly have lined up behind the great field marshal rather than the World War I corporal. Until August 1934, when President Hindenburg died and Hitler won the plebiscite that crowned him Führer of Germany, he had to be careful not to offend Hindenburg and other conservative elites too much.

Another reason Hitler needed to reassure Germans in 1933 that his regime supported Christianity was to deflect growing unease over the anticlerical elements of the Nazi Party. By early 1933, German Catholic bishops had even banned Catholics from joining the Nazi Party (though this ban was lifted in late March 1933). To allay the growing criticism of Nazism as anti-Christian in 1933, Hitler stressed his regime's commitment to Christianity. In his first radio speech to the nation after becoming chancellor, Hitler promised to protect Christianity, since it was the basis for Germany's morality and family life, though in the speech, he did not explicitly claim that he or his party was Christian.[32] Indeed, most of his speeches between 1933–34 that mentioned his support for Christianity stopped short of professing any personal faith in it or Jesus. The closest he came during that time to professing Christian faith publicly was during a mid-February speech in 1933. As in his 1922 profession of faith, he was responding to criticism from the Center Party that Nazism was a danger to Christianity. Hitler countered this opposition by proclaiming that with his regime "Christians and not international atheists" were leading the nation.[33] Even this was not a clear-cut profession of personal faith, though it implied he was a Christian. In his speech to the German parliament on March 23, 1933, he acknowledged the Christian churches as important institutions in the preservation of the German people, and he called it the basis of morality; still, he stopped short of identifying himself or his party as essentially Christian.[34] Yet Hitler knew that he had to appear friendly to Christianity in that address. He was speaking in support of the Enabling Act, a law that would allow him to rule without parliamentary support. Since this was patently unconstitutional, he needed a two-thirds vote. The only way to get that many votes was to bring the Center Party on board. Hitler negotiated with the Center Party before introducing the bill, and they insisted that he publicly ensure religious freedom. He complied to get their votes.[35]

If we compare Hitler's pledges of support for Christianity in February and March 1933 with promises he made to other constituencies (or with his later actions), we realize how empty they really were. For example, in February he told representatives of the German states that he would not think of centralizing everything in his government but would respect the rights of the states. In exchange for Center Party votes for the Enabling Act, he made the same pledge in his March 23 speech. On January 30, 1934, however, he ignored the pledge by dissolving the German state governments. By this time he had consolidated enough power to ignore the opposition. In 1933 and thereafter, he also hypocritically proclaimed himself to be a man of peace to undercut opposition from abroad. Thus, Hitler's already murky professions of faith in 1933–34 carry even less weight, especially since he was not saying the same thing in private that he was saying in public, as we shall discuss later.[36]

However, when we turn to Hitler's view of Jesus, we find a remarkable consistency from his earliest speeches to his latest Table Talks. He expressed admiration for Jesus publicly and privately, without once directly criticizing Him. But his vision of Jesus was radically different from the teachings of the Catholic Church he grew up in. For him, Jesus was not a Jew, but a fellow Aryan. He only rarely stated this explicitly, though he frequently implied it by portraying Jesus as an anti-Semite. However, in April 1921, he told a crowd in Rosenheim that he could not imagine Christ as anything other than blond-haired and blue-eyed, making clear that he considered Jesus an Aryan.[37] In an interview with a journalist in November 1922, he actually claimed Jesus was Germanic.[38] Toward the end of his life, he elaborated further in a November 1944 monologue, where he denied Jesus was a Jew and claimed instead that He was most likely the offspring of a Roman soldier, possibly with a Jewish mother. Since Hitler believed that the ancient Greeks and Romans were mostly Aryan, a Roman father would have given him a substantial dose of Aryan blood. Hitler obviously did not subscribe to the doctrine of the Virgin Birth (nor at any time did he pay credence to any other miracle in the life of Jesus).

In this monologue, Hitler portrayed Jesus as an Aryan fighter against materialism and a staunch opponent of the Jews.[39] In fact, throughout Hitler's career—publicly and privately—he honored Jesus for exemplifying what he considered the most important Aryan moral traits: idealism, socialism, and especially anti-Semitism. Further, he consistently praised Jesus as a great fighter and associated Him with violence and the sword. Hitler's favorite story in the life of Jesus was the account of Him driving the moneychangers out of the temple, because in it, Hitler felt Jesus exemplified all the Aryan characteristics Hitler himself admired. In Hitler's telling of this story, Jesus was an idealistic, valiant fighter cracking a whip to drive the money-grubbing, materialistic Jews out of the temple with violence. Hitler first related this view of Jesus while defending the Twenty-Five Point Program in a speech in August 1920,[40] and he repeated it when professing his Christian faith in his April 12, 1922 speech. There, he stated that Jesus was greatest for being a fighter, not for enduring suffering. Hitler continued, "In boundless love as a Christian and human I read the passage that proclaims how the Lord finally took courage and took up the whip, to drive the usurers, the generation of vipers and adders, out of the temple." Then Hitler blamed the Jews for killing Jesus out of vengeance.[41] In *Mein Kampf*, Hitler again portrayed Jesus as a whip-wielding anti-Semite who was crucified for opposing Jewish materialism.[42]

Hitler appealed to this vision of Jesus as a violent fighter to justify the political violence his party doled out to political enemies. In November 1922 in Munich, he defended himself and his followers against the Bavarian People's Party, who denounced the Nazi Party's violent tactics as un-Christian. Hitler responded, "In any case I am of the conviction that no big difference exists between the whip of Jesus and a rubber truncheon, and the example of Jesus is more valuable to me than the sweet platitudes of their party."[43] Hitler not only invoked Jesus to justify violence against the Jews, but he also claimed in 1929 that if Jesus were on the earth again, He would crack His whip against the Catholic Bavarian People's Party and drive them from city halls and parliament buildings.[44] Perhaps Hitler imagined he was following the example of Jesus by carrying a riding whip for protection, as he was wont to do early in his political career.

Hitler loved the story of Jesus driving the Jews out of the temple with a whip. Here he poses with his whip, which he carried early in his career for protection.
Hitler with whip. From Heinrich Hoffmann, Hitler wie ihn keiner kennt (1938).

In a Christmas speech in 1922, Hitler did not specifically mention a whip, but he did paint Jesus as an idealist fighting against the materialistic Jews who crucified Him because of it.[45] Shortly before

Christmas four years later, he returned to this theme insisting that Jesus had "the greatest fighting disposition" of anyone who had ever lived. He denied that Jesus was an "apostle of peace." Rather he was an arch-foe of the Jews, whom Hitler portrayed as greedy capitalists. Those who continued the struggle against the Jews were building on the example of Jesus, Hitler implied.[46] Two years later on Christmas, he sounded a similar note, stating that Jesus was a "most noble war hero" and a fighter, rather than the Prince of Peace.[47]

However, while honoring Jesus for fighting against the Jews, Hitler also revealed a key difference between his religious views and those of most Christians in his 1926 Christmas speech. After explaining that the Jews had killed Jesus, Hitler portrayed himself as completing Jesus's work, a blasphemous idea if ever there was one. A report of his speech relayed his position: "The work, which Christ had begun, but could not finish, he—Hitler—would complete."[48]

From this and all his other descriptions of Jesus, it appears Hitler saw Jesus's death on the cross as martyrdom, but did not ascribe any other significance to it. Unlike most Christians through the ages who have seen Jesus's death as completing His work of salvation, Hitler apparently thought Jesus's parting words—"It is finished"—merely meant that His life was over. He thought Jesus had failed, unable to fulfill His mission. Not to fear, however—Hitler was coming to the rescue to finish the task that Jesus could not. By 1926, Hitler was clearly in Messianic mode.

Though Hitler did not explicitly mention the resurrection of Jesus in these public speeches, he implied Jesus's death was the end of the matter. Nowhere did he express belief in any of the miracles of Jesus, either. Otto Wagener, a high-ranking Nazi official with close ties to Hitler from 1929 to 1933, reported that Hitler denied the resurrection of Jesus. According to him, Hitler stated, "Immediately after the death of Christ, whom the reactionaries crucified, they set about exterminating, at least imprisoning and depriving of their rights, all those who had accepted Christ before his death. Christ's body was removed from the tomb, to keep it from becoming an object of veneration and a tangible relic of the great new founder of a religion!" However, according to Wagener, Hitler still upheld Jesus as a model who taught socialism by calling people to abandon egotism and embrace the good of the community.[49]

While Hitler appreciated Jesus because he considered him a valiant anti-materialistic anti-Semite, I have never found any evidence that Hitler believed in the deity of Jesus. Richard Steigmann-Gall bases his mistaken claim that Hitler believed in Jesus as God on a mistranslation of Hitler's April 22, 1922 speech (some of which we discussed earlier in this chapter). According to the Norman Baynes' edition of *The Speeches of Adolf Hitler*, during that speech Hitler stated about Jesus, "It points me to the man who once in loneliness, surrounded only by a few followers, recognized these Jews for what they were and summoned men to the fight against them and who, God's truth! was greatest not as sufferer but as fighter."[50] The term that is translated "God's truth!" is "wahrhaftiger Gott," a common German interjection that is rendered in some German-English dictionaries as "good God!" or "good heavens!" In the original German edition, "wahrhaftiger Gott" is set off in commas, indicating that it is indeed an interjection.

Steigmann-Gall, however, mistranslates this phrase in the following sentence: "They point me toward the man who, once lonely and surrounded by only a few followers, recognized these Jews and called for battle against them, and who, as the true God, was not only the greatest as a sufferer but also the greatest as a warrior."[51] Steigmann-Gall uses this mistranslation to argue that Hitler believed in the deity of Jesus. Apparently, he did not understand the colloquial expression used. Hitler certainly was not saying that Jesus was "the true God," as Steigmann-Gall contends. Making matters worse, Steigmann-Gall also mistranslates this passage by interpolating "only . . . also" in the final phrase, even though this is absent from the original German and changes the meaning. Steigmann-Gall's rendition suggests that Hitler did appreciate Jesus as a sufferer to some extent, but the original German negates this entirely, as Baynes' edition makes clear. This is a crucial point, because Steigmann-Gall's version makes Hitler appear more Christian and brings him pretty close to the World Council of Churches' definition of a Christian. But Steigmann-Gall only accomplishes this by twisting Hitler's words. Nowhere have I been able to find any indication that Hitler believed in the deity of Jesus, and all the evidence points in the opposite direction.

While Hitler's positive attitude toward Jesus—at least the Jesus of his imagination—did not seem to change over his career, his position vis-a-vis Christianity is much more complex. Many scholars doubt that as an adult he was ever personally committed to any form of Christianity. They interpret his pro-Christian utterances as nothing more than the cynical ploy of a crafty politician. Almost all historians, including Steigmann-Gall, admit that Hitler was anti-Christian in the last several years of his life.

If he did alter his religious stance, when did this shift occur? Steigmann-Gall follows Max Domarus's and Friedrich Heer's suggestion that Hitler abandoned his childhood faith in 1937.[52] The only direct piece of evidence for this is Hitler's own statement in October 1937 to his propaganda leaders that he had recently overcome his childhood religious conceptions. Hitler continued, "Now I feel as fresh as a colt in the pasture."[53] This is admittedly a significant piece of testimony, since it comes from Hitler himself. Steigmann-Gall thinks that 1937 became the breaking point for Hitler because opposition from the Catholic Church and the Protestant Confessing Church heated up in 1937, turning him against the remnants of Christianity still in his worldview.

A problem with this interpretation, however, is that Hitler never specified exactly what religious conceptions he had just overcome in

1937. Was he abandoning Christianity, deism, pantheism, belief in the miraculous, or appreciation for rites and ceremonies? Even if Hitler was conveying his innermost religious feelings truthfully at this point, his comments were so vague (at least as they were reported) that we do not know exactly what he meant. Further, evidence suggests that Hitler had already abandoned his childhood Catholic faith much earlier, and his contempt for all established religion was already present long before 1937. Finally, in closely examining all of Hitler's religious utterances throughout his career, I have been unable to locate a significant difference between his views *before* 1937 and his views afterward. Alan Bullock seems to agree, remarking that Hitler's attitudes and thoughts expressed in his Table Talks in the 1940s are remarkably similar to the views of *Mein Kampf*.[54]

Derek Hastings has tentatively suggested a different moment of religious crisis for Hitler: 1924. Before 1924, the majority of Hitler's statements about Jesus and Christianity were positive, but in *Mein Kampf* and thereafter, Hitler seemed more antagonistic toward the religion. Hastings points out that Hitler's self-conception altered dramatically in 1924, as he became convinced that he was the coming Führer for all of Germany, rather than the Drummer preparing the way for the coming Führer.[55] Hastings' position is plausible, and I certainly agree that before 1924 Hitler was grooming a public persona that included a Christian identity.[56]

Nonetheless, though Hitler clearly was publicly passing himself off as a Christian between 1919 and 1924, there is considerable evidence he opposed Christianity throughout his career—at least as most people, including Hitler himself, would have understood Christianity. It is difficult to pinpoint when Hitler became estranged from his Catholic upbringing, but it was likely before he left home for Vienna in 1907. Like most Austrians, Hitler was baptized into the Catholic Church soon after birth. Hitler also claimed that while going to school at the cloister of Lambach, he sang in the choir and became enthralled with the church festivals. For a brief time, he aspired to be an abbot, but after reading voraciously about wars and the military, "my temporary aspiration for this profession [abbot] was in any case soon to vanish, making place for hopes more suited to my temperament," he wrote in *Mein Kampf.* [57]

Like most young people in his society, he was confirmed in the Catholic Church. However, despite the fact that confirmation is supposed to be a solemn expression of one's personal Christian faith, Hitler's godfather claimed Hitler seemed disgusted with his confirmation ceremony in 1904.[58] One of Hitler's religion teachers in Linz, Franz Sales Schwarz, made such a negative impression on his students that he alienated most of them from Catholicism.[59] Hitler's boyhood friend Kubizek believed that Hitler had been truly devout in the days when he sang in the Lambach choir, but as he grew older, "his father's freethinking attitude won the upper hand." Kubizek also could not remember Hitler ever going to a church service.[60]

By the time Hitler left home in 1907 to live in Vienna, he was already estranged from Catholicism. Brigitte Hamann, who has done the closest analysis thus far of Hitler's Vienna years, reports that no sources ever mentioned Hitler going to church in Vienna. Further, Hamann claims that almost all the eyewitness accounts of Hitler's time in Vienna note his hatred of the Catholic Church. One source reported that around 1912, "Hitler said the biggest evil for the German people was accepting Christian humility." This certainly jibes with Hitler's later outlook. Though the source base is scant, the evidence we *do* have suggests that Hitler had a negative view of Catholicism already while living in Vienna from 1907 to 1913.[61]

Did the war years, perhaps, bring about a renewed appreciation for religion, as it did for some German troops? In a recent book on Hitler's life as a soldier in World War I, Thomas Weber answers no. According to Weber, even though many frontline soldiers turned to religion in the heat of battle, Hitler, as a messenger, was surrounded by officers who were, for the most part, antireligious and even atheist. Weber states, "There was little chance that he would turn towards religion as a strategy for dealing with the war, when many of the officers of his regiment were full of disdain for religion." Weber also did not discover any evidence or testimony suggesting that Hitler was religiously inclined. On the contrary, Weber writes, "By all accounts, Adolf Hitler was highly critical of religion."

Though the evidence is scarce, almost all of it points to Hitler being more antireligious than religious.[62] In his book on the Christmas truce of 1914, Stanley Weintraub concurs, claiming that Hitler had shed "every vestige of religious observance" and refused to attend the 1914 Christmas service that most of his unit attended.[63] Yet there was still one eyewitness—the chaplain at Pasewalk, where Hitler was hospitalized toward the end of the war after suffering blindness from a gas attack—who reported Hitler was still a faithful Catholic in 1918. In July 1933, the chaplain defended Hitler from charges that he was anti-Catholic by testifying that while Hitler was in Pasewalk, he was a genuine Catholic who devoutly attended Mass.[64]

Hitler remained an official member of the Catholic Church his entire life, but as far as we can tell, as an adult he almost never attended Mass. There is also no evidence he ever went to Confession in his adult life, so he was not exactly a member in good standing. In fact, according to Catholic theology, he was committing mortal sin by avoiding the sacraments. The few times that Hitler did attend church services were for special occasions, such as weddings, funerals for state officials (both Protestant and Catholic), or the Protestant baptism of Goering's child. For example, Hitler attended the requiem Mass in Berlin for the Polish dictator Joseph Pilsudski in May 1935. However, right after the Pilsudski Mass, Goebbels noted in his diary that Hitler was "horrified by the ceremonial nonsense" of the Mass he had just attended. Clearly, Hitler's heart was not really in it (and we do not know if Hitler actually took Holy Communion while he was there).[65] In February 1942, Hitler remarked that he did not want any priests within ten kilometers of his funeral.[66] He also had little appetite for Christian festivals, such as Christmas. His press chief claimed Hitler's distaste for the Christmas celebrations prompted him to try to escape it by going out driving.[67]

Even when he publicly announced his Christian faith in 1922 or at other times, Hitler never professed commitment to Catholicism. Further, despite his public stance upholding Christianity before 1924, he provided a clue in one of his earliest speeches that he was already antagonistic toward Christianity. In August 1920, Hitler viciously attacked the Jews in his speech, "Why Are We Anti-Semites?" One accusation he leveled was that the Jews had used Christianity to destroy the Roman Empire. He then claimed Christianity was spread primarily by Jews.[68] Since Hitler was a radical anti-Semite, his characterization of Christianity as a Jewish plot was about as harsh an indictment as he could bring against Christianity. Hitler was also a great admirer of the ancient Greeks and Romans, whom he considered fellow Aryans. Blaming Christianity for ruining the Roman Empire thus expressed considerable anti-Christian animus. Hitler often discussed both themes—Christianity as Jewish, and Christianity as the cause of Rome's downfall—later in life.

Hitler's anti-Christian outlook remained largely submerged before 1924, because—as Hitler himself explained in *Mein Kampf*—he did not want to offend possible supporters. In August 1924, while he was in Landsberg Prison, Hitler privately told Hess about having to camouflage his opposition to religion, just as he had to hide his enmity toward alcohol. Hitler had remained silent while Hess and fellow Nazis discussed their positions vis-à-vis the Protestant Church, but later he told Hess how he felt. Even though Hitler found playing a religious hypocrite distasteful, he dared not criticize the church, because he knew this might alienate people.[69]

But by the time Hitler wrote *Mein Kampf* in 1924–25, he was walking a tightrope. His political ally, General Ludendorff, was increasingly hostile to the Catholic Church, as were many on the radical Right in Weimar Germany. Hitler did not want to follow them into political oblivion—and indeed Ludendorff did end up politically isolated, perhaps in part because of his antireligious crusade. But Hitler was also sensitive to the anticlerical thrust within and outside his party.[70] Thus, after warning his followers in the first volume of *Mein Kampf* against offending people's religious tastes, he threw caution to the wind in the second volume by sharply criticizing Christianity. In one passage, he complained that both Christian churches in Germany were contributing to the decline of the German people, because they supported a system that allowed those with hereditary diseases to procreate. The problem, he thought, was that the churches focused on the spirit and neglected the physical basis of a healthy life. Hitler immediately followed up this critique by blasting the churches for carrying out mission work among black Africans, who are "healthy, though primitive and inferior, human beings," whom the missionaries turn into "a rotten brood of bastards." In this passage, Hitler harshly castigated Christianity for not supporting his eugenics and racial ideology.[71]

Worse yet, he actually threatened to obliterate Christianity later in the second volume. After calling Christianity fanatically intolerant for destroying other religions, Hitler explained that Nazism would have to be just as intolerant to supplant Christianity:

> A philosophy filled with infernal intolerance will only be broken by a new idea, driven forward by the same spirit, championed by the same mighty will, and at the same time pure and absolutely genuine in itself. The individual may establish with pain today that with the appearance of Christianity the first spiritual terror entered in to the far

freer ancient world, but he will not be able to contest the fact that since then the world has been afflicted and dominated by this coercion, and that coercion is broken only by coercion, and terror only by terror. Only then can a new state of affairs be constructively created.[72]

Hitler's anti-Christian sentiment shines through clearly here, as he called Christianity a "spiritual terror" that has "afflicted" the world. Earlier in the passage, he also argued Christian intolerance was a manifestation of a Jewish mentality, once again connecting Christianity with the people he most hated. Even more ominously, he called his fellow Nazis to embrace an intolerant worldview so they could throw off the shackles of Christianity. *He literally promised to visit terror on Christianity.* Even though several times later in life, especially before 1934, Hitler would try to portray himself as a pious Christian, he had already blown his cover.

Hitler's tirade against Christianity in *Mein Kampf*, including the threat to demolish it, diverged remarkably from his normal public persona. He was usually more circumspect, refraining from open criticism of Christianity. However, many of his colleagues testified that Hitler's personal opinion about Christianity did not match his hypocritical public stance; Hitler, for his part, thought religion itself was hypocritical. According to Wagener, who accompanied Hitler from 1929 to 1933, Hitler honored Jesus as a great socialist but believed the Christian churches had completely perverted His teachings and were, in fact, teaching the exact opposite.[73]

When did Christianity go off the rails? From the very start, according to Hitler, who asserted that he was going to reintroduce the original teachings of Jesus for the first time in history: "*We are the first to exhume these teachings! Through us* alone, and not until now, do these teachings celebrate their resurrection!" By claiming to be the first to exhume Jesus's teachings, Hitler indicated he did not think Christianity had become distorted a couple of centuries after its founding; rather, Christianity had always been a counterfeit. Thus Hitler's appreciation for Jesus—at least his idiosyncratic version of Jesus—did not translate into his favoring Christianity. He saw Jesus and Christianity as fundamentally opposed to each other.[74]

In fact, Hitler specifically bashed Catholicism, reported Wagener. Hitler mentioned that Catholics might have problems with his view of God as one who pervades the cosmos (a view consistent with pantheism). He continued, "Perhaps the adherents of the Roman Church call this 'paganism.' That may well be so. In that case, Christ was a pagan. *I* call pagan their distortions of Christ's ideas and teachings, their cults, their conception of hell and purgatory and heaven, and their worship of saints." He then accused Catholicism of creating many gods, while claiming to be monotheistic.[75]

Others reported on Hitler's private dismissal of Christianity, too. In his memoirs, Rosenberg confirms Hitler privately rejected the Christian conception of God.[76] Hans Ziegler, who edited a Nazi newspaper in Thuringia in the 1920s, had a private conversation with Hitler about religion sometime around 1930. Hitler confessed, "You must know, I am a heathen. I understand that to mean: a non-Christian. Of course I have an inward relationship to a cosmic Almighty, to a Godhead." Hitler thus denied that he was an atheist, but also rejected Christianity.[77]

Goebbels' diaries strikingly corroborate Wagener's, Ziegler's, and Rosenberg's reconstruction of Hitler's religious persona. They are filled with entries that illuminate Hitler's religious hypocrisy and suggest that Hitler really was anti-Christian. In September 1931, Goebbels recorded that Hitler wished to withdraw from the Catholic Church but was waiting for the right moment. Hitler's wish seemed to excite Goebbels, even though he admitted it would cause a scandal. But Goebbels relished the thought that he, Hitler, and other Nazi leaders would someday leave the churches *en masse*. He also wrote that Hitler "even wants sometime later to carry out the fight against it [the Catholic Church]."[78] After reassuring Goebbels that he wanted to fight Catholicism, however, Hitler sanctimoniously cozied up to the Center Party in early 1933 because he needed their political support. Then, when he dissolved the Center Party just a few months later, he insisted that he was a foe only of *political* Catholicism, not of Catholicism as a religious institution. But Goebbels already knew better, and he did not change his assessment later on. In January 1937, Goebbels was with Hitler during an internecine debate on religion and reported, "The Führer thinks Christianity is ripe for destruction. That may still take a long time, but it is coming."[79]

In reading through Goebbels' *Diaries*, Hitler's monologues, and Rosenberg's *Diaries*, it is rather amazing how often Hitler discussed religion with his entourage, especially during World War II. He was clearly obsessed with the topic. On December 13, 1941, for example, just two days after declaring war on the United States, he told his Gauleiter (district leaders) that he was going to annihilate the Jews, but he was postponing his campaign against the church until after the war, when he would deal with them.[80] According to Rosenberg, both on that day and the following, Hitler's monologues were primarily about the "problem of Christianity."[81] In a letter to a friend in July 1941, Hitler's secretary Christa Schroeder claimed that in Hitler's evening discussions at the headquarters, "the church plays a large role." She added that she found Hitler's religious comments very illuminating, as he exposed the deception and hypocrisy of Christianity.[82] Hitler's own monologues confirm Schroeder's impression.

In fact, during World War II, Hitler often expressed hostility toward Christianity but told Goebbels and other anticlerical Nazi leaders they needed to bide their time. Wartime was an inauspicious moment to proceed against the churches, Hitler thought, because he needed to keep the German people united to wage war successfully. In April 1941, Goebbels had a long discussion with Hitler on Christianity, and though Hitler was the "sharpest opponent" of Christianity, he forbade Goebbels from withdrawing from the Catholic Church "for tactical reasons." Goebbels reluctantly complied, even though it grieved him to continue paying the church tax.[83] In his view, Hitler was a staunch but crafty and patient opponent of Christianity. When Hitler told his Gauleiter in December 1941 that the regime would wait until after the war to solve the church problem, he was probably trying to restrain some of the hotheads in his party. But he also promised the day of reckoning would eventually come. He told them, "There is an insoluble contradiction between the Christian and a Germanic-heroic worldview. However, this contradiction cannot be resolved during the war, but after the war we must step up to solve this contradiction. I see a possible solution only in the further consolidation of the National Socialist worldview."[84]

In his memoirs, Hitler's personal lawyer Hans Frank, who became governor of German-occupied Poland (the General Government), also noted the discrepancy between Hitler's public and private religious stance. He implied that Hitler might not have been ill-disposed toward the churches in his early political career, but he portrayed Hitler primarily as an anti-Christian figure who eventually adopted a "demonic Godlessness." However, he noted that Hitler never publicly expressed his anti-Christian attitudes. Hitler always stressed peace with the churches in public, but simultaneously allowed his cronies to wage war on Christianity. At a cabinet meeting in 1937, Hitler commented, "I know that my un-Christian Germanic SS units with their general non-denominational belief in God can grasp their duty for their people (Volk) more clearly than those other soldiers who have been made stupid through the catechism." Hitler's contempt for Christianity could hardly have been more palpable.[85]

Hitler's press chief, Otto Dietrich, confirmed Frank's impression. In private, according to Dietrich, Hitler was uniformly antagonistic to Christianity. Dietrich wrote in his memoirs:

In private conversation he often remarked sarcastically, in reference to churches and priests, that there were some who "boasted of having a direct hook-up with God." Primitive Christianity, he declared, was the "first Jewish-Communistic cell." And he denied that the Christian churches, in the course of their evolution, had developed any genuine moral foundation. Having ordered trials of certain Catholic priests on charges of immorality, he used the findings of the courts as the basis for the broadest generalizations. He considered the Reformation Germany's greatest national misfortune because it "split the country and prevented its unification for centuries."[86]

Dietrich realized that these attitudes were inconsistent with what Hitler was telling the German people about religion. However, in the long term, Hitler hoped to efface the influence of Christianity in Germany. Dietrich stated, "Hitler was convinced that Christianity was outmoded and dying. He thought he could speed its death by systematic education of German youth. Christianity would be replaced, he thought, by a new heroic, racial ideal of God."[87] This confirms the point Goebbels made in his diary—that Hitler hoped ultimately to replace Christianity with a Germanic worldview through indoctrination of children.

Another close friend of Hitler who portrayed him as essentially anti-Christian was Albert Speer. Speer claimed that even though Hitler did not approve of a public campaign against the church, he criticized the churches harshly in private. And while he remained a member of the church, "he had no real attachment to it." Speer recalled a conversation in which Hitler was told that if Muslims had won the Battle of Tours, Germans would be Muslim. Hitler responded by lamenting Germany's fate to have become Christian: "You see, it's been our misfortune to have the wrong religion. Why didn't we

have the religion of the Japanese, who regard sacrifice for the Fatherland as the highest good? The Mohammedan religion too would have
been much more compatible to us than Christianity. Why did it have
to be Christianity with its meekness and flabbiness?" As this conversation reveals, Hitler saw religion not as an expression of truth, but
rather as a means or tool to achieve other ends—namely, the preservation and advancement of the German people or Nordic race.[88] In April
1942, Hitler again compared Christianity unfavorably with Islam and
Japanese religion. In the case of Japan, their religion had protected
them from the "poison of Christianity," he opined.[89]

In his monologues of 1941–42, Hitler frequently bashed Christianity, especially Catholicism. The Catholic Church was founded on
nonsense, he said, and he would rather be excommunicated than
stoop to get the Church's blessing.[90] He called Catholicism a lie that
made a mockery of divine Providence. "I am happy," he said, "that I
have no inner connection with it [Catholicism]."[91] Despite his intense
antipathy for the Christian churches, however, he did not want open
confrontation. He explained,

> I do not trouble myself about doctrinal matters, but I will
> not tolerate it, if a parson (*Pfaffe*) meddles in earthly affairs.
> The organized lie must be broken, so that the state is abso-
> lute lord. In my youth I espoused this point of view: Dyna-
> mite! Today I recognize, that one cannot hurry it along. It
> must slowly decay like a gangrenous limb.[92]

The word Hitler used for "parson" here was *Pfaffe*, which carries
a connotation of contempt. The "organized lie" is presumably the
Catholic Church, since that was the one he was associated with and
surrounded by in his youth. In this passage, Hitler testified not only
that he was anti-church from a young age, but also that he was even
more radical in his younger years. This accords with Hamann's and

Weber's analysis of his early life. And while Hitler's tactics may have changed since his youth—as he now claimed to adopt a more gradualist approach to the church's demise—his goal remained the same: supplanting the church with the state, so the state had total power.

In fact, Hitler contemptuously called Christianity a poison and a bacillus and openly mocked its teachings.[93] In a long diatribe ridiculing many core Christian teachings, Hitler told his colleagues that the Christian concept of heaven was insipid and undesirable. After scoffing at doctrines such as the Fall, the Virgin Birth, and redemption through the death of Jesus, Hitler stated, "Christianity is the most insane thing that a human brain in its delusion has ever brought forth, a mockery of everything divine." He followed this up with a hard right jab to any believing Catholic, claiming that a "Negro with his fetish" is far superior to someone who believes in transubstantiation.[94] Hitler, in his own twisted mind, believed black Africans were subhumans intellectually closer to apes than to Europeans, so to him, this was a spectacular insult to Catholics. In February 1942, Hitler again scoffed at the basic teachings of Christianity, sarcastically relating the story of humanity from a Christian standpoint. He implied that God was responsible for original sin and commented that God's method of redemption by sending his Son was a "murderous subterfuge." Then, according to Hitler, when others did not accept these strange teachings, the church tortured them into submission. In the course of this anti-Christian diatribe, Hitler called the Catholic Church a form of idolatry and "Satanic superstition."[95]

Another theme that surfaced frequently in Hitler's monologues of 1941–42 was that the sneaky first-century rabbi Paul was responsible for repackaging the Jewish worldview in the guise of Christianity, thereby causing the downfall of the Roman Empire. In December 1941, Hitler stated that although Christ was an Aryan, "Paul used his teachings to mobilize the underworld and organize a proto-Bolshevism. With its emergence the beautiful clarity of the ancient world was lost."[96] In fact, since Christianity was tainted from the very start, Hitler sometimes referred to it as "Jew-Christianity."[97] While Hitler often associated Jesus with Aryan traits and socialism, he consistently lambasted Christianity as Jewish and communist. He denigrated the "Jew-Christians" of the fourth century for destroying Roman temples and even called the destruction of the Alexandrian library a "Jewish-Christian deed."[98] Hitler thus construed the contest between Christianity and the ancient pagan world as part of the racial struggle between Jews and Aryans.

In November 1944, Hitler described in greater detail how Paul had corrupted the teachings of Jesus. At first a staunch opponent and persecutor of Christianity, Paul suddenly recognized that he could use this budding movement for his own purposes. Thus, he produced a forgery, Hitler declared: "The fight against the apotheosis of money and the fight against Jewish selfishness and Jewish materialism was altered [by Paul] to become the idea of the inferior races, the slaves, the oppressed, and the financially poor against the ruling class, against the superior race, 'against the oppressor'! The religion of Paul and of what represented Christianity from then on was nothing other than communism!"[99] The idea that Paul and early Christianity embraced slave morality to overthrow the heroic, noble Romans is a Nietzschean theme too, which Hitler gave a racial interpretation.

Hitler's preference for the allegedly Aryan Greco-Roman world over the Christian epoch shines through clearly in Goebbels's diary entry for April 8, 1941. That day, shortly before the invasion of Greece, Hitler informed Goebbels that he would not allow Athens to be bombed. This was quite a remarkable policy decision for the Führer, who had shown absolutely no compunction about annihilating other European cities from the air. Even Coventry, England, with its famously beautiful Christian cathedral, was specifically targeted by the Nazi war machine. Athens, however, was different, explained Goebbels, since "Rome and Athens are Mecca for him [Hitler]...The

Führer is a person entirely oriented toward antiquity. He hates Christianity, because it has deformed all noble humanity." Goebbels even noted that Hitler preferred the "wise smiling Zeus to a pain-contorted crucified Christ," and believed "the ancient people's view of God is more noble and humane than the Christian view." Rosenberg recorded the same conversation, adding that Hitler considered classical antiquity more free and cheerful than Christianity with its Inquisition and burning of witches and heretics. He loved the monumental architecture of the Romans, but hated Gothic architecture. The Age of Augustus was, for Hitler, "the highpoint of history."[100]

From Hitler's perspective, Christianity had ruined a good thing. In July 1941 he stated, "The greatest blow to strike humanity is Christianity," which is "a monstrosity of the Jews. Through Christianity the conscious lie has come into the world in questions of religion."[101] Six months later, he blamed Christianity for bringing about the collapse of Rome. He then contrasted two fourth-century Roman emperors: Constantine, also known as Constantine the Great, and Julian, nicknamed Julian the Apostate by subsequent Christian writers because he fought against Christianity and tried to return Rome to its pre-Christian pagan worship. Hitler thought the monikers should be reversed, since in his view Constantine was a traitor and Julian's writings were "pure wisdom."[102] Hitler also expressed his appreciation for Julian the Apostate in October 1941 after reading *Der Scheiterhaufen: Worte grosser Ketzer* (*Burned at the Stake: Words of Great Heretics*) by SS officer Kurt Egger. This book contained anti-Christian sayings by prominent anticlerical writers, including Julian, Frederick the Great, Nietzsche, Schopenhauer, Goethe, Lagarde, and others.[103] It was a shame, Hitler said, that after so many clear-sighted "heretics," Germany was not further along in its religious development. Hitler then went on a tirade about Paul corrupting Jesus' teachings and destroying the Roman Empire by preaching equality and submission to the divine will. A few days later,

Hitler recommended that Eggers's book should be distributed to millions because it showed the good judgment that the ancient world (meaning Julian) and the eighteenth century (i.e., Enlightenment thinkers) had about the church.[104]

This notion that Christianity was a Jewish plot to destroy the Roman world was a theme Hitler touched on throughout his career, from his 1920 speech "Why Are We Anti-Semites?" to the end of his life. It made a brief appearance in his major speech to the Nuremberg Party Rally in 1929, and reappeared in a February 1933 speech to military leaders.[105] In a small private meeting with his highest military leaders and his Foreign Minister in November 1937, Hitler told them that Rome fell because of "the disintegrating effect of Christianity."[106]

From the way that Hitler bashed a generic "Christianity" as a Jewish-Bolshevik scheme, it seems clear that he was targeting all existing forms of Christianity. His sharpest critiques were leveled at the Catholic Church he grew up in; only rarely did he explicitly divulge his views on Protestantism, and, when he did, he seemed conflicted. He castigated the Protestants for witch-burning, and in July 1941, he was critical of Luther and Protestantism, though he appreciated Luther's courage to revolt against Catholicism. In *Mein Kampf*, Hitler mentioned Luther as a great reformer, but did not elaborate.[107] Wagener remembered Hitler exulting in the German people rising up in the Reformation against the coercive measures of the Catholic Church, and he praised the Swedish king Gustavus Adolphus for saving Germany from the Catholic forces during the Thirty Years' War.[108] What Hitler liked about Protestantism, then, was that it fought against Catholicism. He never expressed any appreciation for their religious position.

He also deprecated Protestantism because it had divided Germany. In a speech to army officers and cadets in February 1942, he lamented that Germans had remained divided for much of their history. The fault for this, he explained, was the Reformation, which led to religious wars. Millions of Germans fought each other, according to Hitler, "only for sheer phantoms." Obviously, Hitler did not think very highly of either Protestantism or Catholicism.[109] In *Mein Kampf*, however, he enjoined them to work together to fight their common enemy: the Jew.[110]

Strangely, Hitler praised the Jesuits for stimulating the Counter-Reformation, whose architecture he appreciated. Luther, on the other hand, had succumbed to a mystical inwardness—according to Hitler—that was inferior to the Jesuit's pursuit of sensuous pleasure (Hitler obviously did not know much about Ignatius of Loyola's own mysticism.) Luther, however, had one thing going for him, Hitler believed: he "did not bind humanity to the letter of the scripture; there are an entire string of utterances, in which he takes a position against the scriptures, in that he ascertains that they contain much that is not good."[111] This is a rather backhanded compliment of the man who made "scripture alone" one of the guiding principles of his life and ministry. If nothing else, it proved Hitler did not have a very high opinion of the Bible.

During a monologue on December 14, 1941, Hitler divulged a decisive distaste for Protestantism. That day, Hitler learned Hanns Kerrl, a Protestant who was his minister for church affairs, had passed away. Hitler remarked, "With the best intentions Minister Kerrl wanted to produce a synthesis of National Socialism and Christianity. I do not believe that is possible." Hitler explained that the form of Christianity with which he most sympathized was that which prevailed during the times of papal decay. Regardless of whether the pope was a criminal, if he produced beauty, he is "more sympathetic to me than a Protestant pastor, who returns to the primitive condition of Christianity," Hitler declared. "Pure Christianity, the so-called primitive Christianity...leads to the destruction of humanity; it is unadulterated Bolshevism in a metaphysical framework."[112] In other words, Hitler preferred Leo X, the great Renaissance patron of the arts who excommunicated Luther, to the Wittenberg monk who called the church back to primitive, Pauline Christianity. According to Rosenberg's account of this same conversation, Hitler specifically mentioned the corrupt Renaissance Pope Julius II, Leo X's predecessor, as being "less dangerous than primitive Christianity."[113]

Hitler's negative attitude toward the Bible, meanwhile, can be traced back to the earliest part of his political career. Hans Frank once asked Hitler what he read as a soldier during World War I. Hitler replied that at first he had read the Christian Gospels and Homer. Later in the war, however, he frequently read Schopenhauer. He continued, "Thus then I could also gladly forgo the Gospels—even though Christ was certainly a true fighter. But the saying about turning the other cheek when one is struck, is not a good prescription for the front." Not surprisingly, he did not approve of all of Jesus' teachings, at least as they were recorded in the New Testament. According to Frank, one saying of Jesus that Hitler *did* like was, "I did not come to bring peace, but the sword." Hitler told Frank that by saying this, Jesus eternally consecrated the use of the sword. Frank further reported that when Mussolini showed Hitler an ancient statue of Jesus, Hitler remarked that the sculpture was proof that Jesus was not a Jew.[114]

Many anti-Semites in early twentieth-century Germany despised the Old Testament as the product of the Jewish spirit, and Hitler was no exception. He saw the Old Testament as the antithesis of everything he stood for. In his view, it taught materialism, greed, and deception. Further, it promoted racial purity for the Jews, since it taught them to avoid mingling with other races. In many respects, Hitler saw the Old Testament as a book instructing the Jews how to triumph in the racial struggle for existence. In his 1920 speech "Why Are We Anti-Semites?," he explained that the Old Testament was vivid proof of the degeneracy of the Jewish race. He stated, "You must excuse me, that I first take the book called the Bible, of which I do not want to affirm that everything in it is absolutely accurate; for we know, that the Jews worked very liberally with it." He then called the Old Testament a "frightful indictment" against the Jewish race. Not only did the Bible teach the Jews to use deceit to supplant other races, Hitler claimed, but also Abraham even gave up his wife to pharaoh so he could do business in Egypt. Jews after Abraham's time have followed his immoral example, he continued. In Hitler's view, then, Abraham was a wicked founding father who set the tone for Jewish life from that time forward.[115] In his speech declaring war on the United States on December 11, 1941, Hitler attacked Roosevelt for supposedly listening to a cabal of Jews, who were allegedly steeped in the greed of the Old Testament.[116] Wagener also remembered Hitler's contempt for the Old Testament, which he considered "suffused with a materialistic ethos that is not our ethos."[117]

In a monologue in June 1942, Hitler again expressed disdain for the Bible, especially the Old Testament. He regretted that the Finnish people's religiosity was based on the Bible because it was permeated with Jewishness. According to Hitler, religious people like the Finns, who during long winters seek their religion in the Bible, "must become mentally crippled" and fall into "religious delusion." Moreover, Hitler lamented that the Bible had been translated into German, because this made Jewish doctrines readily available to the German people. It would have been better, he stated, if the Bible had remained only in Latin, rather than causing mental disorders and delusions.[118]

Though he criticized the Old Testament more often than the New Testament, Hitler did not have much appreciation for the New Testament either, except for the aforementioned story about Jesus driving the moneychangers out of the temple. Around 1928, when discussing the Nazi Party Program with some colleagues, he stated, "The New Testament is full of contradictions, but that did not prevent the spread of Christianity."[119] Since Hitler often remonstrated against Paul as imbuing primitive Christianity with a Jewish spirit, he obviously rejected the Pauline epistles, which comprise about half of the New Testament.

Hitler's disdain, however, was not limited to the Bible. He also rejected the Christian teaching about salvation. According to Goebbels, Hitler stated in May 1943, "The idiocy of the Christian doctrine of salvation is for our time completely unusable. Nonetheless there are scholars, educated people, and men in high positions in public life, who hang on to it as on to a childhood faith. That even today one views the Christian doctrine of salvation as giving direction through a difficult life is completely incomprehensible."[120]

Meanwhile, Hitler not only surrounded himself with many vehemently anti-Christian Nazi officials, but he exulted in their independence from the Christian churches. Many SS members followed Himmler's example and encouragement to withdraw from the churches, and Hitler lauded them for their anti-church attitude.[121] Hitler once advised Mussolini to try to wean the Italian people away from the Catholic Church, lest he encounter problems in the future. When Mussolini asked how to do this, Hitler turned to his military adjutant and asked him how many men in Hitler's entourage attended church. The adjutant replied, "None."[122]

Because Hitler consorted with and promoted Nazi officials with anti-Christian inclinations, it is not surprising that negativity toward Christianity pervaded a good deal of Nazi propaganda. The most notorious piece bashing Christianity was Alfred Rosenberg's *Myth of the Twentieth Century*, which was one of the best-selling works on Nazi ideology in the 1930s, even though Hitler never endorsed it, and at times, even privately distanced himself from it. Other examples of anti-Christian Nazi propaganda include two important programmatic writings that teach the foundations of Nazi racial views: *Handbuch für die Schulungsarbeit in der HJ: Vom deutschen Volk und seinem Lebensraum* (translated as *The Nazi Primer: Official Handbook for Schooling the Hitler Youth*) and *Rassenpolitik*

(*Racial Policy*). The former listed the Christian churches as "implacable opponents" of Nazi racial ideology.[123] The latter, an SS booklet, discussed the churches in a section on opponents of the Nazi regime. It claimed the churches' teachings on human equality contradicted Nazi racial ideology.[124]

In the end, the evidence is preponderant against Hitler embracing any form of Christianity for most of his adult life. Even though he tried to palm himself off as a Christian when it served his political purposes, none of his friends and comrades considered him one. Even though he never officially left the Catholic Church, Schroeder claimed he promised to withdraw from the church immediately after the war to symbolize the dawn of a new historical era.[125] All of Hitler's close associates agreed with Schroeder, testifying that he was antagonistic toward Christianity. He admired the whip-wielding Jesus, whom he considered a fellow Aryan warrior fighting against the allegedly infernal Jews, but he had utter contempt for the Jesus who told His followers to love their enemies and turn the other cheek. He also did not believe that Jesus's death had any significance other than showing the perfidy of the Jews, nor did he believe in Jesus's resurrection. In private conversations and monologues he railed at Christianity because it had followed the lead of that insidious Jewish rabbi Paul. Despite Hitler's disingenuous public statements, and despite his esteem for (his anti-Semitic version of) Jesus, it is abundantly clear that Hitler did not consider himself a Christian. And neither should we.

FIVE

DID HITLER WANT TO DESTROY THE CHURCHES?

ACCORDING TO ERNST VON WEIZSÄCKER, WHOM Hitler appointed ambassador to the Vatican, Heinrich Himmler once told Weizsäcker's wife, "We shall not rest until we have rooted out Christianity."[1] The Security Service of Himmler's SS kept church leaders and organizations under surveillance and continually proposed policies to limit and hinder their activities.[2] The Gestapo arrested hundreds of priests and pastors, some for violating Nazi restrictions or encroachments on the churches, and others on trumped-up charges. Other leading Nazi officials were equally hostile toward the Christian churches. In June 1941, Bormann, who had recently stepped into Hess's vacated position as leader of the Nazi Party Chancellery and had thus become one of the most powerful officials under Hitler, sent a circular letter to all Nazi Gauleiter about the relationship between National Socialism and Christianity. Therein he asserted, "National Socialist and Christian views are irreconcilable. The Christian churches are based on people's ignorance...on the other hand, National Socialism builds on a scientific foundation."[3] Goebbels and Rosenberg wholeheartedly agreed with Bormann and Himmler and hoped to hasten the demise of the Christian churches. Prosecutors at the Nuremberg Trials stressed the intense antagonism of the Nazi regime toward the churches, which was a common perception in the Anglo-American world at the time. And many historians, such as John Conway in *The Nazi Persecution of the Churches, 1933–45*, provide abundant evidence of the Nazi regime's anti-Christian character.

But not all Nazi leaders were on board. Hanns Kerrl, whom Hitler appointed minister for church affairs in 1935, endeavored to synthesize National Socialism and Christianity. Weizsäcker even recalled an angry confrontation between Kerrl and Rosenberg at a cabinet meeting in February 1940 where they argued over the relationship between the National Socialist worldview and Christianity.[4]

What was Hitler's position in the general melee? We have already seen that he was ideologically opposed to the Christian faith, but he was also careful not to offend his mostly Christian constituency by bashing their religion publicly. For political reasons, as we have discussed, he did not favor open confrontation with the churches. The question then emerges whether Hitler wanted to destroy the churches, hoped the churches would continue to exist after accepting Nazi dominion and ideology, or was he indifferent about their continued existence? Did he alter his position on this issue during his political career?

A recent work by Stephen Strehle on church-state separation expands on Conway's argument by situating Hitler's desire for church-state separation in its wider historical context. Strehle argues that

Hitler did indeed intend to destroy the churches.[5] But some historians take a more nuanced approach. The German historian Heike Kreutzer argues that in the first few years after 1930, the Nazi leadership tried to forge a synthesis of National Socialism and Christianity. Once they came to power, the Nazis tried to bring the churches under their control. Only after repeatedly failing to bring the churches to heel did Hitler turn against them. This interpretation implies that Hitler sincerely hoped to work with the churches at first, and only began attacking them when they would not accept his position on church-state relations.[6] Dietmar Süss also does not think that Nazi policy before 1939 aimed at the destruction of the churches; rather, Nazi church policies were designed to suppress the churches' influence step by step. This process radicalized after 1937, when Hitler gave greater sway over church policy to Bormann, Himmler, Rosenberg, and other anticlerical Nazis.[7] Steigmann-Gall, meanwhile, denies that Hitler ever intended to destroy the churches, even during the war, when he privately uttered threats against them.[8]

The problem in weighing the intentions of the Nazi regime toward the churches is that, especially before consolidating power in Germany, Hitler wanted to avoid open conflict with them. He needed to appeal to both Catholics and Protestants to seize power, preserve his popularity, and keep foreign powers off his back. It follows that these concerns might have caused Hitler to mask his animus toward the Christian churches, especially before 1935. However, even taking this into account, Hitler's position toward the churches was complex. When he reflected back on his religious upbringing, he claimed that he hated Christianity from his youth. Once he became a politician, however, his desire to see the end of Christianity was tempered by a realistic acknowledgement that the religion was too deeply rooted in the German people's psyche and emotions simply to abolish it immediately. Even when Hitler privately uttered his most vicious threats against the churches during

World War II, he often indicated that the destruction of the churches would not be a quick and easy project.

In sum, Hitler did want to destroy the churches, but for him, it was a long-term goal that required time and patience. He hoped to accomplish it by gradually increasing restrictions on the churches and, more importantly, wresting the education and training of the youth away from them. Undermining the churches was also subsidiary to many of Hitler's more important goals, such as eliminating the Jews, crushing communism, building German unity, and expanding Germany's borders.

Some of Hitler's close colleagues understood his ambivalent position. His press chief, Otto Dietrich, explained that Hitler's restraint toward religious groups was a political move. In order not to alienate supporters, he sometimes endured attacks from church circles, although he often privately threatened future vengeance against them. Further, Dietrich noted that Hitler's private invective against the churches encouraged Himmler, Bormann, and other anticlericals in his party to attack the churches.[9] Weizsäcker took a similar view of Hitler's position toward the churches. While the official Nazi platform supported "positive Christianity," Weizsäcker explained,

> In practice, things were very different. Hitler himself took care not to attack the Churches openly. But he had from his youth been an enemy of the Church; and without his tacit agreement the rigorous measures that were taken would hardly have been possible. An acquaintance of mine heard him say that in one or two generations the Christian churches would die out of their own accord.[10]

For Hitler, the church question was not a peripheral subject; it was a major topic of conversation. The theme came up repeatedly in his private conversations with Goebbels, Rosenberg, and other officials; in private speeches to party officials; in talks with his secretaries; and in his monologues. In July 1941, he told his entourage, "In the long run National Socialism and the churches cannot exist side by side." When one of his secretaries asked if that meant he was going to launch a new war against the churches, Hitler responded, "No, that does not mean a war; the ideal solution is to do away with the churches by allowing them to shrivel away by themselves gradually and without violence."[11] Indeed, Hitler's desire to destroy the churches through a gradual, non-confrontational approach often brought him into conflict with more zealous anticlerical Nazi officials, who favored more drastic measures against the churches. Because of this, Hitler sometimes served as a moderating influence on anti-church policies. Nonetheless, his ultimate goal was the eradication of the churches, even if he was more patient than some of his comrades.

Before coming to power in 1933, Hitler recognized that an anti-Christian platform would be political suicide, so he consistently portrayed himself in public as supportive of Christianity and the churches. Even so, he was unable to cover up completely the animus toward Christianity that percolated through his party. Thus, in the 1920s and 1930s, he was constantly dogged by accusations that he and his party stood in opposition to Christian ideals. In the early 1930s, the Catholic hierarchy in Germany forbade priests from joining the Nazi Party and enacted other anti-Nazi measures because they perceived Hitler and his movement as intrinsically anti-Catholic. Many of Hitler's most vociferous professions of support for Christianity occurred in speeches where he was overtly countering charges that he was anti-Christian.

Before 1933, then, Hitler's approach was to appease Christians so he could gain their support, build up a mass movement, and take power. He could placate the anticlerical forces in his own party by agreeing with their anti-church agenda in private while *publicly* distancing himself from them. When the fiercely anticlerical General Ludendorff, Hitler's political ally in the Beer Hall Putsch, challenged

Hitler to confront the churches more vigorously, Hitler replied, "I entirely agree with His Excellency, but His Excellency can afford to announce to his opponents that he will strike them dead. But I need, for the building up of a great political movement, the Catholics of Bavaria just as the Protestants of Prussia. The rest can come later."[12] Hitler piously preached peace to the churches, just as he would later proclaim his peaceful intentions to—and even sign nonaggression pacts with—Poland, Denmark, the Soviet Union, and any enemy he was not prepared to face just yet.

In order to build bridges between the Bavarian Catholic milieu and the Nazi Party, Hitler cultivated relationships with a few Catholic priests early in his political career. Interestingly, the two priests Hitler consorted with the most were not in good standing with the Catholic Church. In 1922, Hitler met the Benedictine abbot Alban Schachleiter, who became his devoted follower and remained loyal until his death in 1937. Schachleiter, however, was not actively engaged in the ministry when they met, since his monastery had been dissolved earlier. He was an extremely controversial figure in Catholic circles. In 1926, the Catholic Church banned him from preaching, and in March 1933, he was even forbidden from taking communion.[13] Another Catholic priest that Hitler befriended in his early career was Bernhard Stempfle, who had earlier belonged to the monastic order of the Poor Hermits of St. Hieronymus. Stempfle left his monastery in 1918, moved to Munich, and no longer identified himself as a priest thereafter. He became a journalist for an anti-Semitic newspaper. Despite their marginal status in the Catholic Church, the Nazi press continually referred to Schachleiter as an abbot and Stempfle as a priest, intimating that good Catholics could support the Nazi cause.[14]

Still, Hitler had difficulty playing his juggling act between the churches and the anticlerical forces in his party, because anticlerical Nazis such as Rosenberg—who edited the official Nazi newspaper— often alienated Christians. In 1927, Magnus Gött, a Catholic priest who had previously supported the Nazi Party, wrote to Hitler and expressed his growing doubts about the movement. In two letters responding to Gött's criticisms, Hitler admitted that some Nazis might be renegades, but he played on Gött's Catholic sensibilities by suggesting that Gött should view anticlerical Nazis in the same way as the Apostle Peter, who denied Jesus but later became the first pope. Hitler reassured Gött that Nazism is "a true crusade for the Christianity of the Lord in the highest and noblest sense." He hoped that religious Catholics and Protestants would join and support his movement.[15] In the early 1930s, Hitler and the Nazi Party also began cultivating closer relations to the Protestant Church, especially through the "German Christians," a movement that wanted to import Nazi ideals into the Protestant Church.[16]

Before coming to power, Hitler did not seem to have developed any clear plans or policies for the churches. This is unsurprising, since it fits his method of operation in other arenas, where he had fixed goals but improvised policies. Hitler was often flexible about the means and timing of policies, even when pursuing objects central to his worldview (such as eliminating Jews from Germany). In relation to the churches, he indicated in two private talks with his entourage— on August 6, 1938, and on June 18, 1939—that his goal before coming to power had been to form "a unified German Reich Church." He conceived of this as a loose union of the two major denominations in Germany that would be subordinate to the Nazi state. He did not care about their dogmas, rites, or ceremonies, but they would have to be nationalistic and support the Nazi regime. Uniting the churches under the umbrella of a generic Christianity meshed with Hitler's nationalistic agenda to promote German unity by overcoming the religious division in the country.

As Doris Bergen has demonstrated, the pro-Nazi "German Christian" movement did try to build unity across denominational lines.[17] However, Hitler's vision never really got far, because except for the

German Christians, neither the Catholic Church nor most Protestant leaders had an appetite for such unity in the 1930s. Hitler ultimately blamed the churches for not cooperating with this scheme.[18]

In the first year or two after coming to power, he continually reassured church leaders that he would grant them freedom to worship and continue with their normal activities. At the same time, he sought to bring the churches under his control as much as possible. He was walking a political tightrope; as aforementioned, Franz von Papen, his vice-chancellor, was a member of the Catholic Center Party, and Germany's President Hindenburg, a Protestant, could depose him by invoking emergency powers if he thought Hitler was leading the country into ruin.

After the parliamentary elections in early March 1933, Hitler staged a festive opening for the parliament on March 21 in Potsdam, a city near Berlin where Prussian kings had their palaces. The celebration began with Protestant and Catholic services for the parliamentarians and dignitaries. However, Hitler's seat near the Catholic altar was conspicuously absent. He and Goebbels were instead paying homage to a fallen Nazi storm trooper at a cemetery in Berlin. Hitler excused himself on the grounds that the Catholic Church hierarchy had branded him a renegade and did not want him to participate in the Mass.[19] Interestingly, however, Hitler had summoned Abbot Schachleiter the day before the ceremony to come with haste to Berlin to perform a Mass on March 21 so Hitler could attend Mass that day. Schachleiter declined because his bishop had banned him from performing divine service (and even receiving the sacrament).[20]

The parliamentary episode illustrates that even though Hitler was still trying to portray himself as a loyal Catholic, he would only go so far. In December 1941, Hitler told his colleagues that his decision to skip Mass in the Potsdam ceremony was a masterstroke. In his retelling of this story, he was faced with the question: church or no church. By choosing the latter, he bragged, he had been more revolutionary

Hitler and Goebbels skip the Catholic Mass at the opening of parliament to visit a fallen Nazi at Luisenstadt Cemetery, March 21, 1933.
Hitler and Goebbels at Luisenstadt Cemetery – From Wilfrid Bade, Deutschland Erwacht: Werden, Kampf und Sieg der NSDAP (1933).

than Mussolini, who in his view made too many concessions to the church despite being a freethinker. Of course, Hitler distorted this narrative by not divulging he had invited Schachleiter to come to Berlin to say Mass. Nonetheless, Hitler clearly took pride later in having stayed away from the Mass in Potsdam.[21] Later that day in Potsdam, however, the political ceremony opening the parliament took place in the Garnisonkirche (Garrison Church), where Hitler and Hindenburg addressed the gathered politicians.

Immediately before and after the opening of parliament, Hitler negotiated with the Center Party to get their support for the Enabling Act, which needed a two-thirds margin to pass. The legislation set aside parts of the Weimar Constitution, granting Hitler and his cabinet the right to rule by decree. Hitler personally negotiated with the leaders of the Center Party on March 20 and 22, promising that he would respect their rights and freedoms. He gave the following

Hitler addressing the opening of parliament at Garnisonkirche,
Potsdam, March 21, 1933.
*Hitler at Garnisonkirche, Potsdam. From Wilfrid Bade, Deutschland
Erwacht: Werden, Kampf und Sieg der NSDAP (1933).*

assurances to entice them to vote for the Enabling Act: (1) the state
governments would continue to function, (2) church schools could
continue to operate, (3) the concordats already in force with the German states of Prussia, Bavaria, and Baden would be honored, (4)
judges would remain inviolable, (5) the parliament would continue to
exist, and (6) the president's rights would continue unmolested. The
promises helped secure the Center Party's votes for the Enabling Act.[22]
Unfortunately for the Center Party, Hitler would use the power they
bestowed on him to violate every one of these promises.

Over the next few months, Hitler swept away all political oppo-sition—including the Catholic Center Party—while simultaneously negotiating a concordat with the Catholic Church. Hitler claimed he only wanted to eliminate political Catholicism, not the religious func-tions of the Catholic Church. In a meeting with Bishop Wilhelm Berning on April 26, and in other meetings with Catholic leaders, he insisted that his regime would not restrict organizations sponsored by the Catholic Church. He also feigned being offended by accusa-tions that he would attack Christianity. On the contrary, he lied, he would never think of intervening in the rights of the Church and would not touch the Catholic youth organizations nor interfere with religious education.[23] Two days later, Hitler wrote to Cardinal Adolf Bertram, assuring him that Catholic organizations had nothing to fear.[24] Hitler again expressed his desire to live in peace with the Catholic Church when he met with the papal nuncio, Cesare Ors-enigo, on May 8.[25]

Nonetheless, even while trying to woo Catholic support, Hitler still carried out his ruthless campaign of synchronization (*Gleich-schaltung*) by eliminating all trade unions, including those with religious affiliations. On June 22, 1933, the leader of the German Labor Front, Robert Ley, proclaimed that it was the Führer's will that the German Labor Front be the sole labor organization in the Third Reich. He also announced that Catholic and Protestant unions would now be regarded as enemies of the state.[26] Bertram wrote to Hitler, protesting this move violated his promises in April about the freedom of Catholic organizations. He also requested that Hitler revoke Ley's proclamation.[27] Hitler simply ignored Bertram.

While destroying the Catholic political party and Catholic unions, Hitler continued to pursue negotiations with the Vatican over a Concordat. The impetus for the Concordat came from Germany, not the Vatican, but it remains unclear if it was Hitler's or Papen's initial idea. In any case, Hitler deemed it a good plan, hoping that an agreement with the Vatican would give his regime greater legitimacy, especially in the eyes of German Catholics. He also wanted to placate foreign powers to avoid economic boycotts and keep them from interfering with his rearmament plans later on. Western diplomats in Germany sometimes reported to their governments the worrying news that the Nazi regime was trying to weaken the Christian churches, and Hitler was sensitive to foreign pressure at this point.[28] In July 1933, he told his cabinet that whatever flaws existed in the Concordat could be straightened out later when the foreign policy situation had improved.[29]

The Concordat guaranteed the Catholic Church complete freedom of belief and worship. It allowed the Church to continue appointing its own clergy and operate monastic establishments without government interference. Further, church schools could continue operating, and Catholic instruction would remain in public schools in Catholic regions. Also, the Nazi regime pledged to permit the Catholic Church to continue running organizations for religious, cultural, or charitable purposes. In exchange, the Catholic Church agreed to recognize the legitimacy of the Nazi regime and to abstain from politics.[30] When the Concordat came up for discussion in the cabinet meeting on July 14, 1933, Hitler told his colleagues that it was not up for debate, because it was an unqualified success. He was surprised that the Catholic Church had agreed to it so quickly, but it would produce a "sphere of trust" that would be invaluable to the regime. He was delighted that the Church was essentially acquiescing to his demolition of the Center Party and Catholic trade unions.[31]

Judging from the way that Hitler treated other international treaties and agreements, there is no reason to think he was sincere when he approved the Concordat. Papen's claim in his memoirs that Hitler sincerely wanted peace with the Church in 1933 and was radicalized only later by Goebbels and other anticlerical members of his party seems just as naïve as Papen's promise to his colleagues in January

1933 that he would keep Hitler under control.[32] Carsten Kretschmann is surely correct when he argues, "Hitler's church policy was a policy *with* the Concordat *against* the Concordat."[33] For Hitler, the Concordat was just as binding as his later Nazi-Soviet Non-Aggression Pact, another agreement with an ideological enemy. It did not signal Hitler's real intentions.

While forging a Concordat with the Vatican to win Catholic support for his regime, Hitler simultaneously made moves to bring the German Protestant churches under control. On April 25, 1933, he appointed Ludwig Müller, a chaplain who enthusiastically supported the Nazi Party, his "Plenipotentiary for Questions concerning the Evangelical [i.e., Protestant] Churches."[34] At that time, the Protestant (mostly Lutheran) churches in Germany were divided geographically into separate state churches. Müller's mandate from Hitler was to unify the Protestant churches into a single Reich Church under one bishop. With the help of the German Christian movement, Hitler hoped he could control the newly organized Protestant Reich Church. When Protestant church leaders met in late May to deliberate about a new church constitution and a Reich bishop, the German Christians nominated Müller to fill the new slot. Many Protestant leaders opposed this move, so they tried to preempt Müller's power play by electing as the new Reich bishop Friedrich von Bodelschwingh, an esteemed pastor and director of a Protestant charitable organization. Müller was furious, and with the support of Hitler and the German Christians, he campaigned against Bodelschwingh, successfully pressuring him to resign a month later.[35]

On June 24, the same day Bodelschwingh resigned, the Nazi minister of education and culture appointed August Jäger as state commissioner for Protestant churches in Prussia. Jäger zealously tried to Nazify the Prussian Protestant Church, dismissing church officials and replacing them with German Christians.[36] Not only did Jäger's actions arouse howls of protest from within the church, but also after resigning as Reich bishop, Bodelschwingh met with President Hindenburg to enlighten him about the current controversies in the Protestant Church. Hindenburg responded by meeting with Hitler and sending him a letter, demanding that he mend relations with the Protestant church (the tone of the letter suggests *or else*).[37] Then Hindenburg took an unprecedented step: he published his letter to Hitler in the July 1 newspapers (except the *Völkischer Beobachter*, which refused to carry it), expressing his concern for the church and expressing confidence that Hitler would do something quickly to repair the damage.[38]

Under pressure from the president, Hitler encouraged Müller to continue to forge a new united Reich Church, which came to fruition on July 11, when a new constitution for the German Protestant Church was ratified by the state churches.[39] At the July 14 cabinet meeting—the same day the cabinet discussed the Concordat—Hitler's regime promulgated the Law on the Constitution of the German Evangelical Church, which accepted the newly formed Reich Church. This law also announced that church elections would be held on July 23 for representatives to send to the first church synod under the new constitution.[40] Also, to placate the opposition, Hitler announced on July 14 that the church officials removed by Jäger would be restored to their positions.

Hitler and his regime did everything possible to sway the outcome of the church elections. Goebbels and the Propaganda Ministry instructed the newspapers not to editorialize for anyone other than the German Christians. Nazi newspapers encouraged party members who were Protestant to show up and vote for the German Christians. Uniformed SA troops stood in front of polling places with placards supporting the German Christians. In some places in Germany, ballots only listed the German Christians.[41] Hitler felt these church elections were so important that, despite not being a member of the Protestant Church, he gave a radio address the day before the election and endorsed the German Christian candidates. He told the German nation that he did not want to interfere with matters of church doctrine or teaching, but from the political standpoint, it was necessary to have a church that supported the Nazi state. The German Christians, he maintained, supported his regime, so Germans should cast their ballots for them.[42]

To Hitler's delight, the German Christians won two-thirds of the delegates in this manipulated election. When they met in Wittenberg on September 27, 1933 for the national synod meeting, the German Christians elected Hitler's candidate Müller as the Reich bishop.[43] Hitler had achieved his goal of unifying the Protestant Church under a pro-Nazi Reich bishop. This triumph, however, would unravel quickly, as Müller and the German Christians aroused vigorous opposition to their policies. Hitler had hoped that Protestant bishops, pastors, and other leaders would meekly submit to Müller, especially since he had the power of the state at his back. Later, however, Hitler expressed happiness that this project ultimately collapsed, because he came to recognize that a divided church was easier to dominate. In 1942, he claimed that he had been crazy to try to unite the "state popes"—meaning the Protestant bishops—into a single church. He was thankful that his project failed "through the stupidity of my pope" (i.e., Müller).[44]

Indeed, Müller was an unfortunate choice for Reich bishop, because instead of unifying the Protestant Church, he alienated thousands of pastors by his heavy-handed implementation of Nazi policies. At the synod meeting for the Prussian Protestant Church in Berlin from September 5–6, 1933, Müller and the German Christians incited controversy by pushing through the Aryan paragraph, which forbade converted Jews from serving in church offices. This move aroused Martin Niemöller and other pastors to organize the Pastors' Emergency League, which eventually transformed into the Confessing Church, a branch of the Protestant Church that opposed Nazi encroachments on the church (while simultaneously pledging fidelity to the Nazi state). By the end of 1933, 6,000 pastors, one-third of the total number in Germany, had joined the Pastors' Emergency League. In December, Müller heightened tensions further by merging the Protestant youth organizations into the Hitler Youth without consulting other church leaders.[45] According to Goebbels, Hitler was already disgusted with Müller by that time.[46] The following September, Hitler sent a message to Müller through his foreign minister Konstantin von Neurath. He threatened that if Müller did not straighten out affairs in the Protestant Church, he would never see the Führer again.[47] Müller could not pull it off, and Hitler's confidence in him waned thereafter, even though he continually propped Müller up in the face of opposition from various church leaders. Hitler even refused to allow Müller to resign as Reich bishop in July 1941, when Müller informed him that he wanted to withdraw from the church altogether because he no longer believed its doctrines. Hitler commanded him not to resign, so Müller remained Reich bishop until the collapse of the Third Reich, even though he no longer believed in Christianity.[48]

Hitler was enraged that Niemöller and other Protestant church leaders opposed his hand-picked Reich bishop in 1933, so he summoned Müller, six Protestant bishops, Niemöller, and other Protestant leaders to meet with him, Frick, Göring, and other Nazi officials at the Reich Chancellery in Berlin on January 25, 1934. Immediately before meeting with these clergymen, Hindenburg suggested to Hitler that he should compel Müller to resign. Hitler countered that the Pastors' Emergency League was the real problem, since they were engaging in what he considered political activity. He threatened state action against them if they did not desist.[49] Hitler opened the meeting with the clergy by giving the floor to Göring, who read an excerpt from a phone conversation by Niemöller that the police had tapped earlier that day. Hitler angrily denounced Niemöller's attempt to gain support from President Hindenburg in this church conflict. His tirade had a dampening effect on the church leaders, even though Niemöller bravely defended his actions. Hitler told the church leaders that they would have to work with Müller, whether they liked it or not. He also threatened to withdraw state subsidies from the churches if they did not end their oppositional activities.[50] That night, the Gestapo showed up at Niemöller's home to search for incriminating evidence. A few days, later a bomb mysteriously exploded in Niemöller's house.[51] Nonetheless, Niemöller continued organizing opposition to Müller and Nazi church policies.

Less than two months later, Hitler met with two of the most recalcitrant Protestant bishops, Hans Meiser of Bavaria and Theophil Wurm of Württemberg. He issued a veiled threat, telling them that if they did not cooperate, Christianity would disappear, just as it had in Russia. He also claimed he had no interest in doctrinal issues, though he hastened to add that many passages in the Bible were mistranslated. But, most importantly, he insisted that the churches accept the Nazi "doctrine of blood and race" because it was one of "the irrefutable facts" of the world. Meiser remained firmly opposed to Hitler's church policies and told him that, in light of their disagreements, he would have to take the position of Hitler's "most loyal opposition." This prompted an outburst from Hitler, who shouted that they were traitors and enemies of Germany.[52]

But his tantrum had little effect on Meiser and Wurm, who continued to support the newly emerging Confessing Church. In May 1934, a synod of the Confessing Church issued the Barmen Confession, which rejected the imposition of Nazi standards in the church (while not mentioning Nazi injustices against the Jews, communists, or others). In an attempt to bring the Confessing Church into line, Nazi police forces placed Wurm and Meiser under house arrest in early October 1934. This was a public relations fiasco, as Germans demonstrated in the streets to support their ousted bishops. Further, the Foreign Ministry notified Hitler that many foreign church leaders were loudly protesting the arrests. Perhaps even more worrying to Hitler, his Gauleiter Josef Bürckel warned him that the arrests were creating bad publicity in the Saarland, which might have negative consequences in the upcoming referendum on their joining Germany.[53] On October 26, Hitler intervened, defusing the crisis by releasing the bishops and summoning them to meet with him in Berlin. At his meeting on October 30 with Wurm, Meiser, and Bishop August Marahrens, another Confessing Church supporter, Hitler implied that he had not supported the actions taken against Wurm and Meiser. Hitler further indicated that his attempt to unite the Protestant Church had failed, though he refused to ask Müller to resign. Finally, he once again threatened the bishops that he would withdraw state subsidies from the churches, if they did not come into order.[54]

Two days later Hitler told a gathering of high-level Nazi officials, including Hess, Frick, Göring, Bormann, and others, that he had no intention of capitulating before the church. However, he recognized that his attempt to set up a strong, united Protestant Church had aroused too much opposition among the clergy. Thus, he was altering his policy. Now he recognized that it would be better to foster the fragmentation of the Protestant church into factions, thereby weakening his opposition. He also mentioned his recent exchange with Meiser, who demanded that the church's confession (*Bekenntnis*) be free. Hitler replied that if the confession must be free, so must the state. In this case, the churches would have to raise their own funds without government help.[55] Thus Hitler once again threatened to end state financial support for the churches.

In July 1935, Hitler made another attempt to defuse the Protestant church struggle by placing Hanns Kerrl, who at the time was a minister without portfolio, in charge of church affairs. Kerrl soon began calling himself "Minister for Church Affairs," a designation that Hitler accepted. Kerrl was a long-time party member and faithful disciple of Hitler who sincerely wanted to reconcile Nazism and Christianity. It became obvious fairly quickly that Kerrl would fare no better than Müller in bringing the Protestant Church under control. Thus Kerrl's influence declined precipitously, and by 1937, he and his Ministry had little influence over Hitler or even over church policy.

In January 1937, Kerrl butted heads with Hitler by criticizing the Gauleiter Roever for banning crucifixes from schools in his district. Hitler dismissed Kerrl's objections, noting that every battle had a few tactical mistakes, and he did not think Roever's misstep was all that tragic. Hitler promised to continue the struggle to gain absolute state control of the churches. Tactics might have to be adjusted to the circumstances, he admitted, but he was firm in his commitment to suppress the churches. He offered two approaches, according to Rosenberg: "[E]ither one punctures one vein after the other, or else one wages open combat." Hitler clearly adopted the former, step-by-step approach, but the end result was clear: the churches would eventually be subjugated.[56]

During the conversation with Kerrl, Hitler posed two rhetorical questions: (1) Did the Nazi Party come to power with the churches or without them? (2) Were more people behind the Nazi Party today or earlier? His point was clear—he wanted Kerrl to recognize that the Nazi Party needed the churches even less at that moment than they had before coming to power. Kerrl, however, had the audacity to respond that the Nazi Party was more popular earlier. Hitler—likely astonished by Kerrl's impudence—replied that Kerrl should stop being crazy. Hitler then launched into a long monologue about church affairs, telling the hapless Kerrl that his approach to church affairs was misguided because the correct policy should be to bring the churches completely under the control of the Nazi regime.[57] A month after this dressing down, Kerrl tried to revivify his efforts to unify the warring factions in the Protestant Church, but in February, Hitler applied the brakes to

Kerrl's plans, since he now wanted the church to splinter into factions rather than unify.[58]

Kerrl continued butting heads with Hitler and with other anti-clerical Nazi officials, who often bypassed him when dealing with church affairs. By the late 1930s, the Party Chancellery under Hess and the SS Security Service under Heydrich played an increasingly important role in formulating church policy.[59] Both were intensely anticlerical and favored persecution of the churches. The Security Service placed church officials under surveillance, leading to the arrest of hundreds of pastors, priests, and monks throughout the 1930s. Despite Hitler's own anticlerical tendencies, he was often forced to restrain the radicalism of his underlings due to his concern about foreign and public opinion.[60] However, he seemed to support just about any anti-church measure that did not arouse the ire of the public too much.

Even after Hitler's rebukes in early 1937, Kerrl persisted in trying to build a unified Protestant Church. In January 1940, Hitler told Nazi colleagues that Kerrl was working at odds with Hitler's policies by doing so.[61] A year later, Hitler reminded Kerrl that he had already given him instructions not to unify the Protestant Church under the auspices of the July 1933 constitution (which technically remained a legally binding document, not that Hitler cared). Hitler was clearly irritated that Kerrl was still pursuing a policy of rapprochement with the Protestant Church.[62] When Hitler learned of Kerrl's death in December 1941, he remarked, "Kerrl's motive was undoubtedly noble, but it is nonetheless a hopeless attempt to unite National Socialism and Christianity."[63]

In contrast to Kerrl's attempts to unify Nazism and Christianity, Hitler and many other Nazi officials were pursuing the opposite tactic throughout most of the 1930s. Just a couple of weeks after marshaling all the resources of the Nazi Party to sway the July 1933 Protestant church elections—and even before significant opposition against the outcome had organized—Hitler decided that his party needed to distance itself from the Protestant Church and return to religious neutrality. In a private talk on "Party and Church" to the Nazi Gauleiter on August 5, 1933, he forbade party leaders from influencing developments in the Protestant Church (as they had just done quite vigorously). He prohibited any lectures or discussions about religious issues at party meetings, as well as church hymns being sung. Though party members were free to attend regular church services, party organizations would not be allowed to ask for special worship services.[64] Hitler was apparently concerned the recent events might embolden party officials to forge closer connections to the Protestant Church, so he made sure they understood that was not his intention. On the contrary, he wanted the party to remain separate from the churches.

Over the next few years, Hitler and leading Nazi officials strengthened the barriers between the party and the churches. According to Goebbels, on February 9, 1937, Hitler "inveighed mightily against the churches," calling them "the most brutal institution that one can imagine."[65] That same day, Bormann—maybe at Hitler's instruction, or maybe simply "working toward the Führer"— issued an order that members of the clergy would not be allowed to join the party, and a few months later he expanded the ban to include anyone who was "strongly committed to their religious denomination." Bormann ordered party officials to kick out any members who began studying theology or became clergy.[66] In June 1938, Bormann extended the prohibition even further, forbidding any party leader from taking any kind of leadership position in any religious organization, including the churches.[67] Hitler's direct involvement in issuing these orders is unclear, though Bormann was issuing these directives from the party chancellery, led by Hess, who carried the title "Deputy of the Führer." At a minimum, Hitler likely knew about the measures in advance, and he certainly learned about them afterward, because he received many complaints from church officials about the anti-clerical policies his regime pursued.

Meanwhile, he certainly knew about and approved the Law for the Protection of the National Socialist Workers' Party Insignia of April 1937, which forbade non-party organizations from using Nazi symbols, such as the swastika. One of the organizations targeted by this law was the German Christians, whose symbol was a cross with a swastika. In June, the Ministry of Church Affairs told all church groups to refrain from using Nazi symbols.[68] When the German Christians did not promptly comply, Heydrich warned them in December 1937 to desist, or else the Gestapo would take measures against them.[69] One month earlier, Bormann had also stipulated that party members could not wear uniforms to church functions.[70]

During his first three years in power, Hitler, purely for political reasons, forbade most of the highest leaders in the Nazi Party from leaving the churches (although Rosenberg withdrew from the Protestant Church in 1933). In September 1936, Hitler told his party comrades that he was lifting this earlier restriction—they were free to leave the churches, if they wanted. With a green light from Hitler, Bormann hastily left the Protestant Church.[71] Himmler and Reinhard Heydrich both left the Catholic Church in 1936. Himmler also encouraged, but did not require, other SS men to leave their churches and register simply as "believers in God."

When Hitler privately addressed leading Nazi officials at a conference in Vogelsang in November 1936, he attacked the churches for being out of step with the latest scientific developments. Instead, he claimed, they had chosen to continue preaching anti-scientific dogmas, which alienated many people. Hitler specifically blamed the churches for combating the latest scientific knowledge about races. In addition, Hitler speculated, "All churches, the whole of Christendom is incapable of fighting Bolshevism; a new worldview [i.e., National Socialism] must do it." Thus, Hitler made clear to his party comrades that Nazism was superior to Christianity and would ultimately supplant the churches, because Nazism had the imprimatur of science.[72]

In 1937, the Nazi regime stepped up its campaign of intimidation and persecution of the Confessing Church. In response to increasing restrictions placed on the Protestant Church, pastors disobeyed and sometimes even protested against government intrusions. Hitler ordered the arrest of Niemöller, and on July 1, 1937, he was arrested, charged with inciting rebellion, and incarcerated. Hitler was furious when Niemöller's court case ended in March 1938 with a light sentence that he had already served. Hitler ordered him rearrested, so Niemöller spent the rest of the Nazi period in concentration camps. By November 1937, Nazi police had arrested over seven hundred Protestant pastors in the Confessing Church.[73] In January 1939, Himmler reported to Hitler about his visit with Niemöller at the Oranienburg concentration camp. Hitler then railed against Niemöller, calling him a fanatic and an oppositionist. He vowed he would never release him—and indeed he did not.[74] In fact, late in the war, Hitler ordered Niemöller's execution, though it was not carried out.

While Hitler struggled to bring the Confessing Church to heel in the mid-1930s, he simultaneously whittled away at the Concordat with the Catholic Church. Despite the guarantee in the Concordat that Catholic organizations could continue to function, the Nazi regime gradually eliminated them. During the Röhm Purge in late June and early July 1934, the SS and Gestapo seized the opportunity to murder two lay leaders of Catholic organizations, an editor of a Catholic periodical, and a former priest, none of whom had anything to do with Röhm or the SA, who were the main targets of the Purge.[75] SS Security Service reports indicate that surveillance and pressure from the regime caused a decline in church organizations and publications in the mid-1930s.[76] In addition to clamping down on Catholic organizations, the Nazi regime had persecuted about 12,000

Catholic priests by 1937, and later it began dissolving monasteries, too.[77]

Hitler was especially zealous about gaining control of the hearts and minds of the young people of Germany, which also put him in conflict with the Catholic Church. He told a gathering of the Hitler Youth on May 1, 1937,

> There can be but one German Youth Movement, because there is but one way in which German youth can be educated and trained. The handful of people, who perhaps still cherish within themselves the thought that, beginning with the youth, they will be able to divide the German nation again, will be disappointed. This Reich stands, and is building itself up anew, upon its youth. And this Reich will hand over its youth to no one, but will take its education and its formation upon itself.[78]

Because he wanted the exclusive right to indoctrinate children, Hitler issued a law in 1936 that made the Hitler Youth compulsory. This was a body blow to the Catholic youth organizations, because Baldur von Schirach, head of the Hitler Youth, forbade dual membership in the Hitler Youth and other youth organizations. In March 1939, Hitler promulgated the Youth Service Law, which delivered the coup de grâce to the already weakened Catholic youth organizations by banning them entirely, which was a flagrant violation of the Concordat Hitler had ratified in 1933.[79]

In order to strip away even further the influence of the Catholic Church over the youth in Germany, the Nazi regime began a campaign in 1935 to pressure parents to send their children to public, not parochial, schools. Bormann even drafted a law that year to ban all private schools, arguing that such a move would not violate the Concordat. He claimed that the Concordat gave the Catholic Church the

Nazi poster: "Adolf Hitler's Youth Go to Public School;" this propaganda was aimed at undermining parochial schools, most of which were Catholic.
Nazi Poster: "Adolf Hitler's Youth Go to Public School" – courtesy of Randy Bytwerk.

right to operate schools according to laws governing private schools, so if private schools were abolished, Catholic schools would have no legal right to exist, either.[80] A year later, Hitler endorsed a draft of a school law that would have replaced all parochial schools with public schools and allowed teachers and students to opt out of religious education in the public schools.[81] In 1937, the Ministry of Education was still circulating a draft of the school law to other government and party offices, but apparently it was never publicly proclaimed, because Hitler decided not to officially abrogate the Concordat.[82]

Nonetheless, Nazi Party officials continued pressuring Catholic schools to dissolve. In early 1937, private schools in Berlin were banned, and when a Vatican representative protested this infringement of the Concordat, the German foreign minister declared that it was not contrary to the Concordat. Following Bormann's line of reasoning, the foreign minister argued that all private schools were being closed, not just Catholic ones, so this did not transgress the Concordat.[83] Two years later, Bormann was still complaining that, despite considerable progress in eliminating parochial schools, some were still operating and needed to be closed down. Bormann decreed in 1939 that party officials should dissolve all religious schools, orphanages, and even church camps as quickly as possible, because the churches should have no role in educating children.[84] In February 1937, Bormann had also instructed party officials to ban clergy from teaching religion classes in the public schools.[85] A few months later, the Ministry of Education ordered schools to comply with Bormann's directive.[86] Prior to this (and again after the Nazi period), it had been customary for clergy to provide religious instruction in public schools.

Catholic clergy protested government interference with their activities, which violated the Concordat. Hoping to appease—or maybe intimidate—the Catholic clergy, Hitler met with Cardinal Michael von Faulhaber on November 4, 1936, at his mountain home in Obersalzberg. Hitler reminded Faulhaber of their common enemy—Bolshevism—and encouraged Faulhaber to join forces with Nazism against this threat. He also recounted some of the ways the Catholic Church had been forced to change in the past, such as giving up the geocentric model of the solar system. In a similar fashion, the Catholic Church should abandon its opposition to Nazi ideology, such as racial legislation and compulsory sterilization, which, Hitler insisted, were based on the firm foundation of science.[87] A few days later, Hitler reported to Goebbels that he had presented Faulhaber with a choice: "Either with us against Bolshevism or else [we will wage] a battle against the church."[88] Neither Hitler nor Faulhaber wanted full-scale war at this point, but Hitler was unwilling to cancel the anticlerical measures his regime had already taken that had angered the Catholic clergy. He persisted with his policy of skirmishing with church organizations and officials to reduce the Catholic Church's power; meanwhile, he tried to keep the public pacified.

By early 1937, the Vatican had sent seventy diplomatic protests to the Nazi regime concerning violations to the Concordat.[89] Pope Pius XI was fed up with the constant infractions and finally decided to publicly rebuke the Nazi regime for its continuous transgressions of the Concordat. On March 21, 1937, Catholic priests throughout Germany read the pope's encyclical, *Mit brennender Sorge*, from the pulpit. Hitler, Goebbels, and Kerrl banned the encyclical and threatened anyone possessing a copy with arrest. In fact, Hitler had the chutzpah of accusing the pope of breaching the Concordat by issuing the encyclical—a hypocritical twist, since the point of the encyclical was to protest Hitler's constant violations. Pius's encyclical complained about a wide variety of Nazi actions against the Concordat, including closing parochial schools.[90]

But his protests did absolutely nothing to chasten Hitler. In fact, it riled him up. Initially, Hitler agreed with Goebbels that remaining silent was the best approach, though Goebbels used the opportunity to ban church publications that printed the encyclical. By April 1, Hitler was encouraging Goebbels and the Justice Minister to "let loose against the Vatican" by putting clergy on trial and publicizing the clergy's moral transgressions. In late May, Goebbels gave a major two-hour speech on the clergy trials that was carried on all the radio stations. He smeared the Catholic clergy, accusing them of many vices, including homosexuality. Hitler helped him craft the speech. Goebbels was amazed by Hitler's contributions, claiming Hitler went even farther than he would have gone in attacking the churches. Hitler listened to Goebbels's speech and congratulated him afterward, saying he had been so excited during it that he could not sit down.[91]

Less than two months after Pius issued his encyclical, Hitler held a long discussion about the church question with his Nazi colleagues. He told his comrades, "We must humble the church and make it our servant." He then suggested several means to accomplish this: (1) ban celibacy, (2) confiscate church property, (3) forbid the study of theology before age twenty-four, (4) dissolve monastic orders, and (5) remove the right to educate from the churches. Once these were implemented, Hitler continued, the churches would decline within a few decades to the point that they "will eat out of our hands." Soon thereafter, according to Goebbels, Hitler was seriously contemplating the separation of church and state, which he had threatened earlier and which would have been a major financial blow to the churches.[92]

Though Hitler did not take these drastic measures, he did ramp up his persecution of the Catholic clergy and considered ending the Concordat. In early June, Nazi officials discussed a proposal for rescinding the Concordat.[93] Kerrl told a government official in September 1937 that Hitler was planning a major speech on Reformation Day (October 31), during which he would announce the end of the Concordat and initiate the complete separation of church and state.[94] But Hitler apparently reconsidered. In fact, he never ended up nullifying the Concordat, even though infringements continued unabated in the late 1930s and early 1940s. He also never ended state support for the church (though the subsidies declined considerably, especially during the war).

While carrying on this wrestling match with the churches in the 1930s, the Nazi regime also tried to co-opt Christian festivals by emptying them of their Christian content and imbuing them with Nazi ideology. One of the best examples of this was Christmas. As previously mentioned, Hitler invoked Jesus in some of his Christmas speeches in the 1920s always as a great anti-Semitic Aryan fighter, never as the one who came to bring "peace on earth, goodwill toward men." According to historians Joe Perry and Corey Ross, the Nazi regime tried to de-Christianize the Christmas festivities by emphasizing the pagan Germanic roots of many Christmas traditions. Nazi Christmas celebrations focused on building German unity, not on the birth of Jesus.[95] Nowhere was this more evident than in the *Deutsche Kriegsweihnacht* (*German War Christmas*) books issued during the war by the Nazi regime, which celebrated

DIE GANZE NATUR IST EIN GEWALTIGES RINGEN
ZWISCHEN KRAFT UND SCHWÄCHE,
EIN EWIGER SIEG DES STARKEN ÜBER DEN SCHWACHEN.

ADOLF HITLER

Hitler's Christmas message to the German people in a Nazi book on Christmas: "All of nature is a violent struggle between strength and weakness, an eternal victory of the strong over the weak."
Hitler's Christmas message. From Deutsche Kriegsweihnacht (n.d. [early 1940s]).

Christmas with poems, stories, and songs devoid of religious content. One edition prominently displayed this quotation from Hitler, which set the tone: "All of nature is a powerful struggle between power and weakness, an eternal victory of the strong over the weak."[96] For Germans accustomed to singing "Silent Night" during the holiday season, Hitler's statement would not have seemed like a traditional Christmas message.

By 1939, Hitler's regime had such an antireligious reputation that Hitler felt a need to respond to growing foreign criticism. Hoping to keep Britain, France, and the United States on the sidelines while he expanded toward the East, he tried to deflect these democracies' opposition and win their confidence. In his major speech to the German parliament on the sixth anniversary of the Nazi seizure of power, he insisted that the democracies were wrong to criticize his government as antireligious. His regime had never persecuted anyone for their religious convictions, he assured. On the contrary, it contributed huge sums of tax money to the churches. If the churches did not like the current situation, he was willing to introduce a separation of church and state (as France and the United States already had), which would end church subsidies. He claimed that the Nazi regime had not closed any churches, hindered any church services, nor influenced doctrines or worship services. The only clergy his regime had targeted for persecution were those who criticized the state or used their clerical position for political purposes. Of course, Hitler failed to mention all the church organizations and schools his regime had shut down.[97]

Once the war broke out, Hitler continued playing a cat-and-mouse game with the churches. On the one hand, Hitler hoped to use the war as an excuse to further limit church activities. On the other hand, he hoped to avoid open conflict with the churches during the war, because he wanted to keep the German public firmly united behind the war effort. He did not want negative publicity souring the German people's attitude toward the regime.

At least as early as November 1939, Hitler was telling his comrades that the conflict with the clergy would have to be delayed until after the war. Goebbels agreed, but a month later he again complained to Hitler about the churches. Hitler expressed sympathy for Goebbels' anti-church stance but refused to take any firm action against the church during the war.[98] A few months later, Hitler determined that "for the time being" the regime should not interfere with church liturgies, even if they included words of praise for Jews.[99] The following July, the Interior Minister informed Nazi officials that "the Führer wishes to avoid all measures that are not absolutely necessary, which could impair the relationship between the state and party with the church."[100] In August 1941, after the Gauleiter Sauckel took the unwise step of requiring party officials in his district to withdraw from the church, Hitler reiterated his ban on anti-church activities, lest it destroy German unity and damage the war effort.[101]

While Hitler told his fellow Nazis that he did not want to take strong actions against the church during the war, his secretary testified to a friend—and Goebbels' diaries made clear—that Hitler always reminded the Nazis this was merely a temporary expedient. After the war, he promised, he would reckon with the churches.[102] For instance, in a speech to his Gauleiter in December 1941, Hitler stated, "There is an irresolvable contradiction between the Christian and the Germanic-heroic worldview. This contradiction cannot be resolved during the war, but after the war we must step up to resolve this contradiction." The most effective remedy, he suggested, would be to increase efforts to imbue the German public with the National Socialist worldview, which would effectively supplant the Christian worldview.[103]

Another area where Hitler was unwilling to push hard against the churches was in matters related to the chaplaincy. Hitler knew that chaplains had strong support from most of the military leadership and many rank-and-file soldiers. In April 1940, Bormann asked Hitler to abolish the chaplaincy, but Hitler refused, claiming the time was not ripe yet for such a bold move, even though several months earlier, Hitler and Himmler had discussed their dim view of chaplains in the SS police forces and intimated that they would like to abolish them.[104] Actually, in the branch of the military where the Nazis had the greatest control—Goering's air force—chaplains were persona non grata before 1940.[105] Nonetheless, about a thousand chaplains served in the German armed forces during the war. To maximize casualties among chaplains, the Nazis required that chaplains must serve in the front where the fighting was fiercest, hoping that many would fall in battle.[106]

However, while repeatedly restraining his comrades from rampaging against the religious sensibilities of the German people, Hitler at times sent a different signal. His military adjutant Gerhard Engel recorded that in January 1940 Hitler seemed to be moving toward a more anticlerical position under the influence of Bormann and Himmler. According to Engel, Hitler had seemed more tolerant toward the churches earlier, but by this point, he appeared "determined to fight." Hitler asserted, "The war is in this respect, as in many other matters, a favorable opportunity to settle the church question completely."[107] Hitler hoped to use the war to reduce the churches' power in any way possible. Indeed, in March 1941, Bormann issued a directive clarifying Hitler's July 1940 prohibition against anti-church actions. According to Bormann, some party cadres were misinterpreting Hitler's decree by thinking they were forbidden from placing any restrictions whatsoever on the churches. This was not Hitler's intent at all, according to Bormann. Necessary measures were still allowed, he explained, such as the confiscations of monasteries that were presently occurring in former Austrian territory.[108] Just a week later, Hitler ordered that the church press be completely shut down, ostensibly to save resources and labor needed for the war effort.[109] War exigencies provided a convenient excuse for Hitler to throttle church influence.

During the war, the Nazi regime continued its campaign of limiting the churches in any way it could without inciting too much negative publicity. War-time necessity was often given as an excuse for these restrictions. From 1940 to 1942, about three hundred monasteries and church institutions were closed, and the German army took over many church hospitals. In October 1940, Hitler decreed that the day after an air raid, church services would not be allowed before 10 a.m., so even religious services were limited.[110] In November 1939, Hitler ordered that the Protestant Day of Prayer and Repentance be moved from a Wednesday to a Sunday to help the war effort.[111] He considered an extra workday more important to the war effort than a day of prayer. During the rest of the war, the regime decreed that many church festivals would be shifted to Sunday to benefit the war effort (though some churches simply ignored the decree and cele-brated the holidays as usual).[112] At least one priest was arrested for telling his congregants in 1941 that he would celebrate Corpus Christi Day on the traditional day, whether the state authorities liked it or not.[113]

Many other clergy were harassed or imprisoned by Nazi author-ities. One example was a Catholic priest in Berlin, Bernhard Lichten-berg, arrested on October 23, 1941, for praying for Jews and for those in concentration camps. Under interrogation, Lichtenberg boldly outlined multiple complaints against the Nazi government, including their elimination of religious instruction from schools, the attempt to remove the crucifix from schools, the killing of disabled people, and the persecution of Jews. He stated, "National Socialist ideology is incompatible with the teaching and commands of the Catholic Church." After serving his two-year sentence, he was rearrested (just as Niemöller had been earlier) and died in November 1943 while awaiting transfer to Dachau.[114]

However, while allowing and even encouraging the imprisonment of many clergy, Hitler was more cautious in dealing with bishops. Hitler was furious when Catholic Bishop Clemens August Graf von Galen spoke out boldly in public sermons in July and August 1941 against the Nazi confiscations of monasteries and against the Nazi program of killing disabled people. Though some Nazi officials wanted Galen executed, Hitler demurred, arguing that arresting Galen would damage the war effort. He advised delay, though he placed Galen under surveillance. Hitler also continually assured his comrades that he was only waiting for the right moment to strike. Later, he would destroy Galen and any other church leader who betrayed Germany, he promised.[115] Hitler never made good on this pledge, however, for Galen survived the war.

Later in the war, the Protestant Bishop Wurm was accused of passing information to the Swedish consul, and some Nazi officials wanted him arrested. In March 1943, however, Hitler decided not to indict Wurm, citing "political reasons" for his decision. The Nazi regime had lost face with the earlier arrest of Wurm in 1934, which likely gave Hitler pause. He did not want to repeat that debacle. The restraint likely went against his own personal inclination, for in September 1941, he had joked that he would cure the bishops' "headaches" by taking their heads off.[116]

During the war, Hitler suggested other measures to scale back the influence of the churches. Most of these were ideas he had bandied about earlier. In April 1942, he called it scandalous that churches received money from the state, so he would reduce their subsidies from 900 million marks to 50 million. He also threatened to dissolve all the cloisters and make it more difficult for men to enter the Catholic priesthood.[117] A couple of months later, he promised to end the Concordat.[118] Hitler told Rosenberg in December 1941 that he intended to wrest the youth from the churches completely. No one would be allowed to join the churches until they became adults. Further, Hitler indicated that he would not shrink back from using force against the churches.[119]

Another indication of his hostility toward the churches was his treatment of newly annexed and occupied territories from 1938 to the end of the war. When Hitler annexed Austria to the German Reich in March 1938, he abrogated the Concordat that Austria had with the Vatican but refused to allow Austria to be included in the provisions of the 1933 Concordat between Germany and the Holy See.

This left the Catholic Church in Austria with no formal protection (not that the Concordat had protected the Catholic Church in Germany all that well). The Nazi regime began shutting down Catholic organizations, schools, monasteries, and in 1939 even abolished the church tax. As Hitler expanded into Czechoslovakia and Poland in 1938–39, he likewise refused to apply the Concordat, even to the territories directly annexed to the German Reich. Hitler also denied the Vatican any authority over the Catholic Church in annexed or occupied territories.[120]

In addition, Hitler refused to give his Minister of Church Affairs Kerrl any jurisdiction over church affairs in the newly annexed territories—a highly irregular move, since other Ministries were given jurisdiction there.[121] In November 1940, Bormann explained why the Führer was restricting Kerrl's jurisdiction to Germany's pre-1938 borders. Not only did Hitler oppose Kerrl's continuing attempts to unify the Protestant Church, but he also wanted to give his Gauleiter leeway to take advantage of a "Concordat-free zone."[122] Hitler thus encouraged his Gauleiter to impose restrictions on the churches in all the newly acquired territories, including Austria. Gauleiter Arthur Greiser took advantage of this opportunity by ending state support for the churches in the Wartheland, a territory of Western Poland that Germany annexed in 1939.[123]

In occupied territories with non-German populations, however, Hitler did not care if the people continued practicing their religion, as long as it did not foment any anti-German sentiments. However, he did want to eliminate any Polish leaders who might oppose Nazi rule, and this included the Catholic clergy. Before opening the Polish campaign on September 1, 1939, Heydrich organized SS commando squads who swept into Poland behind the regular army and murdered Polish intellectuals and leaders. They carried a list with 61,000 names, and by December 1939, they had killed about 50,000 men, including Jews, political figures, and intellectuals, but also many

Catholic priests.[124] Quite a few Polish priests were sent to Dachau during the war, too.

To Hitler, it was no issue if the allegedly inferior Poles kept their Catholic faith, as long as they served faithfully as slaves to the "master race." In a meeting with Bormann, Hitler Youth leader Baldur von Schirach, and Hans Frank, governor of the rump state of Poland known as the General Government, Hitler explained he favored allowing them to continue practicing Catholicism. He continued, "Polish priests will be fed by us, and in turn they will direct their herd in the direction we desire. The priests will be paid by us, and in turn they will preach what we desire. If a priest goes against the grain, then he will be dealt with mercilessly. The priests are to keep the Poles mute and stupid."[125] On another occasion, Hitler implied that allowing other countries and peoples to keep their religion was useful, because the churches sapped their strength, which was to Germany's advantage. In December 1941, he stated, "In any case, we would not desire that the Italians or Spaniards lose their Christianity: whoever has it, has bacilli constantly present."[126] In that same monologue, Hitler also boasted that he would "march into the Vatican," expel the Catholic prelates, and then say, "Excuse me, I made a mistake. But then they are gone!" His fait accompli would strike at the very head of the Catholic Church, stripping the German Catholic Church of its international connections.

How serious was Hitler about attacking the Vatican and removing the pope? We know that even though Germany occupied Rome and most of Italy in 1943, the pope remained unscathed in Vatican City during the rest of the war. Nonetheless, there is some evidence that Hitler wanted to take over the Vatican, and the pope was worried about the threat. The journalist Dan Kurzman makes the strongest case to corroborate SS General Karl Wolff's later claim that Hitler commissioned him to kidnap the pope in the fall of 1943.[127] However, many scholars are wary of Wolff's testimony and believe that Hitler's desire to depose the pope never reached the level of an actual plan. It was likely nothing more than a threat, but nonetheless, it was a threat the Vatican took seriously.[128] However, like Galen and Wurm in Germany, the pope was too hot to handle just yet, so Hitler decided to bide his time.

So what was Hitler planning to do to the churches after the war was over? Did he intend to destroy them completely? Historian Steigmann-Gall dismisses this prospect, claiming the widespread view that Hitler would attack the churches after the war is "completely unproven," and the "abolition of the churches altogether was not a Nazi ambition." Steigmann-Gall is likely correct in suggesting Hitler would not have eliminated the churches in one fell swoop at the conclusion of the war. But there is a great deal of evidence that Hitler wanted to fight against the churches once the war was over. Steigmann-Gall himself admits Hitler probably would have continued reducing church power, cutting church revenue, and punishing clergy who interfered with his policies. The ultimate goal of these policies was the complete elimination of the churches, even if it would take a few years or a few decades. Thus, Hitler was working toward the abolition of the churches with an incremental, not cataclysmic, approach.[129]

Interestingly, while Hitler expected the churches to continue to decline in influence, he was not optimistic that they were on the cusp of complete demise. In a conversation with Hitler in January 1940, Rosenberg expressed disgust at the "fetishism" of the German Catholic churches, with their abundance of relics, and Hitler agreed. Rosenberg predicted the religious landscape would look quite different in twenty years, but Hitler objected, claiming it would take two hundred years. Rosenberg reported, "The Führer said a harsh power-political intervention [against the churches] is, of course, conceivable; but only if Germany is completely independent of foreign pressure. Otherwise the inflamed domestic political conflict could cost us our existence."[130]

When Hitler himself discussed his post-war policies toward the churches, his policies often differed. Sometimes he threatened that he would completely destroy the churches, while other times he indicated that the churches could continue to exist, as long as they remained completely subservient to his regime. Hitler told his Gauleiter in May 1942 that he had resolved to destroy the Christian churches after Germany's victory because they were cowardly and had betrayed the country.[131] A few months later, he derided Christianity as a poison bacillus akin to Bolshevism and suggested, "The struggle with the churches will perhaps last several years or under the circumstances maybe a decade, but it will certainly lead to a radical solution."[132] One of Hitler's secretaries thought that if Hitler had won the war, he intended to initiate a vigorous campaign against the churches immediately by withdrawing from the Catholic Church.[133] Weizsäcker, however, read Hitler's intentions differently. "After the war," he stated, "Hitler wanted to allow the Church to continue to exist, but as an instrument of the State, and not under any other conditions."[134]

Hitler's long monologue on religion on October 14, 1941, confirms Weizsäcker's interpretation. Hitler portrayed the churches as completely out of step with modern science, but he admitted Christianity still met a deep metaphysical need that the Nazi Party could not fulfill. Thus, he advised not picking a fight where it was not necessary. Instead, he recommended, "It is best for one to allow Christianity to slowly fade away." As people gained greater understanding of the cosmos, he believed, they would recognize that "the teaching of Christianity leads to complete absurdity." Hitler thought science would ultimately triumph over Christianity.

In the same monologue, he expostulated on future church-state relations. His plan was to allow everyone to have their own private faith, and the churches could continue to exist. However, they would have no voice in government affairs nor be allowed to proclaim any message that contradicted Nazi doctrine. Thus, National Socialist teachings would prevail, especially among the youth.[135] Hitler expressed approximately the same position again in December 1941. Because of the idiocy of Christianity, he expected it to decline, but he would leave the churches to those foolish enough to continue believing. "When we are free from Christianity," he said, "the other peoples [i.e., non-Germans] can keep Christianity."[136]

We gain another glimpse of Hitler's prospects for the churches after the war by examining his plans for rebuilding the bombed-out cities of Germany. Actually, Hitler's scheme to rebuild the cities of Germany began even *before* the war. In 1938, the Nazi regime demolished St. Matthew's Church in Munich and replaced it with a parking lot. When the Nazi regime was formulating plans to build several new urban developments, Bormann issued a directive from Hitler in July 1939 that no churches should be built in them, nor should places be reserved for their later construction. They had no place in the new order Hitler was creating.[137] Later, war damage gave him an opportunity to further limit church activities. In June 1943, he told his entourage that if churches are bombed out, it was not so bad; only those with special artistic value would be rebuilt after the war.[138] Meanwhile, Hitler pored over architectural plans for rebuilding German cities, in which churches were conspicuously absent.[139]

Of course, no one knows exactly what course Hitler would have followed if he had won the war. However, the evidence suggests Hitler would have imposed as many restrictions on the churches as he possibly could and that his ultimate goal was their complete destruction. The timetable for accomplishing this was murky; it might take years or even a couple of centuries and would require long-term education and propaganda, not just repressive police measures. But even if, by some chance, Hitler *had* been willing to live with the churches in perpetuity, they clearly would have faded to only a shadow of what they once were. They would have been completely subservient to the Nazi regime, with no independent voice, no possibility of dissent, and no role in education—certainly not the kind of churches that had existed when Hitler came to power.

SIX

DID HITLER DERIVE HIS ANTI- SEMITISM FROM CHRISTIANITY?

HITLER BLAMED THE JEWS FOR JUST ABOUT everything that he opposed: communism, capitalism, internationalism, liberalism, materialism, egalitarianism, pacifism, and, of course, Christianity. That sneaky rabbi Paul had formulated his version of Christianity, Hitler believed, on the "Jewish-Bolshevik" principles of human equality.[1] When Hitler wrote *Mein Kampf*, he complained that the Christian churches were not sufficiently anti-Semitic. He asked, "In the Jewish question, for example, do not both denominations [Catholic and Protestant] today take a standpoint which corresponds neither to the requirements of the nation nor to the real needs of religion?" A few paragraphs later, he remarked that Protestantism was better than Catholicism in defending the national

147

interests of Germany, but it was still deficient, because it "combats with the greatest hostility any attempt to rescue the nation from the embrace of its most mortal enemy, since its attitude toward the Jews just happens to be more or less dogmatically established."[2] For Hitler, Christianity was essentially Jewish and thus weakened the German effort to combat the Jewish threat. He certainly did not see his anti-Semitism as congruent with the teachings and policies of the Christian churches.

However, while Hitler's anti-Semitism and the Christian churches' stance on the Jews diverged considerably, perhaps Hitler protested a bit too much. Many scholars have noted the intensely anti-Semitic attitudes endemic to the Christian churches in Austria and Germany in the late nineteenth and early twentieth centuries. When Hitler met with leading clergymen, he sometimes reminded them of their anti-Semitic heritage and called on them to cooperate with him in the struggle against the Jews. Also, it is undoubtedly true that Christian prejudice against Jews preceded by centuries the advent of racist anti-Semitism in the nineteenth century, which formed the core of Hitler's outlook. As many scholars have explained, the "new" racial anti-Semitism of the nineteenth century took existing, centuries-old prejudices and retooled them for a secular audience.

In two recent works on the relationship between Christian anti-Semitism and the Holocaust, Robert Michael argues, "It was the long-term and short-term influence of Christian theological anti-Semitism and Christian racist anti-Semitism that provided the most important roots of the Holocaust." He surveys the long, sordid history of Christian anti-Semitism and concludes, "But two millennia of Christian ideas and prejudices, their impact on Christians' behavior, appear to be the major basis of anti-Semitism and of the apex of anti-Semitism, the Holocaust."[3] Richard Steigmann-Gall takes a similar position, insisting that Nazi "anti-Semitism was far from a secular or scientific replacement for Christian forms of Jew-hatred" but was rather "conceived within a Christian frame of reference."[4] Many other scholars have emphasized the Christian and religious roots of Nazi anti-Semitism.[5]

While these historians have blamed the Holocaust on the persistence of religious influences, other scholars blame secularization for the upsurge in racist anti-Semitism in the late nineteenth and early twentieth centuries and for the Holocaust. In his early study of anti-Semitism in Germany, Paul Massing presented the racist form of anti-Semitism that emerged in the late nineteenth century as "essentially un-Christian." While recognizing the persistence of Christian forms of anti-Semitism, he considered the newer racist forms more virulent.[6] Later, Arthur Hertzberg examined the way that the Enlightenment contributed to the modern, secular versions of anti-Semitism.[7] More recently, Stephen Strehle insisted that the Enlightenment and secularization are responsible for both modern anti-Semitism and the Holocaust. He argues, "The impetus of modern anti-Semitism came mainly from sources outside the church."[8] Karla Poewe makes an even stronger claim, stating, "[I]t is not going too far to say that in the 1920s to 1940s to be anti-Semitic meant being anti-Christian and vice versa."[9]

Rather than interpret Nazi anti-Semitism as either the product of religion or the result of secularization, most scholars take a position between these two extremes. As Uriel Tal argued, both traditional Christian anti-Semitism and secular, anti-Christian anti-Semitism played a significant role in shaping Nazi ideology. In Tal's interpretation, "modern anti-Semitism is taken to be a bifurcated movement and the confluence of two streams—the continuation and the product of anti-Jewish Christian tradition and at the same time antagonistic to Christianity itself, including its biblical Jewish sources, its eschatological conception, and its ethical theological elements." Tal argued that Christian anti-Semitism initially shaped the prejudice and hatred toward the Jews, but then, in the nineteenth century, anti-Christian anti-Semitism reshaped that hatred into new, more virulent forms. In the early twentieth century, especially right after World War I, anti-Christian anti-Semitism increased in popularity. Ultimately, Tal believed, the blend of Christian and anti-Christian prejudice toward Jews culminated in the Holocaust.[10]

Many historians have taken a similarly balanced approach. In his analysis of European anti-Semitism, William Brustein examines four main categories of anti-Semitism: religious, racial, economic, and political. All four strands contributed to the anti-Semitic attitudes prevalent in Europe by the early twentieth century, Brustein argues. He does not weigh the importance of each of these against each other, in part because all four factors were usually intertwined. Religiously inspired anti-Semites often complained about the economic dominance of the Jews, for instance, and racial anti-Semites regularly expressed hatred for them because of their alleged involvement in a political world conspiracy. However, while Brustein sees all four factors as important in producing the Holocaust, he admits, "Traditional religious anti-Semitism had lost much of its appeal by the twentieth century, especially in Western Europe."[11]

Catholics in the Middle Ages leveled serious accusations against the Jews in their midst, which spawned hatred, persecution, and sometimes murderous rampages against the Jews. One of the first and most widespread indictments was that they had not only rejected Jesus as the Messiah, but that by killing him, they had committed the despicable crime of deicide. Many Christians insisted this crime still hung over the Jews' heads. Later in medieval times, Catholics began accusing them of committing ritual murders and of desecrating the Christian communion host.[12] In the late nineteenth and early twentieth centuries, these charges were still widespread in Christian circles. Olaf Blaschke has demonstrated the prevalence of anti-Semitism in the late nineteenth-century German Catholic milieu. He concludes that for Catholics, being anti-Semitic was a matter of course, and

"Catholics were anti-Semitic precisely because they wanted to be good Catholics." Blaschke likely overstates his case, but he certainly uncovered a huge fund of Catholic anti-Semitism.[13] Hitler grew up in a Catholic milieu that was often unreflectively anti-Semitic, so it would not be surprising if he imbibed some of its elements in his youth.

The Protestant Church, on the whole, was no more charitable toward the Jews, although when Martin Luther founded Protestantism in the early sixteenth century, he initially was favorably inclined toward them. He hoped that once Christianity was purged of its Romish corruption, the Jews would convert to Christianity. Later, after Jews spurned his proselytizing efforts, Luther turned his vituperation against them. In his infamous pamphlet, "On the Jews and Their Lies," he advocated burning down synagogues and Jewish schools, destroying the Jews' houses and books, forbidding Jews from practicing usury, and forcing them to do manual labor.[14] In the 1870s, the Protestant pastor Adolf Stoecker contributed to the upsurge of anti-Semitism by founding a political party that embraced it. Like most Christian anti-Semites, Stoecker's ideal solution to the "Jewish question" was the Jews' conversion to Christianity and assimilation to German culture. Stoecker eschewed violence, however, stating, "We do not wish to solve the Jewish question in a radical manner with violence, but gradually in a quiet, peaceful manner."[15] Meanwhile, Luther's writings about the Jews and Protestant anti-Judaism remained influential in the early twentieth-century Germany, giving greater popularity and support for Nazi anti-Semitic ideology and policies.[16]

However, while Christian anti-Semitism helped pave the way for racial anti-Semitism, Nazi ideology, and the Holocaust, there were countervailing tendencies in Christianity that also proved significant. Anti-Jewish animus was sometimes tempered by the Christian ethic of loving one's neighbor and even one's enemies. Also, Christians often opposed the biological racism that flourished in intellectual circles in the late nineteenth century. Historian Leon Poliakov remarks, "Judeo-Christian tradition was both anti-racist and anti-nationalist."[17] If one reads the biological racist literature of early twentieth-century Germany, one frequently finds that racist ideologues criticized the Christian churches for their racial egalitarianism.[18]

Christian anti-Semites differed from racial anti-Semites because Christians usually did not object to the Jews as a biological entity; rather, they opposed their religion. If Jews would give up their Jewish religion and be baptized into the Christian faith, they would be accepted as full-fledged members of German society, as they often were. But the secular, racial form of anti-Semitism that flowered around 1900—and which Hitler embraced—regarded conversion and assimilation as the absolute *worst* things that could happen, because then Jews would intermarry with Germans. Hitler believed this would pollute the German bloodline with inferior hereditary traits. Thus, the key difference between Christian anti-Semitism and racial anti-Semitism was that the former wanted to assimilate the Jews into German society while the latter believed it was necessary to eliminate them physically from Germany. Racial anti-Semites usually did not see the churches as allies in their campaign against the Jews.

One of the leading figures in developing the racist anti-Semitism that became prominent in the late nineteenth and early twentieth centuries was Wilhelm Marr, who coined the term anti-Semitism. Marr warned in a popular book in 1879 that the Jews were conquering the Germans in a racial war. This battle of the Germans against the Jews "was from the beginning no *religious* [war], it was a *struggle for existence*, that was waged against the foreign domination of Jewry." Marr, a harsh critic of Christianity, depicted his theory about the racial struggle against Jews as a secular, scientific standpoint.[19] Because he believed the Jews were a race, not a religion, he advocated segregation and discrimination, not assimilation, as the cure for the

"Jewish [q]uestion."[20] Marr, in fact, not only rejected Judaism and Christianity but also monotheism, pantheism and indeed every religion; in 1876, he stated that he regarded "Christianity, as every religion, with its dogmas and articles of faith, as a disease of human consciousness."[21] Marr's antireligious, racist version of anti-Semitism gained many adherents at the end of the nineteenth century, especially as biological racism exploded in popularity among secular-minded intellectuals.

Paul de Lagarde was another anti-Christian who contributed to the popularity of anti-Semitism in the late nineteenth century. Rosenberg considered Lagarde one of the three great prophets of Nazism, along with Wagner and Nietzsche.[22] However, Lagarde's biographer Ulrich Sieg claims that, though Rosenberg and other Nazis honored Lagarde, "it seems highly unlikely that Lagardian ideas influenced Hitler."[23] Lagarde wanted to form a Germanic religion, but not one based on Christianity, which he considered a distorted form of religion, corrupted by the Jews from its earliest days. He viewed true religion not as a set of beliefs or rites but rather a "striving to become better," because "the Good" is one and the same as God. Lagarde's religion, then, was simply living ethically in one's human community.[24] However, Lagarde did not believe the Jews were part of the Germanic community, so he wanted to eliminate them from German society unless they assimilated. Unlike Hitler, Lagarde defined Jews more by their spiritual nature, not their biological traits, so he thought some could overcome their Jewry and participate in the Germanic community.[25]

Hitler's perspective seems much closer to the racist anti-Semitism of Theodor Fritsch, a prominent writer who spread his anti-Semitic views through books, a journal he founded called *Hammer*, and a publishing house. Hitler probably knew about Fritsch from the earliest days of his political career, if not earlier, because the official Nazi newspaper occasionally advertised Fritsch's journal, which was one of the leading outlets of anti-Semitism at that time. Nazi Party membership cards in the early 1920s listed books that every member should know, and of the forty books listed, three were by Fritsch.[26] In 1925, Fritsch sent Hitler a copy of his anti-Semitic tract, *Mein Streit mit dem Hause Warburg*, and, in an article four years later, Hitler mentioned Fritsch as a pioneer in fighting against the Jews.[27] When Fritsch sent Hitler a copy of the thirtieth edition of his famous *Handbuch der Judenfrage* (*Handbook on the Jewish Question*), Hitler thanked Fritsch and said he had already studied this book thoroughly when he lived in Vienna (the claim may or may not be true). Hitler then added, "I am convinced that this [book] worked in a special way to prepare the ground for the National Socialist anti-Semitic movement. I hope that other editions will follow the thirtieth edition and that the book will gradually come to be found in every German family."[28]

Fritsch's religion shared many features in common with Hitler's. He dismissed the Old Testament as tainted by Jewish ideas, and he called Yahweh the father of lies. Fritsch's God was an "infinite, inscrutable, perfect being," unlike the anthropomorphic Jewish God. He argued that Jesus had Germanic blood, and though he respected him for opposing the Jews, he was highly critical of Christianity as it developed after the time of Christ. In any case, he did not think the struggle against the Jews was a religious struggle, even though he sometimes used Christian tropes and quotations from Luther and the Bible to buttress his points. Actually, Fritsch dismissed the Jewish religion as no religion at all—rather, he insisted, it was a sham to cover up their conspiracy against the rest of humanity. Fritsch contended that his anti-Semitism was based on moral considerations, not religious prejudice.[29] Tal categorizes Fritsch and his Hammer Movement as leading purveyors of anti-Christian anti-Semitism, and with good reason.[30]

One of Hitler's closest friends in the early days of the Nazi Party was the anti-Semitic writer Dietrich Eckart, whom Hitler calls his mentor in *Mein Kampf*.[31] Eckart edited the Nazi Party newspaper for two years, and after Eckart's death in late 1923, Hitler would visit Eckart's grave when he passed through Neumarkt. Otto Dietrich remembered that "according to Hitler's own statement [Eckart] had had the greatest influence upon his career. He had been Hitler's best friend and may well be called Hitler's spiritual father. His fanatical racist patriotism and his radical anti-Semitism guided Hitler at the very start of his political career."[32] On Rosenberg's forty-fifth birthday in 1938, Hitler gave him a bust of their mutual friend Eckart.[33] Strangely, however, Hitler once mistakenly claimed that Eckart was a Protestant, so it is not clear how well he actually understood Eckart's religious affiliation.[34]

In fact, Eckart's religion was a mystical faith in the unity of God and humanity derived from a blend of Schopenhauer, Goethe, and the religious mystic Angelus Silesius.[35] Though Eckart honored Jesus for focusing on the spiritual world and rejecting Jewish materialism, he did not think that Christianity had followed his spiritual teachings. Eckart spurned many of the central tenets of Christianity, including the physical resurrection of Jesus, and blamed Paul for corrupting Jesus's pure, spiritual doctrines.[36] Eckart's opposition to many elements of Christianity appears in his posthumously published book that is supposedly a dialogue with Hitler. In 1932, the Nazi Party, in order to counter the image of Hitler as an anti-Catholic, denied that these conversations ever took place, ascribing them to Eckart's fantasy.[37] The book probably does not tell us much about Hitler's religious views, but it does provide an accurate snapshot of Eckart's perspective. In these conversations, Eckart not only rejected the Old Testament and the Pauline epistles, but also many parts of the Gospels, such as Jesus' saying that salvation is of the

Jews. Both denominations of Christianity, Eckart complained, were crawling with Jewish and half-Jewish clergy.[38]

Eckart's main gripe about the Jews was that they reflect a materialistic worldview—they lacked spiritual insight completely, he alleged.[39] His contempt was not directed at their religion, but rather at their character. He asserted, "First the essence, then the religion; not vice-versa!" He blamed many of society's ills on the innate character of the Jews and accused the Jews of being the source of all social injustices in the world. Perhaps even Eckart knew this was hyperbole, but it nevertheless showed his belief that Jews were the main cause of economic oppression. In addition to blaming them for economic oppression, Eckart trotted out some of the standard charges of traditional Christian anti-Semitism, too, accusing the Jews of practicing ritual human sacrifice and claiming Jesus condemned them as children of the devil.[40]

Eckart's stress on the Jews' innate character sounds suspiciously like biological anti-Semitism, though he was not clear about whether this character was hereditary. However, his sweeping condemnation of the Jews did not seem to leave much hope for them mending their ways and becoming good Germans.[41]

Another friend of Hitler from the early days of the Nazi movement who may have influenced his anti-Semitism was Rosenberg. Rosenberg was a Baltic German who, with other émigrés, came to Munich after World War I and the Bolshevik Revolution. Rosenberg quickly established connections with Eckart and Hitler and brought to the Nazi Party an anti-Bolshevik and conspiracy-oriented version of anti-Semitism (one of Rosenberg's émigré associates brought *The Protocols of the Elders of Zion* to Germany.)[42] Rosenberg assisted Eckart in editing the *Völkischer Beobachter* for a couple of years before taking over the helm of the flagship Nazi newspaper. Of those forty books every Nazi Party member should know and which were listed on membership cards in the early 1920s, six of them were by Rosenberg.[43] Though Hitler sometimes privately scoffed at Rosenberg's book, *The Myth of the Twentieth Century* (1930), the book sold more than a million copies during the Nazi period, and many considered it the most important expression of Nazi ideology behind Hitler's *Mein Kampf*. Publicly, Hitler honored Rosenberg highly, granting him the first National Prize that he awarded in 1937. At the award ceremony, Hitler congratulated him for his powerful contribution to the development of the National Socialist worldview.[44]

Rosenberg had become alienated from Christianity as a boy. During his confirmation class, he disliked when the Protestant pastor affirmed belief in miracles and rejected biblical criticism. His science teachers, meanwhile, were teaching him about the long eras of earth history that seemed to run contrary to the biblical account of creation. What really hastened his rupture with the church, however, was Chamberlain's *Foundations of the Nineteenth Century*. Upon reading it, Rosenberg reflected, "the first window into a free world was opened for me."[45] As a result of his youthful apostasy, Rosenberg denied the Virgin Birth, Jesus' ascension, Jesus' resurrection, and indeed all the miracles in the Bible. He claimed the Christian creed was entirely symbolic, not the expression of empirical truths.[46] He still had high esteem for Jesus, but he did not consider him God incarnate, except inasmuch as all humans are manifestations of the divine.[47]

Though he favored religious instruction in the higher grades in school, which would include teaching about Jesus, he also wanted material about Hinduism, Buddhism, and other religions integrated into the lessons.[48] Rosenberg claimed that true religion encompasses not only those who use the concept "God" but also those who prefer the terms "fate" or "providence." It even included others who dispense with any conception of God but are creative artistically, he thought; true religion ultimately embraces Jesus, but also Sophocles, Goethe, Bach, Plato, Rembrandt, and Beethoven.[49] According to

Rosenberg, authentic Aryan religion—unlike Judaism—saw "religion entirely in inner experience, not in stupid faith in historical facts, legends, or even lies."[50] Christians, meanwhile, bitterly attacked Rosenberg's *Myth*, which was universally understood as an assault on their faith.

Rosenberg's 1922 commentary on the Nazi Twenty-Five Point Party Program was the first official work published by the Nazi Party. In it, he explicated that the Jews are a biological race that differed from the German Volk physically and mentally. He believed the Jews were waging a racial struggle against the Germans with a two-pronged strategy of capitalist exploitation and Marxist revolution (Interestingly, the Twenty-Five Points never mentioned Marxism or Bolshevism, but Rosenberg's commentary gives it a prominent role.) Though Rosenberg viewed the conflict between the Germans and Jews as a racial, not a religious, struggle, he still thought the state could intervene against Judaism. Point 24 of the program guaranteed religious freedom except when a religion runs contrary to the German Volk's sense of morality. In the case of Judaism, Rosenberg declared that it was immoral and thus subject to persecution. Rosenberg, like many other biological racists, considered the Jewish faith an expression of their immoral hereditary traits.[51]

Now that we have sketched some of the possible influences on Hitler's anti-Semitism, how did these impact the development of Hitler's worldview? It is not unlikely Hitler picked up some kind of anti-Semitic attitudes in his early years in Austria, since the Austrian and German Catholic milieu was infested with it. However, Hitler's attitude about Jews early in his life is difficult to figure out because the testimony is ambiguous. While he was in Vienna, its Catholic mayor Karl Lueger peddled a populist version of anti-Semitism, and Hitler later praised

Lueger's ability to mobilize the masses. However, he ultimately did not approve of Lueger's form of anti-Semitism, calling it a "sham anti-Semitism which was almost worse than none at all," because any Jew could save himself and his business with "a splash of baptismal water." Hitler viewed this kind of anti-Semitism as superficial, not scientific.[52] Also, Hitler was alienated from Catholicism at an early age, so it is not clear how much credence he would have given to Lueger's anti-Semitic rhetoric. In *Mein Kampf,* Hitler stated that the Pan-Germans such as Schönerer had the right attitude toward anti-Semitism because they based it "on a correct understanding of the importance of the racial problem, and not on religious ideas."[53]

Despite Hitler's claim in *Mein Kampf* that he developed into a consistent racial anti-Semite while in Vienna, historians Brigitte Hamann and Ian Kershaw, who have done the closest analyses of Hitler's early attitudes toward the Jews, do not believe his concocted story. Both conclude that Hitler did not fully develop his harsh anti-Semitic ideology until 1918–19.[54] The shock of German defeat in World War I, the Bolshevik Revolution in Russia, and especially the short-lived communist republic in Munich, which had some Jewish leaders, galvanized anti-Semitic agitation in 1919. Hitler was still in the army when the communists took over in Munich, and his role during that time is murky. After the White forces bloodily suppressed the Bavarian communist regime, Hitler was recruited into an army propaganda unit, where he was trained to ply the troops with ultra-nationalist speeches. One of the nationalist figures who helped train Hitler and his fellow orators was Gottfried Feder, an anti-Semite whose central mission was to combat the alleged economic domination of the Jews. Hitler claimed that after hearing Feder's first lecture, he immediately recognized he "had now found the way to one of the most essential premises for the foundation of a new party."[55] Hitler's anti-Semitism drew heavily from Feder's interpretation of the Jews as greedy, exploitative parasites on the German economy.

Nazi propaganda: "Baptism did not make him a non-Jew." Hitler persecuted Jews on the basis of their race, not their religion.

Nazi propaganda on baptism and Jews. From Ernst Hiemer, Der Giftpilz (1938).

The first expression of Hitler's anti-Semitism—a letter drafted in September 1919—sheds light on Hitler's motivation for opposing the Jews. In this letter, Hitler set forth the fundaments of his anti-Semitic perspective that would remain fixed in his mind to the end of his life. He insisted that being Jewish is a racial, not a religious, category. Their racial character predisposes them to greed and materialism, he asserted, turning them into "the racial tuberculosis of the peoples."

However, he opposed an "emotional anti-Semitism," which results in popular measures against the Jews, such as pogroms. Rather, what is needed, he wrote, was a "rational anti-Semitism," which would introduce discriminatory legislation and whose ultimate goal would be the "removal of the Jews completely."[56] Less than a year later, Hitler wrote another letter, explaining that Jews are parasites in the thrall of mammon. The only solution was to destroy or remove this "racial tuberculosis."[57]

Anti-Semitism was a prominent feature of the Nazi Party Program when Hitler proclaimed it in February 1920. Point Four of the program stipulated, "A fellow German can only be so if he is of German parentage, irrespective of religion." It thus defined a German by one's biological forebears, not by religion. Other discriminatory measures against Jews were designed to curb their political, economic, and cultural influence in Germany. None overtly aimed at their religion, though some interpreted the vague exception clause in Point Twenty-Four, which guaranteed religious freedom, to exclude the Jews from its protection. The program also called for measures against capitalist aggrandizement, especially usury, and though it did not specify that this was directed against Jews, most Nazis would have known that Hitler regularly associated Jews with capitalism, usury, and profiteering. The Twenty-Five Points evinced racial and economic anti-Semitism, but religious anti-Semitism was nowhere to be seen.

In the period 1919 to 1923, one of the main topics in Hitler's speeches was the Jewish threat. In August 1920, Hitler delivered a programmatic speech in Munich on "Why Are We Anti-Semites?" Hitler depicted the Aryans or Nordic people as a race that developed in the northern parts of Europe. Because of the harsh climate, the Aryan race developed a diligent character, viewing labor as a duty to the community. Also, the tough conditions of life weeded out the weak and sickly among them, giving them greater physical stamina and contributing to the development of an inner life. The Jews, on the other hand, never developed an appreciation for labor. In sum, Hitler said, "We see that here two great differences lie in the race: Aryanness means a moral conception of labor and through it what we hear so often today: socialism, sense of community, common welfare before self-interest—Jewry means an egoistic conception of labor and thereby mammonism and materialism, the exact opposite of socialism!" Hitler emphasized these moral and immoral traits of Aryans and Jews were biological and hereditary. In answering the question, "Why Are We Anti-Semites?," Hitler made clear that he opposed the Jews' supposedly hereditary immoral qualities, especially their laziness and greed. His anti-Semitism was not based on religious considerations. To be sure, he did mention a couple of passages from the Hebrew Bible, but these were used to illustrate Jewish greed and immorality, not because he opposed their religious beliefs or practices. Not only do we find zero Christian anti-Semitic themes in this speech, but Hitler specifically distanced himself from Christianity by accusing the Jews of spreading Christianity, a theme he would take up often later, but usually in private, not in public forums.[58]

Only rarely between 1919–23 did Hitler trot out Christian tropes in his anti-Semitic invective. He occasionally mentioned the Jews killing Jesus, but his main point was usually not so much religious as economic. The reason they killed Jesus, in Hitler's telling of the story, was because Jesus preached against their greed and materialism, and they retaliated to defend their materialistic lifestyles. The real problem with the Jews, Hitler thought, was that they were greedy, not that they opposed the Christian religion. Indeed, as we have seen, Hitler thought the Jews reinvented Christianity after Jesus' death, which would make them responsible for the advent of Christian churches.

One other symbol Hitler used occasionally was of the Jew as the devil. In May 1923, he told a crowd in Munich, "The Jew is certainly a race, but not human. He cannot be human in the sense of the image of God, of the Eternal. The Jew is the image of the devil. Jewry means racial tuberculosis of the peoples."[59] By using the symbol of the devil to convey his point that the Jews are evil, Hitler may have appealed to the sensibilities of some religious Germans. However, there is also no reason to suppose that Hitler actually believed in a devil just because he used this symbol, so it fails to prove anything about Hitler's own religious perspective or about the influence of religion on

Nazi propaganda: "The God of the Jews is money. And in order to earn money he commits the greatest crimes." Hitler believed Jews were biologically prone to immorality, including greed.
Nazi propaganda on Jews and greed. From Ernst Hiemer, Der Giftpilz (1938).

his anti-Semitism (just as calling the Aryans "the Prometheus of mankind" in *Mein Kampf* does not mean his Aryan racism was shaped by Greek mythology).[60] It was likely only a figure of speech, not an indication that he thought the Jews were literally in league with some supernatural beings.[61]

Hitler explained in excruciating detail his reasons for opposing the Jews in *Mein Kampf*, and his objections have nothing at all to do with Christian anti-Semitism. Indeed, Hitler specifically denied that Judaism is a religion—or, rather, the Jews' religion just serves as a cover for their parasitical attempts to infiltrate and destroy their host nation: "The Jew has always been a people with definite racial characteristics and never a religion." He accused the Jews of being economic parasites who ply commerce and practice usury in order to subjugate their host people. Their innate biological character, he insisted, made them liars, swindlers, and purveyors of smut and prostitution. But that, Hitler added, wasn't all. To win the biological struggle against the allegedly noble, upright, honest (but sometimes naïve) Aryan people, they fostered racial mixing with Germans, not only with Jewish women, but also with black African soldiers in the Rhineland after World War I. Finally, the Jews had used Marxism to woo the masses so they could politically dominate the country they lived in. Hitler cited the *Protocols of the Elders of Zion* as an indication of the Jews' proclivity to practice deception to gain political advantage. He was a true believer in an international Jewish conspiracy to control the world.[62]

Throughout *Mein Kampf*, Hitler hardly ever mentioned any religious reasons to oppose the Jews, and he even criticized the churches for allowing Jews to assimilate by getting baptized. He claimed Jews only used this baptismal loophole as a ruse to continue their exploitation of the German people.[63] Once, Hitler mentioned that a Jew's "life is only of this world, and his spirit is inwardly as alien to true Christianity as his nature two thousand years' previous was to the great founder of the new doctrine [i.e., Jesus]."[64] This brief comment is the only mention of the opposition of Jews to Christianity in *Mein Kampf,* and it is embedded in a discussion that makes clear that this opposition to Christianity is not really a religious problem, but reflects their worldly materialism. Also, it is included in a very long discussion of the Jewish problem that makes clear that Jews are a race, not a religion. Though Hitler mentioned Luther only once in passing in *Mein Kampf,* he never alluded to Luther's anti-Semitism; in fact, in his speeches before 1923, Hitler only mentioned Luther a few times and never in conjunction with anti-Semitism (though he did cite Goethe and Schopenhauer as opponents of the Jews). He did not praise the churches for being anti-Jewish, but on the contrary criticized them for not being sufficiently anti-Semitic.[65]

In the midst of a passage discussing the Jewish role in disseminating cultural filth in the press, literature, and the theater, Hitler wrote, "It was not to be overlooked, that precisely the Jew, in tremendous numbers, seemed chosen by Nature for this shameful calling. Is this why the Jews are called the 'chosen people?'"[66] By indicating that the Jews were "chosen by Nature"—and for an immoral purpose—Hitler was mocking their claim to be "chosen by God." He was also possibly indicating his pantheistic equating of God and nature, since in this scenario nature shaped the destiny of the Jews. Hitler indicated a similar point in a monologue in December 1941, when he stated, "We do not know what meaning the arrangements have, when we see the Jews destroy other peoples. If nature has created it in order to bring other peoples into motion through its decomposition, then Paul and Trotsky are Jews worthy of the highest respect, because they have contributed the most to this."[67] Note once again that Hitler has nature creating the Jews, indicating that nature is God. Also, the purpose of the Jews in this vision of history is to destroy other peoples who are weak and decaying. Finally, Hitler included Paul as one of the most successful Jews in fulfilling this destructive purpose, again indicating contempt for Christianity as a Jewish institution.

After writing *Mein Kampf,* Hitler's anti-Semitic ideology did not change appreciably. He continued to insist that Jews were a race, not a religion. In a monologue in November 1941, he asserted, "The trick of Jewry was to smuggle itself in as a religion, but without being a religion."[68] Hitler continually railed at the Jews for their inferior biological traits, persistently criticizing them for laziness, economic oppression, deceit, sexual lasciviousness, smut, and their proclivity to engage in political conspiracy, all of which he considered innate hereditary qualities.

After Hitler came to power in 1933, he and his regime endeavored to implement anti-Semitic policies against the Jews as a race, not as a religion. Ironically, when Hitler and his cabinet passed discriminatory legislation against the Jews, they used synagogue records to determine who was a Jew. The reason was simple. The Nazis could not find a biological marker to distinguish Jews from non-Jews. During the Nazi regime, some scientists performed serological studies and other experiments to see if they could find a way to identify Jews scientifically, but these all failed. Some German anthropologists claimed they could identify Jews by skull measurements and facial features, but these were often subjective and inconclusive.

When perusing synagogue records to determine the identity and fate of an individual, however, Nazi officials did not consider the individual's actual membership in the synagogue (a clear religious statement). They looked at his or her grandparents, trying to establish Jewish racial ancestry. Nazi officials identified as Jews individuals who were Catholics, Protestants, agnostics, or atheists, because they did not care what religion these individuals currently embraced. Jews were determined entirely by their genealogy, not by their religion. They were targeted for discrimination (and later extermination) based on their grandparents' religious affiliation.

Why did the Nazis determine Jewish status based on grandparents? In one sense, this could have been a matter of practicality, but also Hitler and other Nazis believed that biological science provided a rationale for not going too far back genealogically. When Nazi officials were debating the way to frame the Nuremberg Laws, some argued that individuals having only one Jewish grandparent could be reabsorbed back into the German Volk, as long as they did not intermarry with Jews. This position won the day and was reflected in the Nuremberg Laws. Hitler reflected this perspective, too, in a monologue in December 1941, when he stated that while those with some recent Jewish heredity often associate with Jews, by the seventh, eighth, or ninth generation, nature takes care of this problem by eliminating the deleterious hereditary traits. He explained that the Mendelian laws of heredity ensured that the Jewish traits would no longer be present by then in the vast majority of cases.[69]

The Crystal Night pogrom against the Jews on November 9–10, 1938, also might seem at first glance like an expression of religious persecution, since that night Nazi ruffians torched multitudes of synagogues and deliberately burned Hebrew Bibles. Dozens of Jews were murdered and thousands were arrested, though most were released within a few weeks with instructions to emigrate. Given Hitler's own contempt for the Hebrew Bible, this burning of the Jewish scriptures should come as no surprise. Indeed, those who construe Crystal Night as an act of Christian religious persecution against Jews are the ones who should be surprised that the Nazis purposely targeted the Jewish holy books and scrolls, because the Hebrew Bible is the Christian Old Testament. In essence, the Nazis were destroying an integral part of the Christian Bible.

The historian Alon Confino recently drew attention to this Bible burning in Nazi Germany in an interesting and provocative essay, but his main argument is puzzling: "There is nothing in racial ideology itself that can explain the symbolic meaning of destroying synagogues and the Bible." Confino, like some of his peers, is subjecting the "racial state" paradigm to critique, attempting to show that even though racial ideology was important, it has "diminished explanatory value." However, later in his essay Confino correctly explains the way that biological determinism shaped the Nazi understanding of culture: "Biology constructed for Germans a moral category of right and wrong because, they believed, of the way it determined their spirit—or, to use current terminology, their culture." In my view, this explains how the burning of Jewish scriptures and synagogues meshes with Nazi racial ideology.[70]

Hitler—and most other Nazis—saw the Jewish religion and other elements of Jewish life as a manifestation of their mental and moral characteristics, which, he believed, were biologically innate.[71] Further, their religion was an expression of their immoral character and served them in their struggle against other races. Thus, in *Mein Kampf*, Hitler claimed that "the Mosaic religion is nothing other than a doctrine for the preservation of the Jewish race," and served as an "ingenious trick" to gain toleration.[72] Confino is right to note that burning Bibles aimed at a cultural, not a racial, target. However, for Hitler, race and culture were intertwined, with culture being an expression of racial character. We should also remember that not only synagogues, but Jewish shops, schools, and orphanages were vandalized on Crystal Night, so Nazis were not singling out Jewish religious places or items for persecution. Anything Jewish was subject to attack.

Confino, however, expands his argument about the religious nature of Nazi anti-Semitism in his book, *A World Without Jews: The Nazi Imagination from Persecution to Genocide*. Therein, Confino argues for "an intimate link between Nazism and Christianity." He explains that Nazis considered it vital to eliminate the Jewish religion, because "by persecuting and exterminating the Jews, the Nazis eliminated the shackles of a past tradition and its morality, thus making it possible to liberate their imagination, to open up new emotional, historical, and moral horizons that enabled them to imagine and to create their empire of death."[73] This last statement has merit,

but there is no reason to think, as Confino does, that the Nazi eradication of Jewish culture and religion is somehow inconsistent with
biological racism. Again, Hitler considered Jewish history and heritage—including Jewish religion and morality—a manifestation of
their innate biological properties.

Less than three months after Crystal Night, in his infamous
speech on January 30, 1939, Hitler ominously warned the Jews,
"Once again I will be a prophet: should the international Jewry of
finance succeed, both within and beyond Europe, in plunging mankind into yet another world war, then the result will not be a Bolshe-
vization of the earth and the victory of Jewry, but the annihilation
of the Jewish race in Europe."[74] Hitler was already preparing for a
war in the east, and he wanted the western democracies, which he
thought were under the influence of Jews, to stay out of it. In this
speech, Hitler portrayed the Jews as a race intent on destroying Germany through economic power and Bolshevism, as indicated in this
"prophecy." Hitler was intent on persecuting the Jews because of their
racial character, which manifested in economic exploitation and
political domination, not because of their religious convictions.

On May 26, 1944, after millions of Jews had already perished in
the Holocaust, Hitler tried justifying his anti-Semitic atrocities to
German generals and other military officers. He explained that race
determines people's abilities. The Nordic race was endowed with
superior biological traits, such as cool mathematical reasoning, the
ability to organize, and artistic and musical creativity. The Jews, on
the other hand, had no creative abilities but possessed a racial tendency to excel in commerce. Hitler then broached the question that
many were probably thinking but dared not ask: Why was Hitler's
regime persecuting the Jews so harshly? Hitler replied, "I have pushed
the Jews out of their positions, and indeed pushed them out ruthlessly.
I have behaved here, just as nature does, not cruelly, but rationally,
in order to preserve the better ones, and I have thereby freed up

hundreds of thousands of positions." If anyone thought to ask whether this could have been solved in a more humane fashion, Hitler pre-empted them: "We stand in a struggle for life and death. If in this struggle our opponents triumph, the German people would be exterminated." If he had not intervened so vigorously, Hitler predicted, Bolsheviks would kill millions of Germans, and "this entire bestiality [i.e., Bolshevism] is organized by the Jews." Hitler was remarkably frank in this speech about his anti-Semitic policy. His justification for annihilating the Jews was based entirely on racial considerations, together with its economic and political ramifications. He appealed to science and nature, not to religion, to justify the Holocaust. Indeed, Hitler made negative comments about Christianity in this speech, undercutting even more the notion that his anti-Semitism was congruent with Christian anti-Semitism.[75]

Hitler provided a similar rationale for exterminating the Jews to the Hungarian leader Admiral Horthy in April 1943. Hitler tried to convince Horthy that the Jews "must be treated like the tuberculosis bacillus, which can infect a healthy body. This is not cruel if you consider that even innocent creatures of nature, like the rabbit and the deer, are shot so that they cannot do harm. Why should you be more kind to these beasts, which want to bring us Bolshevism? Nations which do not fight off the Jews go to seed."[76] Again, in trying to justify his anti-Semitism, Hitler appealed to nature and biology, not to religion.

If Hitler placed race at the center of his ideology and policies, as he did, did he remain true to this vision till the very end? Steigmann-Gall and Robert Michael both suggest either that Hitler changed his view near the end, or that he was never really a convinced racist. They explain that a couple of months before he died, Hitler let the cat out of the bag by writing in his political testament that the Jews were not a racial or biological entity, but rather a spiritual one. This is a startling concession from Hitler, who always maintained the opposite point previous to this time. However, there is a problem here. Steig-mann-Gall's and Michael's argument is based on a questionable source: Hitler's *Politisches Testament: Die Bormann-Diktate.*[77] Kershaw indicates that the source is not reliable, and Hitler's secretary doubted its authenticity.[78] Since this document contradicts everything Hitler ever said on the subject over two-and-a-half decades of his career, it seems safe to dismiss it as either fraudulent or at least distorted. Hitler never denied that the Jews were a racial and biological entity, but on the contrary affirmed it countless times.

It is apparent that Hitler's own reasons for embracing anti-Semitism had little or nothing to do with Christianity or religion. He continually denied that the Jews were a religion, viewing them instead as a race. He rarely invoked Christian themes when railing at the Jews, but he often invoked science, nature, and reason. However, this does not get Christianity entirely off the hook for preparing the soil for the Holocaust. The secularized version of anti-Christian anti-Semitism that became prominent in late nineteenth and early twentieth-century Germany was grafted onto the earlier Christian version of anti-Semitism. Centuries-old caricatures of the Jews were reinterpreted as Jewish biological traits. Further, the Christian churches in Germany and Austria continued to peddle a good deal of anti-Jewish animosity in the early twentieth century, thus giving succor to the Nazi anti-Semitic juggernaut. Both Christian anti-Semitism and anti-Christian anti-Semitism—thus, both religion and secularization—were necessary conditions for the advent of the Nazi Holocaust. The anti-Semitic message that Hitler preached, however, was far more anti-Christian than Christian.

SEVEN

WAS HITLER AN OCCULTIST OR PAGANIST?

SINCE HITLER'S EVIL WAS OF DEMONIC proportions, and since his meteoric political career defies logic, some want to ascribe occult influences to Hitler and his party. How else, they think, can one explain the mesmerizing quality of his speeches and the hypnotic attraction of his stare, on which many of his contemporaries commented? Further, tracing the roots of Hitler's ideology to quack occultists reinforces an image of Hitler as an irrationalist whose thinking came from the lunatic fringe of Austrian and German society. Already in 1958, Wilfried Daim wrote a book purporting to prove that the Viennese occultist Jörg Lanz von Liebenfels (pseudonym of Adolf Josef Lanz) was "The Man Who Gave Hitler His Ideas."[1] Many works since that time have drawn attention to the connections between early twentieth-century occult movements in Vienna and Munich and Hitler as a young man.[2]

One of the more recent books arguing that Hitler's religion was impregnated by occultism is Michael Hesemann's *Hitlers Religion: Die fatale Heilslehre des Nationalsozialismus* (2004). Hesemann insists that Hitler's religion was "nothing less than the key to understanding National Socialism!" He argues that Hitler's religion did not derive from Christianity and, on the contrary, aimed at destroying it. In Hesemann's view, Hitler and his Nazi colleagues imbibed various forms of occultism and esoteric teachings and shaped them into a coherent religion, complete with a doctrine of salvation, a gospel (*Mein Kampf*), a catechism (Rosenberg's *Myth of the Twentieth Century*), belief in a supernatural power, belief in an afterlife, an apocalypse, Messianism, pilgrimage sites, and rites and ceremonies. Hesemann, however, is not a historian, and it shows, because he does not weigh the reliability of his sources sufficiently, nor does he seem to have a firm understanding of some issues (such as Hitler's negativity toward Rosenberg's neo-paganism). He pounces on whatever evidence seems to line up with his position, no matter how shaky or even fraudulent the evidence may be. Nonetheless, even after this is taken into account, he marshals a good deal of evidence to show connections between Hitler and occultists.[3] In the end, however, Hesemann's evidence is not strong enough to support his argument.

Though non-historians, such as Daim and Hesemann, have been more prominent than historians in portraying Nazism as an occult movement, a few historians concur. The prominent historian of Nazi ideology, George Mosse, maintained, "As such, mystical and occult ideas influenced the world view of early National Socialism, and especially of Adolf Hitler, who to the end of his life believed in 'secret sciences' and occult forces.... [T]his mysticism was at the core of much of the irrationalism of the movement, and especially of the world view of its leader."[4] Timothy Ryback has also shown that

Hitler's library contained many books on occult themes. However, despite Ryback's best efforts at examining underlining and other marks in the books, we still cannot be entirely sure the marks were made by Hitler, much less what he meant by them.[5]

Historian Eric Kurlander recently presented a nuanced version of the argument for occult influences on Nazism. He acknowledges the multivalence of Nazi leaders' religious views: some were true devotees of occult practices, while others merely used supernatural themes to appeal to widespread beliefs among the German public. A few Nazi leaders, he admits, even wanted to stomp out occult influences.[6] Those who dabbled in the occult included Himmler and Hess, lending greater credence to a connection between Nazism and occultism. Some leading Nazis, including Himmler and Rosenberg, also embraced neo-paganism, an attempt to revive the pre-Christian Germanic pantheon of gods, along with their rites and ceremonies.

Overall, however, historians generally regard Daim's claim that the occultist Lanz was *the* man who gave Hitler his ideas as a gross overstatement. When Daim interviewed Lanz in 1951, Lanz not only admitted that Hitler had been influenced powerfully by his ideas, but he also told Daim that Hitler had once visited him at his office. Hitler allegedly told Lanz that he was a regular reader of his journal, *Ostara*, and he asked Lanz for some back issues that he did not have. In a letter written a year before Hitler came to power, Lanz exulted that Hitler was his disciple. After World War II, however, he distanced himself from Hitler's policies. While Lanz's testimony is plausible, it is also suspect. He seemed to delight in making his influence seem grandiose, perhaps more than was warranted. For instance, he made the completely implausible claim that one of his disciples was none other than Vladimir Lenin.[7]

After discounting such possibly inflated claims about Lanz's and Hitler's personal contact, however, Daim's stronger point still remains: in his analysis, he demonstrates many parallels between

Lanz's ideology and Hitler's. Lanz was a former Cistercian monk who abandoned Catholicism to found a new religious order, the Order of the New Templars, which was devoted to promoting Ariosophy. This new religion, meaning "Aryan wisdom," used mystical interpretations of biblical passages and other esoteric knowledge to advance the cause of the allegedly superior race, the Aryans. Lanz propagated his ideas through his journal *Ostara*, founded in 1905, which was actually more like a pamphlet series than a journal. It found an eager audience in Vienna and elsewhere, selling tens of thousands of copies. It was readily available in the kiosks of Vienna while Hitler lived there, so he could easily have procured it. Lanz, in fact, was one of the earliest Aryan racial theorists to use the swastika symbol, hoisting his swastika flag above his castle at Werfenstein in 1907, the year Hitler moved to Vienna.[8]

Lanz was extremely eclectic in formulating his racial ideology. For a while, he was a follower of the Pan-German Schönerer, whose biological racism and anti-Semitism seemed to resonate with him.[9] He stayed abreast of scientific racist literature written by nonreligious freethinkers, but he also drew inspiration from occult and esoteric sources, such as theosophy. Under the leadership of Madame Blavatsky, theosophy had tried to blend a mystical racism with a scientific view of an evolutionary hierarchy of races. Despite professing the brotherhood of all humanity, theosophy taught racial inequality, and Blavatsky even endorsed the extermination of inferior races.[10] Lanz also drew inspiration from non-mystical, non-occult sources, such as the physician and racial theorist Ludwig Woltmann. Before founding his own journal, Lanz wrote an extended review of Woltmann's book, *Die politische Anthropologie*, for a freethinking journal and waxed enthusiastic about Woltmann's racist doctrine of Nordic superiority.[11] Woltmann's book had been written for a prize competition for the best work on the political and social implications of Darwinian theory. He synthesized Darwin's theory of natural selection with Arthur

Gobineau's theory of the racial superiority of the Nordic race. Woltmann was a biological and racial determinist, believing that not only
physical characteristics, but also mental and moral traits, are hereditary. Thus, one's destiny is predetermined in one's biological makeup.
Race, according to Woltmann, is the key to historical development,
because some races—the fair-skinned Nordic one especially—were
superior. The Nordic race, he stated, is "the highest product of
organic evolution," and they were the founders of civilization. Further, he believed that races arose through an ongoing racial struggle
for existence, and, like Gobineau, he thought that racial mixing was
deleterious, leading to racial decline.[12]

Though Lanz used the term Aryan rather than Nordic, many of
his ideas about race were similar to those of Woltmann and other
Nordic racists. Lanz believed that "race is the driving force behind
all deeds," determining the destiny of all peoples, or *Völker*. Racial
wisdom was thus the paramount value, motivating him to establish
a religion of race.[13] Lanz warned that the Aryan race was threatened
with decline, and his religion aimed at rescuing and preserving this
endangered, but valuable, race. The key peril confronting Aryans was
racial mixture. One of the more bizarre claims that Lanz made—
based on his mystical interpretation of the Bible—was that the Fall
happened when Eve copulated with an animal, producing progeny
who were half-ape and half-human. These "ape-people" that Eve
bore were the ancestors of the inferior races around the globe, such
as black Africans, and their animal blood tainted all inferior races.
This Fall involved racial mixture with a vengeance, and it dehuman-
ized all non-Aryans, who supposedly had admixtures of animal blood
coursing through their veins.[14]

Unlike Hitler, who despised the Hebrew Bible as the effluvium of
the Jewish mind, Lanz claimed that Moses was a Darwinist who—if
interpreted in the proper mystical sense—taught Aryans how to triumph in the racial struggle through conscious racial selection. Lanz

maintained that the Jews had succeeded historically despite their inferiority because they had appropriated the biblical wisdom that was really intended for Aryans. Aryans should embrace the Bible, including the Old Testament, "as the hard, racially proud and racially conscious book, which proclaims death and extermination to the inferior and world domination to the superior (*Hochwertigen*)." Unfortunately, Lanz continued, a false kind of love had been incorporated into the Bible by some misguided souls.[15]

Elsewhere, Lanz elaborated that the kind of neighborly love and compassion that most people equated with Christianity, and which appeared in the Bible, was based on a misinterpretation hypocritically taught by the inferior races, the so-called "ape-people." The word "neighbor" in the Old Testament really meant, he assured his fellow Aryan racists, one's racial comrade. Thus the command to love our neighbor really "means that we only have to love our racial comrades, thus those who stand closest to our kind and our race."[16] In a 1907 issue of *Ostara*, he warned his fellow Aryans that they were committing race suicide by extending generosity to those of inferior races. Rather, they should always discriminate racially in their charitable giving. (Apparently, Jesus' parable of the Good Samaritan meant nothing to Lanz—or to Hitler.) Ominously, Lanz compared racially inferior people to weeds needing to be pulled.[17] A major theme in this pamphlet and many others was the need to introduce eugenics measures to improve the race.

Many of Lanz's doctrines became core tenets of Hitler's worldview: the primacy of race in determining historical developments, Aryan superiority (with the Aryans being the sole creators of culture), the Darwinian racial struggle, the need for eugenics policies, and the evils of racial mixing.[18] Hitler also shared Lanz's view that Aryans had developed an ancient civilization in the mythical Atlantis.[19] In a passage of *Mein Kampf* that decries racial mixing in a manner reminiscent of Lanz's writings, Hitler admonished the state to elevate the status of marriage, which under the present system was supposedly contributing to biological decline. By hindering the marriages of those he dubbed inferior, he hoped marriages could "produce images of the Lord and not monstrosities halfway between man and ape."[20] By claiming that racial mixture could result in human-ape hybrids, Hitler was pulling a page out of Lanz's repertoire. No wonder Daim was struck by the similarities between Lanz and Hitler and supposed that Hitler's ideology hailed largely from Lanz's writings. Given all these parallels, most historians acknowledge the likelihood that Lanz's Ariosophy influenced Hitler's ideology, either directly or indirectly.

But another like-minded Ariosophist in Vienna, Guido von List, was probably even more influential among early twentieth-century Pan-German nationalists than his colleague Lanz. He introduced the swastika symbol into Aryan racist circles before Lanz, and his ideas were widely discussed in the Pan-German press in Vienna. List and Lanz propagated similar occult racial ideologies, and they belonged to each other's organizations. Before becoming entranced with occult thinking, List wrote for Pan-German publications. He carried this intense nationalist and racist heritage with him into his occult Aryan religion. Like Lanz, he claimed he was recovering ancient Germanic wisdom that had been lost, and he wanted to replace Catholicism with his mystical faith. He preached Aryan supremacy, the need to engage in the struggle for existence against other races, and eugenics measures to improve the vitality of the Aryan race.[21] In 1908, he explained the core of his message: "The high meaning of this custom [of ancient Aryans] lay in the intention of *a planned, widespread breeding of a noble race*, which through strict sexual laws would also remain racially pure."[22] List wanted to reconstitute an ancient Germanic priesthood with esoteric knowledge that could elevate the racially purified and ennobled Aryans to dominate the globe.

We do not know if Hitler had any direct contact with List or the List Society when he lived in Vienna. Brigitte Hamann, however, believes that Hitler's racial ideology had more in common with List than with Lanz. List, for example, taught that the Aryans evolved into a superior race during the Ice Age. They were steeled in body and mind by the harsh conditions, and they had to wage a bitter battle against the elements. Natural selection eliminated the weak, sickly, and less cooperative, leaving the robust, healthy, and more moral members to propagate their superior biological traits.[23] Hitler narrated a similar tale of Aryan origins in his 1920 speech, "Why Are We Anti-Semites?" List also viewed nature as the source of divine power, and according to Nicholas Goodrick-Clarke, he reduced all morality to just one ethical precept: "Live in accordance with Nature."[24] Hitler's ethical views also stressed conformity to nature and its laws.[25]

Those stressing the occultist origins of Hitler's religious views also point out the influence of the Viennese engineer Hanns Hörbiger, who formulated and publicized his World Ice Theory in the early twentieth century. Hitler probably did not encounter Hörbiger's ideas when he lived in Vienna, because Hörbiger only published his theory in 1913, the year Hitler moved to Munich. Despite his scientific training, Hörbiger did not come upon his cosmological theory by amassing empirical evidence. Rather, it came upon him as a startling revelation. He was staring at the moon and suddenly grasped intuitively that it must be a huge ball of ice. He then theorized that the entire cosmos was the product of a universal struggle between ice and fire that had been going on for millions of years. This struggle intersected with human history in certain cosmically significant events, such as the Ice Ages. He believed that the Germans originated in the mythical land of Atlantis in the ice-infested far northern regions.[26]

We do not know when Hitler first heard about Hörbiger's theory, because he did not mention it in his early speeches or writings. In a letter he wrote in July 1938, Himmler claimed that Hitler "has also been a convinced adherent for a long time of this despised doctrine [Hörbiger's World Ice Theory]."[27] (Himmler was also a convinced adherent to "this despised doctrine.") The first time Hitler himself mentioned Hörbiger seems to be during a monologue in late January 1942. During that talk, Hitler said he was reading a book about the origin of human races and speculated that mythology contains many elements of truth. Specifically, he referred to the Atlantis myth that circulated in Nordic racist circles in the early twentieth century. He stated, "I can only explain it such, that one of the Nordic natural catastrophes extinguished a humanity that possessed a higher culture." In the midst of the discussion, which contained many wild speculations about mythology and cosmology, Hitler said, "I am favorably disposed toward the World Ice Theory of Hörbiger."[28] Thus, it is also likely the book Hitler referenced earlier was Hörbiger's work. At the very least, he appeared to be Hörbiger's disciple, because all these themes come from Hörbiger's hare-brained, all-encompassing theory of cosmic evolution.

In fact, Hörbiger's theory made quite an impression on Hitler. In February 1942, he claimed that Hörbiger should be honored along with Ptolemy and Copernicus in the observatory he planned to build in Linz, because the World Ice Theory was a major scientific discovery.[29] An SS document from August 1942 also testifies that in the spring of 1942, Hitler told Himmler the harsh winter of 1941–42 and other recent climatic conditions convinced him more than ever that the World Ice Theory of Hörbiger was correct.[30] Though we do not know when Hitler first became fascinated with Hörbiger's Ice Theory, he clearly thought it was a profound and important idea by early 1942.

When Hitler moved back to Munich after serving in World War I, he encountered another small but vibrant occult movement that would intersect with his fledgling Nazi Party. During World War I, the occult-oriented Rudolf von Sebottendorff embraced Ariosophy, and, after the war, he began organizing a movement in Munich to spread the ideals of Aryan supremacy. Sebottendorff admitted that two of the greatest influences on him were List and Lanz. Like other Ariosophists, he was fascinated by the ancient Germanic gods, ancient rune inscriptions that allegedly contained esoteric messages, and German mythology. In August 1918, shortly before the end of the war, he founded the Thule Society in Munich as an organization to foster German nationalism and Aryan racism. The Thule Society adopted the swastika as its symbol and "Heil" as its greeting, thus contributing to later Nazi practices.[31]

In June 1918, Sebottendorff acquired the *Münchner Beobachter* as the mouthpiece for the Thule Society. In order to attract young Germans to his movement, he featured sports articles in this newspaper. However, its real purpose was to advance his racist and ultra-nationalist views, so he also published articles on these themes. One early article he wrote was "Keep Your Blood Pure," which sounds remarkably similar to Hitler's racial philosophy in *Mein Kampf*. In this essay, Sebottendorff asserted that race is the key to understanding history. He was incensed that Christianity had led some Germans to embrace racial equality. He wrote,

> Encouraged by Christianity they propagated the doctrine of the equality of humans. Gypsies, Hottentots, Brazilian natives, and Germans are supposedly completely equal in value. Too bad the great teacher, nature, teaches otherwise. It teaches: This equality is nonsense. It is the greatest lie that humanity has ever been talked into. To the destruction of us Germans. There are higher and lower races! If one values the racial mish-mash, the "Tschandalen" [this was Lanz's term for inferior human races that had resulted from a human-ape hybrid] the same as the

Aryans—the noble humans—then one commits a crime
against humanity. . . . Wherever one looks in the past, the
bearers of Germanic blood have always been the bearers
and creators of culture.[32]

The affinities with Hitler's worldview are obvious: racial inequality, the role of nature in confirming racial inequality, and the Aryans
as the sole creators of culture. When Hitler came to power in 1933,
Sebottendorff boasted that he had laid the intellectual foundation for
Nazism.

Sebottendorff's view of Christianity was similar to Hitler's, too.
He criticized many of its features, especially its tendency to promote
human equality. While appreciating Luther's anti-Semitism, he noted
that it was nonetheless deficient, because it was based on religious,
not racial, considerations.[33] He also dismissed the notion that people
should turn the other cheek. Rather, he proclaimed, they should strike
back until their opponent remained on the ground. Strangely, Sebottendorff thought Jesus approved of this pugnacity, for he continued,
"That was also the opinion of our Savior: He came to bring the
sword."[34]

The Thule Society connected in interesting ways with the early
Nazi Party, lending plausibility to the notion that occultism exercised
influence initially over Hitler and the party. Anton Drexler and Karl
Harrer, the cofounders of the German Workers' Party (later renamed
the National Socialist German Workers' Party, or Nazi Party for
short), received considerable impetus from Sebottendorff to establish
their party.[35] Many other leading figures in the early Nazi movement
were either members of the Thule Society or visited their meetings.
Hess was the most prominent Thule Society member to rise in the
ranks of the Nazi Party, and he remained committed to occult practices throughout his career in the Nazi Party. Some secondary works
also list other early Nazi Party luminaries as members, such as

Eckart, Rosenberg, and Gottfried Feder. These three did indeed attend or speak to the Thule Society, but contrary to some accounts, they were guests, not members.[36] Another early Nazi Party member who played a leading role in the Thule Society was the Munich publisher Julius Friedrich Lehmann, a leading figure in the Pan-German movement who befriended Hitler.[37] One important way the Thule Society contributed to the early development of the Nazi Party was by selling its newspaper, which they had renamed the *Völkischer Beobachter*, to the Nazis in late 1920.[38] The paper had already established a readership among Munich's Pan-German nationalists and racists. Aside from political speeches, especially by Hitler, the *Völkischer Beobachter* became one of the most important propaganda tools of the early Nazi Party.

A different movement, neo-paganism, also held sway over some leading Nazis, especially Himmler and Rosenberg. Neo-paganism, the attempt to resurrect the old Germanic gods and goddesses, sometimes overlapped with occultism, though some neo-paganists were staunch opponents of it. Both schools of thought were anti-Christian in their orientation. The occultist Sebottendorff, for example, tried to resurrect the worship of Wotan and other ancient Germanic gods. Himmler and Rosenberg saw neo-paganism as a way to bring Germans back to their original pre-Christian religion. Neo-paganism countered the universalizing tendencies of Christianity and emphasized the distinctiveness of the Aryan race, even in their religion.

Despite all these historical connections between Hitler and occultists, the popular idea that Hitler was an occultist—or at least powerfully influenced by occultism—faces serious objections, leading many scholars to reject the idea that Hitler was heavily influenced by the occult.[39] First, many of the ideas that Hitler allegedly cribbed from Lanz or other occult writers were not ideas distinctive to the occult scene. Second, many of the ideas and terminology that *were* distinctive to Lanz and other occultists are absent from Hitler's speeches and writings. Third, Hitler explicitly rejected mystical religious notions on numerous occasions. Finally, the Nazi regime persecuted occultists.

Nicholas Goodrick-Clarke has done the most careful study of the Ariosophists Lanz and List in his work *The Occult Origins of National Socialism*. One remarkable finding of his study is that—despite his catchy title—National Socialism did *not* have occult origins. After acknowledging the many points of agreement between Ariosophy and Hitler's worldview, Goodrick-Clarke still concludes, "Ariosophy is a symptom rather than an influence in the way that it anticipated Nazism."[40] The problem with concluding that strong parallels between Ariosophy and Nazism mean the former influenced the latter is that it ignores the wider historical context. Historians well-versed in the racist ideology that blossomed in the 1890s and thereafter in German-speaking lands recognize that many of the racial ideas Ariosophy purveyed were widespread outside the occult milieu, too, such as Aryan racism, social Darwinism, eugenics, and the perils of racial mixing. Thus, Hitler and other Nazis may have imbibed them from a large variety of sources—most of them having no connection with the occult. In fact, many elements of their racial ideologies were not original to Lanz, List, Sebottendorff or other Ariosophists, but were culled from non-occult sources.

Aryan or Nordic racism was such a prominent feature in the Viennese press when Hitler lived there, and the multitude of racial theories were so similar, that Hamann claims it is impossible to know which specific sources informed Hitler's racial thought. She notes, "Around 1900 the new race doctrines were ubiquitous, like a religious doctrine."[41] Lanz and List were only two among many Austrian and German thinkers pushing Aryan supremacy, and they were by no means the most influential. Woltmann, a physician whose social Darwinist racial ideas inspired Lanz, was far more influential than Lanz himself, and he had nothing whatsoever to do with the occult. Woltmann considered his racial ideology completely scientific, and he never appealed to esoteric knowledge. One of the more powerful influences on Woltmann was Gobineau, whose ideas were gaining greater circulation in the 1890s and thereafter through the Gobineau Society, founded by Ludwig Schemann. Neither Gobineau nor Schemann, both powerful influences on the development of Nordic racism in the early twentieth century, were purveyors of occultism. Chamberlain, whose influence on Hitler's racism is undisputed, was likewise teaching Germanic supremacy before Lanz and List took up the cause, and he had far greater reach than these fringe occultists. Theodor Fritsch, one of the most influential anti-Semitic publicists in the early twentieth century and whose work Hitler endorsed, also did not peddle occult philosophies.[42]

The Gobineau Society, meanwhile, was not the only organization imbued with Aryan racism. In *Mein Kampf*, Hitler acknowledged he was influenced by Georg von Schönerer's Pan-German Party while living in Vienna. Schönerer and his party preached biological racism, Aryan supremacy, and other themes that would later become central features in Hitler's ideology. The Bayreuth Circle, of which Chamberlain was a member, disseminated Wagner's (and Chamberlain's) racist outlook. No one doubts that Wagner influenced Hitler. The Pan-German League, an ultra-nationalist organization that attracted many intellectuals and scholars (not to be confused with Schönerer's political party), was imbued with social Darwinist racism, too.[43] Thus, Hitler had a plethora of non-occult sources at hand to shape his racist worldview. And while the parallels between his outlook and the racial ideas of the Ariosophists are significant, the similarities were likely mostly the product of common influences.

But even if Hitler *was* influenced by Lanz, List, or other Ariosophists—which still might be true—it does not prove he was also affected by any of the specifically occult ideas they were peddling. Hitler read prolifically, but—as he explained himself in *Mein Kampf*—he did not simply swallow everything he read. Hitler explained that his method of reading was not the same as most intellectuals, because "they lack the art of sifting what is valuable for them in a book from that which is without value, of retaining the one forever, and, if possible, not even seeing the rest, but in any case not dragging it around with them as useless ballast."[44] Hitler read selectively, incorporating what he considered important into his worldview and discarding the rest: "The art of reading as of learning is this: *to retain the essential, to forget the non-essential.*"[45] No single thinker shaped Hitler's worldview, which was an amalgam of ideas circulating widely in early twentieth-century Austria and Germany.

Are there other ways we can determine whether Hitler embraced the occult elements of the Ariosophists? If Hitler actually imbibed their occult teachings, it should be possible to point to specific statements that Hitler made reflecting or endorsing such views. Most of the secondary works that argue for occult influences on Hitler, however, fail to locate any such evidence. Lanz and List used specific terminology in their writings that one never finds in Hitler's own speeches or writings. For instance, Lanz called the superior Aryan race the "asische" race, and the inferior mixed races were the "Tschandalen." These terms are absent in Hitler's speeches and writings. I also wonder if Hitler might have been put off by Lanz's continual use of the term "blond race" to describe Aryans.[46] Indeed, Hitler at times referred to the Aryan race as having blond hair and blue eyes, but he did not call it the "blond race," since this would have placed him outside its orbit. More importantly, Hitler never appealed to esoteric or mystical knowledge, such as runes, to ground or justify his racial thought. Thus, despite the similarities, many scholars rightly reject the idea that Hitler's thought was shaped significantly by the occultist elements in Lanz's or List's worldview.[47]

The notion that the Thule Society infused Hitler with occultism is likewise bedeviled by serious objections. Hitler was not a member of the Thule Society, and it is doubtful he ever attended their meetings.[48]

Further, though its leader was an occultist and undoubtedly imparted an occult and neo-pagan flavor to the organization to some extent, not all members were occultists. The primary purpose of the Thule Society was not to promote occultism, but to rally the ultra-nationalist and racist forces in Munich society. Lehmann, who probably influenced Hitler more than Sebottendorff did, was a leading member of the Thule Society, but he was not involved in the occult scene.[49] He was an ultra-liberal Protestant who leaned more toward materialism than occultism.[50] Hastings maintains that the Thule Society had a Catholic wing to it, too, and he even disputes the claim that the Thule Society had a powerful influence on the early Nazi movement.[51]

If Hitler did not imbibe the specifically esoteric ideas of Lanz, List, Sebottendorff, or other occultists, what about Hörbiger's Ice Theory? We have solid evidence (even multiple strands of it) that Hitler believed in Hörbiger's "revelation." Does this prove that Hitler had occult tendencies? It certainly indicates that Hitler was open to quack hypotheses. However, Hörbiger tried to pass off his theory as scientific, and he was sorely disappointed when most scientists dismissed it as nonsense. Despite its lack of scientific credibility, Hitler was convinced it was a dramatic scientific advance.[52] That is why he proposed teaching Hörbiger's ideas as a part of astronomy at an observatory that also featured Copernican theory.

Even if Hitler's acceptance of Hörbiger's ideas and the myth of Atlantis might indicate a slight propensity toward mysticism, Hitler more often than not dismissed all kinds of mysticism, whether occultism or neo-paganism, as superstitious nonsense. In Mein Kampf, Hitler spurned the right-wing nationalists who enthused about Germanic prehistory, especially those wanting to resurrect ancient Germanic religions. He stated, "Especially with the so-called religious reformers on an old Germanic basis, I always have the feeling that they were sent by those powers which do not want the resurrection of our people." Hitler had no interest in neo-paganism or mysticism, which he considered counterproductive politically, because it would lead to religious squabbling and destroy German unity.[53]

At the Nuremberg Party Rally in September 1938, Hitler confronted head-on the neo-paganism in his own party. Some Germans were becoming unsettled at Rosenberg's and Himmler's attempts to resurrect ancient Germanic gods, rites, and shrines. Hitler reassured his followers that this did not represent the official party position, nor did it correspond with his own perspective. He discussed this matter while explaining the role of architecture in building the new National Socialist culture. He criticized medieval Christian mysticism, which had given rise to Gothic "cathedrals'" mystical narrowness and somberness." Hitler then portrayed his movement as a modern movement that embraced reason, rather than mysticism: "National Socialism is a cool and highly-reasoned approach to reality based upon the greatest of scientific knowledge and its spiritual expression." Because of the scientific underpinnings of Nazi ideology, "we have no desire of instilling in the Volk a mysticism that transcends the purpose and goals of our teachings." He then insisted that his party was a purely political organization focused on the German people as a race. It was not a religious cult for worship or mystical ceremonies. Thus, the buildings created by his regime would focus on gathering places for the German people, not sites of worship. He asserted, "Hence the National Socialist Movement will not tolerate subversion by occult mystics in search of an afterlife." This speech was an open rebuke to Himmler, Rosenberg, and other neo-pagans, who were building shrines and formulating rites and ceremonies to honor ancient Germanic gods.[54]

This negativity toward neo-paganism and mysticism in his public speeches matched Hitler's private utterances. At a private gathering in 1923, General Ludendorff's wife, Mathilde von Kemnitz, began waxing eloquently about the new Nordic religion she was promoting. Hitler tried to cut her off, stating, "As far as I am concerned, the universe has only astronomical meaning."[55] In August 1935, Hitler told Goebbels, "Rosenberg, Himmler and Darré must put an end to their cultic nonsense."[56] Speer remembered Hitler as utterly contemptuous of Himmler's penchant for Germanic mythology. Despite his admiration for Himmler's devotion to the Nazi cause and his organizational skills, behind his back Hitler derided his religious tendencies, exclaiming, "What nonsense! Here we have at last reached an age that has left all mysticism behind it, and now he wants to start that all over again. We might just as well have stayed with the church. At least it had tradition. To think that I may some day be turned into an SS saint! Can you imagine it? I would turn over in my grave." He also contemptuously dismissed Rosenberg's *Myth* as "stuff nobody can understand."[57] Hitler's military adjutant likewise recalled that Hitler disapproved of Himmler's plans to reintroduce the cult of Wotan and Thor.[58] In October 1941, Hitler ranted again about the foolishness of trying to resurrect the cult of Wotan.[59]

Even Rosenberg recognized that Hitler was not sympathetic with his efforts to revive Germanic paganism. In his reminiscences on the Nazi movement, he remarked that Artur Dinter, an early Nazi Party leader who was forced out of the movement in the 1920s, had been a dangerous element. He had styled himself a religious reformer, but Hitler opposed his sectarian tendencies, often speaking sarcastically about these kinds of religious sects. Rosenberg then confessed that Hitler was even suspicious of Rosenberg's own studies of Germanic prehistory. Hitler, he recalled, was not interested in the huts of the ancient Germans, but rather looked to the temples of Greece as cultural models.[60] Hitler proved more enamored with copying the classical styles of ancient Greece and Rome than resurrecting ancient Germanic culture, including Germanic pagan religions. However, interestingly, when discussing his admiration for the Greco-Roman world and its culture, Hitler never expressed any desire to revive the polytheistic religions.

In addition to rejecting neo-paganism, Hitler did not put any faith in astrology, nor did he base his decisions on horoscopes. In an interview in the 1950s, Hitler's personal photographer and friend Heinrich Hoffmann dismissed as fantasy the speculations that Hitler used an astrologer. He admitted that Hitler read a good deal about astrology and the occult, but "as a matter of principle Hitler stood opposed to astrology." Nevertheless, Hoffmann thought Hitler was superstitious in some ways, because on occasion he would flip a coin to make a decision.[61] Dietrich, Hitler's press chief, substantiated Hoffmann's report, claiming that when Hitler was out driving and did not know where he wanted to go, he would sometimes flip a coin to decide. However, Dietrich continued, "This was, by the way, the only concession Hitler made to superstition. Of course he often expressed supreme belief in himself and his 'racial destiny.' But contrary to widespread opinion, he would have nothing to do with astrology or any kind of occultism." According to Dietrich, despite Hitler's close relationship with Hess, he thought less of Hess for his mystical and occult inclinations.[62] Indeed, when Hess flew to Britain in May 1941 on his bizarre mission to broker a peace deal, Hitler was enraged and blamed Hess's lunacy on his occultism. According to Hans Frank, Hitler angrily denounced Hess as a traitor and claimed he had perpetrated his deed through the influence of "the astrological clique" around him. Hitler added, "It is thus time radically to clear away this astrological nonsense."[63]

With the encouragement of other anti-occultists in his regime, especially Goebbels and Bormann, Hitler initiated a campaign against occultists in the aftermath of Hess's escapade. Bormann wrote to SS officer Reinhard Heydrich on May 14, 1941, telling him about Hitler's decision: "The Führer wishes that the strongest measures be directed against occultists, astrologists, medical quacks, and the like, who lead the people astray into stupidity and superstition."[64] Heydrich then orchestrated the police crackdown against occultists on

June 9, 1941, arresting or interrogating many spiritists, theosophists, anthroposophists, Christian Science practitioners, and astrologers. The German police closed down presses and confiscated publications propagating occultism.[65] A few days later, Goebbels exulted triumphantly in his diary: "All astrologers, hypnotists, Anthroposophists, etc., arrested and their entire activity crippled. Thus finally this swindle has ended. Peculiarly not a single clairvoyant foresaw that he would be arrested. A bad professional sign!"[66] One of the more bizarre aspects of this anti-occult campaign is that it was directed by Himmler's police forces, despite Himmler's own fascination with the occult. Indeed, Himmler released the astrologer, Wilhelm Wulff, from custody, under the condition that he ply his occult art for Himmler. Thus he became Himmler's personal astrologer at the same time other astrologers were being persecuted.[67]

This police action in 1941 was the culmination of several years of escalating hostility and persecution directed at occult individuals and organizations during the Third Reich. Despite (or maybe because of) his claims that he was an inspiration for Hitler and the early Nazi movement, Sebottendorff was jailed and forbidden to speak shortly after Hitler came to power.[68] In two of the best historical studies on occultism and parapsychology in early twentieth-century Germany, Corinna Treitel and Heather Wolffram both argue that the Nazi regime was mostly oppositional toward occultism, despite some influence of occultism on a few high-ranking Nazi leaders. The SS Security Service, the intelligence-gathering wing of the SS, kept tabs on occult organizations from the earliest days of the regime, labeling them "enemies of the state." In 1937, the Nazi regime banned theosophical organizations. Treitel concludes, "Although the occult may have played a minor part in the 'fool's paradise' inhabited by top Nazi leaders, the fact remains that escalating hostility was the dominant theme in the regime's response to the occult movement."[69] Concerning Hitler himself, Treitel insists that he "despised occultists' mystical inclinations."[70] Wolffram concurs, explaining that despite exceptions, the overall attitude of the Nazi regime toward parapsychology and occultism was negative. Already in 1934, three of the largest German states—Prussia, Saxony, and Baden—outlawed fortune telling in public and banned publications on horoscopes, card reading, and dream interpretation. In 1935 and again in 1938, the Nazi regime denied parapsychologists permission to travel to the International Congress for Parapsychology, and they persecuted them along with other occultists after the Hess debacle.[71]

Despite his general negativity toward occult practices, Hitler did indulge in one form of occult activity: dowsing. A dowser, Gustav Pohl, claimed that he could detect harmful "earth rays" that caused cancer. A study of his dowsing in one city determined that he had identified rays in certain locations that corresponded precisely to the incidence of cancer in that city. Many Germans were impressed by this claim, including Hitler. Ever fearful of ill health, he hired Pohl to dowse the Chancellery in Berlin in 1934 to make sure that he was safe from these deleterious rays.[72] However, it may be that Hitler changed his mind about dowsing, for in July 1941, the Nazi regime banned dowsing and other occult methods of fending off "earth rays."[73]

Despite this one dowsing incident, his acceptance of Hörbiger's Ice Theory, and his ruminations about a mythical Atlantis, Hitler's attitude toward the occult and neo-paganism was generally negative. Though his racial ideology may have been influenced by the Ariosophists, he never incorporated their esoteric and mystical ideas into his thought. He rejected astrology, clairvoyance, and other occult practices. When he was with Goebbels, Bormann, and others who shared his anti-occult sensibilities, he was sarcastic and made fun of some of his closest colleagues who indulged in occult tendencies, including Hess and Himmler. He called Rudolf Steiner's anthroposophy a Jewish scheme to destroy Germans.[74] Michael Rissmann is on target when he explains, "Occult tendencies were foreign to Hitler, if one follows the reliable sources, already in his years in Vienna.... According to his own opinion, Hitler did not think in mystical-esoteric, but in rational categories."[75] Hitler was certainly diabolically evil, but he did not base his evil philosophy on occultism or neo-paganism.

EIGHT

WHO WAS HITLER'S LORD?

ONE OF THE MOST FAMOUS QUOTATIONS FROM Hitler's *Mein Kampf* is, "Hence today I believe that I am acting in accordance with the will of the Almighty Creator: *by defending myself against the Jew, I am fighting for the work of the Lord.*"[1] Some construe this to mean Hitler believed in the Christian God and saw his war fighting against Jews as part of a religious battle that had been waged for centuries.[2] Even though Hitler did not overtly appeal to Christianity in this statement, his use of the terms "Almighty Creator" and "Lord" would have been understood by many of his contemporaries (and those who currently ignore Hitler's many anti-Christian utterances) as the Christian God. Anti-Semites in the Catholic or Protestant churches would have applauded him for doing "the work of the Lord."

Nonetheless, there are major problems with suggesting that this statement indicates Hitler's Lord was the Christian God. The aim of Hitler's anti-Semitism—the "Lord's work" he thought he was doing—was radically different from the goal of traditional Christian anti-Semitism (as mentioned in chapter six).

The context itself suggests Hitler had some other kind of God in mind. Hitler was fulminating against the "Jewish doctrine of Marxism," which he thought "rejects the aristocratic principle of Nature." In the sentence immediately preceding his famous quotation about doing the work of the Lord, Hitler stated, "Eternal Nature inexorably avenges the infringement of her commands."[3] Four important points emerge from this. First, Hitler personified nature in this passage, ascribing to it characteristics that would normally be associated with God. Second, Hitler called nature eternal. If he thought nature existed forever, as this statement indicated, then the God he believed in could not have created nature sometime in the past. Thus Hitler's God was not even a deistic, much less a theistic, God. The "Almighty Creator" he mentioned in the following sentence could not have created nature, making it highly probable that Hitler's "Creator" *was* nature. Third, Hitler believed that nature's commands defined morality, since he claimed nature issues commands.

Finally, the juxtaposition of these two sentences implies the nature he deified in the first sentence is the Almighty Creator and Lord he mentioned in the following sentence, especially since the two sentences are linked by the word "hence" (in the original German, this was the word "so"): "Eternal nature inexorably avenges the infringement of her commands. Hence today I believe that I am acting in accordance with the will of the Almighty Creator: *by defending myself against the Jew, I am fighting for the work of the Lord.*" Thus, the "Lord" on whose behalf Hitler was fighting the Jews *was none other than nature deified.* Samuel Koehne seems to agree with this interpretation, stating in a recent article, "At times he [Hitler] conflated this 'divine will' and 'Nature,' or the 'commands' of 'Eternal Nature' and the 'will of the Almighty Creator.'"⁴

When Hitler called nature eternal in *Mein Kampf*, this was not just a slip of the pen (or typewriter). He referred to nature as eternal on several occasions throughout his career. In an essay he wrote in January 1923, Hitler castigated those who were vacillating between bravery and cowardice, claiming they would ultimately fail because "[e]ternal nature denies them strength in the struggle for existence."⁵ In *Mein Kampf*, Hitler repeatedly described nature and natural laws as eternal. He derided those who "fall into the lunacy of believing that he has really risen to be lord and master of Nature." Rather, he asserted, nature's rules are eternal and thus inescapable.⁶ At the 1937 Nuremberg Party Congress, he boasted that his regime had finally brought the German people a worldview that was consistent with the "eternal organic laws of nature."⁷ In a monologue in 1941, he mentioned that humans are powerless against the "eternal law of nature."⁸ Twice he called natural laws eternal in a speech in early 1942.⁹ Given his rather frequent reference to nature and its laws as eternal, it seems that Hitler did not believe they were created by some being outside nature.

I am not, of course, the first person to conclude Hitler was a pantheist. In 1935, a religious commentator George Shuster placed the dominant German religious beliefs in the 1930s into five categories: Catholicism, Lutheranism, Judaism, neo-pantheism, and negativity toward religion. Though Hitler was influenced by the first two, his deepest cravings evinced pantheism, according to Shuster.¹⁰ Pius XI did not specifically mention Hitler in his encyclical "Mit brennender Sorge," but he did combat therein the "pantheistic confusion" he saw in Nazi ideology.¹¹ Shortly after World War II, the German theologian Walter Künneth interpreted Hitler's religion as a form of apostasy from Christianity. He argued that when Hitler used terms like God, Almighty, and Creator, as he was wont to do, he redefined these terms in a pantheistic direction. Künneth stated, "In proper translation Hitler meant by 'Creator' the 'eternal nature,' by 'Almighty' and 'Providence' he meant the lawfulness of life, and by the 'will of the Lord' he meant the duty of people to submit themselves to the demands of the race."[12] Thus, even when Hitler was using words traditionally associated with Christian theism, he was redefining them.

Robert Pois argues not only that Nazism advocated a religion of nature, but that it was central to the Nazi project. Their "religion was one which could and did serve to rationalize mass-murder," he asserts. He only spends a few pages discussing Hitler's own religious views, but he does portray Hitler as a pantheist who exalted "pitiless natural laws" above humanity. "What Hitler had done," according to Pois, "was to wed a putatively scientific view of the universe to a form of pantheistic mysticism presumably congruent with adherence to 'natural laws.'" In Pois's view, Hitler's pantheistic perspective was part of the Nazi revolt against the Christian faith and its values. Hitler "had virtually deified nature and he most assuredly identified God (or Providence) with it."[13] Pois might overstate the role played by the "religion of nature" in the Nazi Party, but he does demonstrate that it was not uncommon. André Mineau argues that the SS was inclined toward pantheism, stating, "The SS view of religion was a form of naturalistic pantheism that had integrated the biological paradigm."[14]

A number of other scholars who have analyzed Hitler's religion concur it was pantheistic. Michael Rissmann asserts Hitler defined God as an abstract lawfulness of nature, not as a personal deity. He notes that Hitler sought knowledge about God not from scripture or revelation, but by studying science and history. The way he wanted to impart his awe of "God" (Rissmann uses scare quotes here) was to build planetariums and museums.[15] Michael Hesemann agrees with this analysis, claiming that the observatory and planetarium Hitler wanted to build near Linz would serve as "a shrine [*Heiligtum*] of

National Socialist pantheism, camouflaged as an observatory."[16] Even Friedrich Heer, who stresses Hitler's early affinity with Christianity, believes that Hitler gradually moved closer to a pantheistic position. He argues that Hitler's concept of the "Lord God" blended over time into a more impersonal "Providence" and eventually drifted even further into worship of nature and its "pitiless law."[17] Other scholars characterizing Hitler's religion as pantheistic include Dirk Bavendamm, Fritz Redlich, Paul Weindling, and François Bédarida.[18]

Not everyone agrees, of course, that Hitler was a pantheist. Richard Steigmann-Gall explicitly denies that he was, arguing that Hitler's religion was a supernatural one, not a religion of nature.[19] Even though he claims (wrongly, in my view) that Hitler's religious understanding shifted in the mid-1930s, he does not think Hitler's drift away from institutionalized Christianity meant a rejection of a supernatural Creator God. Unlike Steigmann-Gall, Thomas Schirrmacher, in the most extensive and thorough analysis of Hitler's religion to date, emphasizes the *anti*-Christian character of Hitler's theology. However, Schirrmacher interprets Hitler as a non-Christian monotheist, specifically rejecting the idea that Hitler was a pantheist or deist. Oddly, however, Schirrmacher admits Hitler used the terms God, Almighty, and Creator synonymously with the rule of nature and the laws of nature.[20]

Before I explain Hitler's pantheistic religion in greater depth, it is important to understand that pantheism was an influential religious perspective in German-speaking lands (and elsewhere in Europe) before and during Hitler's time. By the early twentieth century, two forms of pantheism had emerged, which I will call mystical pantheism and scientific pantheism (some scholars call the former idealistic or spiritualistic monism and the latter materialistic or naturalistic monism.)[21] Mystical pantheists believed that the cosmos had a mind or will that was supreme, while scientific pantheists stressed determinism, i.e., the strict rule of natural laws. According to scientific pantheism, the laws of nature are an expression of the will of God and thus inescapable and ironclad. Mystical pantheism disagreed with this view, denying that science could fathom the mind of the universe. Mystical pantheism sometimes had affinities or even overlapped with animism, polytheistic nature-gods, or occultism. Scientific pantheism, on the other hand, shared similarities with atheism.

Both forms of pantheism emerged in the seventeenth and eighteenth centuries and gained prominence through Baruch Spinoza and his followers in the Radical Enlightenment. Mystical pantheism became an important and intellectually respectable position in the early Romantic movement in the 1790s. Nicholas Riasanovsky argues that pantheism was the very core of the early Romantic movement, even though most of the Romantics later abandoned pantheism. The famous German poet and mystic Novalis stated that poets "find everything in nature.... For them nature has all the variety of an infinite soul." The key ideologist of the German Romantic movement, Friedrich Schlegel, wanted to found a new religion wherein "God is created through the world." Interestingly, Riasanovsky explains that the purpose of pantheism "was to make men and women God. More precisely, they were parts of God; but because all divisions were ultimately unreal, they were, in effect, God himself." Or, as Novalis stated, "God is I."[22] German idealist philosophy of the early nineteenth century gave further impetus to pantheism. The most influential German philosopher during that time, Georg Wilhelm Friedrich Hegel, was often considered by contemporaries—and some scholars today—as a pantheist. Though Hegel's vision of God was ambiguous (maybe purposely so), even those scholars who do not identify him as a pantheist often locate him somewhere between pantheism and atheism.[23]

Some forms of anti-Semitism in the late nineteenth century favored pantheism as an antidote to the supposedly Jewish features of monotheism. For instance, Eduard von Hartmann, who is sometimes regarded as a forerunner of Freud because of his philosophizing about the unconscious, promoted pantheism as a replacement for Christianity in 1874. He believed Christianity was in its death throes. Hartmann was a popularizer of Schopenhauer's philosophy, though he blended it with Schelling's pantheism. Hartmann praised pantheism as the original religion of the Aryans, while denigrating monotheism as an inferior Semitic religion.[24]

Scientific or naturalistic pantheism came to the fore in the late nineteenth century, as science gained prestige through its many successes. The intensely anticlerical Darwinian biologist Ernst Haeckel was a leading exemplar of scientific pantheism in the late nineteenth and early twentieth centuries. He usually called his philosophy monism, because he stressed the unity of spirit and matter, but he also sometimes described his religion as pantheism.[25] In 1898, while writing to his colleague (and later his biographer) Wilhelm Bölsche, Haeckel accepted Bölsche's invitation to come to a "pantheistic baptismal celebration."[26] In his best-selling *Riddle of the Universe*, Haeckel wrote that pantheism was the worldview of modern science, because it unites God, or energy, with the world, or substance. He also said, however, that in his view atheism and pantheism were identical, and he quoted Schopenhauer approvingly: "Pantheism is only a polite atheism."[27]

Haeckel always insisted that his pantheism was mechanistic and deterministic, because he considered spirit just another name for energy, which was subject to natural laws. According to Todd Weir, Haeckel defined "God as the summation of the laws of causation."[28] He staunchly fought against all mystical conceptions of pantheism or monism. At the 1913 meeting of the German Monist League, he presented a lecture (in absentia) on "Monism and Mysticism" that directly combated mysticism of every sort, including Hartmann's mystical pantheism, vitalism, and occultism. Everything in the cosmos is subject to the laws of physics, he asserted.[29] During the Nazi

The Nazi regime honored the German Darwinian biologist and pantheist Ernst Haeckel by including his portrait in the 1936 "Exhibition of Great Germans" in Berlin.
Haeckel' photo in Nazi Exhibition. From Ausstellung grosse Deutsche in Bildnessen ihrer Zeit (1936).

period, some scholars and government officials dismissed Haeckel's monism as materialistic. However, many others defended him against the accusation of materialism by pointing to his pantheism.[30] Indeed, one of Hitler's contemporaries, the political theorist Eric Voegelin, noticed the resemblance between Haeckel's and Hitler's religious views, stating, "Hitler's ideas on religion were those of a relatively primitive monism, approximately corresponding to Haeckel's *Welträtsel* at the turn of the century."[31]

One of the more interesting cases of pantheism in the early twentieth century was the commanding general of the Austrian army in World War I, Franz Conrad von Hötzendorf. Conrad's worldview was in many respects similar to Hitler's. In the 1870s, Conrad was powerfully influenced by reading Schopenhauer and Darwin.

According to his biographer, Lawrence Sondhaus, "By the end of the century Conrad, like other Austro-Hungarian officers, developed a worldview that accepted, on Darwinistic grounds, struggle among nations and nationalities as 'natural' and, indeed, necessary."[32] In his private notes from the early 1920s, he wrote, "The recognition of the struggle for existence as the fundamental principle of all earthly events is the only realistic and rational foundation of politics. Only through struggle is preservation and thriving possible." He jotted down a view of morality pretty similar to Hitler's, too: "What is 'right'? 'Right' is what the stronger one wants [or wills]."[33] Conrad rejected theistic conceptions of God, embracing instead an impersonal Almighty (*Allmacht*—a term Hitler also frequently used) that is identical with nature and nature's laws.[34]

Another early twentieth-century figure who shared many affinities with Hitler's religious views was Hans F. K. Günther, whom Hitler admired for his writings on Nordic racism. Hitler was so enthusiastic about Günther's work that he pressed Wilhelm Frick to appoint him to a professorship in social anthropology at the University of Jena in 1930, and Hitler attended his inaugural lecture. When Hitler instituted a Nazi Party Prize for Art and Science at the 1935 Nuremberg Party Rally, he bestowed the first prize for science on Günther.[35] In 1934, Günther discussed Nordic religion in his book *Piety of a Nordic Kind*. (The copy of this book that I examined was owned by the Adolf Hitler School, an elite Nazi educational institution, so, clearly the Nazis approved of this work.) In this book, Günther examined the religiosity of the Indo-Germanic people, not the specific content of their religions, yet he admitted that pantheism or some kind of mysticism is more compatible with Nordic religious inclinations than theism is. Like Hitler, he believed that the world is eternal, and he dismissed as an "Eastern" invention the idea that God created the world ("Eastern" likely meant Jewish in this context—it clearly was not referring to South or East Asian religions.) He also denied body-soul dualism, the need for redemption, and the existence of an afterlife, claiming instead that true religion should focus on this world. He insisted that authentic Indo-German religiosity should pursue some form of "natural religion" rather than theistic religion.[36] Though Günther did not make clear what his own view of God was, he clearly rejected theism and deism, while sympathizing with pantheism.[37] Further, many of his beliefs, such as focusing on this world rather than a supernatural realm and rejection of a personal afterlife, are congruent with Hitler's religious perspective.

Martin Bormann's outspoken pantheistic views also seem similar to Hitler's religion, and though he probably did not influence Hitler, he was able to disseminate his views to other Nazi Party leaders. In June 1941, Bormann, the head of the Nazi Party apparatus and one of the most powerful figures in the final four years of the Third Reich, issued a statement on the relationship between National Socialism and Christianity to all the Gauleiter. He told them that Nazis do not understand God as a human-like being sitting somewhere in the cosmos, but rather as the vastness of the universe itself. He continued,

> The force which moves all these bodies in the universe, in accordance with natural law, is what we call the Almighty or God. The assertion that this world-force can worry about the fate of every individual, every bacillus on earth, and that it can be influenced by so-called prayer or other astonishing things, is based either on a suitable dose of naiveté or on outright commercial effrontery.[38]

Bormann then equated morality with the laws of nature, which are the will of God. Though Rosenberg was critical of Bormann's style, even he noted the content of Bormann's missive was similar to Hitler's ruminations during his Table Talks.[39]

Bormann also equated God with nature in his private correspondence. In February 1940, he wrote to Rosenberg and encouraged him to help develop a handbook of moral instruction for the youth, so they could replace religion classes with moral education. One of the moral laws that Bormann wanted included was "love for the all-ensouled nature, in which God manifests himself even in animals and plants." Bormann hoped this manual would not base its morality on any religious dogmas, such as creation or the afterlife.[40] In February 1944, he wrote to his mistress, "Anyone who feels himself to be a creature of this life and encompassed by this life, in other words, by the will of All-Highest, of Omnipotence, of Nature, that is to say, by the will of God,—anyone who feels himself to be merely one of the countless meshes of the web we call a people—cannot be frightened by the hardships of this existence."[41] From all this, it is clear Bormann believed that nature is God.

The prevalence of pantheism in Hitler's milieu, however, does not definitively prove Hitler was a pantheist, since many other religions were even more widespread in Austrian and German society, such as Catholicism, Protestantism, agnosticism, and atheism. However, it demonstrates that pantheism was a viable option, especially among those with an anticlerical bent. When we examine Hitler's religious statements in depth, we find that he often expressed views of nature and God that seem closer to pantheism than to any other religious position. Also, his friends and associates noticed that he had an extremely intense love of nature. His boyhood friend August Kubizek noted that Hitler loved nature "in a very personal way.... He viewed nature as a whole. He called it the 'Outside.' This word from his mouth sounded so familiar, as though he had called it 'Home.' Actually he felt at home in nature.... Nature exerted on him an entirely unusual influence, as I have never observed with other people."[42] Loving nature, of course, does not make one a pantheist, but Hitler's intense love of nature (and his contempt for organized religion) could easily have guided him in that direction.

In fact, considerable evidence suggests that Hitler did see nature as divine. In *Mein Kampf,* Hitler deifies nature to such an extent that most translators, including the most common one by Ralph Manheim, often capitalize the word "Nature." We cannot know for sure if this would have met with Hitler's approval, since in German all nouns are capitalized, including *Natur.* Nonetheless, all five

Hitler loved nature profoundly; he, Hess, and his entourage taking a morning hike in the Bavarian Alps.
Hitler and entourage hiking in the Alps. From Heinrich Hoffmann, Hitler in seinen Bergen (1935).

translations I have examined, including one billed as the "Official Nazi Translation," capitalize "Nature" in many places.[43]

Indeed, nature is quite obviously deified in several extended passages of *Mein Kampf*. In one section, Hitler explained the foreign policy implications of the tendency of human populations to increase (this was Malthus's population principle, which Darwin adopted as a fundamental part of his theory of biological evolution). Hitler portrayed nature as an active force, intervening by natural laws—especially the law of natural selection—to keep the population in check. He stated, "By thus brutally proceeding against the individual and immediately calling him back to herself [nature] as soon as he shows himself unequal to the storm of life, she keeps the race and species strong, in fact, raises them to the highest accomplishments." He then assured his readers that though it seems inhumane, nature is actually a "cruel queen of wisdom," because her ways are ultimately benevolent:

> While Nature, by making procreation free, yet submitting survival to a hard trial, chooses from an excess number of individuals the best as worthy of living, thus preserving them alone and in them conserving their species, man limits procreation, but is hysterically concerned that once a being is born it should be preserved at any price. This correction of the divine will seems to him as wise as it is humane.... For as soon as procreation as such is limited and the number of births diminished, the natural struggle for existence which leaves only the strongest and healthiest alive is obviously replaced by the obvious desire to 'save' even the weakest and most sickly at any price, and this plants the seed of a future generation which must inevitably grow more and more deplorable the longer this mockery of Nature and her will continues.[44]

Not only did Hitler oppose limiting population growth by birth control as unnatural, but he thought it violated the "will" of nature, which he also called the "divine (*göttliche*) will." In this quote, as well as in the surrounding context, nature was an actor guiding history, not a passive object.

Another passage of *Mein Kampf* reeking of pantheism is the opening portion of the chapter on "Nation and Race." Nazis considered this chapter so important that they published it separately as a propaganda pamphlet so it could be used in schools and Nazi organizations.[45] In this chapter, Hitler deplored racial crossing, which, he wrote, was "contrary to the will of Nature for a higher breeding of all life." He then asserted that nature does not "desire" the mating of strong individuals with weaker ones. Shortly thereafter, he claimed that racial crossing lowers the level of the higher race, leading to biological degeneration. He continued, "To bring about such a development is, then, nothing else but to sin against the will of the eternal creator. And as a sin this act is rewarded. When man attempts to rebel against the iron logic of Nature, he comes into struggle with the principles to which he himself owes his existence as a man." Interestingly, after earlier mentioning that the "will of Nature" opposes racial crossing, he now invoked the "will of the eternal creator." It is noteworthy that the translator capitalized "Nature" in the passage, but not "eternal creator." Hitler, however, used the terms "nature" and "creator" interchangeably in his writings and speeches. And in this passage, after mentioning the "eternal creator" just once, he quickly returned again to nature, conflating the "iron logic of Nature" with the "will of the eternal creator."[46]

Hitler then fulminated against pacifists who thought they could overcome nature, or be a "conqueror of Nature." On the contrary, he asserted, humans are subject to natural laws, and he in fact construed humans to be the product of nature. He stated, "At this point someone or other may laugh, but this planet once moved through the ether for

Hitler posing with his dog in the Alps.
Hitler with his dog in the Alps. From Heinrich Hoffmann, Hitler wie ihn keiner kennt (1938).

millions of years without human beings and it can do so again someday if men forget that they owe their higher existence, not to the ideas
of a few crazy ideologists, but to the knowledge and ruthless application of Nature's stern and rigid laws." Since Hitler claimed here that
humans "owe their higher existence" to nature, it seems that he is
also ascribing nature's superiority to humans—far different from the
Christian belief of man made in the image of God.

In the first chapter of the second volume of *Mein Kampf*, Hitler
returned to this theme of the supremacy of nature. He explained this

"folkish" philosophy, which he embraced, centered on racial inequality and racial struggle. Those upholding this worldview are duty-bound "to promote the victory of the better and stronger, and demand the subordination of the inferior and weaker in accordance with the eternal will that dominates this universe. Thus, in principle, it serves the basic aristocratic idea of Nature." Once again, Hitler clearly deified nature, since the laws of nature correspond with the "eternal will" that rules the cosmos. A few sentences later, Hitler identified God with nature yet again, stating, "Anyone who dares to lay hands on the highest image of the Lord [i.e., the Aryans] commits sacrilege against the benevolent creator of this miracle and contributes to the expulsion from paradise. And so the folkish philosophy of life corresponds to the innermost will of Nature," since it fosters "higher breeding." The first sentence using the terms Lord, creator, and paradise are clear allusions to biblical terminology and appeal to a Christian mentality. However, the following sentence then equates these concepts of God with nature, which has a will.[47] Thus, in these and other passages of *Mein Kampf*, Hitler seems to equate nature with God, not only by juxtaposing the two concepts but also by ascribing a will and actions to nature that are normally reserved for a deity.

In his public speeches, Hitler also occasionally conflated nature with Providence or God. During one speech to the Nazi Women's Organization in September 1934, he used the terms nature and Providence interchangeably:

> That, of course, is the wonderful thing about Nature and Providence. No conflict is possible in the relations between the two sexes as long as each fulfills the task assigned to it by Nature.... After this revolt [women's liberation] a shift took place which was not in accordance with Nature's design, and it prevailed until both sexes returned to what an eternally wise Providence assigned to them.[48]

He then adjured each sex to fulfill "the task assigned to it by Nature and Providence." He also proclaimed that the Nazi regime was assigning women their proper role "in accordance with the decrees of Nature and Providence." Interestingly, as in *Mein Kampf,* the translators again capitalize nature, indicating Hitler was deifying it. After all, Hitler himself assigned to nature the same characteristics as Providence, such as promulgating decrees.[49]

In a September 1938 speech on Nazi architecture, Hitler blasted fellow Nazis who wanted to erect religious buildings and introduce forms of worship. He denied that Nazism had anything to do with such activities. He then intimated, however, that nature was worthy of some measure of worship, stating, "Our worship is exclusively the cultivation of the natural, and for that reason, because natural, therefore God-willed. Our humility is the unconditional submission before the divine laws of existence so far as they are known to us men: it is to these we pay our respect. Our commandment is the courageous fulfillment of the duties arising from those laws."[50] While rejecting the neo-paganism and mysticism of some of his associates, he approved of some kind of nature worship, though he did not want to develop rites and ceremonies for it.

In addition to these public statements, Hitler's associate Otto Wagener also remembered Hitler making private comments that seem pantheistic. Once, Hitler asserted, "For me, God is the Logos of St. John, which has become flesh and lives in the world, interwoven with it and pervading it, conferring on it drives and driving force, and constituting the actual meaning and content of the world." Obviously, Hitler was not referring to Jesus as the Logos who became flesh, because he is not describing the Logos as God becoming an individual human. Rather, for him, the Logos was a God who is closely interconnected with the cosmos, "pervading" the entire world. Hitler's God was not really the Logos of the Gospel, who created a world distinct from Himself. Hitler even recognized this disparity between his views and Christianity, because he admitted that many people would construe his position as pagan.[51]

Wagener also recalled Hitler discussing the celebration of Christmas. After noting that Christmas had originated as a pagan ceremony at the time of the winter solstice, Hitler indicated his approval for celebrating Christmas, but not in honor of Jesus's birth. He asked, "Now, why shouldn't our young people be led back to nature?" He hoped that Christmas festivities could lead children away from the church and "into the great outdoors, to show them the powerful workings of divine creation and make vivid to them the eternal rotation of the earth and the world and life." He desired the Hitler Youth to introduce Christmas traditions in which "the young people should be led back *to nature*, they should recognize nature as the giver of life and energy.... [I]t is only in the freedom of nature that a human being can also open himself to a higher morality and a higher ethic."[52] Thus, Christmas Hitler-style would draw young people away from the church while fostering veneration for nature as the highest entity.

In his monologues during the war, Hitler frequently intimated that nature was his God. In July 1941, he told his guests, "I believe whoever looks into nature with open eyes is the most pious person." He admitted man did not know the origin of the laws of nature and continued, "Thus people came up with the beautiful concept of the Almighty, whose rule they venerate. We do not want to bring people up as atheists. In every person lives the ability to form the conception—as far as its rule is concerned—of what one calls God." Bormann, who chronicled the event, apparently understood Hitler to be talking about nature as God, because immediately after the word "God," he added a clarifying note to this transcript: "Namely the rule of the laws of nature in the entire universe." Hitler's remarks certainly suggest that he considered nature identical with—or at least tightly interwoven with—God, and Bormann confirmed this.[53] Several months later, Hitler lampooned the Christian vision of deity for its anthropomorphism. If the Christian view of God was correct, he commented sarcastically, "then the ant would have to conceive of God as an ant, just as every animal would conceive of God, i.e., Providence, the laws of nature, in its own form." Thus, not only did Hitler reject the Christian conception of God, but he also equated God, Providence, and the laws of nature, thereby manifesting his pantheism.[54]

In a monologue in February 1942, Hitler discussed his plans for the observatory and planetarium he wanted to erect near his former hometown of Linz, Austria, which he intended to turn into a cultural capital of his Third Reich. Perched on a hill above Linz, the planetarium would replace the Catholic baroque pilgrimage church currently located there. The church—this "temple of idols," Hitler called it—would be torn down to make way for the observatory, which would become a Nazi pilgrimage site. The slogan on the observatory would read, "The heavens proclaim the glory of the Eternal One." Hitler dreamed of tens of thousands of visitors flowing through this planetarium every Sunday, so they could comprehend the immense vastness of the universe. Thus Sunday would be a time to venerate nature, not the Christian God. Hitler hoped this contemplation of nature would instill in Germans a kind of religiosity that would replace the "superstition" of the churches. He wanted people to be religious, but in an anticlerical (*pfaffenfeindlichen*) fashion. "We can do nothing better," he said, "than to direct ever more people to these wonders of nature." At the observatory, Hitler thought, people could learn, "A person can comprehend this and that, but he cannot dominate nature; he must know that he is a being dependent on the creation."[55] Hitler envisioned this observatory and planetarium as the new temples for the worship of nature. He was so serious about building the observatory that he had one of his favorite architects, Professor Gieseler, begin drawing up plans for it in 1942.[56]

Another way that Hitler endowed nature with the attributes usually associated with God was by portraying it as the source of morality. In *Mein Kampf*, Hitler argued humans can never master nature but have to submit to its laws. An individual

> ... must understand the fundamental necessity of Nature's rule, and realize how much his existence is subjected to these laws of eternal fight and upward struggle. Then he will feel that in a universe where planets revolve around suns, and moons turn about planets, where force alone forever masters weakness, compelling it to be an obedient slave or else crushing it, there can be no special laws for man. For him, too, the eternal principles of this ultimate wisdom hold sway. He can try to comprehend them; but escape them, never.[57]

Nature dictates moral and social laws to humans, just as it controls the physical laws of the universe. Hitler reiterated this theme of nature being the source of morality several times in *Mein Kampf*, including passages discussed earlier in this chapter.

Hitler also spoke often about the sway of nature over the course of history. In a major speech to the 1937 Nuremberg Party Congress, he explained that the life of the peoples (Völker) follows a "lawfulness determined by nature." According to Hitler, those who investigate historical developments will discover that human life is dominated by the instincts Providence has given them to procreate and preserve their lives. They will find "thereby that the maintaining of human life in general goes no other way than that prescribed in nature. They are the same elementary drives and powers of self-preservation, which are also characteristic of all other beings on this earth. They determine the struggle for life and thereby the way of life for humans."[58] Those who think they can escape from natural laws are committing a fallacy and lack historical and scientific knowledge. Only those with such ignorance, Hitler affirmed, would try "to introduce the paragraphs of a League of Nations or Geneva statutes in the place of a law of almighty nature that has been valid since the beginning of all life on this earth." Hitler's appeal to the laws of "almighty nature" underscores his pantheistic tendencies. Thereafter he stressed the inescapable validity of "the unbreakable laws of nature," especially the law of the struggle for existence. The entire thrust of this portion of his speech was that humans are subject to nature, who alone dictates morality.[59]

In a February 1942 speech to officers and cadets, Hitler laid out his basic philosophy justifying his war of conquest. He appealed to nature's laws as the proper guide to human behavior: "For we all are beings of nature, which—as far as we can survey—only knows one hard law;... We humans cannot extract ourselves from this law." If someone naively tries to evade the laws of nature by saying, "'I mean well,'" Hitler claimed, "nature or Providence does not ask about your intentions or your desires," but it operates according to its own laws. Here Hitler equated nature and Providence, and he conflated them in the ensuing sentences, too, referring to the "will of Providence," the "right of nature," and the "eternal laws of nature" as being the same thing.[60]

Hitler also identified the laws of nature with God in a monologue in November 1941. He explained that he did not know anything about the world beyond this one (*Jenseits*) but *did* know something about divinity:

> Somehow this all flows into a knowledge of the helplessness of humanity in the face of the eternal law of nature. It is not harmful, if we only come to the knowledge that the entire salvation of humanity lies in trying to comprehend the divine Providence and not believing that he can

rebel against that law. If people humbly conform to the laws, that is wonderful.[61]

In this passage, Hitler equated "divine Providence" with natural laws that are also eternal. All we as humans can do, Hitler claimed, is learn those laws and obey them.

A few weeks later, he again warned against thinking that man could somehow supersede nature's laws. Even if they seem harsh, Hitler insisted, people have no recourse but to submit. He conjectured, "If one takes his own life, he as matter and as spirit and soul returns back into nature. The toad does not know what it was before, and we do not know it about us, either! The thing to do, therefore, is to investigate the laws of nature, so that one does not set oneself against them; that would be to oppose the firmament!"[62] The notion Hitler expressed here that one's body and soul flow back into nature smacks of pantheism. The idea that the laws of nature should guide moral action also suggests Hitler saw nature as the source of moral law.

According to Hitler's secretary Christa Schroeder, Hitler often discussed religion and the churches with the secretaries. She testified, "He had no kind of tie to the church. He considered the Christian religion an outdated, hypocritical and human-ensnaring institution. His religion was the laws of nature." Schroeder confirmed what seems obvious from reading through Hitler's monologues: he rejected Christianity and worshipped nature. Further, she sketched his commitment to a deified nature as tightly knit with his view of human evolution and morality, since he saw humans as "a member of creation and a child of nature, and for us the same laws are valid as for all living organisms." He even mentioned the law of nature most important to him: "In nature the law of struggle rules from the beginning. Everything unfit for life and everything weak is eliminated." Hitler thus saw nature as a justification for his violent policies.[63]

If Hitler's religion was pantheistic—as I have demonstrated—was it closer to mystical or scientific pantheism? In light of Hitler's emphasis on the eternal validity and inescapable, ironclad character of natural laws, it seems to tilt more toward scientific pantheism. As we have seen, Hitler believed that cosmic and human history were entirely subject to laws that can be understood scientifically. He specifically rejected mysticism as a source of knowledge. At the 1933 Nuremberg Party Congress, he expressed a deterministic perspective, not only in relation to natural occurrences, but also in human history. He explained that in nature there are no chance events because everything is subject to the law of cause and effect. Just as humans need to understand the cause of a disease in order to cure it, so they need to comprehend the laws that rule human history. The rise and decline of peoples is not mysterious, Hitler maintained, but it follows from specific causes that people can investigate and understand.[64] This deterministic perspective lines up with many comments Hitler made throughout his career where he pronounced the inevitable sway of natural laws over the affairs of humanity.

Hitler's determinism, however, sat in uneasy tension with his stress on willpower. How could one exert one's will if everything in the universe is determined by prior natural causes? It should be noted that many politicians and thinkers—such as Karl Marx and Vladimir Lenin, for instance—have shared Hitler's dilemma of how to square determinism with willful action. One way that Nazis as biological determinists (and Marxists as economic determinists) were able to bridge the determinism-free will divide was to insist that their activity was in line with the inevitable flow of historical developments. In Hitler's perspective, Providence (or Nature or Fate or God) was smiling favorably upon his efforts, precisely because he was acting in harmony with the inescapable laws of nature. His and Germany's successes did not come from prayer or mystical rites or ceremonies but resulted from taking action in accordance with the laws of nature.

Hitler illustrated this belief when he told officer cadets in Berlin in December 1940 how they could achieve victory. In stirring them up to "kill or be killed," he stated, "We can emerge victorious from this arduous battle, if only we realize its unchangeable, necessary and inevitable nature. The individual cannot shrink from it [sic], it is the fate of the entire Volk. Hence, at this hour, I would like to speak to you on the inevitability not only of this [battle], but of struggle as such."[65] In the rest of the speech, Hitler instructed them about the laws of nature applicable to the war they were fighting, and he admonished them to wage war in concert with these insuperable laws.

How, then, can we best make sense of Hitler's concept of God when quite often he seems pantheistic, but occasionally he sounds deistic or even theistic? One option is that Hitler was a pantheist but used more traditional religious language to appeal to his audience and win the support of those who did not share his views. Given the preponderance of his pantheistic terminology and the many times he deified nature, together with the way he juxtaposed "Creator" with "eternal nature," I believe this is the best explanation. Unlike with Christianity, Hitler had little or no reason to pose as a pantheist, because this would not have appealed to a very large constituency. However, he had very strong political reasons to pose as a believer in a more traditional kind of God. Savvy politician that he was, he wanted to appeal to Germans of all religious persuasions, so he used more traditional God-language to win popular support. This is consistent with his own statements about the relationship between religion and propaganda, and it squares with what we know about his hypocritical use of Christian themes.

Another strong possibility is that Hitler's view of God was not pantheistic, but *panen*theistic. Friedrich Tomberg argues this, claiming that Hitler embraced a panentheism that believed "everything is in nature, but nature is in God."[66] This would allow Hitler to equate nature with God, because panentheists see nature as divine. However, they also see God as having an existence beyond nature, too. A panentheist could construe God as intervening in history in some ways, though usually not in miraculous events. This could correspond roughly with the way Hitler described God blessing or favoring the German Volk. A third possibility is Hitler simply had his metaphysics muddled. He was not a rigorous thinker, and he admitted that he did not know much about the nature of God, so perhaps he did not know himself whether to believe in a pantheistic, panentheistic, deistic, or theistic God. He admitted more than once that God is inscrutable, which makes it plausible that he would be unable to decide among these options.

While I freely admit that it is impossible to know with ironclad certainty whether Hitler was a pantheist, panentheist, deist, or a theist, it seems Hitler's position was closest to pantheism. When he used language that suggested other positions, it was usually in public speeches, where he was simply using traditional God-language to appeal to the religious beliefs of his audience. However, as is evident in many places where he used the terms God and nature interchangeably, he was often employing traditional religious terminology, but defining those terms in non-traditional ways. For Hitler, God was Nature.

NINE

WAS HITLER A CREATIONIST?

ONE OF THE MOST SERIOUS OBJECTIONS LODGED against the interpretation of Hitler as a pantheist is his use of the term "Creator" in his writings and speeches. Hitler occasionally referred to an Almighty Creator or Eternal Creator, and he sometimes asserted humans were made in the image of God. If Hitler believed in a God who created nature as a distinct entity, separate from himself as deity—as monotheistic religions have traditionally taught—then he would not be a pantheist. He would most likely be a deist, since he generally spurned the idea that God intervened miraculously in history.

In his speech to the 1935 Nuremberg Party Congress, Hitler called God "the Creator" of the German Volk. However, he also implied that God would not intervene miraculously on behalf of his chosen people. They would have to work and fight to gain the Almighty's favor and blessing. Hitler stated, "In the long run God's favor will be given only to him who deserves it. He who speaks and acts in the name of a people created by the Almighty continues to act under this commission so long as he does not sin against the substance and the future of the work of the Creator that has been placed in his hand. Therefore it is good that the conquest of power is always bound up with hard fighting."[1] Hitler's God was not one who intervened supernaturally in historical developments. Rather, he rewarded people according to the way they worked and fought. God did not break into the cause and effect relationship governed by natural law.

In January 1943, Hitler again called God "Creator" yet implied this version was not a miracle-working deity; rather, he expected humans to make their own way in the world. In a statement read by Goebbels on behalf of Hitler, the Führer asserted, "The Almighty will be a just judge. It is our task to fulfill our duty in such a manner that we prove ourselves to Him as the Creator of the world, in accordance with his law on the struggle for existence." Hitler was not referring to God's judgment as some miraculous intervention in history, for earlier in the same speech he insisted, "In this mightiest struggle of all time, we cannot expect that Providence give us victory as a present. Each and every people will be weighed, and what is judged too light will fall." God's judgment is thus not a decision of a personal deity but the result of natural causation: those who work hard and fight bravely win. It is also interesting to note that, according to this speech, one of the things Hitler's God established was the Darwinian law of the struggle for existence.[2]

Admittedly, Hitler still sometimes sounds like a deist in his speeches and in *Mein Kampf*. However, I am not persuaded he really embraced deism. First, he never specified anything about how God created the world, and he often mentioned God creating the laws of the struggle for existence and natural selection to rule the biological world.[3] This seems to suggest that God created biological organisms through natural processes, not by fiat. Second, in many cases where Hitler referred to a Creator, such as a few of the passages from *Mein Kampf* discussed in chapter eight, he used it in a context that also referenced "eternal nature" or equated his Creator with nature (or both). This suggests he was not intending his use of the term to imply that God created nature at a finite point in the past, as a deist or theist would believe. God or nature was a "Creator," but it is not clear at all from Hitler's discourse if he believed God created through natural or supernatural processes. Third, Hitler often spoke about nature creating organisms, again implying nature is synonymous with the Creator.[4] Fourth, Hitler explicitly rejected the creation stories of the Judeo-Christian tradition. Finally, Hitler embraced an evolutionary account of the origins of humanity.

Let's explore these last two points in greater depth. Never did Hitler express belief in the biblical creation story—which, after all, derived from the Jewish scriptures. (we have already seen that Hitler's anti-Semitism led him to spurn the Old Testament as a Jewish document.) He obviously did not embrace young-earth creationism (which is what most Americans mean today when they use the term creationism), since on quite a few occasions he mentioned the earth existing for hundreds of thousands, or even millions, of years. For example, in *Mein Kampf,* he warned pacifists that their naiveté would have disastrous consequences, because "this planet once moved through the ether for millions of years without human beings and it can do so again some day if men forget that they owe their higher existence, not to the ideas of a few crazy ideologists, but to the knowledge and ruthless application of Nature's stern and rigid laws."[5] Wagener recalled that Hitler speculated about the bizarre theories of a Viennese writer, Hans Goldzier, who claimed that electricity radiating from the earth's interior helped produce plants, animals, and humans. Hitler admitted that this conjecture might be nonsense, but he did not think science had adjudicated the issue yet, and he certainly did not think Christianity had any answers about origins. He protested that "the churches offer up creation myths...[b]ut the thinking man of the modern age must consign them to the realm of tall tales."[6] In general, Hitler regarded the Old Testament creation stories as delusional inventions of the Jewish mind.

On October 24, 1941, Hitler spoke at great length to his entourage about the controversy between science and religion, and specifically between evolution and Christianity. Hitler opened this lengthy monologue on evolution by claiming that the church's teachings are contrary to modern research. In fact, as Hitler expounded on this science-religion controversy, he clearly came down on the side of science and bashed the church, asserting, "The definition of the church is a misuse of the creation for earthly purposes." He also divulged his pantheistic tendencies: "Whoever sees God only in an oak or in a tabernacle and not in the Whole, cannot be pious deep inside; he remains stuck in the outward." In addition, Hitler praised the French Enlightenment thinkers' anticlericalism and the progress of science. After expostulating on the glories of science and the ignorance of the church, Hitler pronounced his belief in the evolution of humans. He stated, "There have been humans at the rank at least of a baboon in any case for 300,000 years at least. The ape is distinguished from the lowest human less than such a human is from a thinker like, for example, Schopenhauer."[7] Hitler clearly accepted evolutionary theory, including human evolution, and rejected religious teachings to the contrary.

Nor was this an isolated statement. One of Hitler's secretaries, Christa Schroeder, remembered that on several occasions the Führer discussed religion, the church and biological evolution with his secretaries. After explaining that Hitler rejected the church, she provided a lengthy description of Hitler's views on human evolution:

Science does not yet clearly know from which root human beings have arisen. We are certainly the highest stage of evolution of any mammal, which evolved from reptiles to mammals, perhaps through apes, to humans. We are a member of creation and children of nature, and the same laws apply to us as to all living organisms. And in nature the law of the struggle rules from the beginning. Everything incapable of living and everything weak will be eliminated.[8]

Schroeder thus confirmed in considerable detail that Hitler believed in human evolution through the process of struggle and selection.

Two other associates of Hitler testify that belief in Darwinian evolution was integral to his ideology. Wagener remembered a conversation in the summer of 1931 when Hitler professed, "Everywhere in life only a process of selection can prevail. Among the animals, among plants, wherever observations have been made, basically the stronger, the better survives. The simpler life forms have no written constitution. Selection therefore runs a natural course. As Darwin correctly proved: the choice is not made by some agency—nature chooses." This not only demonstrates Hitler believed in Darwinian natural selection, but it also suggests he saw the process as non-teleological, i.e., not directed by some deity. Wagener claimed that Hitler based his support for killing the weak and the sick on this vision of natural selection.[9] Otto Dietrich generally concurred, stating that Hitler's "evolutionary views on natural selection and survival of the fittest coincided with the ideas of Darwin and Haeckel." Hitler was not an atheist, according to Dietrich, but believed in a Supreme Being who "had created laws for the preservation and evolution of the human race. He believed that the highest aim of mankind was to survive for the achievement of progress and perfection." Thus, evolutionary thought was central to Hitler's goals and policies.[10]

In his two books, Hitler discussed evolutionary theory as vital to his theory of racial struggle and eugenics. Several times throughout *Mein Kampf*, he specifically employs the term "struggle for existence" ("Kampf um das Dasein"); in fact, the phrase or its plural appears three times in a passage several pages long where Hitler described why the Germans should be both pro-natalist and expansionist.[11] Historian Robert Richards, however, inexplicably claims that Hitler's views in this passage are un-Darwinian, because—according to Richards— a Darwinian should supposedly want population expansion only within restricted borders, which would allow the fit to triumph over the unfit. Richards argues expanding into new territory would lessen the struggle, allowing the fit and less fit "to have fairly equal chances."[12] Richards, however, miscalculates here because he leaves out one of the most important factors in Hitler's reasoning: the living space (*Lebensraum*) is to be taken from allegedly inferior races. Thus, expanding is *part* of the Darwinian racial struggle that allows the allegedly fitter Nordic race to outcompete allegedly inferior races. Contra Richards, Hitler's discussion makes perfect sense in a Darwinian world if unequal races are waging a struggle for existence. In fact, the whole idea of *Lebensraum* was first formulated by Friedrich Ratzel, a Darwinian biologist who later became a geographer.[13] In addition, many pro-natalist eugenicists with impeccable Darwinian credentials, such as Alfred Ploetz or Max von Gruber, agreed with Hitler's position on expansionism (indeed, they may have influenced Hitler in this matter).

Later in *Mein Kampf*, in the chapter on "Nation and Race," Hitler discussed biological evolution in the context of racial purity. He argued that racial mixing is deleterious to biological organisms, precisely because it would stymie biological evolution. His reasoning was thus: If two organisms at different levels mate, this will result in offspring below the level of the higher parent—"consequently, it will later succumb in the struggle against the higher level." Hitler did not use the term "struggle for existence" here, but he described this struggle as a contest between organisms in which the stronger prevail and the weaker are eliminated. He then stated, "If this law did not prevail, any conceivable higher evolution (*Höherentwicklung*) of organic living beings would be unthinkable."[14]

Richards, for his part, objects to my translation of this sentence, claiming that I am playing a "sly trick" by translating *Entwicklung* as "evolution," which Ralph Manheim renders as "development" in the standard translation. There are three major problems with Richards' criticism, however. First, even if, for the purposes of argument, we concede that "development" is the proper rendering of *Entwicklung* in this context, we still end up with Hitler believing in biological evolution. Hitler has just described a struggle between living organisms that leads to the victory of the stronger and the elimination of the weaker. In that context, what would the "higher development of organic living beings" mean? "Higher development" certainly implies that a change is transpiring. Further, just two paragraphs later, Hitler maintained the "struggle is always a means for improving a species' health and power of resistance and, therefore, a cause of its higher development (*Höherentwicklung*)." Again, "improving" a species and bringing about its "higher development" is not the language of one committed to fixity of species. Hitler used the term "higher development" (*Höherentwicklung*) yet again in the following paragraph when discussing biological organisms. Thus, even if we do not translate *Entwicklung* as "evolution," it is still clear that evolution is exactly what Hitler meant.

Second, in the 1920s (and even thereafter), German biologists regularly used the term *Entwicklung* to mean "evolution." To be sure, it also meant "development," and in most contexts this is a preferable translation, especially when the context has nothing to do with biology.

Within the context of biology itself, *Entwicklung* could have different meanings, and biologists did use it to mean embryological development. Examining the context in "Nation and Race," however, it is obvious Hitler is referring to biological organisms, but he clearly did not mean embryological development. Richards, meanwhile—who does not consider the context of any of the quotes I used—conjures out of thin air a historical "fact" to refute my thesis. He states, "By the end of the nineteenth century, the terms *Entwicklung* and 'development' as referring to species' evolution had declined in use in both Germany and England, though in German *Entwicklungslehre* would still be used to mean the theory of evolution."[15]

This claim simply does not pass muster. I have examined the biological journals and books of Darwinian biologists of the early twentieth century, and they regularly used the term *"Entwicklung"* to refer to evolution. I could provide hundreds of examples (including passages in German biology textbooks), but a couple of telling ones will suffice. The Nazi government's manual setting forth the official biology curriculum used the term *Entwicklung* repeatedly to refer to evolution. It stipulated, for example, that in the eighth class teachers should provide an "overview of the *Entwicklung* of life in the course of geological history." Here, *Entwicklung* quite obviously means biological evolution, and the context proves it. Immediately after this comment, the manual discussed evidence for biological evolution and told teachers they should cover *"Darwinismus."* It next instructed them to teach the "Origin and *Entwicklung* [obviously meaning evolution] of humans and human races."[16] One more example: In the 1943 edition of a book published in a series on "National Socialist Pedagogy in School Instruction," Paul Brohmer claimed that "the *Entwicklung* of living organisms during earth history from simpler to higher forms—including humans—is not disputed."[17] Would translating this as "evolution" really be a "sly trick"? I have used two examples from Nazi publications to underscore that Nazis accepted biological evolution. The term *Entwicklung* was used widely in Germany at the time to mean evolution, Richards' specious claim notwithstanding.

The final major problem with Richards' critique is that, except for Ralph Manheim, who never translates *Entwicklung* as evolution, other translators of *Mein Kampf* do render it as "evolution" when the context is a discussion of biological organisms changing over time. In 1938, Charles Grant Robertson, a scholar at the University of Birmingham who specialized in the German language, published an excerpt of Hitler's *Mein Kampf* that contained the relevant passage quoted above from "Nation and Race." Robertson prefaced his translation by commenting, "The racial thought of Herr Hitler begins with a popularized conception of Darwin's evolutionary hypotheses, which are turned to surprising uses." Then he translated *Entwicklung* as evolution: "If this law [struggle] did not prevail, any higher evolution of all organic life would be unthinkable."[18]

The following year, two different English translations of *Mein Kampf* appeared, one in Britain by James Murphy and another in the United States by Barrows Mussey. Both translate *Entwicklung* as evolution in certain contexts. Mussey, for example, translates the relevant passages from "Nation and Race" thus: "[f]or if this law did not hold, any conceivable evolution of organic living things would be unthinkable....Always struggle is a means to improve the health and stamina of the species, and thus a cause of its evolution. By any other process all development and evolution would cease, and the very reverse would take place."[19] Giving it a little looser translation, Murphy uses both "evolution" and "development" in his version: "[f]or if such a law did not direct the process of evolution then the higher development of organic life would not be conceivable at all." On the following page, Murphy's translation again makes clear that he believes Hitler's prose reflected an evolutionary viewpoint: "If Nature does not wish that weaker individuals should mate with the stronger, she wishes even less that a superior race should intermingle with an inferior one; because in such a case all her efforts, throughout hundreds of thousands of years, to establish an evolutionary higher stage of being, may thus be rendered futile."[20] In addition to passages from *Mein Kampf*, various translators of Hitler's other works, such as the *Second Book* and his speeches, translate *Entwicklung* as evolution when the context requires it. If my translation of *Entwicklung* as evolution is a sly trick, then, apparently, there are quite a few of us sly tricksters around.

Hitler's main point in discussing biological evolution in "Nation and Race" was to insist that different species—and then he extrapolated to races—should not interbreed, because this would undermine the evolutionary process. In the midst of this passage, Hitler stressed the distinction between species by stating, "the fox is always a fox, the goose a goose, the tiger a tiger, etc." This meant, according to Hitler, that the fox could not be a humanitarian toward a goose. By implication, an Aryan could not be a humanitarian toward other races, as Hitler explains later in the chapter.

Richards maintains that this brief statement proves Hitler was committed to the fixity of species. If, indeed, Hitler meant that, over geological time, these species always remained the same, then Richards would be right. However, there is no reason to interpret this phrase as applying to geological history, especially since this brief comment is tucked in the midst of a passage that embraced evolution. Again, Richards completely ignores the context. It's more likely Hitler meant a shorter timeframe when discussing foxes remaining foxes. He, like other Nazi ideologists that sometimes spoke about the unchanging nature of the Aryan race, only meant that it did not vary significantly during shorter time spans, such as thousands of years. They were not implying that species and races were static over millions of years, since often they made clear they did indeed believe in evolution over millions of years.

Hitler, like many biologists during his time, embraced hard heredity, the idea that species could not change through direct environmental influences. August Weismann, the pioneer in advocating hard heredity in the late nineteenth century (as did many eugenicists of the early twentieth-century Germany), did not see any contradiction between it and Darwinism. Nor did Hitler or most Nazi ideologists. In fact, many scholars have noticed this Darwinian thrust in *Mein Kampf*.[21]

Hitler's commitment to biological evolution comes through again in his *Second Book* of 1928. In the opening pages of the book, Hitler described the history of the earth in a way that is clearly evolutionary, and he included humans in his evolutionary account:

> The history of the world in the ages when humans did not yet exist was initially a representation of geological occurrences. The clash of natural forces with each other, the formation of a habitable surface on this planet, the separation of water and land, the formation of the mountains, plains, and the seas. That is the history of the world during this time. Later, with the emergence of organic life, human interest focuses on the appearance and disappearance of its thousandfold forms. Man himself finally becomes visible very late, and from that point on he begins to understand the term 'world history' as referring primarily to the history of his own development—in other words, the representation of his own evolution. This development is characterized by the never-ending battle of humans against animals and also against humans themselves. Finally, out of the unclear tangle of individual beings, formations rise—families, tribes, peoples, states. The portrayal of their genesis and dissolution alone is the replication of the eternal struggle for survival.[22]

It should go without saying that this sketch of the earth's history, being driven as it is by the struggle for survival among organisms, is Darwinian. Apparently, however, it does not go without saying, because Richards insists this passage is not Darwinian at all, but rather Hegelian.[23]

However, as discussed in chapter two, Hitler overtly rejected Hegelianism in two separate monologues. And if we examine this passage from the *Second Book* more closely, we find that it has nothing to do with Hegelianism and everything to do with biological evolution driven by the struggle for existence. Nowhere in this passage did Hitler state or even imply that earth's history was being driven by Hegel's Universal Reason, or *Geist*. It also is noteworthy that this first chapter of Hitler's unpublished book is entirely about the "struggle for survival," and the term he used, "Lebenskampf"—or literally, "struggle for life,"—is one Darwin used as a synonym for the "struggle for existence." (Indeed, the original subtitle of Darwin's *Origin of Species* was *The Preservation of Favoured Races in the Struggle for Life*.)

Hitler opened the chapter arguing that the struggle for life is the driving force in human history and in politics. What is driving this struggle? Not Hegelian Geist, but the "self-preservation instinct" that manifests itself in two motivations: "hunger and love." By love, Hitler explained he simply meant reproduction. He then stated, "In truth, these two impulses [hunger and love] are the rulers of life." Thus biological instincts, not Hegelian Geist or rationality, drive history forward, in Hitler's view. In fact, Hitler wrote, "Whatever is made of flesh and blood can never escape the laws that condition its development. As soon as the human intellect believes itself to be above that, that real substance that is the bearer of the spirit is destroyed." This is a direct rejection of Hegelianism, as it gives primacy to the body and nature over the spirit. Hitler is founding his view of development on biology, not Hegelian Geist.[24]

Further, in the paragraph immediately preceding the one block-quoted above and which Richards wrongly calls Hegelian, Hitler wrote:

> The types of creatures on the earth are countless, and on an individual level their self-preservation instinct as well as the longing for procreation is always unlimited; however, the space in which this entire life process plays itself out is limited. It is the surface area of a precisely measured sphere on which billions and billions of individual beings struggle for life and succession. In the limitation of this living space lies the compulsion for the struggle for survival, and the struggle for survival, in turn, contains that precondition for evolution.[25]

Here Hitler argued that reproduction outstrips the available resources, causing a struggle for life. This is the same Malthusian point upon which Darwin founded his theory of natural selection. Anyone reading these first three pages of Hitler's *Second Book* should realize why the translator used the term "evolution" here: Hitler was describing biological change in organisms that occurs because of a struggle caused by their superfecundity. This certainly sounds like Darwinian evolution to me.

If we have any lingering doubts about Hitler's attitude toward human evolution or the importance of it in his ideology, however, we can examine his speeches for clues. What we find is that on numerous occasions, Hitler discussed human evolution, including the following concepts: population pressure causes a struggle for existence between organisms; this struggle results in selection of the strongest or fittest; and this selection leads to biological progress. For instance, in January 1927, Hitler told a Munich audience that the earth and the entire cosmos is part of an evolutionary process that has been going on for millions of years. As part of this evolutionary process, biological organisms were involved in a constant struggle "where the stronger overthrows or destroys the weaker." As always, Hitler stressed that humans were no exception to the laws of nature. He stated, "In the process of evolution humans arose, just as animals, and their vocation was struggle for their existence."[26] In a speech later that year, Hitler again expressed his belief that humans were descendants of animals. At the time, he was countering pacifist thinking by asserting the necessity of a struggle between organisms, including humans. He stated,

> You are the product of this struggle. If your ancestors had not fought, today you would be an animal. They did not gain their rights through peaceful debates with wild animals, and later perhaps also with humans, through the comparative adjustment of relations by a pacifist court of arbitration, but rather the earth has been acquired on the basis of the right of the stronger.[27]

Hitler thus thought that the forefathers of humans were animals, and humans would still be animals if they had not been elevated by the struggle for existence. In April 1928, Hitler again stressed the importance of the struggle for existence, claiming that "struggle is the precondition for every higher evolution" and humans cannot exempt themselves from this natural law.[28]

In a September 1928 speech, Hitler was even more explicit, providing a long discussion of the necessity of the struggle for existence in the evolutionary process. He explained that the struggle for existence occurs because a limited amount of land is beset by an unlimited number of organisms. This is precisely the Malthusian explanation that Darwin gave for the struggle for existence. Hitler then asserted that humans cannot escape this struggle, to which they owe their very existence. The world has existed for millions of years without humans, he said, and "you owe your existence as a human exclusively to the higher breeding that you owe to the struggle itself, because struggle, the father of all things, causes selection, because the result is always that the rotten and decaying things disappear, and what remains must be the healthy ones, so that your eternal struggle also means an eternal process of improvement." This is a clear statement of Darwinian evolutionary theory: the Malthusian population imbalance causing a struggle for existence that leads to the selection of the fittest, ultimately producing biological progress.[29]

In a written statement from 1929, Hitler alluded to his belief in human evolution. He was emphasizing the antipacifist stance of the Nazi Party, which saw struggle as a basic and ineluctable law of nature. He wrote that the National Socialist idea considers struggle the precondition for the "ascent of all living organisms, including humans. The National Socialist idea sees in struggle the promoter of everything strong, the remover of every sick weakness, and thus the purifier of all organisms." By describing this selection of organisms through a struggle as a process that leads to biological progress, Hitler clearly demonstrated he believed in human evolution.[30]

Another time he indicated this belief was in a 1937 speech for the opening of the Munich House of German Art. Hitler was horrified by modernist art, and he accused modernist artists of being atavistic, i.e., throwbacks to creatures at earlier evolutionary stages. He said, "When we know today that the evolution of millions of years, compressed into a few decades, repeats itself in every individual, then this art, we realize, is not 'modern.' It is on the contrary to the highest degree 'archaic,' far older probably than the Stone Age." Not only does this statement show Hitler believed that humans evolved over millions of years, but it also demonstrates that Hitler believed in Haeckel's theory of evolutionary recapitulation. Haeckel had theorized (and Darwin and many other Darwinists agreed with him) that during embryonic development, organisms repeated the evolutionary stages their ancestors had traversed. Whether Hitler ever read Haeckel or not, he accepted Haeckel's recapitulation theory, which he applied to humans.[31]

In a speech to military officers and cadets in May 1942, Hitler explained the reason that Germany needed to fight expansionist wars. He told them that struggle determines who will fill the space on the earth's surface. "This struggle," he affirmed, "leads in effect to an unswerving and *eternal selection*, to the selection *of the better and tougher*. We thus see in this struggle an element of the building up of all living things." This struggle is a law of nature that produces "progressive evolution" (*Vorwärtsentwicklung*). Hitler acknowledged that the natural processes of struggle and selection caused biological change in organisms. Since he was discussing warfare among humans and conflict between different peoples (Völker), he obviously was applying these evolutionary insights to humans.[32]

In June 1944, Hitler explained his views on war to an audience of army officers in a remarkably candid speech. He opened it by basing his philosophy of war on natural law:

> Among the processes that are essentially immutable, that remain the same throughout all time, and that only change in the form of the means applied, is war. Nature teaches us with every gaze into its workings, into its events, that the principle of selection dominates it, that the stronger remains victor and the weaker succumbs. It teaches us that what often appears to someone as cruelty, because he himself is affected or because through his education he has turned away from the laws of nature, is in reality necessary, in order to bring about a higher evolution of living organisms.[33]

Hitler then insisted that humans must follow the ways of nature, not the allegedly misguided path of humanitarians. If they pursue humanitarianism, Hitler warned, they will be supplanted by other organisms that take the struggle seriously. Hitler then reminded these officers that "it has only been a few million years ago, that human-like figures have been active on this earth, scarcely 300,000 years, provable by skeletons, and scarcely 10,000 years through traces of a so-called human culture." Thus, not only did Hitler clearly believe humans evolved, but he also based his philosophy of war on it. War, he stated, is an immutable process and the necessary condition for "natural selection of the stronger and simultaneously the process of the elimination of the weaker."[34]

In a monologue in March 1942, Hitler affirmed his belief in human evolution in a conversation about why men shave off their beards. According to Hitler, shaving was "nothing but the continuation of an evolution that has been proceeding for millions of years: Gradually humans lost their hair."[35] While Hitler's opinion about the relationship between shaving and evolution is ridiculous, the notion that humans lost their hair over millions of years demonstrates he believed they were once hairy creatures, such as apes.

In addition to all these statements from Hitler himself, another piece of evidence that shows he believed in human evolution is the Nazi propaganda pamphlet from 1944 titled *Wofür kämpfen wir?*(*Why Are We Fighting?*), which explained the ideological basis for the expansionist war Germany was fighting. In a letter published in the front of the pamphlet, Hitler personally endorsed the book and instructed German officers to use it regularly to indoctrinate their soldiers in the National Socialist worldview. The pamphlet teaches the importance of struggle between organisms and biological selection, which improves species, and that humans should strive to advance their own species: "We believe therefore *in the task of improving humans.*" This task corresponds to the laws of nature, which are God-given, so waging struggle to improve the human species fulfills the will of God: "Our racial idea is only the 'expression of a worldview,' which recognizes in the higher evolution of humans a divine command."[36]

We should also note that there was an official Nazi position on evolution. According to Hitler and his comrades, the education of the youth in the National Socialist worldview was one of the most important functions that the Nazi regime performed. Because of racism's centrality to Nazi ideology, biology was one of the most important subjects, and the Nazi regime increased biology instruction in the schools. They also made sure it conformed to *their* ideology. The official Nazi biology curriculum included large doses of evolution, including human evolution. Not only did the schools teach human evolution, but SS training manuals, Racial Policy Office lectures, Nazi periodicals, and many other Nazi publications also explained the importance of human evolution for the Nazi worldview. Some of Germany's leading evolutionary anthropologists were SS officers or lectured to Nazi organizations. Evolutionary biologists and anthropologists were promoted, appointed to professorships, and generally feted by the Nazi regime. While this may not be solid evidence about what Hitler personally thought on the matter, it is powerful circumstantial evidence.[37]

As I have demonstrated above, Hitler did indeed believe in human evolution. It was not a peripheral element of his worldview, either. It helped shape his understanding of the human struggle for existence, natural selection among humans and human races, eugenics, pronatalism, killing the disabled, and expansionism. Of course, Hitler's evolutionary views were synthesized with many other influences, such as anti-Semitism and nationalism; it was by no means the *sole* influence on his ideology or policies. But in addition to all the times Hitler explicitly broached the topic of human evolution, he even more frequently discussed the racial struggle for existence, the struggle for existence within the Nordic race, natural selection, and many other Darwinian themes. He often abbreviated these terms as "racial struggle," "struggle," and "selection," just as many of his contemporaries, including biologists and eugenicists, did, but key issue here is the concept, not the exact terminology. When Hitler spoke about the "selection" of the strongest organisms and the elimination of the weakest, it did not matter whether he used the exact term "natural selection" (though he did at times). He was obviously describing it, and that is the crucial issue.

Despite the importance of human evolution to his worldview, Hitler did once appear to express doubt about human evolution. In a private conversation in January 1942, Hitler said the following:

> Where do we get the right to believe that humanity was not already from its earliest origins what it is today? Looking at nature teaches us that in the realm of plants and animals, transformations and further developments occur. But never within a genus has evolution made such a wide leap, which humans must have made, if they had been transformed from an ape-like condition to what they are now.[38]

Note that Hitler continued to believe plants and animals evolved, so he was not denying all forms of biological evolution. Nor was he adopting creationism. He merely seemed to be suggesting that somehow humans might be an exception to the evolutionary rule in nature. In fact, he did not even explicitly *deny* human evolution, though he certainly expressed doubt about it.

Admittedly, if this statement were all we knew about Hitler's opinions about the topic, we would have to conclude that he was not committed to the idea of human evolution. In light of this evidence, however, why do I continue to think Hitler believed in human evolution? Primarily because, as I have already demonstrated, Hitler often expressed belief in human evolution in various ways throughout this political career. This included an extended discussion of evolution in a monologue less than three months earlier, a stray comment less than two months after his January 1942 monologue, and extended discussions of human evolution in speeches in May 1942 and June 1944. Apparently Hitler's doubt did not stick, and he returned to his belief in human evolution very quickly. His doubt about human evolution was a brief episode, a mere blip on the screen. Would it be fair to characterize someone as a disbeliever in some religion, ideology, or idea, just because in one private conversation they expressed doubt about it?

Further, Hitler prefaced his January 1942 comment with the revelation that he had recently been reading a book on the origin of human races. Most likely, his thoughts reflected this recent reading, not his long-standing convictions. This seems especially probable because in the same January 1942 monologue, Hitler also speculated about many bizarre theories, such as Hörbiger's World Ice Theory. If, indeed, Hitler was basing his reflections on his reading of Hörbiger or one of Hörbiger's disciples, as seems likely based on his comments about Atlantis and mythology, then Hitler may not have been denying human evolution at all. Hörbiger put forward many quirky ideas in his book on the World Ice Theory, and his theory of biological evolution was certainly strange. He denied that humans evolved from apes, which is one of Hitler's main points in this monologue. However, Hörbiger was not denying human evolution overall. Rather, he thought that humans had evolved through a teleological process that resembled embryological development. He explicitly endorsed Haeckel's biogenetic law, which stated that organisms traverse their evolutionary past in the course of their embryological development. Thus, Hörbiger believed that humans had developed from simpler organisms, but these were in some sense proto-human organisms (just as an embryo of a human is already human). Hörbiger thus denied that humans evolved from other animals. Instead, he asserted, other animals were the chance side-products that evolved from the proto-human organisms.[39] Hörbiger's ideas were completely out of line with the teachings of evolutionary biologists in the early twentieth century, but he still believed in some kind of evolution. Thus, even if, in January 1942, Hitler was giving up his belief in human evolution from apes, this would not necessarily mean that he rejected biological evolution or even human evolution entirely.

Also, the reason that Hitler provided in January 1942 for doubting human evolution was that there was a "wide leap" between apes and humans. Yet Hitler explicitly contradicted this point many times in his career. In fact, just three days earlier, Hitler had taken the opposite position. On January 22, 1942, Hitler was discussing the superiority of vegetarianism when he remarked, "The apes, our relatives in antiquity, are pure herbivores."[40] By calling apes "our relatives," he was implying an evolutionary relationship and certainly contradicting the position he took just three days later that saw an immense gulf between apes and humans. In fact, less than three months earlier, he had clearly stated his belief that humans had indeed evolved and reasoned, "The ape is distinguished from the lowest human less than such a human is from a thinker like, for example, Schopenhauer."[41] In a 1933 speech at the Nuremberg Party Rally, he stated, "The gulf between the lowest creature which can still be styled man and our highest races is greater than that between the lowest type of man and the highest ape."[42] These last two comments paraphrase statements Haeckel made in many of his works; two examples are "the difference between the lowest primitive humans and the highest evolved cultured humans is in this respect greater than that between the former and the apes" and *"the differences between the highest and the lowest humans is greater than that between the lowest human and the highest animal."*[43] Hitler's multiple statements about the closeness of primitive humans and apes suggest the reason for Hitler's doubt about human evolution in January 1942—that there was a "wide leap" between humans and animals—was a fleeting thought, not a permanent feature of his intellectual architecture. The preponderance of evidence is that Hitler embraced Darwinian theory and was *not* a creationist.

What about the many times that Hitler mentioned a Creator, and the times he claimed that humans were created in the image of God? In chapter eight, I explained why I am convinced that Hitler equated the Creator with nature. However, even if Hitler did believe in some kind of Creator distinct from nature, this would not make Hitler a creationist opponent of Darwinian evolution. There are many evolutionists around today (e.g., Francis Collins, director of the National Institutes of Health) who believe that God created the cosmos and then allowed biological organisms to emerge through the process of Darwinian evolution. This includes most theists and deists who accept biological evolution. Some of these theistic evolutionists even believe that humans are created in the image of God, despite their evolutionary origins. Many Catholic thinkers, for instance, take this position today. So even if Hitler did believe in some kind of Creator Being distinct from nature, this would not make him a creationist. For someone to argue that Hitler was a creationist, they would have to show that Hitler believed that species or kinds of organisms were specially created by some kind of superior being. I do not know of any such evidence. Even Schirrmacher, while interpreting Hitler as a monotheist (wrongly, in my view), still admits that Hitler was a theistic evolutionist, not a creationist.[44]

In fact, on occasion Hitler stated that nature had placed living organisms, including humans, on earth. In the midst of a discussion in *Mein Kampf* about the necessity of humans engaging in a struggle because of the imbalance between reproduction and the available living space (*Lebensraum*), Hitler asserts, "Nature knows no political boundaries. First, she puts living creatures on this globe and watches the free play of forces. She then confers the master's right on her

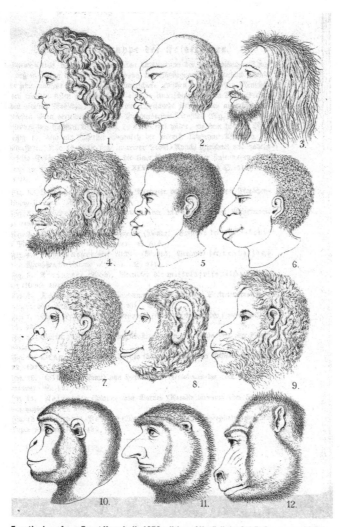

Frontispiece from Ernst Haeckel's 1870 edition of Natürliche Schöpfungsgeschichte, a book on biological evolution, showing that the highest human is further from the lowest human than the lowest human is from the highest primate.
Frontispiece from Haeckel's book. From Ernst Haeckel, Natürliche Schöpfungsgeschichte, 2nd ed. (1870).

favorite child, the strongest in courage and industry."[45] In other words, nature is the source of living organisms—not some Creator God—and lets these organisms fight it out among themselves. Nature is not actively intervening or doing miracles but rather allowing its laws to prevail.

In a speech in December 1940, Hitler mentioned humans owe their existence to nature: "For it is nature which places man on this earth and leaves it to him." To be sure, Hitler also mentioned Providence a few times in this part of his speech, but he equated Providence with nature, as when he stated, "Providence or nature has placed man on this earth."[46] For Hitler, Providence and nature were one and the same. It is hard to see how any self-respecting theist or even deist could make statements about nature placing living organisms and humans on the earth, as Hitler did. His comments are completely antithetical to a creationist perspective. However, they make perfect sense if Hitler embraced pantheism.

Hitler can only be termed a creationist, then, if the term creationism is expanded to mean a belief that some kind of God created something or other at sometime or other. This is not how most people use the term creationist. Indeed, using such an expanded definition of creationism means all theists and deists would be creationists, no matter what position they held about the age of the earth or biological evolution. Ironically, this expanded definition of creationism would even include Charles Darwin, at least at the time he wrote *Origin of Species*, since he confessed therein that the laws of nature that he was proposing were "laws impressed on matter by the Creator."[47] In the second edition of the *Origin of Species*, Darwin even added the word "Creator" to the final sentence: "There is grandeur in this view of life, with its several powers, having been originally breathed by the Creator into a few forms or into one; and that, whilst this planet has gone cycling on according to the fixed law of gravity, from so simple a beginning endless forms most beautiful and most wonderful have been, and are being, evolved."[48] In the end, however, I doubt even this wide definition fits Hitler, because he viewed the universe as eternal and thus uncreated.

TEN

WAS HITLER'S MORALITY BASED ON RELIGION?

ON APRIL 10, 1923, HITLER FULMINATED, "THE liberation [of Germany] requires more than diligence; to become free requires pride, will, spite, hate, hate, and once again, hate."[1] A year earlier, he told a Munich crowd, "Christianity prescribes to us faith, hope and love. Love and hope cannot help us; only faith can, because it begets the will."[2] Hitler preached hate, spurned Christian love, and later ordered the murder of millions of innocent people, including Jews, Gypsies, Slavs, and people with disabilities.

It is unsurprising, then, that some regard him as a Nietzschean-style nihilist who cast aside all moral restraint. The notion that Hitler was a Nietzschean promoting an aristocratic morality and spurning the so-called slave morality of Christianity was a position already popularized in the 1930s and 1940s by Hermann Rauschning, a Nazi leader who jumped ship well before Hitler launched his war of aggression and genocide. Rauschning became a vociferous critic of Hitler from exile. On the basis of his personal contacts with Hitler, he claimed Hitler was an "Antichrist" waging a "deliberately planned battle against the dignified, immortal foundation of human society; the message from Mount Sinai." Rauschning called this "Hitler's Battle Against the Ten Commandments." According to Rauschning, Hitler said he was fighting against "the curse of so-called morals, idolized to protect the weak from the strong in the face of the immortal law of battle, the great law of divine nature. Against the so-called ten commandments [sic], against them we are fighting."[3] Rauschning's work is controversial and must be used cautiously, because he is not always accurate in his description of Hitler's religious and philosophical stance. Nonetheless, it is interesting he intimated that Hitler's religious position was either pantheistic or at least close to pantheism, since he put the words "divine nature" in Hitler's mouth. He also testified that Hitler stated, "For our Volk it is decisive, whether they uphold the Jewish Christian faith with its morality of sympathy, or a strong heroic faith in God in nature, in God in one's own Volk, in God in one's own destiny, in one's own blood."[4]

More recently, the German philosopher Gunnar Heinsohn has taken Rauschning's position even further, arguing that the reason Hitler wanted to annihilate the Jews was to extinguish their moral teaching promoting the sanctity of life. No doubt Heinsohn is correct when he explains that Hitler embraced a social Darwinist position that was the polar opposite of Judaism's ethics, which forbade murder and enjoined loving one's neighbor.[5] However, the problems with Heinsohn's position are legion. First, most Christians believe in the Ten Commandments, too, and the prohibition against murder is just as pronounced in the Christian tradition as in Judaism, so why didn't Hitler kill all Christians in his zeal to eliminate this ethical code?

Second, even disbelievers in Judaism, such as atheists and agnostics, perished in the Nazi Holocaust if they had Jewish ancestry, which contradicts Heinsohn's claim that the Jews were persecuted on the basis of their beliefs. Third, Hitler targeted many non-Jewish groups for annihilation, such as people with disabilities, Gypsies, and Slavs. Heinsohn has things backwards: Hitler did not kill Jews in order to rid the world of the Jewish command, "Thou shalt not murder." Rather, he killed Jews (and others) because he had *already* dispensed with the Judeo-Christian belief in the sanctity of life.

Rauschning and Heinsohn are right, at least, that Hitler rejected the Judeo-Christian position on the sanctity of human life. But it does not necessarily follow that Hitler was a nihilist. In fact, despite the immorality of Hitler's worldview and policies, his atrocities were not based on a nihilistic or atheistic worldview. As we have already seen, Hitler was a pantheist who based his morality on the laws of nature. Many scholars have recently explored the moral dimension of Hitler's worldview and Nazi ideology and policies and concluded that—misguided and pernicious as Hitler's thought and deeds were—they flowed from a consistent ethical position. When Hitler pursued policies that most of us consider evil, he was not, in his mind, abandoning moral considerations. On the contrary, he was convinced that what he was doing was not only morally justified, but morally praiseworthy.

I argued this point extensively in my previous book, *Hitler's Ethic: The Nazi Pursuit of Evolutionary Progress*, where I identify Hitler's ethical position as a racist form of evolutionary ethics. Hitler believed that whatever promoted evolutionary progress was morally good, and anything that hindered progress or led to biological degeneration was reprehensible. In his view, any moral system, code, or commandments must be judged according to how it contributes to the biological advancement (or regression) of humanity. His belief that the Aryan or Nordic race was superior to all other races led him to this corollary: Whatever benefits the Nordic race is moral.[6] Wolf-gang Bialas's recent analysis of Nazi ethics agrees largely with this interpretation of Hitler's thought. Bialas states, "The Nazi worldview clearly had an ethical dimension, rooted in notions of an evolutionary ethic that legitimized the struggle for existence."[7] Indeed, so many historians have argued that social Darwinism was a central tenet of Nazi ideology that this idea is considered commonplace.[8]

Since Hitler based his ethical views on natural laws, especially evolutionary laws, this means that Christian ethics were not sacrosanct. Some elements of Christian morality might, in Hitler's view, comport with the laws of nature and thus be valid. Other Christian command-ments, however, needed to be discarded as relics of the benighted, pre-scientific past. Indeed, many historians have noted the fundamentally anti-Christian thrust of Hitler's ethics. Alan Bullock, an early biogra-pher of Hitler, explains, "In Hitler's eyes Christianity was a religion fit only for slaves; he detested its ethics in particular. Its teaching, he declared, was a rebellion against the natural law of selection by strug-gle and the survival of the fittest."[9] Another biographer, Joachim Fest, notes that Hitler wanted to replace Judeo-Christian morality with the "indubitable will of Nature."[10] Claudia Koonz, in her insightful study titled *The Nazi Conscience*, argues that Nazism preached and practiced a coherent moral ideology that was an "absolutist secular faith" con-trary to Christianity.[11] The Holocaust historian Robert Wistrich also stresses the anti-Christian character of the Nazi moral vision, stating, "For at the heart of Nazism, despite its cunning pretense of 'positive Christianity,' there was a deep-seated rejection of the entire civilization that had been built on Judeo-Christian ethics."[12] Ulf Schmidt, who specializes in the history of medicine and medical ethics under Nazism, likewise interprets Nazi ideology as a departure from Christian moral teaching. He asserts, "Nazism reveals a fundamental break with Judeo-Christian ethics, an attack against a traditional belief system based on altruism and compassion."[13] Bialas insists that Nazi ethics was fundamentally a rejection of bourgeois and Christian values, resting instead on social Darwinist foundations.[14]

Swimming against this current of thought, Steigmann-Gall has emphasized the compatibility of Nazi ethics with Christian ethics.[15] Hitler often preached about concern for the poor, opposition to greed and usury, the need for diligence, the destructive character of sexual licentiousness, and many other themes that would resonate with any good Christian. The Nazis also presented themselves as being pro-marriage, pro-family, pro-children, anti-abortion, and anti-homosexuality, thus promoting moral values that appealed to a conservative Christian constituency.

Clever politician that he was, Hitler at times stressed these points of convergence between his moral views and Christianity. In an interview in December 1922, he averred that Christianity was the "only possible ethical foundation of the German people."[16] A couple of years later, he reiterated this in *Mein Kampf* but also implied it was a temporary expedient, not a fixed principle. He explained that religion performs a useful function by cultivating morality among the masses. Religion, he thought, should be judged according to its utility, which implies that its truthfulness was irrelevant to him. Hitler believed that by promoting morality, religion was performing a useful function, at least at present, so it should not be undermined. This passage in *Mein Kampf* suggests that Hitler did have some affinity with Christian ethics, while simultaneously illustrating his skepticism toward Christianity as a religious system.[17] A couple of weeks after coming to power in 1933, Hitler told his fellow Germans that he wanted "to fill our culture once more with the spirit of Christianity" by purging smut and immorality from literature, the theater, and the press.[18] Hitler knew how to appeal to the conservative Christians whose political support he needed.

Once, Hitler even suggested—contra Rauschning's claim—that the Ten Commandments were valid moral laws. In a monologue where he extolled the Enlightenment and criticized Christian dogmas as unscientific, he nonetheless praised Judeo-Christian ethics, stating, "The Ten Commandments are laws of order that are absolutely praiseworthy."[19] By the time he made this statement in October 1941, German physicians following his orders had murdered over 70,000 Germans with disabilities, and German killing squads operating in Soviet territories had massacred multitudes of Jews and communist officials. Hitler was seriously confused—or more likely incredibly hypocritical—if he thought he was upholding the Ten Commandments. However, as in *Mein Kampf*, it could be that he thought the Ten Commandments were good instructions for the masses to keep them in order but not applicable to those enlightened enough to operate according to the laws of nature. Indeed, Hitler usually appealed to the laws of nature, rather than to any kind of religious revelation, as the source of morality.

Another way that Hitler's morality diverged from Christian norms was that he ignored or reinterpreted what Jesus called the most important commandment: "You shall love the Lord your God with all your heart, with all your soul, and with all your strength." Hitler did love nature, so perhaps in some sense he did love his pantheistic God. However, Jesus was quoting from the Old Testament, where the Lord specified was Yahweh. Hitler certainly did not love that God, whom he identified as the God of the Jews. Further, Hitler continually insisted that God was inscrutable and unknowable, unlike in Christianity, where one could cultivate a personal, loving relationship with Him. One cannot communicate with the impersonal kind of God that Hitler believed in. (I do not give much weight to Hitler's public invocations to God in his speeches, since they seem to have been intended for his audience, not as a sincere effort to communicate with God.) In any case, Hitler never *encouraged* people to love God and cultivate a relationship with Him, so whatever positions he took on other questions of ethics, he missed the central tenet of Christian morality.

The centerpiece of Hitler's ethics was not to love God but to follow the laws of nature, which he identified with God's will. On the sixth anniversary of the Nazi seizure of power, Hitler enjoined his nation to follow the "power of the most holy rights of nature." How can anyone understand these laws of nature that should guide their actions? Hitler dismissed the notion that there is any kind of "special morality" to guide human conduct and the policy of the state. Rather, the state "knows only the laws of life and necessities understood by people through reason and knowledge."[20] Hitler thus rejected any appeal to revelation. Instead, moral knowledge had to come through human reason as it explored and discovered the laws of nature. Hitler appealed to science, not mysticism or divine revelation, as the source of moral instruction.

What Hitler thought he discovered through reason was that nature was ruled by the struggle for existence, and humans could not escape this natural law. He believed that the struggle for existence had produced everything, including humanity, and would continue to lead to biological progress. Gilmer Blackburn expresses a view widely shared by historians when he explains the primacy of struggle in Hitler's worldview: "If the Nazi dictator entertained convictions that could be termed 'religious,' his creed began and ended with the struggle for existence."[21] In Hitler's view, then, morality consisted of submitting to the universal law of the struggle for existence by fighting one's enemies and triumphing—or else perishing—in the contest. Only through this struggle could humanity thrive and progress. Trying to evade the struggle would only lead to decline and biological degeneration.

Hitler's publicist Otto Dietrich explained Hitler upheld a "philosophy of nature" that he considered "the final truth about life. He took such principles as the struggle for existence, the survival of the fittest and strongest, for the law of nature and considered them a 'higher imperative' which should also rule in the community life of

Cover of Nazi journal proclaims, "Life Requires Struggle," reflecting Hitler's stress on the importance of the Darwinian struggle for existence.
Nazi journal, "Leben erfordert Kampf"; From Der Schulungsbrief (1942).

men. It followed for him that might was right, that his own violent methods were therefore absolutely in keeping with the laws of nature." Dietrich explained how this evolutionary ethic fit in with Hitler's religious views, too. According to Dietrich,

> [Hitler's] evolutionary views on natural selection and survival of the fittest coincided with the ideas of Darwin and Haeckel. Nevertheless, Hitler was no atheist. He professed

a highly general, monotheistic faith. He believed in guidance from above and in the existence of a Supreme Being whose wisdom and will had created laws for the preservation and evolution of the human race. He believed that the highest aim of mankind was to survive for the achievement of progress and perfection.... He was acting, he believed, on the command of this Supreme Being.[22]

Fighting in the struggle for existence was thus an ethical imperative with divine sanction.

In *Mein Kampf,* Hitler explained why struggle was necessary and even beneficial for humans. If races at different levels mate, he claimed, the offspring will be inferior to the higher parent, so "it will later succumb in the struggle against the higher level. Such mating is contrary to the will of Nature for a higher breeding of all life." Rather than mate with inferior specimens, the "stronger must dominate and not blend with the weaker, thus sacrificing his own greatness. Only the born weakling can view this as cruel, but he after all is only a weak and limited man; for if this law did not prevail, any conceivable higher development (*Entwicklung*) of organic living beings would be unthinkable." In this passage Hitler clearly personified nature, calling the struggle for existence the "will of Nature," but he also referred to it as "the will of the eternal creator." Hitler stated that humans cannot overcome nature, but only discover its laws and comply with them. Violating the natural order by trying to escape the struggle for existence is to commit a "sin," a term Hitler explicitly used in this passage.[23]

In his 1937 speech to the Nuremberg Party Congress, Hitler expounded on this theme. He congratulated his regime for operating in greater harmony with the "eternal organic laws of nature" than any previous German government. He then discussed the twin causes of human evolution, which were the instincts of preservation and reproduction. As a gift of Providence, these drives, Hitler said, "determine the struggle for life and thus the way of life of humans." He then scoffed at those who thought they could contravene the laws of nature and extinguish the instinct for preservation: "For only then [if the self-preservation instinct could be eliminated] could one try to implement the statutes of a League of Nations or the Geneva Convention, in the place of the law of the all-powerful nature (*Allgewalt Natur*) that has been valid since the beginning of all life on this earth." He then asserted that the "unbreakable laws of nature" will continue to hold sway over the struggle for existence between humans in the future.[24] Hitler's use of the term "all-powerful nature" (*Allgewalt Natur*) implies pantheism, since it ascribes to nature a characteristic—omnipotence—exclusive to deity. Further, he clearly invoked natural laws, especially the struggle for existence, as the arbiter of morality.

During the war, Hitler continued to justify his policies by appealing to the laws of nature emanating from the Almighty, or Providence. In January 1943, he explained the religious and moral basis for his aggressive policies: "The Almighty will be a just judge. It is our task to fulfill our duty in such a manner that we prove ourselves to Him as the Creator of the world, in accordance with His law on the struggle for existence."[25] Later in the war, he asserted that the Almighty ordained the law of struggle between peoples. "Whether man agrees to or rejects this harsh law makes absolutely no difference," he said. "Man cannot change it; whoever tries to withdraw from this struggle for life does not erase the law but only the basis of his own existence."[26]

Hitler understood that many people recoiled from this pitiless vision of the world and the harsh morality he deduced from it. Thus he hammered on this theme quite often in his speeches and writings to convince his contemporaries that what appeared harsh and immoral was actually a beneficial process. In a monologue in December 1941, he told his entourage, "One may find it dreadful, how in nature one devours the other." He then set forth examples from the animal world to illustrate his point that killing is a normal, natural process, and he invoked divine sanction for this cruelty in nature: "If I want to believe in a divine command, it can only be: to preserve the species! One should also not value the individual life so highly at all. If its continuance were necessary, it would not perish."[27] Hitler often devalued the lives of individuals, who were only significant, in his estimation, for their contribution to the advancement of the German people and humanity. One of the Nazis' weekly proverbs quoted Hitler saying, "The individual must and will as always perish; only the Volk must remain." Hitler believed that this knowledge about the insignificance of the individual should foster humility. He told Cardinal Michael von Faulhaber in a conversation in November 1936, "The individual is nothing. Cardinal Faulhaber will die, Alfred Rosenberg will die, Adolf Hitler will die. Thus one should be inwardly humble before God."[28] I know it is almost impossible to fathom, but Hitler apparently thought of himself as humble.

Hitler deduced two key principles from the need to wage the struggle for existence: the right to destroy those who are weaker and the right to take living space, i.e., land, from them. These themes reverberate through many of Hitler's speeches and writings, and found their ultimate fulfillment in his genocidal policies during World War II. In *Mein Kampf*, Hitler set forth the fundaments of his worldview, which

> finds the importance of mankind in its basic racial elements. In the state it sees on principle only a means to an end and construes its end as the preservation of the racial existence of man. Thus, it by no means believes in an equality of the races, but along with their difference it recognizes their higher or lesser value and feels itself obligated, through this

knowledge, to promote the victory of the better and stronger, and demand the subordination of the inferior and weaker in accordance with the eternal will that dominates this universe. Thus, in principle, it serves the basic aristocratic idea of Nature and believes in the validity of this law down to the last individual.[29]

In Hitler's view, the victory of the stronger over the weaker is part of God's plan. Even though he only mentioned the "subordination" of the weak in this passage, elsewhere he made clear that this really meant death to the weak. In another passage in *Mein Kampf* which addresses the need to promote population expansion, he articulated the social Darwinist perspective that this process would result in the weak perishing in the competition for limited resources. He explained,

For as soon as procreation as such is limited and the number of births diminished, the natural struggle for existence which leaves only the strongest and healthiest alive is obviously replaced by the obvious desire to 'save' even the weakest and most sickly at any price, and this plants the seed of a future generation which must grow more and more deplorable the longer this mockery of Nature and her will continues.

He then spelled out the consequences of his pro-natalist policy more clearly: "A stronger race will drive out the weak, for the vital urge in its ultimate form will, time and again, burst all the absurd fetters of the so-called humanity of individuals, in order to replace it by the humanity of Nature which destroys the weak to give his place to the strong."[30] Hitler spurned humane ideals and human rights in favor of a conflict model of society, in which the only right is whatever the stronger can impose on the weaker.

In a March 1928 speech on "The Struggle of the Day or Struggle for Destiny," Hitler set forth in great detail his philosophy of struggle and its implications for morality. Therein, as in his *Second Book*, written at about the same time, he claimed that struggle derived from the biological drives of hunger and love. In other contexts, Hitler lumped these two together as the self-preservation instinct. The ensuing struggle not only pits humans against animals, but also entails combat between different human races. In the struggle for existence in nature, many organisms are exterminated, so, Hitler queried, why should we suppose that this would be different for human races, some of which are not far separated from apes? Hitler warned against moralizing about this struggle or the destruction of the inferior creatures of the earth (such as other human races), stating, "On this earth the right of the stronger holds sway, the right of struggle and the right of victory; if you think that rights prevail, then you are deceiving yourself." The struggle is good in itself, Hitler claimed, because it prevents degeneration, which would otherwise occur.[31]

In a 1937 speech to construction workers, Hitler expounded on the "eternal law of life," which is "the law of selection, and the stronger and healthier has received the right to life from nature. And that is rightly so. Nature does not recognize the weakling, the coward, or the beggar," but only those strong enough to prevail in the struggle, which can be seen everywhere in the organic world. He invited them to gaze at the woods or the meadows or to investigate human history. Everywhere they would find confirmation of the principle, "Woe to him who is weak!" Hitler hoped to win these workers' support for strengthening Germany, particularly for his remilitarization program. Ultimately he was preparing the German people—though he did not yet dare say it openly—for expansionist warfare.[32]

During World War II, Hitler continually justified his genocidal policies by appealing to the laws of nature, especially in "secret speeches" given to military cadets and officers. (Some of these "secret speeches" had thousands in attendance; in this respect, they were hardly secret. However, they are called "secret speeches" because they were not open to the general public and not published at the time, as many of Hitler's speeches were.) In May 1944, Hitler lectured his military leadership about the reasons they needed to be relentlessly harsh in the war. Hitler insisted that nature knows nothing of tolerance, but rather eliminates the weak:

> There is no tolerance in nature. Nature is, if I take 'tolerant' as a human concept, the most intolerant thing that has ever existed. It destroys everything that is not capable of living, that will not or cannot defend itself; it eliminates them, and we are only a speck of dust in this nature; a human is nothing other than a small bacteria or small bacillus on one such planet. If he removes himself from these laws, he does not alter the laws, but rather he ends his existence.

Hitler thus reduced the significance of human life to that of dust or microorganisms, while exalting nature, whose laws define morality. Later in this speech, Hitler broached the topic of his harsh anti-Jewish policies, and though he did not specifically mention the mass extermination of the Jews, he certainly implied it. He insisted that his policy of "driving out" the Jews was "just as nature does it, not brutal, but rational, in order to preserve the better ones [i.e., the Germans]." He then answered those who might wonder if this could have been accomplished in a less cruel fashion: "We stand in a struggle for life and death." Anything that helped the Aryans preserve their race in this struggle was morally right, Hitler informed them.[33] Thus, cruelty, oppression, murder, and even genocide were morally justified, in his view, if they advanced the cause of the German people.

During his Nuremberg Party Congress address in 1929, Hitler indicated one of the corollaries to his view that the strong should prevail over the weak: infanticide for those deemed inferior. He hoped to take the "natural process of selection" into his own hands if he came to power by "acting deliberately according to racial laws." One measure he mentioned theoretically as a way to improve the Aryan or Nordic race was infanticide. Remarkably, he speculated that if 700–800,000 of the weakest children out of one million born were eliminated, this would result in a strengthening of the German people. He then praised Sparta for having practiced infanticide, and he criticized modern European societies for setting up institutions to care for the weak and sickly. Hitler's shocking suggestion that killing the weakest 70 to 80 percent of all children at birth might be beneficial should not be seen as a serious policy proposal. However, it does shed light on Hitler's morality, which grants rights only to the stronger, while consigning the weaker to the trash bin (or crematorium).[34] Further, it presaged Hitler's support for killing the disabled (including infants), which he began implementing under the cover of war in 1939–40.

Otto Wagener remembered Hitler making similar harsh comments about the role of natural selection among humans. According to Wagener, Hitler stated, "Weaklings, runts, sick individuals are cast out of their communities by the healthy ones; some of them are even killed, disposed of. That is the will of nature. What is healthy abhors that which is sick, the productive abhors the life of the drone, purposeful striving abhors indifferent depravity." Hitler then remonstrated against modern institutions that allegedly coddled the infirm, while healthy Germans had to struggle to make ends meet. He again praised the Spartans for their infanticide. Wagener recalled Hitler saying later, "The elimination of worthless life is therefore dictated by nature, a consequence of the purpose of human existence, as well as the existence of all life." Killing the disabled as "lives unworthy of life" was simply a part of the natural, divinely ordained struggle. As Hitler asserted, "For God and nature cannot want a mother to give birth to sickly, deformed human beings, useless for life!" Here again we see the conflation of God and nature, with this pantheistic deity determining the proper course of action.[35] By killing approximately 200,000 disabled Germans during World War II, Hitler thought he was pleasing God.

When Hitler spoke about the triumph of the stronger in the struggle for existence, he was of course rooting for the home team: the German people, whom he believed to be racially superior, because they had substantial portions of so-called Aryan or Nordic racial elements in their blood. Though at times Hitler called the German Volk a creation of God and indeed "the highest image of the Lord," on many other occasions he actually deified the German Volk. In his

Nazi school poster used to teach about compulsory sterilization: "Eradication of the Sick and Weak in Nature/ Whatever does not meet the demands of existence perishes. – Walter Gross" (Head of Nazi Office of Racial Policy).

Nazi School Poster: "Ausmerzung." From Alfred Vogel, Erblehre und Rassenkunde in bildlicher Darstellung (1938).

May Day speech in 1923, he told his audience that National Socialists needed to learn to love their Fatherland and Volk with a fanatical love that "allows no other idols beside it."[36] Seeing divinity in the German Volk is consistent with a pantheistic view, where God pervades everything.

Hitler's devotion to the German Volk was in some ways even more pronounced than his devotion to the inscrutable God, because the German Volk was closer at hand. Hitler never quite figured out how to worship his unknowable Providence, but he did find ways to serve the German people (or, at least, he thought he was serving them). He often claimed that the German Volk was supreme on this earth and the object of his complete faith and commitment. In October 1935, he denied that he was subject to anyone except his own conscience. Then he continued, "And this conscience has but one single commander (*Befehlsgeber*): our Volk!"[37] Two days earlier, he made a similar statement: "The Volk alone is our Lord (*Herr*), and we serve this Volk according to our best knowledge and conscience."[38] Both these statements would be blasphemous for anyone believing in a monotheistic god that transcends the German Volk. If Hitler had been a monotheist, he should have confessed God as the commander of his conscience, not the Volk. If he were a Christian, he should have confessed Jesus as his Lord.

This does not mean that Hitler saw any contradiction between serving his (pantheistic) God and serving the German Volk. Before a plebiscite in March 1936, Hitler said he would accept the election results as "the voice of the Volk, which is the voice of God."[39] In February 1937, he told a Munich crowd of the "Old Fighters," i.e., the early Nazi Party members, "I have only one great faith: that is faith in my Volk." Again, this seems blasphemous from a monotheistic perspective, because it suggests that his faith in the German Volk was even more important than his faith in God. Later in that speech, however, he expressed faith in both the Volk *and* God. He also alluded to the Nazi struggle with the Confessing Church by remarking that the only real "Confessing Church" is "the National Socialist movement, which confesses: We believe in our Germany and believe in our Volk and believe in our Lord God," who would not abandon them if they remained loyal to the Volk.[40]

Ultimately, Hitler did not think the Volk replaced God, even if he did sometimes call the Volk the only object of his faith, his only Lord, and his only commander. There was still some sense in which he viewed the German Volk as the creation or emanation of God. In a February 1926 speech, he harshly castigated those who despised the German Fatherland. He opposed this cowardice and was determined to "set up the Fatherland as the only God there is, besides the heavenly God."[41] Here and elsewhere, Hitler exalted the Volk to the highest position on earth, while still maintaining belief in some kind of God above.

For Hitler, the preservation and advancement of the Volk was the highest goal in life, and ethical and moral principles were determined by their ability to advance the German Volk. He stated this position many times in many ways. For instance, in *Mein Kampf*, Hitler asserted that National Socialists only have one doctrine: the Volk and Fatherland. Looking out for the interests of the Volk by fighting for its freedom and nourishment is a *"mission allotted it by the creator of the universe."*[42] Just a few days after he came to power in February 1933, he preached to his fellow Germans that the Volk was the highest value they could pursue. They were engaged in a struggle in which the goal was "the preservation of this Volk and this soil, the preservation of this Volk for the future, in the realization that this alone can constitute our reason for being. It is not for ideas that we live, not for theories or fantastic party programs; no, we live and fight for the German Volk, for the preservation of its existence, that it may undertake its own struggle for existence."[43] For Hitler, the good of the Volk was the final arbiter of all policies.

Every human institution had to bow down and pay homage to the Volk—including all religions. At the Nuremberg Party Congress of 1935, Hitler elevated service to the German Volk as the highest purpose of life. All institutions—and he specifically mentioned religions—must serve this higher purpose.[44] The value of a religion had nothing to do with its truth or falsity, but only with its ability to help or hinder the advancement of the German Volk. This included Christianity, as Hitler made clear in a November 1937 address to an elite Nazi school when he explained that he was establishing the state on a new foundation. It was not founded on Christianity, he said, nor on the supremacy of the state, but rather on the primacy of the People's Community (*Volksgemeinschaft*). Anything that stood in opposition to the German Volk—whether religious divisions or political parties—would be ruthlessly suppressed.[45]

It did not matter one whit to Hitler how cruel, oppressive, or brutal his policies were. What mattered was solely whether or not they succeeded in elevating the German Volk. In August 1923, Hitler shouted that the German people needed to exert its will to become free, and it did not matter what instruments they used to attain this goal. He thundered, "May this weapon be humane or not! If it gains freedom for us, it is right before our conscience and before our Lord God!"[46] Hitler served a God and cultivated a conscience that did not care if some people were exterminated in the global struggle for existence. His God only cared about the strongest, the ablest, and the most intelligent—and Hitler was convinced that the German people embodied these traits better than any other race.

How did Hitler's vision of the supremacy of the German Volk and his utter disregard for other peoples fit into the Christian command to love your neighbor as yourself, which Jesus called the second most important commandment? Interestingly, Hitler seemed to think that the German people were inherently unselfish—it was part of their nature to care for their fellow Germans. Once he came to power, he inaugurated an annual Winter Relief Campaign to help the poor and disadvantaged. He even thought the noble Aryans had a biological, hereditary predisposition to work hard and sacrifice for the sake of the community, as he explained in an August 1920 speech. He stated, "Aryanness means a moral conception of labor and through it what we talk about so often today: socialism, a sense of community, common welfare before self-interest." Altruism was a key part of Hitler's morality. Ominously, however, this speech was entitled "Why Are We Anti-Semites?," and he made clear that Jews were not part of the moral community. Their biological character was allegedly egotistical, selfish, and greedy. Hitler clearly did not believe in loving one's Jewish neighbors.[47]

Indeed, according to Dietrich Eckart, Hitler rejected the usual understanding of loving one's neighbor because he thought the Jews had tricked Luther into translating the Hebrew word in the commandment as "neighbor." (Incidentally, in many passages of this supposed dialogue, both Hitler and Eckart come across as dilettantish in biblical matters, making goofy mistakes about geography, biblical language, etc.) Rather, Hitler said, the word translated as "neighbor" should instead be rendered as "racial comrade" (*Volksgenosse*).[48] While Eckart's dialogue with Hitler is not an entirely reliable source for Hitler's position, it does seem to reflect Hitler's stance in this case: Love your neighbors, but only if they are racial comrades. Ironically, when Jesus was challenged to define "neighbor," he told the parable of the Good Samaritan, which takes an approach completely opposite to Hitler's, since the parable encourages people to love even those who are considered ethnic or racial enemies.

Hitler's insistence that Germans should hate or harm their racial enemies, rather than love them, demonstrates once again his opposition to Christian morality. He overtly rejected Jesus' command to love your enemy and turn the other cheek. In his "Why Are We Anti-Semites?" speech, he opposed the notion that humans should treat everyone else with respect. If someone from another race tries to undermine the German race, Hitler said, he could not remain indifferent. Rather, "In that case I say that I belong to those who, when they receive a slap to the left cheek, give back two or three [blows]."[49] When Hans Frank asked Hitler what he read at the Western Front during World War I, Hitler replied that at first he read the Gospels. Later, he gladly set them aside, he said, in part because "the story about turning the other cheek, when one receives a blow, is not a good prescription for the Front."[50] In December 1941, Goebbels recorded in his diary that Hitler rejected Christianity because of its Sermon on the Mount morality. Christianity, Hitler claimed, "is Jewish in its entire essence. A religion that proceeds from the principle that one should love his enemies, may not kill, and must offer the left cheek when struck on the right one, is not suitable for a manly doctrine of defending one's Fatherland. Christianity is in fact a doctrine of decay. For a modern person it deserves only intellectual disdain."[51] Hitler's contempt for Christian morality, including some of the Ten Commandments (such as the prohibition on killing), was palpable. Certainly many versions of Christianity had interpreted loving one's enemies and turning the other cheek in such a way that did not apply to many areas of life, such as warfare. However, no one committed to Christian morality would directly criticize a commandment of Jesus—or one of the Ten Commandments—as Hitler did.

Not only did Hitler not consider other races part of the same moral community with the German Volk, but he also construed them as competitors in the racial struggle for existence. Thus he held that destroying people of other races is not only morally permissible, but morally good and right. In his speech to the Nuremberg Party Congress in 1933, Hitler instructed his comrades about the "eternal laws of life," which they needed to comprehend and comply with if they were to emerge victorious in the struggle between races. One of the most important of these laws, he averred, was that races are radically unequal. He parroted a view common to scientific racists of his time when he proclaimed, "The distance between the lowest, so-called human and our highest race is greater than that between the lowest human and the highest ape." Hitler further insisted that the biological inequality of the human races implies those races have different value. Races that are more "highly evolved" (*höher entwickelte*) are "qualitatively higher-standing races," while some are "qualitatively worse." According to Hitler, the higher races had historically suppressed the lower ones, according to the "right of the stronger," a right that was rational and completely in tune with nature.[52]

In 1933, Hitler could not publicly spell out what suppressing other races meant, because he was still trying hard to deceive the world into thinking he was a man of peace so he could remilitarize without outside interference. However, after the genocidal war on the Eastern Front was in full swing, Hitler divulged his racial philosophy in all its brutality to his entourage. In a monologue in October 1941, Hitler expounded his philosophy of conquest and racial annihilation. He planned to sift through the people in the conquered territories of the East to find racially desirable elements that could be preserved. However, Russians living in the cities "must completely die off. We need not have any pangs of conscience about this," because "we do not have any responsibility toward these people." The Germans' task, Hitler asserted, was to settle these territories with Germans and treat the natives as American Indians had been treated.[53]

Hitler denied, however, that he had any hatred for these people. Rather, he was acting with cool deliberation. He remarked, "I am approaching this matter ice-cold. I feel that I am only the executor of a historical will [i.e., a will guiding historical development]." When someone eats Canadian wheat, that person does not think about the Indians, Hitler reminded his colleagues. Rights and laws were "an invention of humans!" "Nature does not recognize surveying and notaries," Hitler asserted. "Heaven only recognizes power." He then sarcastically dismissed the "principle that all humans should love one another," because its proponents, such as Christian missionaries, contradict it by teaching that those who do not accept their message will burn in hell. Thus, instead of trying to avoid their hypocrisy by actually keeping the commandment to love one another, Hitler threw the commandment completely overboard, as least as it applied to racial relations.[54]

Hitler considered expansionist warfare a part of the God-ordained racial struggle. This was a constant theme in *Mein Kampf* and in many of his speeches, especially during World War II. It was also the primary message of his *Second Book*, where he claimed that the earth is not given once and for all to anyone, but rather is on loan from Providence to those courageous enough to take possession of it and strong enough to hold onto it. Once again, Hitler thought the stronger race had God on its side, even as it crushed the weaker. "Therefore," he asserted, "every healthy native people sees nothing sinful in the acquisition of land, but rather something natural." The "modern pacifist," he continued, "who repudiates this most holy right" lives off past injustices. Thus, Hitler brushed aside two of the Ten Commandments that forbade coveting land and stealing, insisting instead that taking land from other people through warfare is a "most holy right" that enjoys Providence's blessing.[55]

In a December 1940 speech, Hitler enunciated similar social Darwinist themes that virtually quoted from his *Second Book* and reiterated major points he made in *Mein Kampf*. In this speech to officer cadets, Hitler explained at length the philosophy behind his expansionist warfare. War is part of a struggle that is unavoidable, according to Hitler, because "Providence or nature has placed man on this earth. Man begins to multiply on this earth. This does not take place in a vacuum: his struggle begins as he encounters the other beings who populated this earth before him and who live there besides him."

Struggle ensues among humans because there is limited living space (*Lebensraum*).[56]

Hitler argued that there were only two possibilities to resolve the tension between prolific reproduction and the limited living space: decreasing reproduction or increasing the living space. If people restrict their fertility, Hitler claimed, "the biological consequences are grave: this undermines the process of natural selection, the breeding of the fittest." Hitler proposed following a different path: "It is the natural way and the one willed by Providence: namely that man should adjust the *Lebensraum* to his numbers. In other words, that he should partake in the struggle for this earth. For it is nature which places man on this earth and leaves it to him. Truly, this earth is a trophy cup for the industrious man. And this rightly so, in the service of natural selection."[57] Again Hitler equated nature and Providence, and claimed that nature was the source of human existence.

The moral justification for expansionist warfare that Hitler offered these young officer cadets was that it conformed to natural law, specifically the struggle for existence and natural selection. Hitler repeated this theme often in speeches he delivered to military cadets and officers during the war.[58] In a February 1942 address, he expostulated that man cannot escape from the laws of nature, especially the "law that gives the right to life to the stronger and takes the life of the weaker." The only way to withdraw from the struggle that nature and Providence impose upon man, Hitler explained, is to die. He set forth the harsh but inescapable rule that "when the individual lives, he hinders the life of another, and if he dies, he makes the path free for the life of a new individual." Not only did Hitler call this principle the "will of Providence," but he claimed that no better principle was imaginable than "the principle of the eternal selection of the better over the weaker." People ignore these wise but harsh laws at their peril, according to Hitler, because those not strong enough to prevail in the struggle have forfeited their right to exist.[59]

In a monologue in October 1941, Hitler contrasted his philosophy of expansionist warfare with Christianity. He presented war as essentially a struggle over land and resources, and, as he did so often in other venues, justified killing in warfare by appealing to the pitiless struggle in nature. War, he stated, "corresponds to the principle in nature, ever to bring about selection through struggle: The law of existence demands uninterrupted killing, so that the better will live. Christianity is rebellion against this fundamental principle, a protest against the creation; followed consistently, it would lead to the breeding of the inferior."[60] Even though he did not proclaim this point publicly, he recognized that his philosophy of expansionist warfare with victory to the stronger and death to the weaker was not consistent with the Christian emphasis on helping the weak. In Hitler's view, Christian morality was fundamentally flawed because it did not conform to the ruthless, but ultimately beneficial, laws of nature. Though he believed that Providence and nature were smiling on his war of annihilation, he had no illusion that his views on ethics were consistent with Christian morality.

Hitler's belief that nature imposed a moral imperative to expand the population had profound implications for his views on sexual morality. His pro-natalist sexual morality had some points of contact with traditional Christian views, since the Catholic Church opposed contraception, abortion, prostitution, and homosexuality. However, Hitler's opposition was based on entirely different premises. Hitler only opposed them to the extent that they interfered with increasing the number of healthy Nordic babies, which was the ultimate goal of his sexual morality. In the case of contraception and abortion, Hitler favored contraception and abortion for those deemed biologically inferior. In July 1933, Hitler passed a decree that resulted in the compulsory sterilization of about 350–400,000 Germans with disabilities. While prohibiting abortion for healthy

Germans, abortions for Germans with disabilities were required, and Jews and other racial "undesirables" were allowed to practice abortion.

One of the most important commandments in Hitler's sexual morality was *thou shalt not mix your blood with other races*. While the Catholic Church forbade intermarriage between Catholics and non-Catholics, Hitler forbade intermarriage and sexual relations between Germans and Jews, regardless of their religious convictions. For Hitler, it was a sin—punishable by law after the Nuremberg Laws were promulgated in 1935—for a Catholic of Aryan descent to marry a Catholic with Jewish grandparents. Hitler also forbade intermarriage of Germans with Slavs but encouraged German intermarriage with the Norwegians or Dutch, because they were deemed fellow Nordic peoples.

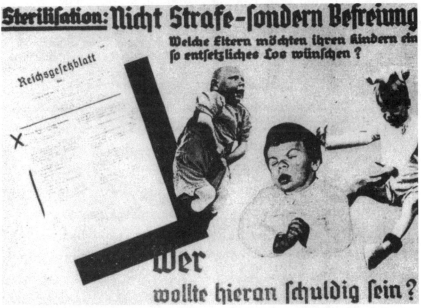

Nazi poster supporting the compulsory sterilization program: "Sterilization: Not Punishment—but rather Liberation."
Nazi poster on sterilization program. From Volk und Rasse (1936).

Hitler posed as a supporter of traditional marriage and the family in his public speeches, especially before coming to power. This was not entirely hypocritical because he thought that in general marriage and family life were conducive to producing children. However, in private Hitler overtly criticized Christian morality for its sexual restrictions that sometimes interfered with population expansion. In December 1940, he told his colleagues that he was worried about the "sexual problem," by which he meant primarily prostitution and sexually transmitted diseases. However, while recommending early marriage—a point that Christians could approve—he explicitly rejected Christian sexual morality as too restrictive. Goebbels noted that Hitler was not prudish but viewed sexual morality from an entirely different perspective than Christians did. Hitler thought, "We must also view this question [sexual morality] from the standpoint of its utility for the Volk. That is our morality." The main point, according to Hitler, was to get as many children as possible for the Volk.[61]

Because he favored marriage and procreation, Hitler was incensed that the Catholic Church taught celibacy for priests and nuns. In his view, this robbed the German people of its potential and weakened it in its struggle with other races. In October 1941, Hitler lamented that Catholicism encouraged some women to forgo marriage. However, even more important than marriage, Hitler intoned, was that women bear children: "Nature doesn't care at all, whether beforehand a declaration is made in the presence of witnesses! Nature wants the woman to have a child." This demonstrates once again that, for Hitler, nature dictated morality. In this case, the morality it dictated was that extramarital sexual relations were perfectly fine, as long as they resulted in more healthy German babies.[62]

In monologues during the war, Hitler discussed ideas about how to increase the Nordic population. One of his proposals was to send "racially highly valuable" units of men into some areas with poor racial characteristics to "freshen up" the blood of the population. Hitler admitted that this program of extramarital procreation would be controversial, but he lashed out at those who would restrict sexual relations to marriage, accusing them of hypocrisy.[63] In response to the increasing casualties on the Eastern Front, Hitler also contemplated introducing polygamy after the war to offset the imbalance between men and women. Once again, Hitler exalted nature and its will above the sanctity of marriage.[64]

In a final analysis, Hitler's morality was based on what he perceived to be the will of nature, not on the Ten Commandments or any other religious revelation. He viewed some elements of Christian morality as beneficial but rejected the universal thrust of Christian ethics, insisting instead that the command to love and help others is only applicable within one's racial community. He completely rejected other parts of Christian morality, such as caring for the sick and

A Nazi periodical lauds "The German Mother" with a saying by Hitler: "Every child that she brings into the world is a battle that she wins for the existence or non-existence of her Volk."
"The German Mother." From Neues Volk, 1936.

disabled, because he thought nature favored the strong at the expense of the weak. Thus, he considered killing the weak, sick, and "inferior" to be in harmony with nature and its laws. By murdering people with disabilities and exterminating Jews and Gypsies, he thought he was fulfilling the divine commands of nature, which was his God.

CONCLUSION

IN MID-JANUARY OF 1940, HITLER WAS DISCUSSING with his colleagues a rather frequent topic of his conversations and monologues: the church. After he sarcastically imitated Niemöller, the Confessing Church leader who was incarcerated in a concentration camp, someone in his entourage indicated to him that posterity might not be able to figure out what Hitler's own religious views were, because he never openly stated his beliefs.[1] The person who brought this to Hitler's attention had clearly noticed the discrepancy between his private expressions of intense antipathy to Christianity and his public religious image. Since many in Hitler's entourage were also intensely anti-Christian, perhaps they were trying to provoke him to state his personal religious views publicly. In any case, this observation about the inscrutability of Hitler's religious views still has merit today—even though we have far more information about Hitler available to us than most of his contemporaries had.

That, of course, does not mean everyone draws the same conclusion. As we have seen, some people today interpret Hitler as an atheist, while others insist he was a Christian. In fact, he has been described as an adherent of just about every major religious position in twentieth-century European society (excepting Judaism, of course), which included agnosticism, pantheism, panentheism, occultism, deism, and non-Christian theism.

Interestingly, when Hitler was confronted in January 1940 with the observation that people might not know where he stood religiously, he suggested that, on the contrary, it should not be difficult for people to figure it out. After all, he asserted, he had never allowed any clergy to participate in his party meetings or even in funerals for party comrades. He continued, "The Christian-Jewish pestilence is surely approaching its end now. It is simply dreadful, that a religion has even been possible, that literally eats its God in Holy Communion."[2] Hitler clearly thought that anyone should be able to figure out that he was not a Christian. Nonetheless, Rosenberg reported in his diary later that year that Hitler had determined that he should divulge his negative views about Christianity in his last testament "so that no doubt about his position can surface. As head of state he naturally held back—but nevertheless after the war clear consequences will follow."[3] Many times, Hitler told his colleagues that he would reckon with Christianity after the successful conclusion of the war.

Interestingly, even in these conversations, Hitler only indicated what he did *not* believe. He did not explain at that time what he *did* believe about God, the after-life, or other religious issues. Indeed, it is much easier to figure out what Hitler did not believe than to figure out the actual content of his religious convictions and feelings. Probably, this is partly because Hitler considered God ineffable. Hitler's

God was not one who revealed himself clearly to humanity, but a mysterious being who superseded human knowledge.

So, what did Hitler *not* believe? He continually rejected Christianity, calling it a Jewish plot to undermine the heroic ideals of the (Aryan-dominated) Roman Empire. He did not accept the deity of Jesus, the resurrection of Jesus, or indeed any of the miracles of Jesus. There is no evidence that he believed in a triune God. Though he esteemed Jesus as an Aryan fighter against Jewish materialism who was martyred for his anti-Jewish stance, he did not ascribe to Jesus's death any significance in human salvation. Indeed, he did not believe in salvation at all in the Christian sense of the term, because he denied a personal afterlife. Despite his public invocations to God, Hitler also did not believe in the efficacy of prayer. His God responded to people and judged them according to their works, not their words. Although he spurned Christianity, this did not lead him to disbelieve in every form of deity, however. He overtly rejected atheism, associating it with "Jewish-Bolshevism." Further, he explicitly condemned mysticism, occultism, and neo-paganism. Thus, it is evident Hitler was neither a Christian, atheist, occultist, nor neo-paganist.

While this narrows the range of religious options slightly, it still leaves us with agnosticism, pantheism, panentheism, deism, and non-Christian theism. A reasonable case could be made for more than one of these options. In order solve this puzzle, however, one must not only examine the full panoply of Hitler's religious statements but also decipher how to weigh those statements. Are his private statements more revealing of his true convictions than his public speeches? Probably, but even his private statements must be used cautiously. Are his books a better indication of his personal beliefs than his speeches? This is likely, because he seemed to be more systematic in explaining his worldview in *Mein Kampf* and in his *Second Book*. However, they also served propaganda purposes and must be used carefully as well. There also remains the question of whether Hitler even had a coherent metaphysic; if not, perhaps there is no single answer to what Hitler's religion was.

One problem is that Hitler often portrayed God as an impersonal force, yet sometimes he implied God did take a personal interest in humanity, or at least in the German people's destiny. Though he usually insisted that God does not intervene in the natural cause-and-effect relationships in the universe, at times he seemed to ascribe a role to Providence in history. When he survived assassination attempts, for instance, he took it as a sign from Providence that he was specially chosen to fulfill a divine mission. Until the very end of World War II, he thought his God would not fail to bring victory to the German people.

One of the reasons that I do not think Hitler was a theist is because he did not seem to think God could contravene the laws of nature. Hitler often called the laws of nature eternal and inviolable, thus embracing determinism. He interpreted history as a course of events determined by the racial composition of people, not by their religion or other cultural factors. The way to understand humanity and history, according to Hitler, was to study the laws of nature. He considered science, not religious revelation, the most reliable path to knowledge. What Hitler thought science revealed was that races are unequal and locked in an ineluctable struggle for existence, which would determine the future destiny of humanity.

Whether Hitler construed the laws of nature as the creation of a deistic or theistic God, or the emanation of a pantheistic God, he clearly grounded his morality on the laws of nature, which he consistently portrayed as the will of God. Since nature brought about biological improvement through struggle, Hitler defined moral goodness as whatever contributed to biological progress.[4] Evil or sin, in Hitler's opinion, was anything that produced biological degeneration. Thus, Hitler thought he was operating in complete harmony with God's will by sterilizing people with disabilities and forbidding the intermarriage of Germans and Jews. Killing the weak to make way for the strong was part of the divine plan revealed in nature, in Hitler's view. Thus, even murdering disabled Germans, launching expansionist wars to wrest territory from allegedly inferior races, and murdering millions of Jews, Sinti, Roma, Slavs, and others defined as subhumans, was not only morally permissible but also obedience to the voice of God. After all, that was how nature operated, producing superabundantly and then destroying most of the progeny in the Darwinian struggle for existence. Hitler often reminded his fellow Germans that even if this seemed ruthless, it was actually wise. In any case, he warned that they could not moralize about it, because humans were completely subject to the laws of nature.

In the end, while recognizing that Hitler's position was somewhat muddled, it seems evident his religion was closest to pantheism. He often deified nature, calling it eternal and all-powerful at various times throughout his career. He frequently used the word "nature" interchangeably with God, Providence, or the Almighty. While on some occasions he claimed God had created people or organisms, at other times (or sometimes in the same breath) he claimed nature had created them. Further, he wanted to cultivate a certain veneration of nature through a reinvented Christmas festival that turned the focus away from Christianity. He also hoped to build an observatory-planetarium complex in Linz that would serve as a religious pilgrim-age site to dazzle Germans with the wonders of the cosmos. Overall, it appears a pantheist worldview was where Hitler felt closest to home.

Since it is so difficult to pinpoint exactly what Hitler's religion was, it might seem his religion was historically inconsequential. However, hopefully this study of Hitler's religion sheds light on a number of important issues. First, his anti-Christianity obviously shaped the persecution of the Christian churches during the Third Reich. Second, his religious hypocrisy helped explain his ability to appeal to a broad constituency. Third, his trust that his God would reward his efforts and willpower, together with his sense of divine mission, imbued him with hope, even in hopeless circumstances. This helps us understand why he was so optimistic until the very end, when it should have been obvious much earlier that the game was up. Finally, and most importantly, his religion did not provide him any transcendent morality. Whatever Hitler's stance on other religious issues, his morality was entirely of this world, derived from his understanding of the workings of nature. In my view, this was the most pernicious element of his religion. Hitler followed what he considered the dictates of nature by stealing, killing, and destroying. Ultimately, however, he perished, because his God could not give him life.

A NOTE ON SOURCES

WHILE MOST PRIMARY SOURCES ON HITLER'S religion are relatively uncontroversial, a few are contested, especially individuals' memoirs and personal recollections of conversations with Hitler. When confronted with sources that some scholars consider problematic, my policy has been either not to use them at all, or else only to use them when the point they are making is confirmed by a good deal of independent testimony. Occasionally I may mention a well-known source I consider unreliable or only partly reliable to take issue with its claims.

The authenticity of most of Hitler's speeches and writings are uncontroversial, and I use them liberally. However, some have questioned Hitler's Table Talks as a reliable source for discovering Hitler's views on religion. In an interesting piece of detective work, Richard Carrier demonstrates convincingly that the English version of Hitler's Table Talk is based on the translation of a problematic and possibly inauthentic text. Thus, I do not use nor cite the English translation of Hitler's Table Talk. However, even Carrier admits that the two German editions edited by Henry Picker and Werner Jochmann are generally reliable. Carrier was hoping that debunking Hitler's Table Talk would demolish the image of Hitler as an anti-Christian that many scholars have built on this flawed document. Unfortunately for Carrier, Hitler is every bit as anti-Christian in the Jochmann and Picker editions.[1]

The Picker and Jochmann editions of Hitler's Table Talk monologues are very similar—indeed verbatim—in many passages. Each contains some passages not found in the other one. However, when comparing the many passages they share in common, most of them are identical, though occasionally there are very minor differences. Oddly, Carrier maintains that Picker is probably more reliable than Jochmann, but this is not the opinion of most scholars. I have read both editions and will rely mostly on Jochmann, though many of the passages I quote are in both editions. I will only use Picker sparingly and to confirm points Hitler made elsewhere, not to try to establish some unique point. We also need to remember that these monologues are not transcriptions of Hitler's talks, but are reconstructions based on notes taken during the monologues. Based on some testimony of those present at these monologues, the renditions we have are generally accurate, since they were written immediately afterwards.

The only book Hitler published during his lifetime, *Mein Kampf*, poses a different kind of problem. It is notoriously unreliable as a memoir, and many scholars—myself included—consider some of the vignettes about his earlier life completely fictitious. It does, however, accurately convey Hitler's ideology, as does Hitler's *Second Book*, which was only discovered after World War II.

Two other contemporary sources—Joseph Goebbels' diaries and the recently recovered Alfred Rosenberg diaries—confirm the general account of Hitler's monologues. My book is one of the first to use Rosenberg's diaries, which do not divulge anything that overturns our previous knowledge about Hitler, but rather corroborate other sources and provide some interesting details. While memoirs by Hitler's associates are important sources, some were written before 1945 by erstwhile friends and allies who had turned against Hitler. Often they had an axe to grind and wanted to protect their own image. Others were written after 1945 by those who wanted to distance themselves from Hitler's views. I have examined a large variety of accounts by everyone from Hitler's secretaries to Hitler's architect friend Albert Speer to Hitler's political cronies, Hans Frank and Alfred Rosenberg. While there are some contradictions between these various accounts, they generally agree on the general outlines of Hitler's religion.

Probably the most controversial piece of memoir literature about Hitler's religion has been Hermann Rauschning's writings. Some historians, such as Theodor Schieder, have defended Rauschning from his dismissive treatment by other historians (such as Eberhard Jäckel).[2] However, Schieder recognizes that Rauschning's account of his conversations with Hitler was not verbatim and also included some of Rauschning's opinions. Pia Nordblom argues against the idea that Rauschning's works were a conscious falsification, while also admitting they constituted an interpretation of Hitler, not an accurate transcript of conversations.[3] Rauschning's portrayal of Hitler's general position is plausible, but some of his details run up against considerable countervailing evidence. For instance, Rauschning claims that Hitler considered Jesus to be Jewish, which is a position Hitler often contradicted from the early 1920s through the 1940s.[4] I have taken Rauschning's perspective into account, and even if his conversations with Hitler were completely accurate, it would have little effect on my interpretation. In this book, I acknowledge Rauschning's position when relevant, but ultimately I do not consider his writings reliable enough to use extensively.

Another controversial source containing an extensive conversation with Hitler about religion is Dietrich Eckart's *Der Bolschewismus von Moses bis Lenin: Zwiegespräch zwischen Adolf Hitler und mir* (1924). I use Eckart's work to illuminate Eckart's position and also the religious perspectives in Hitler's milieu, but I do not consider it a reliable source for Hitler's own words on religion. In 1932, the Nazi propaganda leadership denied that Eckart's book was reliable, calling the recorded conversations a fictional fantasy. The Nazis at that point were combating those who were using Eckart's book to demonstrate that Hitler was anti-church.[5] But even if Eckart's work were a verbatim account of Hitler's words, it would merely reinforce my interpretation of Hitler's religion.

Concerning Hitler's secretaries' testimony, Christa Schroeder claims that Albert Zoller's book, *Hitler privat*, was based on interrogations with her, but Zoller added a significant amount of material from other sources and may even have invented some of it. Since Schroeder disputes its reliability, I have not used Zoller.[6] Instead, I have relied on Schroeder's own work, *Er War Mein Chef: Aus dem Nachlass der Sekretärin von Adolf Hitler*. Much of her testimony is also confirmed by Traudl Junge. Unfortunately, one crucial paragraph in Junge's memoirs that discusses Hitler's religion and Hitler's belief in human evolution is cribbed from Schroeder's earlier book. Junge had a co-author, so I do not know which one of them plagiarized. Because of this problem, however, I have used Schroeder instead of Junge, even though they both say essentially (and sometimes exactly) the same thing.

One final questionable source that makes a difference in interpreting Hitler's worldview is *The Testament of Adolf Hitler: The Hitler-Bormann Documents, February–April 1945*. The editor,

Francois Genoud, was the same figure Carrier criticized for his mishandling of the Table Talk manuscripts. In this case, Genoud claimed that he translated this *Testament* into French, but the original documents have been lost. It is possible Genoud invented them or at least falsified them. Ian Kershaw, the preeminent biographer of Hitler, considers the *Testament* an unreliable source.[7] However, even if these documents were genuine, it would not greatly alter my interpretation of Hitler's religion. This document portrays Hitler in most respects exactly like the monologues—as a virulent anti-Christian who attacked Christianity as a Jewish invention. One relevant statement in the *Testament*, however, is likely completely inaccurate. At one point, Hitler stated that the Jews are not really a biological entity, but a spiritual one. Richard Steigmann-Gall and Robert Michael pounce on this to argue that Hitler was a religious, not a racial, anti-Semite.[8] This statement runs contrary to an avalanche of evidence from every reliable source we have, so it is reasonable to dismiss it as unreliable. Hitler clearly believed the Jews were a biological, not a religious entity, a point he explained quite often.

Overall, I have tried to steer clear of sources that are disputed or controversial, relying instead on a vast fund of primary sources that confirm each other. Where I use English language sources, in most cases I have read the original German to verify the accuracy of the translation.

Finally, I need to note that I try to convey Hitler's thoughts as accurately as possible by using his own terms and wording. Unfortunately, the English language, unlike the German language, does not have a verb tense to indicate indirect discourse. Thus, I want to emphasize that when I use terminology or phrasing that might seem wrong-headed or even objectionable—for instance, describing Jews as parasitic or using the term Aryan—I am not conveying my own thoughts, but Hitler's.

I have also followed two additional practices for the ease of the reader. First, whenever the term "anti-Semite " or "anti-Semitism" is used, I employ the Webster's Dictionary-approved form in all references, including quoted material, for consistency. Second, the Chicago Manual of Style, which this book follows, allows the *initial* letter in quoted material to be changed to either capital or lowercase so that it remains grammatically correct with the surrounding text, thereby forestalling any confusion for the reader. In any instance, however, where capitalization of the initial letter may be crucial to the larger academic point being discussed, brackets have been used.

ACKNOWLEDGMENTS

LIKE ALL SCHOLARSHIP, THIS WORK WOULD HAVE been impossible without the previous work of many scholars, whose work I have used. My citations reflect my deep debt to these many men and women. I am especially indebted to Eric Kurlander, Charles Bellinger, Richard Ravalli, Tom Johnson, Kelly Gonser, Eric Nystrom, Caleb Hampton, and Derek Cowell, who read the manuscript and provided helpful comments. I appreciate Randy Bytwerk for helping me with a couple of the illustrations. Thanks also to Julie Reuben for her help in obtaining obscure sources through Inter-Library Loan. Thanks to California State University, Stanislaus, for providing a research leave to complete this project. I also thank my agent, Steve Laube, and the Regnery History editor, Alex Novak, for believing in the value of this book project and for bringing it to publication. Most of all, thanks to my dear wife and my precious children for their love and support.

NOTES

INTRODUCTION

1. Cass Jones, "Controversy over Adolf Hitler Statue in Warsaw Ghetto," *Guardian*, December 28, 2012, http://www.theguardian.com/world/2012/dec/28/adolf-hitler-statue-warsaw-ghetto.

2. Hitler, *Mein Kampf*, trans. Ralph Manheim (Boston: Houghton Mifflin, 1943), 161. Unless indicated otherwise, all quotations from *Mein Kampf* will be from the Manheim translation, though I have examined the original German to verify the accuracy of the quotations.

3. Hitler, speech on March 28, 1936, in Max Domarus, *The Complete Hitler: A Digital Desktop Reference to His Speeches and Proclamations, 1932-1945*, 4 vols. (Wauconda, IL: Bolchazy-Carducci Publishers, 2007), 2:802.

4. Sam Jones, John Hooper, and Tom Kington, "Pope Benedict XVI Goes to War with 'Atheist Extremism,'" September 16, 2010, http://www. theguardian.com/world/2010/sep/16/pope-benedict-xvi-atheist-extremism.

5. Richard Dawkins, "Ratzinger Is an Enemy of Humanity," September 22, 2010, http://www.theguardian.com/commentisfree/belief/2010/sep/22/ ratzinger-enemy-humanity.

6. Otto Strasser, *Hitler and I*, trans. Gwenda David and Eric Mosbacher (Boston: Houghton Mifflin, 1940), 93.

7. Quoted in Rainer Bucher, *Hitler's Theology: A Study in Political Religion*, trans. Rebecca Pohl (London: Continuum, 2011), vii.

8. Kevin Spicer, *Hitler's Priests: Catholic Clergy and National Socialism* (DeKalb: Northern Illinois University Press, 2008); Robert P. Ericksen, *Theologians Under Hitler (Gerhard Kittel, Paul Althaus, and Emanuel Hirsch)* (New Haven: Yale University Press, 1985).

9. Doris Bergen, *Twisted Cross: The German Christian Movement in the Third Reich* (Chapel Hill: University of North Carolina Press, 1996), 7.

10. I have discussed these points at great length in my earlier books, *From Darwin to Hitler: Evolutionary Ethics, Eugenics, and Racism in Germany* (New York: Palgrave Macmillan, 2004), and *Hitler's Ethic: The Nazi Pursuit of Evolutionary Progress* (New York: Palgrave Macmillan, 2009). I discuss them further in the last two chapters of this book.

11. Scholars interpreting Nazism as a political religion include: Michael Burleigh, "National Socialism as a Political Religion," *Totalitarian Movements and Political Religions* 1, no. 2 (2000): 1–26; Michael Burleigh, *The Third Reich: A New History* (New York: Hill and Wang, 2000), Introduction; Klaus Vondung, "National Socialism as a Political Religion: Potentials and Limits of an Analytical Concept," *Totalitarian Movements and Political Religions* 6, no. 1 (2005): 87–95; Klaus Vondung, *Magie und Manipulation: Ideologische Kult und politische Religion des Nationalsozialismus* (Göttingen: Vandenhoeck und Ruprecht, 1971): 7–13; Milan Babik, "Nazism as a Secular Religion," *History and Theory* 45 (2006): 375–96; Karla Poewe, *New Religions and the Nazis* (New York:

Routledge, 2006), Introduction; Claus-Ekkehard Bärsch, *Die politische Religion des Nationalsozialismus : die religiöse Dimension der NS-Ideologie in den Schriften von Dietrich Eckart, Joseph Goebbels, Alfred Rosenberg und Adolf Hitler* (Munich: W. Fink, 1998), 350 and passim; and various scholars in *Der Nationalsozialismus als politische Religion*, ed. Michael Ley and Julius H. Schoeps (Bodenheim bei Mainz: Philo Verlagsgesellschaft, 1997).

12. Scholars who reject the notion that Nazism is a political religion include: Richard J. Evans, "Nazism, Christianity and Political Religion: A Debate," *Journal of Contemporary History* 42, no. 1 (2007): 5–7; Richard J. Evans, *The Third Reich in Power* (New York: Penguin, 2005): 257–59; Neil Gregor, "Nazism—A Political Religion? Rethinking the Voluntarist Turn," in *Nazism, War and Genocide*, ed. Neil Gregor (Exeter: University of Exeter Press, 2005): 1–21; Richard Steigmann-Gall, "Nazism and the Revival of Political Religion Theory," *Totalitarian Movements and Political Religions* 5, no. 3 (2004): 376–396; and Stanley Stowers, "The Concepts of 'Religion,' 'Political Religion,' and the Study of Nazism," *Journal of Contemporary History* 42 (2007): 9–24.

13. Christine von Braun, "Und der Feind ist Fleisch geworden: Der rassistische Antisemitismus," *Der ewige Judenhass: Christlicher Antijudaismus, Deutschnationale Judenfeindlichkeit, Rassistischer Antisemitismus*, eds. Christine von Braun and Ludger Heid (Berlin: Philo, 2000): 149–213, esp. 150; Michael Hesemann, *Hitlers Religion: Die fatale Heilslehre des Nationalsozialismus* (Munich: Pattloch, 2004): 16–18, 441; Anton Grabner-Haider and Peter Strasser, *Hitlers mythische Religion: Theologische Denklinien und NS-Ideologie* (Vienna: Böhlau Verlag, 2007); and Werner Reichelt, *Das braune Evangelium: Hitler und die NS-Liturgie* (Wuppertal: Peter Hammer Verlag, 1990), 90 and passim.

14. "Der Schwur unter dem Lichtdom," in *Der Parteitag der Ehre vom 8. bis 14. September 1936: Offizieller Bericht über den Verlauf des Reichsparteitages mit sämtlichen Kongressreden*, 2nd ed. (Munich:

Zentralverlag der NSDAP, Franz Eher Nachf., 1936), 173; emphasis in original.

15. "Der Schwur unter dem Lichtdom," in *Der Parteitag der Ehre vom 8.* bis 14. September 1936: *Offizieller Bericht über den Verlauf des Reichsparteitages mit sämtlichen Kongressreden*, 2nd ed. (Munich: Zentralverlag der NSDAP, Franz Eher Nachf., 1936): 173–77; emphasis in original.

16. Hitler, closing speech at Nuremberg Party Congress, 1937, in Christian Dube, "Religiöser Sprache in Reden Adolf Hitlers: Analysiert an Hand ausgewählter Reden aus den Jahren 1933–1945," diss., University of Kiel, 2004, 251.

17. Robert Ley, in "Der Appel der Politischen Leiter," in *Der Parteitag Grossdeutschland vom 5.* bis 12. September 1938: *Offizieller Bericht über den Verlauf des Reichsparteitages mit sämtlichen Kongressreden* (Munich: Zentralverlag der NSDAP, Franz Eher Nachf., 1938), 210.

18. Derek Hastings, *Catholicism and the Roots of Nazism: Religious Identity and National Socialism* (Oxford: Oxford University Press, 2010): 181–82; see also 163–64.

19. Ian Kershaw, *The 'Hitler Myth': Image and Reality in the Third Reich* (Oxford: Oxford University Press, 1987), 39; David Redles, *Hitler's Millennial Reich: Apocalyptic Belief and the Search for Salvation* (New York: New York University Press, 2005) discusses Hitler's messianism, but I do not find his work particularly reliable, because it draws heavily from questionable sources.

20. Goebbels, diary entry on October 14, 1925, in *Die Tagebücher von Joseph Goebbels*, ed. Elke Fröhlich, part I: *Aufzeichnungen 1923–1941*, vol. 1: *June 1924–Dec. 1930* (Munich: K. G. Saur, 1987), 365.

21. Werner Reichelt, *Das braune Evangelium: Hitler und die NS-Liturgie* (Wuppertal: Peter Hammer Verlag, 1990): 134–35; see also a slightly different version in Klaus Scholder, *Die Kirchen und das Dritte Reich*, vol. 2: *Das Jahr der Ernüchterung 1934 Barmen und Rom* (n.p.: Siedler Verlag, n.d.): 143.

22. Hitler, *Mein Kampf,* trans. Ralph Manheim (Boston: Houghton Mifflin, 1943): 116.

23. Hitler, monologue on October 14, 1941, in *Monologe im Führerhauptquartier 1941–1944: Die Aufzeichnungen Heinrich Heims,* ed. Werner Jochmann (Hamburg: Albrecht Knaus, 1980): 82–83.

24. Hitler, *Mein Kampf,* trans. Ralph Manheim (Boston: Houghton Mifflin, 1943): 383; I have translated "Weltanschauung" as "worldview" instead of "philosophy" in this passage.

25. Hitler, *Mein Kampf,* trans. Ralph Manheim (Boston: Houghton Mifflin, 1943): 454–55.

26. Hitler, speech on August 27, 1933, quoted in Miles Ecclesiae [pseudonym of Karl Spiecker], *Hitler gegen Christus: Eine katholische Klarstellung und Abwehr* (Paris: Societe d'editions europeennes, 1936): 29.

27. Hitler, "Die Kulturtagung im Opernhaus," in *Der Parteitag der Ehre vom 8. bis 14. September 1936: Offizieller Bericht über den Verlauf des Reichsparteitages mit sämtlichen Kongressreden,* 2nd ed. (Munich: Zentralverlag der NSDAP, Franz Eher Nachf., 1936): 67; emphasis in original. Hitler made essentially the same point in "Die Verleihung des Deutschen Nationalpreises," September 6, 1938, in *Der Parteitag Grossdeutschland vom 5. bis 12. September 1938: Offizieller Bericht über den Verlauf des Reichsparteitages mit sämtlichen Kongressreden* (Munich: Zentralverlag der NSDAP, Franz Eher Nachf., 1938): 76.

28. Walter Künneth, *Der große Abfall: Eine geschichtstheologische Untersuchung der Begegnung zwischen Nationalsozialismus und Christentum,* 2nd ed. (Hamburg: Friedrich Wittig Verlag, 1948), 20 ch. 2.

29. Detlev Peukert, "The Genesis of the 'Final Solution' from the Spirit of Science," in *Reevaluating the Third Reich,* ed. Thomas Childers and Jane Caplan (New York: Holmes and Meier, 1993): 234–52.

30. Claudia Koonz, *The Nazi Conscience* (Cambridge: Belknap Press of Harvard University Press, 2003): 1–2, 6; other scholars interpreting Nazism as primarily secular include Michael Prinz and Rainer Zitelmann,

"Vorwort," in *Nationalsozialismus und Modernisierung*, ed. Michael Prinz and Rainer Zitelmann (Darmstadt: Wissenschaftliche Buchgesellschaft, 1991); Richard Shorten, *Modernism and Totalitarianism: Rethinking the Intellectual Sources of Nazism and Stalinism, 1945 to the Present* (New York: Palgrave Macmillan, 2012): 2–4; Michael Rissmann, *Hitlers Gott: Vorsehungsglaube und Sendungsbewusstsein des deutschen Diktators* (Zürich: Pendo, 2001): 12–13, 195, 205.

31. Richard Steigmann-Gall, *The Holy Reich: Nazi Conceptions of Christianity, 1919–1945* (Cambridge: Cambridge University Press, 2003): 12.

32. Todd H. Weir, *Secularism and Religion in Nineteenth-Century Germany: The Rise of the Fourth Confession* (Cambridge: Cambridge University Press, 2014): 273–76.

33. Todd H. Weir, *Secularism and Religion in Nineteenth-Century Germany: The Rise of the Fourth Confession* (Cambridge: Cambridge University Press, 2014): 2–3.

34. Owen Chadwick, *The Secularization of the European Mind in the Nineteenth Century* (Cambridge: Cambridge University Press, 1975): 16–17, and passim.

35. This seems to be roughly the position of Richard J. Evans in *The Third Reich in Power* (New York: Penguin, 2005); and in "Nazism, Christianity and Political Religion: A Debate," *Journal of Contemporary History* no. 42, 1 (2007): 5–7; and Alan Bullock, *Hitler and Stalin: Parallel Lives* (New York: Alfred A. Knopf, 1992): 386.

36. See Richard Weikart, *Hitler's Ethic: The Nazi Pursuit of Evolutionary Progress* (New York: Palgrave Macmillan, 2009).

37. World Council of Churches, "The Basis of the WCC," www.oikoumene.org/en/about-us/self-understanding-vision/basis, accessed March 22, 2014.

38. Robert Ericksen and Susanne Heschel, eds. *Betrayal: German Churches and the Holocaust* (Minneapolis: Fortress Press, 1999): 10.

39. Quoted in Benjamin Lazier, *God Interrupted: Heresy and the European Imagination between the World Wars* (Princeton: Princeton University Press, 2008): 76.

40. Todd Weir, "The Riddles of Monism: An Introductory Essay," in *Monism: Science, Philosophy, Religion, and the History of a Worldview*, ed. Todd Weir (New York: Palgrave Macmillan, 2012): 16.

41. Benjamin Lazier, *God Interrupted: Heresy and the European Imagination between the World Wars* (Princeton: Princeton University Press, 2008): 8–9.

42. Nicholas Riasanovsky, *The Emergence of Romanticism* (New York: Oxford University Press, 1992), 71, quote at 79.

43. Kurt Hildebrandt, "Die Bedeutung der Abstammungslehre für die Weltanschauung," *Zeitschrift für die gesamte Naturwissenschaft* 3 (1937–1938): 23.

44. Max von Gruber to Heinrich Friedjung, March 20, 1885, in Wiener Stadt- und Landesbibliothek, Aut. 163.011.

45. See also Weikart, *Hitler's Ethic: The Nazi Pursuit of Evolutionary Progress* (New York: Palgrave Macmillan, 2009), ch. 1, "Hitler as Moral Crusader and Liar."

ONE: WAS HITLER A RELIGIOUS HYPOCRITE?

1. Hitler, "Die 'Hetzer' der Wahrheit," April 12, 1922, in *Hitler: Sämtliche Aufzeichnungen, 1905–1924*, ed. Eberhard Jäckel (Stuttgart: Deutsche Verlags-Anstalt, 1980), 623–24.

2. Goebbels, diary entry of December 29, 1939, in *Die Tagebücher von Joseph Goebbels*, ed. Elke Fröhlich, Part I: *Aufzeichnungen 1923–1941*, vol. 7: *Juli 1939-März 1940* (Munich K. G. Saur, 1998), 250.

3. Hitler, speech of November 10, 1938, in Max Domarus, *The Complete Hitler: A Digital Desktop Reference to His Speeches and Proclamations, 1932–1945* (Wauconda, IL: Bolchazy-Carducci Publishers, 2007), 2:1245.

4. "Hitler vor Kreisleitern auf der Ordensburg Volgelsang am 29. April 1937," in Adolf Hitler, *"Es spricht der Führer": 7 exemplarische Hitler-Reden,* ed. Hildegard von Kotze and Helmut Krausnick (Gütersloh: Sigbert Mohn Verlag, 1966), 167–68.

5. Hitler, monologue on December 17, 1941, in *Monologe im Führerhauptquartier 1941–1944: Die Aufzeichnungen Heinrich Heims,* ed. Werner Jochmann (Hamburg: Albrecht Knaus, 1980),153.

6. Hitler, *Mein Kampf,* 99.

7. Andrew G. Whiteside, *The Socialism of Fools: Georg Ritter von Schönerer and Austrian Pan-Germanism* (Berkeley: University of California Press, 1975), 252–53, see also 205–10.

8. Hitler, *Mein Kampf,* 108–19.

9. Ibid., 118–19.

10. Ibid., 562–64; quote at 564.

11. Ibid., 119.

12. Ibid., 116.

13. "Programme of the NSDAP, 1920," in *The Third Reich and the Christian Churches,* ed. Peter Matheson (Grand Rapids, MI: William B. Eerdmans, 1981), 1.

14. Rudolf Hess to Ilse Pröhl, August 20, 1924, in *Rudolf Hess Briefe 1908–1933,* ed. Wolf Rüdiger Hess (Munich: Langen Müller, 1987), 350–51.

15. Joseph Goebbels, diary entry for September 12, 1931, in *Die Tagebücher von Joseph Goebbels,* ed. Elke Fröhlich, Part I: *Aufzeichnungen 1923–1941,* vol. 2/II: *Juni 1931–September 1932* (Munich K. G. Saur, 2004), 96.

16. Alfred Rosenberg, *The Memoirs of Alfred Rosenberg,* ed. Serge Lang and Ernst von Schenck, trans. Eric Posselt (Chicago: Ziff-Davis Publishing Co., 1949), 258–59.

17. Rosenberg, diary entry for June 28, 1934, in *Das politische Tagebuch Alfred Rosenbergs aus den Jahren 1934/35 und 1939/40,* ed. Hans-Günther Seraphim (Göttingen: Musterschmidt-Verlag, 1956), 32.

18. "Testimony of Johanna Wolf," Nuremberg, February 24, 1948, United States Holocaust Memorial Museum Archives, RG 6.005.01, Interrogation of Hitler's Secretaries.

19. Hitler, speech on November 8, 1941, in Max Domarus, *The Complete Hitler: A Digital Desktop Reference to His Speeches and Proclamations, 1932–1945* (Wauconda, IL: Bolchazy-Carducci Publishers, 2007), 4:2511–12.

20. Hitler, speech on August 26, 1934, in *The Speeches of Adolf Hitler, April 1922–August 1939*, ed. Norman H. Baynes (Oxford: Oxford University Press, 1942), 1:386–87.

21. Hitler, speech on November 23, 1937, in Max Domarus, *The Complete Hitler: A Digital Desktop Reference to His Speeches and Proclamations, 1932–1945* (Wauconda, IL: Bolchazy-Carducci Publishers, 2007), 2:980.

22. Hitler, speech on January 30, 1939, in Christian Dube, "Religiöser Sprache in Reden Adolf Hitlers: Analysiert an Hand ausgewählter Reden aus den Jahren 1933–1945" (diss., University of Kiel, 2004), 312–14.

23. Hitler, speech on May 1, 1937, in Max Domarus, *The Complete Hitler: A Digital Desktop Reference to His Speeches and Proclamations, 1932–1945* (Wauconda, IL: Bolchazy-Carducci Publishers, 2007), 2:893.

24. Hitler, monologue on December 13, 1941, in *Hitlers Tischgespräche im Führerhauptquartier*, ed. Henry Picker (Frankfurt: Ullstein, 1989), 80.

TWO: WHO INFLUENCED HITLER'S RELIGION?

1. Christa Schroeder, *Er War Mein Chef: Aus dem Nachlass der Sekretärin von Adolf Hitler*, ed. Anton Jaochimsthaler, 2nd ed. (Munich: Langen Müller, 1985), 218.

2. Hitler, monologue on May 19, 1944, in *Monologe im Führerhauptquartier 1941–1944: Die Aufzeichnungen Heinrich Heims*, ed. Werner Jochmann (Hamburg: Albrecht Knaus, 1980), 411; he also mentioned Kant,

Schopenhauer, and Nietzsche in a monologue on October 25, 1941, in *Monologe im Führerhauptquartier*, 107.

3. Goebbels, diary entry for May 13, 1943, in *Die Tagebücher von Joseph Goebbels*, ed. Elke Fröhlich, part II: *Diktate 1941–1945*, vol. 8: *April–Juni 1943* (Munich K. G. Saur, 1993), 290.

4. Weikart, *Hitler's Ethic: The Nazi Pursuit of Evolutionary Progress*, provides a book-length discussion of Hitler's social Darwinism.

5. One of the earliest attempts to explore the roots of Nazi ideology was William McGovern, *From Luther to Hitler: The History of Fascist-Nazi Political Philosophy* (Cambridge, MA: Riverside Press, 1941). Despite the title, McGovern was not arguing that Luther was the sole influence on Hitler, but he explored a wide variety of influences, including Luther, social Darwinism, Nietzsche, and others.

6. August Kubizek, *Adolf Hitler: Mein Jugendfreund* (Graz: Leopold Stocker Verlag, 1953), 227.

7. "Ansprache Hitlers vor Generalen und Offizieren am 26. Mai 1944 im Platterhof," in Hans-Heinrich Wilhelm, "Hitlers Ansprache vor Generalen und Offizieren am 26. Mai 1944," *Militärgeschichtliche Mitteilungen* 2 (1976): 144.

8. Otto Dietrich, *The Hitler I Knew*, trans. Richard and Clara Winston (London: Methuen, 1957), 77, 150; see also Hans Frank, *Im Angesicht des Galgens: Deutung Hitlers und seiner Zeit auf Grund eigener Erlebnisse und Erkenntnisse* (Munich-Gräfelfing: Friedrich Alfred Beck Verlag, 1953), 46.

9. Christa Schroeder, *Er War Mein Chef: Aus dem Nachlass der Sekretärin von Adolf Hitler*, ed. Anton Jaochimsthaler, 2nd ed. (Munich: Langen Müller, 1985), 77.

10. Hitler, "Der Klassenkampf ein Börsenbetrug," March 1, 1922, in *Hitler: Sämtliche Aufzeichnungen, 1905–1924*, ed. Eberhard Jäckel (Stuttgart: Deutsche Verlags-Anstalt, 1980), 589.

11. Hitler, "Deutsche Student und deutscher Arbeiter als Träger der deutschen Zukunft," February 26, 1923, in *Hitler: Sämtliche Aufzeichnungen,*

1905–1924, ed. Eberhard Jäckel (Stuttgart: Deutsche Verlags-Anstalt, 1980), 837.

12. Hitler, "Volksrepublik oder Judenstaat," February 17, 1922; "Die 'Hetzer' der Wahrheit," April 12, 1922; "Politik und Rasse. Warum sind wir Antisemiten?" April 20, 1923, in *Hitler: Sämtliche Aufzeichnungen, 1905–1924*, ed. Eberhard Jäckel (Stuttgart: Deutsche Verlags-Anstalt, 1980), 577, 620, 909.

13. Hitler, *Mein Kampf*, 232, 305.

14. Hitler, monologue on October 24, 1941, in *Monologe im Führerhauptquartier 1941–1944: Die Aufzeichnungen Heinrich Heims*, ed. Werner Jochmann (Hamburg: Albrecht Knaus, 1980), 105.

15. Arthur Schopenhauer, "The World as Will and Idea," in *The Works of Schopenhauer*, abridged edition, ed. Will Durant (New York: Frederick Ungar Publishing, 1928), 163.

16. Christopher Janaway, *Schopenhauer* (Oxford: Oxford University Press, 1994), 5–6, 29–30, 38.

17. Arthur Schopenhauer, "The World as Will and Idea," in *The Works of Schopenhauer*, abridged edition, ed. Will Durant (New York: Frederick Ungar Publishing, 1928), 34; one of the few works to discuss at any length Schopenhauer's influence on Hitler is Stephen Strehle, *The Dark Side of Church/State Separation: The French Revolution, Nazi Germany, and International Communism* (New Brunswick, NJ: Transaction Publishers, 2013), 166–70.

18. Hans Sluga, *Heidegger's Crisis: Philosophy and Politics in Nazi Germany* (Cambridge, MA: Harvard University Press, 1993), 79–81, also points out other tensions between Schopenhauer and Hitler.

19. Christopher Janaway, *Schopenhauer* (Oxford: Oxford University Press, 1994), 28–29, 38.

20. Christopher Janaway, *Schopenhauer* (Oxford: Oxford University Press, 1994), 39; ellipses in Janaway; Michael Tanner, *Schopenhauer* (New York: Routledge, 1999), 12–13.

21. Weikart, *Hitler's Ethic: The Nazi Pursuit of Evolutionary Progress*, ch. 2–3.

22. Barbara Hannan, *Riddle of the World: A Reconsideration of Schopenhauer's Philosophy* (Oxford: Oxford University Press, 2009), 9.

23. Christopher Janaway, *Schopenhauer* (Oxford: Oxford University Press, 1994), 38.

24. Arthur Schopenhauer, "The World as Will and Idea," in *The Works of Schopenhauer*, abridged edition, ed. Will Durant (New York: Frederick Ungar Publishing, 1928), 165.

25. For Hitler's view on this matter, see Richard Weikart, *Hitler's Ethic: The Nazi Pursuit of Evolutionary Progress* (New York: Palgrave Macmillan, 2009), 114–17; for the views of other social Darwinists about this, see Weikart, *From Darwin to Hitler: Evolutionary Ethics, Eugenics, and Racism in Germany* (New York: Palgrave Macmillan, 2004), ch. 4.

26. Christopher Janaway, *Schopenhauer* (Oxford: Oxford University Press, 1994), 5.

27. Arthur Schopenhauer, "On the Sufferings of the World," in *Life, Death and Meaning: Key Philosophical Readings on the Big Questions*, ed. David Benatar (Lanham, MD: Rowman and Littlefield Publishers, 2004), 400.

28. Arthur Schopenhauer, "Religion: A Dialogue," in *The Works of Schopenhauer*, abridged edition, ed. Will Durant (New York: Frederick Ungar Publishing, 1928), 465–98, esp. 483, 490, 496.

29. Arthur Schopenhauer, "The World as Will and Idea," in *The Works of Schopenhauer*, abridged edition, ed. Will Durant (New York: Frederick Ungar Publishing, 1928), 163.

30. Alfred Rosenberg, diary entry for April 9, 1941, in Alfred Rosenberg Diary, 531, http://collections.ushmm.org/view/2001.62.14; accessed January 22, 2014.

31. Goebbels, diary entry for April 8, 1941, in *Die Tagebücher von Joseph Goebbels*, ed. Elke Fröhlich, part I: *Aufzeichnungen 1923–1941*, vol. 9: *Dezember 1940–Juli 1941* (Munich K. G. Saur, 1998), 234.

32. Jacob Golomb and Robert S. Wistrich, eds., *Nietzsche, Godfather of Fascism?: On the Uses and Abuses of a Philosophy* (Princeton: Princeton University Press, 2002), 8.

33. Martin Schwab, "Selected Affinities: Nietzsche and the Nazis," in *Nazi Germany and the Humanities*, eds. Wolfgang Bialas and Anson Rabinbach, eds. (Oxford: Oneworld, 2007), 160–61.

34. Steven E. Aschheim, The Nietzsche Legacy in Germany, 1890–1990 (Berkeley: University of California Press, 1992), 111, 239–40.

35. Simon May, *Nietzsche's Ethics and His War on 'Morality'* (New York: Oxford University, The Clarendon Press, 1999), 132; other scholars stressing the affinities between Nietzsche and Nazism are Richard Wolin, *The Seduction of Unreason: The Intellectual Romance with Fascism from Nietzsche to Postmodernism* (Princeton: Princeton University Press, 2004), ch. 1; Richard Shorten, *Modernism and Totalitarianism: Rethinking the Intellectual Sources of Nazism and Stalinism, 1945 to the Present* (New York: Palgrave Macmillan, 2012), 193, 208; Stephen Strehle, *The Dark Side of Church/State Separation: The French Revolution, Nazi Germany, and International Communism* (New Brunswick, NJ: Transaction Publishers, 2013), 170–84; and Erich Sandvoss, *Hitler und Nietzsche* (Göttingen: Musterschmidt-Verlag, 1969).

36. Hans Sluga, *Heidegger's Crisis: Philosophy and Politics in Nazi Germany* (Cambridge, MA: Harvard University Press, 1993), 15, 42, 125, 131.

37. Max Whyte, "The Uses and Abuses of Nietzsche in the Third Reich: Alfred Baeumler's 'Heroic Realism,'" *Journal of Contemporary History* 43 (2008): 171–94; quote at 193; another work discussing the Nazi reception of Nietzsche is Yvonne Sherratt, *Hitler's Philosophers* (New Haven: Yale University Press, 2013), ch. 3.

38. David B. Dennis, *Inhumanities: Nazi Interpretations of Western Culture* (Cambridge: Cambridge University Press, 2012), 250–51, 260; quote at 258.

39. Rosenberg, diary entries for September 17, 1936 and December 26, 1936, in Alfred Rosenberg Diary, 69, 133–35, http://collections.ushmm.org/view/2001.62.14; accessed January 22, 2014.

40. Heinrich Härtle, *Nietzsche und der Nationalsozialismus* (Munich: Zentralverlag der NSDAP, Franz Eher Nachf., 1937), 5–6, 162–64.

41. Steven E. Aschheim, *The Nietzsche Legacy in Germany, 1890–1990* (Berkeley: University of California Press, 1992), 239.

42. Max Whyte, "The Uses and Abuses of Nietzsche in the Third Reich: Alfred Baeumler's 'Heroic Realism,'" *Journal of Contemporary History* 43 (2008): 178.

43. Carol Diethe, *Nietzsche's Sister and the Will to Power: A Biography of Elisabeth Foerster-Nietzsche* (Urbana and Chicago: University of Illinois Press, 2003), 151–57; H. F. Peters, *Zarathustra's Sister: The Case of Elisabeth and Friedrich Nietzsche* (New York: Crown Publishers, 1977), 218–26; Max Whyte, "The Uses and Abuses of Nietzsche in the Third Reich: Alfred Baeumler's 'Heroic Realism,'" *Journal of Contemporary History* 43 (2008): 193.

44. Heinrich Hoffmann, *Hitler wie ihn keiner kennt. 100 Bilddokumente aus dem Leben des Führers* (Berlin: Zeitgeschichte-Verlag, 1938), 108.

45. Max Domarus, *The Complete Hitler: A Digital Desktop Reference to His Speeches and Proclamations, 1932–1945* (Wauconda, IL: Bolchazy-Carducci Publishers, 2007), 4:2803.

46. Max Whyte, "The Uses and Abuses of Nietzsche in the Third Reich: Alfred Baeumler's 'Heroic Realism,'" *Journal of Contemporary History* 43 (2008): 192.

47. Ernst Hanfstaengl, *Unheard Witness* (Philadelphia: J. B. Lippincott, 1957), 217–18.

48. Dietrich, *The Hitler I Knew*, 149–50.

49. Hitler, "Warum musste ein 8. November kommen?" *Deutschland Erneuerung* 8 (Apr. 1924): 203.

50. Hitler, closing speech to the Nuremberg Party Congress, September 1933, in *The Speeches of Adolf Hitler, April 1922–August 1939*, ed. Norman H. Baynes (Oxford: Oxford University Press, 1942), 1:478.

51. Hitler, speech on January 30, 1942, in Max Domarus, *The Complete Hitler: A Digital Desktop Reference to His Speeches and Proclamations, 1932–1945* (Wauconda, IL: Bolchazy-Carducci Publishers, 2007), 4:2571.

52. Goebbels, diary entry for January 30, 1941, in *Die Tagebücher von Joseph Goebbels*, ed. Elke Fröhlich, part I: *Aufzeichnungen 1923–1941*, vol. 9: *Dezember 1940–Juli 1941* (Munich K. G. Saur, 1998), 117.

53. Leon Stein, *The Racial Thinking of Richard Wagner* (New York: Philosophical Library, 1950), 92–93.

54. For example, Robert Michael, *Holy Hatred: Christianity, Antisemitism, and the Holocaust* (New York. Palgrave Macmillan, 2006), 146–47.

55. Stein, *The Racial Thinking of Richard Wagner*, 78, 96, 98, quote at 95; Alan David Aberbach, *The Ideas of Richard Wagner: An Examination and Analysis of His Major Aesthetic, Political, Economic, Social and Religious Thought* (Lanham, MD: University Press of America, 1984), 267–69.

56. Joachim Köhler, *Wagners Hitler: The Prophet and His Disciple*, trans. Ronald Taylor (Cambridge, UK: Polity Press, 2000), 216, 226.

57. Stein, *The Racial Thinking of Richard Wagner*, 92–94, quote at 94; Alan David Aberbach, *The Ideas of Richard Wagner: An Examination and Analysis of His Major Aesthetic, Political, Economic, Social and Religious Thought* (Lanham, MD: University Press of America, 1984), 268.

58. Joachim Köhler, *Wagners Hitler: The Prophet and His Disciple*, trans. Ronald Taylor (Cambridge, UK: Polity Press, 2000), 213–16, quote at 216.

59. Stein, *The Racial Thinking of Richard Wagner*, 76–77; Alan David Aberbach, *The Ideas of Richard Wagner: An Examination and Analysis of His Major Aesthetic, Political, Economic, Social and Religious Thought* (Lanham, MD: University Press of America, 1984), 282, 306–8.

60. Richard Wagner, "Hero-dom and Christendom," p. 275, http://users. belgacom.net/wagnerlibrary/prose/waghero.htm, accessed April 8, 2014.

61. Houston Stewart Chamberlain to Adolf Hitler, October 7, 1923, in Houston Stewart Chamberlain, *Briefe, 1882–1924 und Briefwechsel mit Kaiser Wilhelm II*, 2 vols. (Munich: F. Bruckmann, 1928), 2:124.

62. Hitler, speech on Janaury 18, 1927, in *Hitler: Reden, Schriften, Anordnungen, Febraur 1925 bis Januar 1933*, vol. II: *Vom Weimarer Parteitag bus zur Reichstagswahl Juli 1926–Mai 1928*, ed. Bärbel Dusik, part 1: *Juli 1926–Juli 1927* (Munich:K. G. Saur, 1992-2003), 129–30.

63. David B. Dennis, *Inhumanities: Nazi Interpretations of Western Culture* (Cambridge: Cambridge University Press, 2012), 261, 264.

64. Geoffrey Field, *Evangelist of Race: The Germanic Vision of Houston Stewart Chamberlain* (New York: Columbia University Press, 1981), 447–48.

65. Houston Stewart Chamberlain to Ludwig Schemann, May 27, 1893, in Ludiwg Schemann Papers, Freiburg University Library, IV B 1/2.

66. Uriel Tal, *Christians and Jews in Germany: Religion, Politics, and Ideology in the Second Reich* (Ithaca: Cornell University Press, 1975), 280; William I. Brustein, *Roots of Hate: Anti-Semitism in Europe before the Holocaust* (Cambridge: Cambridge University Press, 2003), 133.

67. Richard Weikart, *From Darwin to Hitler: Evolutionary Ethics, Eugenics, and Racism in Germany* (New York: Palgrave Macmillan, 2004), 124–25.

68. George L. Mosse, *Toward the Final Solution: A History of European Racism* (New York: Howard Fertig, 1985), 107.

69. Houston Stewart Chamberlain, *Die Grundlagen des neunzehnten Jahrhunderts*, 13th ed., 2 vols. (Munich: F. Bruckmann, 1919), 1:222–23.

70. Geoffrey Field, *Evangelist of Race: The Germanic Vision of Houston Stewart Chamberlain* (New York: Columbia University Press, 1981), 302–11; Houston Stewart Chamberlain, *Mensch und Gott: Betrachtungen über Religion und Christentum* (Munich: F. Bruckmann, 1921), 31.

71. Chamberlain, *Die Grundlagen des neunzehnten Jahrhunderts*, 1:256, 266–73.

72. Ibid., 1:273–93.

73. Geoffrey Field, *Evangelist of Race: The Germanic Vision of Houston Stewart Chamberlain* (New York: Columbia University Press, 1981), 306.

74. Ibid., 305.

75. Houston Stewart Chamberlain, *Die Grundlagen des neunzehnten Jahrhunderts*, 13th ed., 2 vols. (Munich: F. Bruckmann, 1919), 1:287.

76. Rosenberg, diary entry on December 14, 1941, in Rosenberg Diary, 625–27, http://collections.ushmm.org/view/2001.62.14; accessed January 22, 2014.

77. Chamberlain, *Die Grundlagen des neunzehnten Jahrhunderts*, 1:690–98; quote at 696-97.

78. Hitler, monologue on December 13, 1941, in *Monologe im Führerhauptquartier 1941–1944: Die Aufzeichnungen Heinrich Heims*, ed. Werner Jochmann (Hamburg: Albrecht Knaus, 1980), 151.

79. Weikart, *Hitler's Ethic: The Nazi Pursuit of Evolutionary Progress*, 14.

80. For Lehmann's influence on Hitler, see Sigrid Stöckel, ed., *Die 'rechte Nation' und ihr Verleger: Politik und Popularisierung im J. F. Lehmanns Verlag, 1890–1979* (Berlin: Lehmanns, 2002); and Timothy W. Ryback, *Hitler's Private Library: The Books that Shaped His Life* (New York: Alfred A. Knopf, 2008), 109–11.

81. Melanie Lehmann, *Verleger J. F. Lehmann. Ein Leben im Kampf um Deutschland. Lebenslauf und Briefe* (Munich: J. F. Lehmann, 1935), 22–25, 100–1.

THREE: WAS HITLER AN ATHEIST?

1. Ernst Hanfstaengl, *Unheard Witness* (Philadelphia: J. B. Lippincott, 1957), 72.

2. Alan Bullock, *Hitler: A Study in Tyranny*, revised ed. (NY: Harper and Row, 1964), 389–90.

3. Alan Bullock, *Hitler and Stalin: Parallel Lives* (New York: Alfred A. Knopf, 1992), 386.

4. Hitler, speech on November 8, 1941, in Max Domarus, *The Complete Hitler: A Digital Desktop Reference to His Speeches and Proclamations, 1932–1945* (Wauconda, IL: Bolchazy-Carducci Publishers, 2007), 4:2513.

5. Hitler, monologue on January 8–9, 1942, in *Monologe im Führerhauptquartier 1941–1944: Die Aufzeichnungen Heinrich Heims*, ed. Werner Jochmann (Hamburg: Albrecht Knaus, 1980), 185–87.

6. Hitler, monologue on February 20–21, 1942, in *Monologe im Führerhauptquartier 1941–1944: Die Aufzeichnungen Heinrich Heims*, ed. Werner Jochmann (Hamburg: Albrecht Knaus, 1980), 288.

7. Christa Schroeder, *Er War Mein Chef: Aus dem Nachlass der Sekretärin von Adolf Hitler*, ed. Anton Jaochimsthaler, 2nd ed. (Munich: Langen Müller, 1985), 61–62.

8. George Lachmann Mosse, *The Crisis of German Ideology: Intellectual Origins of the Third Reich* (NY: Grosset and Dunlap. 1964), 13, 106–7, and passim; George L. Mosse, *Toward the Final Solution: A History of European Racism* (New York: Howard Fertig, 1985), 205–6 and passim.

9. Jeffrey Herf, *Reactionary Modernism: Technology, Culture, and Politics in Weimar and the Third Reich* (Cambridge: Cambridge University Press, 1984), esp. chs. 8–9. Other historians portraying Nazism as primarily irrational and anti-Enlightenment are (among many others): Fritz Stern, *The Politics of Cultural Despair: A Study in the rise of the Germanic Ideology* (Garden City, NY: Anchor Books, 1965); and Anton Grabner-Haider and Peter Strasser, *Hitlers mythische Religion: Theologische Denklinien und NS-Ideologie* (Vienna: Böhlau Verlag, 2007).

10. Dirk Bavendamm, *Der junge Hitler: Korrekturen einer Biographie, 1889–1914* (Graz: Ares Verlag, 2009), 455; Friedrich Tomberg, *Das Christentum in Hitlers Weltanschauung* (Munich: Wilhelm Fink, 2012), 151–62.

11. Stanley G. Payne, *A History of Fascism, 1914–1945* (Madison: University of Wisconsin Press, 1995), 203.

12. Detlev Peukert, "The Genesis of the 'Final Solution' from the Spirit of Science," in *Reevaluating the Third Reich*, ed. Thomas Childers and Jane Caplan (New York: Holmes and Meier, 1993), 234–52.

13. Eric Kurlander stresses the amalgamation of rational and irrational in "Hitler's Monsters: The Occult Roots of Nazism and the Emergence of the Nazi 'Supernatural Imaginary,' *German History* 30, 4 (2012): 528–549.

14. Quoted in S. Körner, *Kant* (Baltimore: Penguin, 1955), 96.

15. Robert Richards, *The Romantic Conception of Life: Science and Philosophy in the Age of Goethe* (Chicago: University of Chicago Press, 2004).

16. H. Stuart Hughes, *Consciousness and Society: The Reorientation of European Social Thought, 1890–1930*, rev. ed. (New York: Vintage, 1977).

17. Hans F. K. Günther, *Rassenkunde des deutschen Volkes*, 3rd ed. (Munich: J. F. Lehmanns Verlag, 1923), 14.

18. Hans F. K. Günther, *Frömmigkeit nordlicher Artung*, 3rd ed. (Jena, E. Diederichs, 1936).

19. Hitler, monologue on May 19, 1944, in *Monologe im Führerhauptquartier 1941–1944: Die Aufzeichnungen Heinrich Heims*, ed. Werner Jochmann (Hamburg: Albrecht Knaus, 1980), 411.

20. Hitler, monologue on October 24, 1941, in *Monologe im Führerhauptquartier 1941–1944: Die Aufzeichnungen Heinrich Heims*, ed. Werner Jochmann (Hamburg: Albrecht Knaus, 1980), 103–4.

21. Hitler, monologue on July 2, 1942, in *Hitlers Tischgespräche im Führerhauptquartier*, ed. Henry Picker (Frankfurt: Ullstein, 1989), 405.

22. Hans Frank, *Im Angesicht des Galgens: Deutung Hitlers und seiner Zeit auf Grund eigener Erlebnisse und Erkenntnisse* (Munich-Gräfelfing: Friedrich Alfred Beck Verlag, 1953), 205.

23. Paul R. Hinlicky, *Before Auschwitz: What Christian Theology Must Learn from the Rise of Nazism* (Eugene: Cascade Publishers, 2013), 140.

24. August Kubizek, *Adolf Hitler: Mein Jugendfreund* (Graz: Leopold Stocker Verlag, 1953), 114.

25. Paul Hoser, "Hitler und die katholische Kirche. Zwei Briefe aus dem Jahr 1927," *Vierteljahrshefte für Zeitgeschichte* 42, 3 (1994): 489.

26. Otto Wagener, *Hitler—Memoirs of a Confidant*, ed. and trans. Henry Ashby Turner (New Haven: Yale University Press, 1978), 65.

27. Hitler, monologue on February 27, 1942, in Monologe im Führerhauptquartier 1941–1944: Die Aufzeichnungen Heinrich Heims, ed. Werner Jochmann (Hamburg: Albrecht Knaus, 1980), 301–2; see also Hitler, monologue on February 20–21, 1942, in Monologe im Führerhauptquartier 1941-1944: Die Aufzeichnungen Heinrich Heims, ed. Werner Jochmann (Hamburg: Albrecht Knaus, 1980), 285–87.

28. Hitler, monologue on October 24, 1941, in Monologe im Führerhauptquartier 1941–1944: Die Aufzeichnungen Heinrich Heims, ed.Werner Jochmann (Hamburg: Albrecht Knaus, 1980), 105.

29. Hitler, monologue on Feburary 27, 1942, in *Monologe im Führerhauptquartier 1941–1944: Die Aufzeichnungen Heinrich Heims*, ed. Werner Jochmann (Hamburg: Albrecht Knaus, 1980), 301–2.

30. Hitler, speech to Nuremberg Party Congress, September 1935, in Christian Dube, "Religiöser Sprache in Reden Adolf Hitlers: Analysiert an Hand ausgewählter Reden aus den Jahren 1933–1945," (diss., University of Kiel, 2004), 228–29.

31. Hitler, speech on September 6, 1938, in Norman H. Baynes, ed., *The Speeches of Adolf Hitler, April 1922–August 1939*, 2 vols. (Oxford: Oxford University Press, 1942), 1:395–96.

32. Hitler, speech at Nuremberg Party Congress, September 1933, in Christian Dube, "Religiöser Sprache in Reden Adolf Hitlers: Analysiert an Hand ausgewählter Reden aus den Jahren 1933–1945," (diss., University of Kiel, 2004), 199–210.

33. Rainer Zitelmann, *Hitler: Selbstverständnis eines Revolutionärs* (Hamburg: Berg, 1987), 372–77.

34. Rosenberg, diary entry for February 7, 1940, in Alfred Rosenberg Diary, 377, at http://collections.ushmm.org/view/2001.62.14, accessed January 22, 2014; "Ansprache Hitlers vor Generalen und Offizieren am 26. Mai 1944 im Platterhof," in Hans-Heinrich Wilhelm, "Hitlers Ansprache vor

Generalen und Offizieren am 26. Mai 1944," *Militärgeschichtliche Mitteilungen* 2 (1976): 146.

35. Goebbels, diary entry for May 12, 1943, in *Die Tagebücher von Joseph Goebbels*, ed. Elke Fröhlich, part II: *Diktate 1941-1945*, vol. 8: *April-Juni 1943* (Munich K. G. Saur, 1993), 281.

36. Hitler, *Mein Kampf*, trans. Ralph Manheim (Boston: Houghton Mifflin, 1943), 268.

37. Paul Hoser, "Hitler und die katholische Kirche. Zwei Briefe aus dem Jahr 1927," *Vierteljahrshefte für Zeitgeschichte* 42, 3 (1994): 488.

38. Cardinal Michael Faulhaber, "Bericht Faulhabers über eine Unterredung mit Hitler," November 4–5, 1936, in *Akten Kardinal Michael von Faulhabers, 1917–1945*, vol. 2: *1935–1945*, ed. Ludwig Volk (Mainz: Matthias-Grünewald, 1978), 2:187.

39. Goebbels, diary entry for April 23, 1940, in *Die Tagebücher von Joseph Goebbels*, ed. Elke Fröhlich, part I: *Aufzeichnungen 1923–1941*, vol. 8: *April–November 1940* (Munich K. G. Saur, 1998), 69.

40. Hitler, monologue on November 11, 1941, in *Monologe im Führerhauptquartier 1941–1944: Die Aufzeichnungen Heinrich Heims*, ed. Werner Jochmann (Hamburg: Albrecht Knaus, 1980), 135; see also Hitler, monologue on October 14, 1941, in *Monologe im Führerhauptquartier 1941–1944: Die Aufzeichnungen Heinrich Heims*, ed. Werner Jochmann (Hamburg: Albrecht Knaus, 1980), 84–85.

41. Michael Burleigh, *Sacred Causes: Religion and Politics from the European Dictators to Al Qaeda* (New York: Harper Collins, 2006), 100; for a similar view, see Rainer Bucher, *Hitler's Theology: A Study in Political Religion*, trans. Rebecca Pohl (London: Continuum, 2011), 26.

42. Hitler, monologue on October 24, 1941, in *Monologe im Führerhauptquartier 1941–1944: Die Aufzeichnungen Heinrich Heims*, ed. Werner Jochmann (Hamburg: Albrecht Knaus, 1980), 102–3.

43. Walter Schellenberg, *The Schellenberg Memoirs*, ed. Louis Hagen (London: Andre Deutsch, 1956), 112.

44. Hitler, New Year's Proclamation, January 1, 1943, in Max Domarus, *The Complete Hitler: A Digital Desktop Reference to His Speeches and Proclamations, 1932–1945* (Wauconda: Bolchazy-Carducci Publishers, 2007), 4:2737.

45. Albert Speer, *Inside the Third Reich*, trans. Richard and Clara Winston (New York: Avon Books, 1970), 605.

46. Hitler, monologue on April 9, 1942, in *Hitlers Tischgespräche im Führerhauptquartier*, ed. Henry Picker (Frankfurt: Ullstein, 1989), 210.

47. Hitler monolgue on December 13, 1941, in *Monologe im Führerhauptquartier 1941–1944: Die Aufzeichnungen Heinrich Heims*, ed. Werner Jochmann (Hamburg: Albrecht Knaus, 1980), 150–51.

48. Hitler monologue on February 17, 1942, in *Monologe im Führerhauptquartier 1941–1944: Die Aufzeichnungen Heinrich Heims*, ed. Werner Jochmann (Hamburg: Albrecht Knaus, 1980), 279.

49. Hitler, monologue on February 26, 1942, in *Monologe im Führerhauptquartier 1941–1944: Die Aufzeichnungen Heinrich Heims*, ed. Werner Jochmann (Hamburg: Albrecht Knaus, 1980), 297.

50. Hitler, *Mein Kampf*, trans. Ralph Manheim (Boston: Houghton Mifflin, 1943), 131.

51. Hitler, *Mein Kampf*, trans. Ralph Manheim (Boston: Houghton Mifflin, 1943), 306.

52. Hitler, monologue on November 11, 1941, in *Monologe im Führerhauptquartier 1941–1944: Die Aufzeichnungen Heinrich Heims*, ed. Werner Jochmann (Hamburg: Albrecht Knaus, 1980),135.

53. Hitler, monologue on December 13, 1941, in *Monologe im Führerhauptquartier 1941–1944: Die Aufzeichnungen Heinrich Heims*, ed. Werner Jochmann (Hamburg: Albrecht Knaus, 1980), 150–51.

54. Hitler, monologue on September 23, 1941, in *Monologe im Führerhauptquartier 1941–1944: Die Aufzeichnungen Heinrich Heims*, ed. Werner Jochmann (Hamburg: Albrecht Knaus, 1980), 67.

55. Detlev Peukert, "The Genesis of the 'Final Solution' from the Spirit of Science," in *Reevaluating the Third Reich*, ed. Thomas Childers and Jane Caplan (New York: Holmes and Meier, 1993), 241–42, quote at 247.

56. Hitler, "Politik, Idee und Organisation," July 4, 1926, in *Hitler: Reden, Schriften, Anordnungen, Februar 1925 bis Januar 1933*, vol. II: *Vom Weimarer Parteitag bus zur Reichstagswahl Juli 1926–Mai 1928*, part 1: *Juli 1926–Juli 1927*, ed. Bärbel Dusik, (Munich: K. G. Saur, 1992–2003), 17.

57. Hitler, "Die deutsche Not und unser Weg," January 15, 1928, in *Hitler: Reden, Schriften, Anordnungen, Februar 1925 bis Januar 1933*, vol. II: *Vom Weimarer Parteitag bus zur Reichstagswahl Juli 1926–Mai 1928*, part 2: *August 1927–May 1928*, ed. Bärbel Dusik, (Munich: K. G. Saur, 1992–2003), 611; see also Hitler, speech on September 13, 1935, in Max Domarus, *The Complete Hitler: A Digital Desktop Reference to His Speeches and Proclamations, 1932–1945* (Wauconda: Bolchazy-Carducci Publishers, 2007), 2:699.

58. Goebbels, diary entry for December 14, 1941, in *Die Tagebücher von Joseph Goebbels*, ed. Elke Fröhlich, Teil II: *Diktate 1941–1945*, Band 2: *Oktober–Dezember 1941* (Munich: K. G. Saur, 1996), 507.

59. Quoted in Thomas Schirrmacher, *Hitlers Kriegsreligion: Die Verankerung der Weltanschauung Hitlers in seiner religiösen Begrifflichkeit und seinem Gottesbild*, 2 vols. (Bonn: Verlag für Kultur und Wissenschaft, 2007), 1:224.

60. Pius XI, *Mit brennender Sorge*, in March 10, 1937 papal encyclical, available online at http://www.vatican.va/holy_father/pius_xi/encyclicals/documents/hf_p-xi_enc_14031937_mit-brennender-sorge_en.html; accessed February 7, 2014.

61. Thomas Schirrmacher, *Hitlers Kriegsreligion: Die Verankerung der Weltanschauung Hitlers in seiner religiösen Begrifflichkeit und seinem Gottesbild*, 2 vols. (Bonn: Verlag für Kultur und Wissenschaft, 2007), 2:22–24.

62. Hitler, speech on February 15, 1933, in Max Domarus, *The Complete Hitler: A Digital Desktop Reference to His Speeches and Proclamations, 1932–1945* (Wauconda: Bolchazy-Carducci Publishers, 2007), 1:253.

63. Hitler, speech on March 23, 1933, in Max Domarus, *The Complete Hitler: A Digital Desktop Reference to His Speeches and Proclamations, 1932–1945* (Wauconda: Bolchazy-Carducci Publishers, 2007), 1:279.

64. Hitler, radio address on October 14, 1933, in Max Domarus, *The Complete Hitler: A Digital Desktop Reference to His Speeches and Proclamations, 1932–1945* (Wauconda: Bolchazy-Carducci Publishers, 2007), 1:369–70.

65. Hitler, speech on April 26, 1942, in Max Domarus, *The Complete Hitler: A Digital Desktop Reference to His Speeches and Proclamations, 1932–1945* (Wauconda: Bolchazy-Carducci Publishers, 2007), 4:2617.

66. Hitler, monologue on July 11–12, 1941, in *Monologe im Führerhauptquartier 1941–1944: Die Aufzeichnungen Heinrich Heims*, ed. Werner Jochmann (Hamburg: Albrecht Knaus, 1980), 40.

67. Hitler, monologue on October 24, 1941, in *Monologe im Führerhauptquartier 1941–1944: Die Aufzeichnungen Heinrich Heims*, ed. Werner Jochmann (Hamburg: Albrecht Knaus, 1980), 105.

68. Hitler, monolgue on Feb. 27, 1942, in *Monologe im Führerhauptquartier 1941–1944: Die Aufzeichnungen Heinrich Heims*, ed. Werner Jochmann (Hamburg: Albrecht Knaus, 1980), 301–2.

69. Hitler, speech in Sonthofen, November 23, 1937, in Max Domarus, *The Complete Hitler: A Digital Desktop Reference to His Speeches and Proclamations, 1932–1945* (Wauconda: Bolchazy-Carducci Publishers, 2007), 2:980–81.

70. Michael Rissmann, *Hitlers Gott: Vorsehungsglaube und Sendungsbewusstsein des deutschen Diktators* (Zürich: Pendo, 2001), 190.

71. Alfred Rosenberg, *The Memoirs of Alfred Rosenberg*, ed. and with commentaries by Serge Lang and Ernst von Schenck, trans. Eric Posselt (Chicago: Ziff-Davis Publishing Co., 1949), 258–59.

72. Hans Frank, *Im Angesicht des Galgens: Deutung Hitlers und seiner Zeit auf Grund eigener Erlebnisse und Erkenntnisse* (Munich-Gräfelfing: Friedrich Alfred Beck Verlag, 1953), 204.

73. Hitler, speech on February 10, 1933, in Max Domarus, *The Complete Hitler: A Digital Desktop Reference to His Speeches and Proclamations, 1932–1945* (Wauconda: Bolchazy-Carducci Publishers, 2007), 1:247.

74. Max Domarus, *The Complete Hitler: A Digital Desktop Reference to His Speeches and Proclamations, 1932–1945* (Wauconda: Bolchazy-Carducci Publishers, 2007), 1:29.

75. Hitler, speech of July 31, 1937, in Max Domarus, *The Complete Hitler: A Digital Desktop Reference to His Speeches and Proclamations, 1932–1945* (Wauconda: Bolchazy-Carducci Publishers, 2007), 2:918.

76. Max Domarus, *The Complete Hitler: A Digital Desktop Reference to His Speeches and Proclamations, 1932-1945* (Wauconda, IL: Bolchazy-Carducci Publishers, 2007), 2:1326-27, n. 163.

77. Hitler, speech on June 6, 1937, in Max Domarus, *The Complete Hitler: A Digital Desktop Reference to His Speeches and Proclamations, 1932–1945* (Wauconda: Bolchazy-Carducci Publishers, 2007), 2:903.

78. Hitler, proclamation on January 1, 1945, in Max Domarus, *The Complete Hitler: A Digital Desktop Reference to His Speeches and Proclamations, 1932–1945* (Wauconda: Bolchazy-Carducci Publishers, 2007), 4:2992.

79. Ian Kershaw, *The 'Hitler Myth': Image and Reality in the Third Reich* (Oxford: Oxford University Press, 1987), 21–25.

80. Hitler, speech on September 7, 1932, in Max Domarus, *The Complete Hitler: A Digital Desktop Reference to His Speeches and Proclamations, 1932–1945* (Wauconda: Bolchazy-Carducci Publishers, 2007), 1:165.

81. Hitler, speech on March 14, 1936, in Max Domarus, *The Complete Hitler: A Digital Desktop Reference to His Speeches and Proclamations, 1932–1945* (Wauconda: Bolchazy-Carducci Publishers, 2007), 2:790.

82. Hitler, speech on June 27, 1937, in Norman H. Baynes, ed., *The Speeches of Adolf Hitler, April 1922–August 1939*, 2 vols. (Oxford: Oxford University Press, 1942), 1:410–11.

83. Hitler, speech on April 9, 1938, in Max Domarus, *The Complete Hitler: A Digital Desktop Reference to His Speeches and Proclamations, 1932–1945* (Wauconda: Bolchazy-Carducci Publishers, 2007), 2:1088–89.

84. Walter Schellenberg, *The Schellenberg Memoirs*, ed. Louis Hagen (London: Andre Deutsch, 1956), 111.

85. Michael Rissmann, *Hitlers Gott: Vorsehungsglaube und Sendungsbewusstsein des deutschen Diktators* (Zürich: Pendo, 2001), 176.

86. Albert Speer, *Inside the Third Reich*, trans. Richard and Clara Winston (New York: Avon Books, 1970), 459.

87. Hitler, speech on January 30, 1945, in Christian Dube, "Religiöser Sprache in Reden Adolf Hitlers: Analysiert an Hand ausgewählter Reden aus den Jahren 1933–1945," (diss., University of Kiel, 2004), 388.

88. Hitler, "Die deutsche Not und unser Weg," January 15, 1928, in *Hitler: Reden, Schriften, Anordnungen, Febraur 1925 bis Januar 1933*, vol. II: *Vom Weimarer Parteitag bus zur Reichstagswahl Juli 1926–Mai 1928*, part 2: *August 1927–May 1928*, ed. Bärbel Dusik (Munich: K. G. Saur, 1992–2003), 611.

89. Hitler, speech on September 7, 1938, in Max Domarus, *The Complete Hitler: A Digital Desktop Reference to His Speeches and Proclamations, 1932–1945* (Wauconda: Bolchazy-Carducci Publishers, 2007), 2:1145; see also Hitler, speech on September 3, 1939, in Max Domarus, *The Complete Hitler: A Digital Desktop Reference to His Speeches and Proclamations, 1932–1945* (Wauconda: Bolchazy-Carducci Publishers, 2007), 3:1783.

90. Hitler, monologue on February 27, 1942, in *Monologe im Führerhauptquartier 1941–1944: Die Aufzeichnungen Heinrich Heims*, ed. Werner Jochmann (Hamburg: Albrecht Knaus, 1980), 301–2.

91. Hitler, monologue on August 20, 1942, in *Monologe im Führerhauptquartier 1941–1944: Die Aufzeichnungen Heinrich Heims*, ed. Werner Jochmann (Hamburg: Albrecht Knaus, 1980), 354.

92. Hitler, monologue on February 20, 1938, in Max Domarus, *The Complete Hitler: A Digital Desktop Reference to His Speeches and Proclamations, 1932–1945* (Wauconda: Bolchazy-Carducci Publishers, 2007), 2:1021.

93. "Hitler vor Bauarbeitern in Berchtesgaden über nationalsozialistische Wirtschaftspolitik am 20. Mai 1937," in Adolf Hitler,*"Es spricht der Führer": 7 exemplarische Hitler-Reden*, ed. Hildegard von Kotze and Helmut Krausnick (Gütersloh: Sigbert Mohn Verlag, 1966), 217.

94. Hitler, monologue on January 1, 1944, in Max Domarus, *The Complete Hitler: A Digital Desktop Reference to His Speeches and Proclamations, 1932–1945* (Wauconda: Bolchazy-Carducci Publishers, 2007), 4:2861.

95. Hitler, speech on May 1, 1933, in Max Domarus, *The Complete Hitler: A Digital Desktop Reference to His Speeches and Proclamations, 1932-1945* (Wauconda, IL: Bolchazy-Carducci Publishers, 2007), 1:316.

96. Hitler, speech at Nuremberg Party Congress, 1935, in Christian Dube, "Religiöser Sprache in Reden Adolf Hitlers: Analysiert an Hand ausgewählter Reden aus den Jahren 1933–1945," (diss., University of Kiel, 2004), 231.

97. Hitler, "Rede im Sportpalast 1940," in Christian Dube, "Religiöser Sprache in Reden Adolf Hitlers: Analysiert an Hand ausgewählter Reden aus den Jahren 1933–1945," (diss., University of Kiel, 2004), 326, 330.

98. Hitler, speech on July 4, 1944, in Max Domarus, *The Complete Hitler: A Digital Desktop Reference to His Speeches and Proclamations, 1932–1945* (Wauconda: Bolchazy-Carducci Publishers, 2007), 4:2911.

99. Hitler, *Mein Kampf*, trans. Ralph Manheim (Boston: Houghton Mifflin, 1943), 627, 683.

100. Hitler, speech on September 6, 1938, in Max Domarus, *The Complete Hitler: A Digital Desktop Reference to His Speeches and Proclamations, 1932–1945* (Wauconda: Bolchazy-Carducci Publishers, 2007), 2:1147. I have modified the translation slightly to reflect the original German better; see the German edition of Domarus for the German original.

101. Hitler, New Years' Proclamation on January 1, 1940, in Max Domarus, *The Complete Hitler: A Digital Desktop Reference to His Speeches and Proclamations, 1932–1945* (Wauconda: Bolchazy-Carducci Publishers, 2007), 3:1911–12. Unfortunately, the English translation of this interpolates the word "intervention" in this sentence, which is absent from the German original.

102. Hitler, monologue on January 17–18, 1942, in *Monologe im Führerhauptquartier 1941–1944: Die Aufzeichnungen Heinrich Heims*, ed. Werner Jochmann (Hamburg: Albrecht Knaus, 1980), 210.

103. Hitler, speech on March 10, 1940, in Max Domarus, *The Complete Hitler: A Digital Desktop Reference to His Speeches and Proclamations, 1932–1945* (Wauconda: Bolchazy-Carducci Publishers, 2007), 3:1952.

104. Hitler, speech on January 30, 1943, in Max Domarus, *The Complete Hitler: A Digital Desktop Reference to His Speeches and Proclamations, 1932–1945* (Wauconda: Bolchazy-Carducci Publishers, 2007), 4:2749–50.

FOUR: WAS HITLER A CHRISTIAN?

1. Miles Ecclesiae [pseudonym of Karl Spiecker], *Hitler gegen Christus: Eine katholische Klarstellung und Abwehr* (Paris: Societe d'editions europeennes, 1936), 34; on Spiecker's opposition to Nazism, see also *Confronting the Nazi War on Christianity: The Kulturkampf Newsletters, 1936-1939*, ed. Richard Bonney (Bern: Peter Lang, 2009). Another contemporary of Hitler portraying him as anti-Christian is Waldemar Gurian, *Hitler and the Christians* (London: Sheed and Ward, 1936).

2. Robert P. Ericksen, *Complicity in the Holocaust: Churches and Universities in Nazi Germany* (Cambridge: Cambridge University Press, 2012), 46.

3. Heinrich Hoffmann, *Hitler wie ihn keiner kennt. 100 Bilddokumente aus dem Leben des Führers* (Berlin: Zeitgeschichte-Verlag, 1935), 57; Hoffmann, *Hitler wie ihn keiner kennt. 100 Bilddokumente aus dem Leben des Führers* (Berlin: Zeitgeschichte-Verlag, 1938), 73. I contacted the Hoffmann Photoarchive via e-mail and was informed that the cross is on the original negative.

4. Neil Gregor, *How to Read Hitler* (New York: Norton, 2005), 77; see also Rainer Bucher, *Hitler's Theology: A Study in Political Religion*, trans. Rebecca Pohl (London: Continuum, 2011), 26.

5. Michael Burleigh, *The Third Reich: A New History* (New York: Hill and Wang, 2000), 255, 259; Michael Burleigh, *Sacred Causes: Religion and Politics from the European Dictators to Al Qaeda* (New York: Harper Collins, 2006), 101; see also Doris Bergen, *Twisted Cross: The German Christian Movement in the Third Reich* (Chapel Hill: University of North Carolina Press, 1996), 1.

6. Robert P. Ericksen, *Complicity in the Holocaust: Churches and Universities in Nazi Germany* (Cambridge: Cambridge University Press, 2012), 46, 53; broadly supporting this position are Friedrich Tomberg, *Das Christentum in Hitlers Weltanschauung* (Munich: Wilhelm Fink, 2012); Claudia Koonz, *The Nazi Conscience* (Cambridge: Belknap Press of Harvard University Press, 2003), 79; Friedrich Meinecke, *The German Catastrophe: Reflections and Recollections*, trans. Sidney B. Fay (Boston: Beacon Press, 1950), 81.

7. Richard Steigmann-Gall, "Christianity and the Nazi Movement: A Response," *Journal of Contemporary History* 42 (2007): 186; Richard Steigmann-Gall, "Rethinking Nazism and Religion: How Anti-Christian Were the 'Pagans'?" *Central European History* 36 (2003): 75–105.

8. Richard Steigmann-Gall, *The Holy Reich: Nazi Conceptions of Christianity, 1919–1945* (Cambridge: Cambridge University Press, 2003), 3, 60, 252–59. Agreeing with Steigmann-Gall's portrayal of Hitler as Christian is Robert Michael, *Holy Hatred: Christianity, Antisemitism, and the Holocaust* (New York: Palgrave Macmillan, 2006), 156–57; however, Michael is not particularly reliable, making such specious claims as that Hitler took regular communion until age 30 (p. 173). For critiques of Steigmann-Gall's position, see Richard Weikart, review of Richard Steigmann-Gall, *The Holy Reich*, in *German Studies Review* 27 (2004): 174–76; the special edition of *Journal of Contemporary History* (vol. 42, no. 1, 2007) devoted to critiques of Steigmann-Gall; and Mark Edward Ruff, "The Nazis' *Religionspolitik*: An Assessment of Recent Literature," *The Catholic Historical Review*, 92 (2006), 252–66.

9. "Programme of the NSDAP, 1920," in *The Third Reich and the Christian Churches*, ed. Peter Matheson (Grand Rapids: William B. Eerdmans, 1981), 1.

10. Samuel Koehne, "Nazism and Religion: The Problem of 'Positive Christianity,'" *Australian Journal of Politics and History* 60 (2014): 28–42.

11. Samuel Koehne, "The Racial Yardstick: 'Ethnotheism' and Official Nazi Views on Religion," *German Studies Review* 37 (2014): 575–96.

12. Richard Steigmann-Gall, *The Holy Reich: Nazi Conceptions of Christianity, 1919–1945* (Cambridge: Cambridge University Press, 2003), 14.

13. On Hitler's appeal to Protestants in Munich, see Björn Mensing, "'Hitler hat eine göttliche Sendung,': Münchens Protestantismus und der Nationalsozialismus," in *Irrlicht im leuchtenden München? Der Nationalsozialismus in der "Hauptstadt der Bewegung,"* eds. Björn Mensing and Friedrich Prinz (Regensburg: Friedrich Pustet, 1991), 92–123.

14. Samuel Koehne, "Reassessing *The Holy Reich*: Leading Nazis' Views on Confession, Community and 'Jewish' Materialism," *Journal of Contemporary History* 48 (2013): 423–45.

15. Steigmann-Gall, "Christianity and the Nazi Movement," *Journal of Contemporary History* 42 (2007): 186.

16. *Mein Kampf*, 459.

17. Hitler, "Warum sind wir Antisemiten?" August 31, 1920, in *Hitler: Sämtliche Aufzeichnungen, 1905-1924*, ed. Eberhard Jäckel (Stuttgart: Deutsche Verlags-Anstalt, 1980), 220–21.

18. Hitler, "Wer kann uns retten?" December 8, 1922, in *Hitler: Sämtliche Aufzeichnungen, 1905–1924*, ed. Eberhard Jäckel (Stuttgart: Deutsche Verlags-Anstalt, 1980), 756.

19. Hitler, "Die nationalsozialistische Bewegung und die Beamten und Angestellten," April 6, 1923, in *Hitler: Sämtliche Aufzeichnungen, 1905–1924*, ed. Eberhard Jäckel (Stuttgart: Deutsche Verlags-Anstalt, 1980), 867.

20. Hitler, "Die nationalsozialistische Bewegung und die Beamten und Angestellten," April 6, 1923, in *Hitler: Sämtliche Aufzeichnungen,*

1905–1924, ed. Eberhard Jäckel (Stuttgart: Deutsche Verlags-Anstalt, 1980), 865.

21. Hitler, "Rede auf einer Versammlung des Deutschen Kampfbundes," September 27, 1923, in *Hitler: Sämtliche Aufzeichnungen, 1905–1924*, ed. Eberhard Jäckel (Stuttgart: Deutsche Verlags-Anstalt, 1980), 1018.

22. Hitler, "Regierung und Partei," December 4, 1922, in *Hitler: Sämtliche Aufzeichnungen, 1905–1924*, ed. Eberhard Jäckel (Stuttgart: Deutsche Verlags-Anstalt, 1980), 754.

23. This is also the view of Samuel Koehne, "The Racial Yardstick: 'Ethnotheism' and Official Nazi Views on Religion," *German Studies Review* 37 (2014): 575–96.

24. Hitler, speech on February 24, 1939, in Norman H. Baynes, ed., *The Speeches of Adolf Hitler, April 1922–August 1939*, 2 vols. (Oxford. Oxford University Press, 1942), 1:402.

25. Hitler, speech on October 5, 1937, in Norman H. Baynes, ed., *The Speeches of Adolf Hitler, April 1922–August 1939*, 2 vols. (Oxford: Oxford University Press, 1942), 1:393; also in "Der Führer zur Eröffnung des Winterhilfswerks 1937/38," in Heinrich Hoffman, *Das Führer und das Winterhilfswerk: Bilddokumente* (n.p.: n.d. [probably 1937 or 1938]), 34–36.

26. Goebbels, diary entry on December 28, 1939, in *Die Tagebücher von Joseph Goebbels*, ed. Elke Fröhlich, part I: *Aufzeichnungen 1923–1941*, vol. 7: *Juli 1939–März 1940* (Munich: K. G. Saur, 1998), 248.

27. Hitler, "Die 'Hetzer' der Wahrheit," April 12, 1922, in *Hitler: Sämtliche Aufzeichnungen, 1905–1924*, ed. Eberhard Jäckel (Stuttgart: Deutsche Verlags-Anstalt, 1980), 623.

28. Hitler, speech on December 15, 1925, in *Hitler: Reden, Schriften, Anordnungen, Febraur 1925 bis Januar 1933*, vol. I: *Die Widergründung der NSDAP Februar 1925–Juni 1926*, ed. Clemens Vollnhals (Munich: K. G. Saur, 1992–2003), 237.

29. Hitler, speech on December 19, 1926, in *Hitler: Reden, Schriften, Anordnungen, Febraur 1925 bis Januar 1933*, vol. II: *Vom Weimarer*

Parteitag bus zur Reichstagswahl Juli 1926–Mai 1928, part 1: *Juli 1926–Juli 1927*, ed. Bärbel Dusik (Munich: K. G. Saur, 1992–2003), 106.

30. Hitler, "Der Reichsbanneraufmarsch—ein Erfolg des monarchistischen Gedankens der Bayerischen Volkspartei," May 24, 1927, in *Hitler: Reden, Schriften, Anordnungen, Febraur 1925 bis Januar 1933*, vol. II: *Vom Weimarer Parteitag bus zur Reichstagswahl Juli 1926–Mai 1928*, part 1: *Juli 1926–Juli 1927*, ed. Bärbel Dusik (Munich: K. G. Saur, 1992–2003), 317–18; emphasis in original.

31. Hitler, "Bayer[ische] Volkspartei u[nd] Bayer[ischer] Kurier—Die Stützen von Thron und Altar," February 29, 1928, in *Hitler: Reden, Schriften, Anordnungen, Febraur 1925 bis Januar 1933*, vol. II: *Vom Weimarer Parteitag bus zur Reichstagswahl Juli 1926–Mai 1928*, part 2: *August 1927–May 1928*, ed. Bärbel Dusik (Munich: K. G. Saur, 1992–2003), 695.

32. Hitler, radio speech on February 1, 1933, in Max Domarus, *The Complete Hitler: A Digital Desktop Reference to His Speeches and Proclamations, 1932–1945* (Wauconda: Bolchazy-Carducci Publishers, 2007), 1:233.

33. Hitler, speech on February 15, 1933, in Max Domarus, *The Complete Hitler: A Digital Desktop Reference to His Speeches and Proclamations, 1932–1945* (Wauconda: Bolchazy-Carducci Publishers, 2007), 1:253.

34. Hitler, speech on March 23, 1933, in Max Domarus, *The Complete Hitler: A Digital Desktop Reference to His Speeches and Proclamations, 1932–1945* (Wauconda: Bolchazy-Carducci Publishers, 2007), 1:279, 283.

35. Guenter Lewy, *The Catholic Church and Nazi Germany* (New York: McGraw-Hill, 1964), 33.

36. Many scholars agree with this assessment, including Michael Rissmann in *Hitlers Gott: Vorsehungsglaube und Sendungsbewusstsein des deutschen Diktators* (Zürich: Pendo, 2001), 26–28, 34.

37. Hitler, speech on April 21, 1921, in *Hitler: Sämtliche Aufzeichnungen, 1905–1924*, ed. Eberhard Jäckel (Stuttgart: Deutsche Verlags-Anstalt, 1980), 367.

38. Hitler, interview with *Acht-Uhr-Blatt*, November 11, 1922, in *Hitler: Sämtliche Aufzeichnungen, 1905–1924*, ed. Eberhard Jäckel (Stuttgart: Deutsche Verlags-Anstalt, 1980), 727.

39. Hitler, monologue on November 30, 1944, in *Monologe im Führerhauptquartier 1941–1944: Die Aufzeichnungen Heinrich Heims*, ed. Werner Jochmann (Hamburg: Albrecht Knaus, 1980), 412–13.

40. Hitler, "Warum sind wir Antisemiten?" August 31, 1920, in *Hitler: Sämtliche Aufzeichnungen, 1905–1924*, ed. Eberhard Jäckel (Stuttgart: Deutsche Verlags-Anstalt, 1980), 220–21.

41. Hitler, "Die 'Hetzer' der Wahrheit," April 12, 1922, in *Hitler: Sämtliche Aufzeichnungen, 1905–1924*, ed. Eberhard Jäckel (Stuttgart: Deutsche Verlags-Anstalt, 1980), 623.

42. Hitler, *Mein Kampf*, 307.

43. Hitler, "Positiver Antisemitismus der Bayerischen Volkspartei," November 2, 1922, in *Hitler: Sämtliche Aufzeichnungen, 1905–1924*, ed. Eberhard Jäckel (Stuttgart: Deutsche Verlags-Anstalt, 1980), 718.

44. Hitler, "Politik der Woche," April 13, 1929, in *Hitler: Reden, Schriften, Anordnungen, Februar 1925 bis Januar 1933*, vol. III: *Zwischen den Reichstagswahlen, Juli 1928–September 1930*, part 2: *März 1929–Dezember 1929* (Munich: K. G. Saur, 1992–2003), 200.

45. Hitler, "Rede auf einer NSDAP-Versammlung," December 17, 1922, in *Hitler: Sämtliche Aufzeichnungen, 1905–1924*, ed. Eberhard Jäckel (Stuttgart: Deutsche Verlags-Anstalt, 1980), 769–70.

46. Hitler, speech on December 18, 1926, in *Hitler: Reden, Schriften, Anordnungen, Februar 1925 bis Januar 1933*, vol. II: *Vom Weimarer Parteitag bus zur Reichstagswahl Juli 1926–Mai 1928*, part 1: *Juli 1926–Juli 1927*, ed. Bärbel Dusik (Munich: K. G. Saur, 1992–2003), 105–6; also in *Der Aufstieg der NSDAP in Augenzeugenberichten*, ed. Ernst Deuerlein, 2nd ed. (Düsseldorf: Karl Rauch Verlag, 1968), 266.

47. Hitler, speech on December 11, 1928, in *Hitler: Reden, Schriften, Anordnungen, Februar 1925 bis Januar 1933*, vol. III: *Zwischen den*

Reichstsagswahlen, Juli 1928–September 1930, part 1: *Juli 1928–Februar 1929* (Munich: K. G. Saur, 1992–2003), 350.

48. Hitler, speech on December 18, 1926, in *Aufstieg der NSDAP in Augenzeugenberichten*, 266.

49. Otto Wagener, *Hitler—Memoirs of a Confidant*, ed. and trans. Henry Ashby Turner (New Haven: Yale University Press, 1978), 139–40, 238, quote at 316.

50. Baynes, 1:19.

51. Steigmann-Gall, *Holy Reich*, 37.

52. Friedrich Heer, *Der Glaube des Adolf Hitler: Anatomie einer politischen Religiosität* (Munich: Bechtle Verlag, 1968), 310.

53. Max Domarus, *The Complete Hitler: A Digital Desktop Reference to His Speeches and Proclamations, 1932–1945* (Wauconda: Bolchazy-Carducci Publishers, 2007), 2:959.

54. Alan Bullock, *Hitler and Stalin: Parallel Lives* (New York: Alfred A. Knopf, 1992), 726; Alan Bullock, *Hitler: A Study in Tyranny*, revised ed. (New York: Harper and Row, 1964), 672.

55. Ian Kershaw discusses this shift in Hitler's attitude toward himself in *The 'Hitler Myth': Image and Reality in the Third Reich* (Oxford: Oxford University Press, 1987), 21–25.

56. Derek Hastings, "Faith of the Future Führer? The Evolution of Hitler's Early Religious Identity," paper presented to the German Studies Association Conference, October 6, 2013; Derek Hastings, *Catholicism and the Roots of Nazism: Religious Identity and National Socialism* (Oxford: Oxford University Press, 2010), esp. 181–82; Derek Hastings, "How 'Catholic' Was the Early Nazi Movement? Religion, Race, and Culture in Munich, 1919–1924," CEH 36 (2003): 383–433.

57. Hitler, *Mein Kampf*, 6.

58. Brigitte Hamann, *Hitler's Vienna: A Dictator's Apprenticeship*, trans. Thomas Thornton (New York: Oxford University Press, 1999), 19.

59. Friedrich Heer, *Der Glaube des Adolf Hitler: Anatomie einer politischen Religiosität* (Munich: Bechtle Verlag, 1968), 30.

60. August Kubizek, *Adolf Hitler: Mein Jugendfreund* (Graz: Leopold Stocker Verlag, 1953), 114.

61. Hamann, *Hitler's Vienna: A Dictator's Apprenticeship*, 249–50, 302.

62. Thomas Weber, *Hitler's First War: Adolf Hitler, the Men of the List Regiment, and the First World War* (Oxford: Oxford University Press, 2010), 52, 135–36.

63. Stanley Weintraub, *Silent Night: The Story of the World War I Christmas Truce* (New York: The Free Press, 2001), 71.

64. "'Der NS-Staat trägt etwas vom Gottesstaat in sich': Katholiken über den Aufbau des Dritten Reiches 1933," Der Spiegel (1965), accessed October 1, 2013, http://www.spiegel.de/spiegel/print/d-46169577.html.

65. Goebbels, diary entry for May 19, 1935, in *Die Tagebücher von Joseph Goebbels*, ed. Elke Fröhlich, part I: *Aufzeichnungen 1923–1941*, vol. 3/I: *April 1934–Februar 1936* (Munich: K. G. Saur, 2005), 234.

66. Hitler, monologue on February 27, 1942, in *Monologe im Führerhauptquartier 1941–1944: Die Aufzeichnungen Heinrich Heims*, ed. Werner Jochmann (Hamburg: Albrecht Knaus, 1980), 303.

67. Dietrich, *The Hitler I Knew*, 181–82.

68. Hitler, "Warum sind wir Antisemiten?" August 31, 1920, in *Hitler: Sämtliche Aufzeichnungen, 1905–1924*, ed. Eberhard Jäckel (Stuttgart: Deutsche Verlags-Anstalt, 1980), 191.

69. Rudolf Hess to Ilse Pröhl, August 20, 1924, in *Rudolf Hess Briefe 1908–1933*, ed. Wolf Rüdiger Hess (Munich: Langen Müller, 1987), 350–51.

70. Othmar Plöckinger, *Geschichte eines Buches: Adolf Hitlers "Mein Kampf" 1922–1945* (Munich: R. Oldernbourg, 2006), 82–84.

71. Hitler, *Mein Kampf*, 403.

72. Ibid., 454–55.

73. Otto Wagener, *Hitler—Memoirs of a Confidant*, ed. and trans. Henry Ashby Turner (New Haven: Yale University Press, 1978), 65, 139–40, 316.

74. Ibid.

75. Wagener, *Hitler—Memoirs of a Confidant*, 224.

76. Alfred Rosenberg, *The Memoirs of Alfred Rosenberg*, ed. and with commentaries by Serge Lang and Errnst von Schenck, trans. Eric Posselt (Chicago: Ziff-Davis Publishing Co., 1949), 259.

77. Hans Severus Ziegler, *Adolf Hitler aus dem Erleben dargestellt* 3rd ed. (Göttingen: Verlag K. W. Schütz: Göttingen, 1965), 119–20.

78. Goebbels, diary entry on September 12, 1931, in *Die Tagebücher von Joseph Goebbels*, ed. Elke Fröhlich, part I: *Aufzeichnungen 1923–1941*, vol. 2/II: *Juni 1931–September 1932* (Munich: K. G. Saur, 2004), 96.

79. Goebbels, diary entry for January 5, 1937, in *Die Tagebücher von Joseph Goebbels*, ed. Elke Fröhlich, part I: *Aufzeichnungen 1923–1941*, vol. 3/II: *März 1936–Februar 1937* (Munich: K. G. Saur, 2001), 316.

80. Goebbels, diary entry for December 13, 1941, in *Die Tagebücher von Joseph Goebbels*, ed. Elke Fröhlich, part II: *Diktate 1941–1945*, vol. 2: *Oktober–Dezember 1941* (Munich: K. G. Saur, 1996), 498–500.

81. Alfred Rosenberg, diary, entry for December 14, 1941, 625, accessed January 22, 2014 http://collections.ushmm.org/view/2001.62.14.

82. Christa Schroeder, *Er War Mein Chef: Aus dem Nachlass der Sekretärin von Adolf Hitler*, ed. Anton Jaochimsthaler, 2nd ed. (Munich: Langen Müller, 1985), 120.

83. Goebbels, diary entry for April 29, 1941, in *Die Tagebücher von Joseph Goebbels*, ed. Elke Fröhlich, part I: *Aufzeichnungen 1923–1941*, vol. 9: *Dezember 1940–Juli 1941* (Munich: K. G. Saur, 1998), 279–80.

84. Goebbels, diary entry for December 13, 1941, in *Die Tagebücher von Joseph Goebbels*, ed. Elke Fröhlich, part II: *Diktate 1941–1945*, vol. 2: *Oktober–Dezember 1941* (Munich: K. G. Saur, 1996), 499–500.

85. Hans Frank, *Im Angesicht des Galgens: Deutung Hitlers und seiner Zeit auf Grund eigener Erlebnisse und Erkenntnisse* (Munich-Gräfelfing: Friedrich Alfred Beck Verlag, 1953), 204.

86. Dietrich, *The Hitler I Knew*, 154.

87. Ibid.,156.

88. Speer, *Inside the Third Reich*, 141–43, 175.

89. Hitler, monologue on April 4, 1942, in *Hitlers Tischgespräche*, 184.

90. Hitler, monologue on November 11, 1941, in *Monologe im Führerhauptquartier 1941–1944: Die Aufzeichnungen Heinrich Heims,* ed. Werner Jochmann (Hamburg: Albrecht Knaus, 1980), 134; and monologue on March 31, 1942, in *Hitlers Tischgespräche,* 173.

91. Hitler, monologue on February 27, 1942, in *Monologe im Führerhauptquartier 1941–1944: Die Aufzeichnungen Heinrich Heims,* ed. Werner Jochmann (Hamburg: Albrecht Knaus, 1980), 303.

92. Hitler, monologue on December 13, 1941, in *Monologe im Führerhauptquartier 1941–1944: Die Aufzeichnungen Heinrich Heims,* ed. Werner Jochmann (Hamburg: Albrecht Knaus, 1980), 150.

93. Hitler, monologue on December 13, 1941, in *Monologe im Führerhauptquartier 1941–1944: Die Aufzeichnungen Heinrich Heims,* ed. Werner Jochmann (Hamburg: Albrecht Knaus, 1980), 150–51; and monologue on April 4, 1942 in *Hitlers Tischgespräche,* 184.

94. Hitler, monologue on December 13, 1941, in *Monologe im Führerhauptquartier 1941-1944: Die Aufzeichnungen Heinrich Heims,* ed. Werner Jochmann (Hamburg: Albrecht Knaus, 1980),150.

95. Hitler, monologue on February 27, 1942, in *Monologe im Führerhauptquartier 1941–1944: Die Aufzeichnungen Heinrich Heims,* ed. Werner Jochmann (Hamburg: Albrecht Knaus, 1980), 301–2.

96. Hitler, monologue on December 13, 1941, in *Monologe im Führerhauptquartier 1941–1944: Die Aufzeichnungen Heinrich Heims,* ed. Werner Jochmann (Hamburg: Albrecht Knaus, 1980), 150–51. Dietrich Eckart had previously bashed Paul in Dietrich Eckart, *Der Bolschewismus von Moses bis Lenin. Zwiegespräch zwischen Adolf Hitler und mir* (Munich: Hoheneichen Verlag, 1924), 26–29, 199, 203.

97. Hitler, monologue on February 17, 1942, in *Monologe im Führerhauptquartier 1941–1944: Die Aufzeichnungen Heinrich Heims,* ed. Werner Jochmann (Hamburg: Albrecht Knaus, 1980), 279.

98. Hitler, monologue on July 5, 1942, in *Hitlers Tischgespräche,* 422.

99. Hitler, monologue on November 30, 1944, in *Monologe im Führerhauptquartier 1941–1944: Die Aufzeichnungen Heinrich Heims*, ed. Werner Jochmann (Hamburg: Albrecht Knaus, 1980), 412–13.

100. Goebbels, April 8, 1941, in *Die Tagebücher von Joseph Goebbels*, ed. Elke Fröhlich, part I: *Aufzeichnungen 1923–1941*, vol. 9: *Dezember 1940–Juli 1941* (Munich: K. G. Saur, 1998), 234; Alfred Rosenberg Diary, entry for April 9, 1941, 531, accessed January 22, 2014, http://collections.ushmm.org/view/2001.62.14.

101. Hitler, monologue on July 11–12, 1941, in *Monologe im Führerhauptquartier 1941–1944: Die Aufzeichnungen Heinrich Heims*, ed. Werner Jochmann (Hamburg: Albrecht Knaus, 1980), 41.

102. Hitler, monologue on January 27, 1942, in *Monologe im Führerhauptquartier 1941–1944: Die Aufzeichnungen Heinrich Heims*, ed. Werner Jochmann (Hamburg: Albrecht Knaus, 1980), 236.

103. *Der Scheiterhaufen: Worte grosser Ketzer*, ed. Kurt Eggers (Dortmund: Im Volkschaft-Verlag, 1941).

104. Hitler, monologues on October 21 and 25, 1941, in *Monologe im Führerhauptquartier 1941–1944: Die Aufzeichnungen Heinrich Heims*, ed. Werner Jochmann (Hamburg: Albrecht Knaus, 1980), 96–98, 106.

105. Hitler, "Appell an die deutsche Kraft," August 4, 1929, in *Hitler: Reden, Schriften, Anordnungen, Febraur 1925 bis Januar 1933*, vol. III: *Zwischen den Reichstsagswahlen, Juli 1928–September 1930*, part 2: *März 1929–Dezember 1929* (Munich: K. G. Saur, 1992–2003), 351; Reinhard Müller, "Hitlers Rede vor der Reichswehrführung 1933: Eine neue Moskauer Überlieferung," *Mittelweg 36*, 1 (2001), 77.

106. Hitler, "Hossbach Memo," November 5, 1937, in Max Domarus, *The Complete Hitler: A Digital Desktop Reference to His Speeches and Proclamations, 1932–1945* (Wauconda: Bolchazy-Carducci Publishers, 2007), 2: 966.

107. Hitler, *Mein Kampf*, 213.

108. Wagener, *Hitler—Memoirs of a Confidant*, 20–21.

109. Hitler, "Hitler vor Offizieren und Offiziersanwärtern am 15. Februar 1942," in *"Es spricht der Führer": 7 exemplarische Hitler-Reden*, ed. Hildegard von Kotze and Helmut Krausnick (Gütersloh: Sigbert Mohn Verlag, 1966), 311.

110. Hitler, *Mein Kampf,* 562–65.

111. Hitler, monologue on July 21, 1941, in *Monologe im Führerhauptquartier 1941–1944: Die Aufzeichnungen Heinrich Heims,* ed. Werner Jochmann (Hamburg: Albrecht Knaus, 1980), 42–43.

112. Hitler, monologue on December 14, 1941, in *Monologe im Führerhauptquartier 1941–1944: Die Aufzeichnungen Heinrich Heims,* ed. Werner Jochmann (Hamburg: Albrecht Knaus, 1980), 152.

113. Alfred Rosenberg Diary, entry for December 14, 1941, 627–29, accessed January 22, 2014, http://collections.ushmm.org/view/2001.62.14. Rosenberg's account confirms the account given in the monologues.

114. Hans Frank, *Im Angesicht des Galgens: Deutung Hitlers und seiner Zeit auf Grund eigener Erlebnisse und Erkenntnisse* (Munich-Gräfelfing: Friedrich Alfred Beck Verlag, 1953), 46, 238, 294.

115. Hitler, "Warum sind wir Antisemiten?" August 31, 1920, in *Hitler: Sämtliche Aufzeichnungen, 19051924,* ed. Eberhard Jäckel (Stuttgart: Deutsche Verlags-Anstalt, 1980), 187.

116. Hitler, speech on December 11, 1941, in Max Domarus, *The Complete Hitler: A Digital Desktop Reference to His Speeches and Proclamations, 19321945* (Wauconda: Bolchazy-Carducci Publishers, 2007), 4:2543.

117. Otto Wagener, Hitler—*Memoirs of a Confidant,* ed. and trans. Henry Ashby Turner (New Haven: Yale University Press, 1978), 206.

118. Hitler, monologue on June 5, 1942, in *Hitlers Tischgespräche im Führerhauptquartier,* ed. Henry Picker (Frankfurt: Ullstein, 1989), 355.

119. Ernst Hanfstaengl, *Unheard Witness* (Philadelphia: J. B. Lippincott, 1957), 147.

120. Goebbels, diary entry for May 12, 1943, in *Die Tagebücher von Joseph Goebbels,* ed. Elke Fröhlich, part II: *Diktate 1941–1945,* vol. 8: *April–Juni 1943* (Munich: K. G. Saur, 1993), 281.

121. Hitler, monologue on December 13, 1941, in *Monologe im Führerhauptquartier 1941–1944: Die Aufzeichnungen Heinrich Heims*, ed. Werner Jochmann (Hamburg: Albrecht Knaus, 1980), 150.

122. Heinz Linge, *Bis zum Untergang: Als Chef des Persönlichen Dienstes bei Hitler*, 2nd ed. (Munich: Herbig, 1980), 131.

123. *The Nazi Primer: Official Handbook for Schooling the Hitler Youth*, ed. Fritz Brennecke, trans. Harwood L. Childs (New York: Harper and Brothers, 1938), 9–10.

124. *Rassenpolitik* (Berlin: Der Reichsführer SS, SS-Hauptamt, n.d.), 3–6.

125. Christa Schroeder, *Er War Mein Chef: Aus dem Nachlass der Sekretärin von Adolf Hitler*, ed. Anton Jaochimsthaler, 2nd ed. (Munich: Langen Müller, 1985), 68–69.

FIVE: DID HITLER WANT TO DESTROY THE CHURCHES?

1. Ernst von Weizsäcker, *Memoirs of Ernst von Weizsäcker*, trans. John Andrews (Chicago: Henry Regnery, 1951), 281.

2. Heinz Boberach, ed., *Berichte des SD und der Gestapo über Kirchen und Kirchenvolk in Deutschland, 1934–1944* (Mainz: Matthias-Grünewald-Verlag, 1971); Wolfgang Dierker, *Himmlers Glaubenskrieger: Der Sicherheitsdienst der SS und seine Religionspolitik, 1933–1941* (Paderborn: Ferdinand Schöningh, 2002).

3. Martin Bormann, "Rundschreiben des Leiters der Parteikanzlei an alle Gauleiter betr. Verhältnis von Nationalsozialismus und Christentum," June 9, 1941, in *Dokumente zur Kirchenpolitik des Dritten Reiches*, vol. 5: *1939–45*, ed. Gertraud Grünzinger and Carsten Nicolaisen (Gütersloh: Gütersloher Verlagshaus, 2008), 5:307.

4. Ernst von Weizsäcker, *Memoirs of Ernst von Weizsäcker*, trans. John Andrews (Chicago: Henry Regnery, 1951), 281.

5. Stephen Strehle, *The Dark Side of Church/State Separation: The French Revolution, Nazi Germany, and International Communism* (New Brunswick: Transaction Publishers, 2013), 123.

6. Heike Kreutzer, *Das Reichskirchenministerium im Gefüge der nationalsozialistischen Herrschaft* (Düsseldorf: Droste Verlag, 2000), 33–34, passim.

7. Dietmar Süss, "Nationalsozialistische Religionspolitik," in *Die katholische Kirche im Dritten Reich: Eine Einführung, ed.* Christoph Kösters and Mark Edward Ruff (Freiburg im Breisgau: Herder Verlag, 2011), 50–63.

8. Richard Steigmann-Gall, "Religion and the Churches," in *Nazi Germany: The Short Oxford History of Germany*, ed. Jane Caplan (Oxford: Oxford University Press, 2008), 166.

9. Dietrich, *The Hitler I Knew*, 155.

10. Ernst von Weizsäcker, *Memoirs of Ernst von Weizsäcker*, trans. John Andrews (Chicago: Henry Regnery, 1951), 281.

11. Hitler, monologue on July 11–12, 1941, in *Monologe im Führerhauptquartier 1941–1944: Die Aufzeichnungen Heinrich Heims*, ed. Werner Jochmann (Hamburg: Albrecht Knaus, 1980), 40–41.

12. John Conway, *The Nazi Persecution of the Churches, 1933–45* (New York: Basic Books, 1968), 5.

13. Roman Bleistein, "Abt Alban Schachleiter, OSB: Zwischen Kirchentreue und Hitlerkult," *Historisches Jahrbuch* 115 (1995): 174–75; Ernst Hanfstaengl, *Unheard Witness* (Philadelphia: J. B. Lippincott, 1957), 85–87.

14. Kevin Spicer, *Hitler's Priests: Catholic Clergy and National Socialism* (DeKalb: Northern Illinois University Press, 2008), 35–38.

15. Paul Hoser, "Hitler und die katholische Kirche. Zwei Briefe aus dem Jahr 1927," *Vierteljahrshefte für Zeitgeschichte* 42, 3 (1994): 487–92.

16. Heike Kreutzer, *Das Reichskirchenministerium im Gefüge der nationalsozialistischen Herrschaft* (Düsseldorf: Droste Verlag, 2000), 33–34.

17. Doris Bergen, *Twisted Cross: The German Christian Movement in the Third Reich* (Chapel Hill: University of North Carolina Press, 1996), ch. 6.

18. Gerhard Engel, *Heeresadjutant bei Hitler 1938–1943: Aufzeichnugen des Majors Engel*, ed. Hildegard von Kotze (Stuttgart: Deutsche Verlags-Anstalt, 1974), 30–31, 49.

19. "Erklärung Hitlers über sein Fernbleiben vom katholischen Gottesdients," March 21, 1933, in *Dokumente zur Kirchenpolitik des Dritten Reiches*, vol. 1: *Das Jahr 1933* ed. Carsten Nicolaisen, (Munich: Christian Kaiser Verlag, 1971), 1:22–23.

20. Roman Bleistein, "Abt Alban Schachleiter, OSB: Zwischen Kirchentreue und Hitlerkult," *Historisches Jahrbuch* 115 (1995): 178; Kevin Spicer, *Hitler's Priests: Catholic Clergy and National Socialism* (DeKalb: Northern Illinois University Press, 2008), 83.

21. Hitler, monologue on December 13, 1941, in *Monologe im Führerhauptquartier 1941–1944: Die Aufzeichnungen Heinrich Heims*, ed. Werner Jochmann (Hamburg: Albrecht Knaus, 1980), 151–52.

22. Rudolf Morsey, "Ermächtingungsgesetz und Reichskonkordat 1933," in *Die katholische Kirche im Dritten Reich: Eine Einführung, ed.* Christoph Kösters and Mark Edward Ruff (Freiburg im Breisgau: Herder Verlag, 2011), 39–40.

23. "Protokoll der Konferenz der Diözesanvertreter in Berlin," April 25–26, 1933, in *Katholische Kirche und Nationalsozialismus: Dokumente*, ed. Hans Müller (Munich: Deutscher Taschenbuch Verlag, 1965), 128–30; "Aktennotiz ohne Unterschrift," June 7, 1933, in *Akten zur deutschen auswärtigen Politik 1918–1945: Aus dem Archiv des deutschen Auswärtigen Amtes*, ed. Hans Rothfels et al, Serie C: *1933–1937: Das Dritte Reich: Die ersten Jahre*, vol. 1, part 1: *30. Januar bis 15. Mai 1933* (Göttingen: Vandenhoeck und Ruprecht, 1971), 344–45.

24. Hitler to Cardinal Bertram, April 28, 1933, in *Akten zur deutschen auswärtigen Politik 1918–1945: Aus dem Archiv des deutschen Auswärtigen Amtes*, ed. Hans Rothfels et al, Serie C: *1933–1937: Das*

Dritte Reich: Die ersten Jahre, vol. 1, part 1: *30. Januar bis 15. Mai 1933* (Göttingen: Vandenhoeck und Ruprecht, 1971), 358.

25. Peter Godman, *Hitler and the Vatican: Inside the Secret Archives that Reveal the New Story of the Nazis and the Church* (New York: Free Press, 2004), 32–33.

26. "Verfügung R. Leys gegen die konfessionellen Arbeitervereine," June 22, 1933, in *Dokumente zur Kirchenpolitik des Dritten Reiches*, vol. 1: *Das Jahr 1933* ed. Carsten Nicolaisen, (Munich: Christian Kaiser Verlag, 1971), 1:66–67.

27. Cardinal Bertram to Hitler, June 25, 1933, in *Katholische Kirche und Nationalsozialismus: Dokumente*, ed. Hans Müller (Munich: Deutscher Taschenbuch Verlag, 1965), 174–75.

28. Abraham Ascher, *Was Hitler a Riddle? Western Democracies and National Socialism* (Stanford: Stanford University Press, 2012), 162–63.

29. *Die Regierung Hitler*, part 1: *1933/34*, vol. 1: *30. Januar bis 31. August 1933*, ed. Karl-Heinz Minuth (Boppard am Rhein: Harald Doldt Verlag, 1983), 683.

30. Concordat, in *The Third Reich and the Christian Churches*, ed. Peter Matheson (Grand Rapids: William B. Eerdmans, 1981), 29–33.

31. *Die Regierung Hitler*, part 1: *1933/34*, vol. 1: *30. Januar bis 31. August 1933*, ed. Karl-Heinz Minuth (Boppard am Rhein: Harald Doldt Verlag, 1983), 683.

32. Franz von Papen, *Memoirs*, trans. Brian Connell (London: Andre Deutsch, 1952), 261, 280.

33. Carsten Kretschmann, "Eine Partie für Pacelli? Die Scholder-Repgen-Debatte," in *Das Reichskonkordat 1933: Forschungsstand, Kontroversen, Dokumente*, ed. Thomas Brechenmacher (Paderborn: Ferdinand Schöningh, 2007), 13.

34. "Hitler Beruft Ludwig Müller zu seinem Bevollmächtigten für die evangelisch Kirche," April 25, 1933, in *Dokumente zur Kirchenpolitik des Dritten Reiches*, vol. 1: *Das Jahr 1933* ed. Carsten Nicolaisen, (Munich: Christian Kaiser Verlag, 1971), 1:42–43.

35. Ernst Christian Helmreich, *The German Churches under Hitler: Background, Struggle, and Epilogue* (Detroit: Wayne State University Press, 1979), 135–40.

36. Ibid.

37. Heinrich Schmid, *Apokalyptisches Wetterleuchten* (Munich: Verlag der Evangelisch-Lutherischen Kirche in Bayern, 1947), 31.

38. Klaus Scholder, *Die Kirchen und das Dritte Reich*, vol. 1: *Vorgeschichte und Zeit der Illusionen 1918–1934* (Frankfurt: Propyläen, 1977), 465–66.

39. Heike Kreutzer, *Das Reichskirchenministerium im Gefüge der nationalsozialistischen Herrschaft* (Düsseldorf: Droste Verlag. 2000), 42.

40. "Gesetz über die Verfassung der Deutschen Evangelischen Kirche," July 14, 1933, in *Dokumente zur Kirchenpolitik des Dritten Reiches*, vol. 1: *Das Jahr 1933* ed. Carsten Nicolaisen, (Munich: Christian Kaiser Verlag, 1971), 1:107–9.

41. Ernst Christian Helmreich, *The German Churches under Hitler: Background, Struggle, and Epilogue* (Detroit: Wayne State University Press, 1979), 140–43.

42. "Rundfunkansprache Hitlers am Vorabend der Kirchenwahlen," July 22, 1933, in *Dokumente zur Kirchenpolitik des Dritten Reiches*, vol. 1: *Das Jahr 1933* ed. Carsten Nicolaisen, (Munich: Christian Kaiser Verlag, 1971), 1:119–21.

43. Kreutzer, *Das Reichskirchenministerium im Gefüge der nationalsozialistischen Herrschaft*, 42.

44. Hitler, monologue on August 29, 1942, in *Monologe im Führerhauptquartier 1941–1944: Die Aufzeichnungen Heinrich Heims*, ed. Werner Jochmann (Hamburg: Albrecht Knaus, 1980), 374.

45. Heike Kreutzer, *Das Reichskirchenministerium im Gefüge der nationalsozialistischen Herrschaft* (Düsseldorf: Droste Verlag, 2000), 45.

46. Goebbels, diary entry on December 8, 1933, in *Die Tagebücher von Joseph Goebbels*, ed. Elke Fröhlich, part I: *Aufzeichnungen 1923–1941*, vol. 2/III: Oktober 1932–März 1934 (Munich: K. G. Saur, 2006), 332.

47. "Aufzeichnung des Reichsministers des Auswärtigen Freiherrn von Neurath," September 20, 1934, in *Akten zur deutschen auswärtigen Politik 1918–1945: Aus dem Archiv des deutschen Auswärtigen Amtes,* ed. Hans Rothfels et al, Serie C: *1933–1937: Das Dritte Reich: Die ersten Jahre,* vol. 3, part 1: *14. Juni bis 31. Oktober 1934* (Göttingen: Vandenhoeck und Ruprecht, 1973), 407.

48. "Schreiben des Chefs der Reichskanzlei an Reichsbischof Müller," July 27, 1941, in *Dokumente zur Kirchenpolitik des Dritten Reiches,* vol. 5: *1939–45,* ed. Gertraud Grünzinger and Carsten Nicolaisen (Gütersloh: Gütersloher Verlagshaus, 2008), 5:317–18.

49. Klaus Scholder, *Die Kirchen und das Dritte Reich,* vol. 2: *Das Jahr der Ernüchterung 1934 Barmen und Rom* (n.p.: Siedler Verlag, n.d.), 2:59.

50. Theophil Wurm, "Der Empfang der Kirchenführer bei dem Reichskanzler in Berlin am 25.1.1934"; Bishop D. Schöffel (Hamburg), "Schreiben des Landesbischofs der Ev.-luth. Kirche im Hamburgischen Staate an Landesbischop Wurm," February 12, 1934; and Martin Niemöller, "Rundschreiben vom 16. Februar 1934," in *Dokumente zur Kirchenpolitik des Dritten Reiches,* vol. 2: *1934/35,* ed. Carsten Nicolaisen (Munich: Christian Kaiser Verlag, 1975), 2:23–29.

51. Conway, *The Nazi Persecution of the Churches,* 74.

52. Bishop Wurm, "Aufzeichnungen," March 13, 1934, in Heinrich Schmid, *Apokalyptisches Wetterleuchten* (Munich: Verlag der Evangelisch-Lutherischen Kirche in Bayern, 1947), 60–62.

53. Klaus Scholder, *Die Kirchen und das Dritte Reich,* vol. 2: *Das Jahr der Ernüchterung 1934 Barmen und Rom* (n.p.: Siedler Verlag, n.d.), 2:333–34, 349.

54. Bishop Wurm, "Den Gemeinden in geeigneter Form bekanntzugeben"; "Bericht Landesbischof Meisers an den bayerischen Ministerpräsidenten," November 2, 1934, in *Dokumente zur Kirchenpolitik des Dritten Reiches,* vol. 2: *1934/35,* ed. Carsten Nicolaisen (Munich: Christian Kaiser Verlag, 1975), 2:196–98.

55. "Reichsstatthalterkonferenz in der Reichskanzlei vom 1. November 1934," in *Die Regierung Hitler*, vol. 2: *1934/35*, part 1: *August 1934–Mai 1935*, ed. Friedrich Hartmannsgruber (Munich: R. Oldenbourg Verlag, 1999), 134.

56. Alfred Rosenberg, diary entry for January 18, 1937, in Alfred Rosenberg Diary, 143, accessed January 22, 2014, http://collections.ushmm.org/view/2001.62.14.

57. Rosenberg, diary entry for January 18, 1937, in Alfred Rosenberg Diary, 145, accessed January 22, 2014, http://collections.ushmm.org/view/2001.62.14; see also Goebbels, diary entry for January 14, 1937, in *Die Tagebücher von Joseph Goebbels*, ed. Elke Fröhlich, part I: *Aufzeichnungen 1923–1941*, vol. 3/II: *März 1936–Februar 1937* (Munich: K. G. Saur, 2001), 328.

58. Rosenberg, diary entry for February 14, 1937, in Alfred Rosenberg Diary, 161–63, accessed January 22, 2014, http://collections.ushmm.org/view/2001.62.14.

59. "Erlass über die Zusammenfassung der Zuständigkeiten des Reichs und Preussens in Kirchenangelegenheiten," July 16, 1935; Lammers, "Vermerk der Reichskanzlei," August 15, 1935, in *Dokumente zur Kirchenpolitik des Dritten Reiches*, vol. 3: *1935–37*, ed. Gertraud Grünzinger and Carsten Nicolaisen (Gütersloh: Christian Kaiser Verlag, 1994), 3:1–3; Heike Kreutzer, *Das Reichskirchenministerium im Gefüge der nationalsozialistischen Herrschaft* (Düsseldorf: Droste Verlag, 2000), 73–79, 322–23; Ernst von Weizsäcker, *Memoirs of Ernst von Weizsäcker*, trans. John Andrews (Chicago: Henry Regnery, 1951), 282.

60. Wolfgang Dierker, *Himmlers Glaubenskrieger: Der Sicherheitsdienst der SS und seine Religionspolitik, 1933–1941* (Paderborn: Ferdinand Schöningh, 2002), 130–31, 535–36; Heinz Boberach, ed., *Berichte des SD und der Gestapo über Kirchen und Kirchenvolk in Deutschland, 1934–1944* (Mainz: Matthias-Grünewald-Verlag, 1971), 901–4.

61. Goebbels, diary entry for January 17, 1940, in *Die Tagebücher von Joseph Goebbels*, ed. Elke Fröhlich, part I: *Aufzeichnungen 1923–1941*, vol. 7:

Juli 1939–März 1940 (Munich: K. G. Saur, 1998), 275; see also Rosenberg, diary entry for January 19, 1940, in Alfred Rosenberg Diary, 361, accessed January 22, 2014, http://collections.ushmm.org/view/2001.62.14.

62. Lammers, "Schreiben des Chefs der Reichskanzlei an den Reichskirchenminister," February 19, 1941, in *Dokumente zur Kirchenpolitik des Dritten Reiches*, vol. 5: *1939–45*, ed. Gertraud Grünzinger and Carsten Nicolaisen (Gütersloh: Gütersloher Verlagshaus, 2008), 5:241.

63. Rosenberg, diary entry for December 14, 1941, in Alfred Rosenberg Diary, 627, accessed January 22, 2014, http://collections.ushmm.org/view/2001.62.14.

64. Rudolf Hess, "Anordnung des Stellvertreters des Führers," January 12, 1934, in *Dokumente zur Kirchenpolitik des Dritten Reiches*, vol. 2: *1934/35*, ed. Carsten Nicolaisen (Munich: Christian Kaiser Verlag, 1975), 2: 10–11.

65. Goebbels, diary entry for February 9, 1937, in *Die Tagebücher von Joseph Goebbels*, ed. Elke Fröhlich, part I: *Aufzeichnungen 1923–1941*, vol. 3/ II: *März 1936–Februar 1937* (Munich: K. G. Saur, 2001), 365.

66. Martin Bormann to Reichsschatzmeister der NSDAP, July 14, 1939, in United States Holocaust Memorial Museum Archives, Alfred Rosenberg Correspondence, Lena Fishman Collection, RG-06.022.01*1; also in *Dokumente zur Kirchenpolitik des Dritten Reiches*, vol. 4: *1937–39*, ed. Gertraud Grünzinger and Carsten Nicolaisen (Gütersloh: Christian Kaiser/ Gütersloher Verlagshaus, 2000), 4: 369.

67. Bormann, "Anordnung des Stellvertreters des Führers betr. Betätigung in Glaubensgemeinschaften," June 1, 1938, in *Dokumente zur Kirchenpolitik des Dritten Reiches*, vol. 4: *1937–39*, ed. Gertraud Grünzinger and Carsten Nicolaisen (Gütersloh: Christian Kaiser/Gütersloher Verlagshaus, 2000), 4: 209–10.

68. "Erlass des Reichskirchenministers betr. Führung von Bezeichnungen der NSDAP durch kirchliche Vereine und Gruppen," June 3, 1937, in *Dokumente zur Kirchenpolitik des Dritten Reiches*, vol. 4: *1937–39*, ed.

Gertraud Grünzinger and Carsten Nicolaisen (Gütersloh: Christian Kaiser/ Gütersloher Verlagshaus, 2000), 4: 78.

69. Heydrich, "Schreiben des Geheimen Staatspolizeiamtes an die Reichsgemeinde der Deutschen Christen," December 21, 1937, in *Dokumente zur Kirchenpolitik des Dritten Reiches*, vol. 4: *1937–39*, ed. Gertraud Grünzinger and Carsten Nicolaisen (Gütersloh: Christian Kaiser/ Gütersloher Verlagshaus, 2000), 4: 172.

70. Bormann, "Rundschreiben des Stabsleiters des Stellvetreters des Führers," November 11, 1937, in *Dokumente zur Kirchenpolitik des Dritten Reiches*, vol. 4: *1937–39*, ed. Gertraud Grünzinger and Carsten Nicolaisen (Gütersloh: Christian Kaiser/Gütersloher Verlagshaus, 2000), 4: 124.

71. Rosenberg, diary entry for September 17, 1936, in Alfred Rosenberg Diary, 73, accessed January 22, 2014, http://collections.ushmm.org/ view/2001.62.14.

72. Rosenberg, diary entry for November 22, 1936, in Alfred Rosenberg Diary, 115, accessed January 22, 2014, http://collections.ushmm.org/ view/2001.62.14.

73. Conway, *The Nazi Persecution of the Churches, 1933–45*, 212–13; Ernst Christian Helmreich, *The German Churches under Hitler: Background, Struggle, and Epilogue* (Detroit: Wayne State University Press, 1979), 213–14.

74. Gerhard Engel, diary entry for January 17, 1939, in Gerhard Engel, *Heeresadjutant bei Hitler 1938–1943: Aufzeichnugen des Majors Engel*, ed. Hildegard von Kotze (Stuttgart: Deutsche Verlags-Anstalt, 1974), 43–44.

75. Conway, *The Nazi Persecution of the Churches, 1933–45*, 92.

76. Heinz Boberach, ed., *Berichte des SD und der Gestapo über Kirchen und Kirchenvolk in Deutschland, 1934–1944* (Mainz: Matthias-Grünewald-Verlag, 1971), xli.

77. William Patch, "The Catholic Church, the Third Reich, and the Origins of the Cold War: On the Utility and Limitations of Historical Evidence," *Journal of Modern History* 82 (2010): 405.

78. Hitler, speech on May 1, 1937, quoted in John Conway, *The Nazi Persecution of the Churches, 1933–45* (New York: Basic Books, 1968), 178.

79. H. W. Koch, *The Hitler Youth: Origins and Development 1922–1945* (New York: Stein and Day, 1976), 111, 219.

80. Martin Bormann, "Der Stellvertreter des Führers an den Reichsminister für Wissenschaft, Erziehung und Volksbildung," September 18, 1935, in *Die Regierung Hitler*, vol. 2: *1934/35*, part 1: *August 1934–Mai 1935*, ed. Friedrich Hartmannsgruber (Munich: R. Oldenbourg Verlag, 1999), 794–95.

81. Martin Bormann, "Schreiben des Stellvertreters des Führers an den Staatssekretär im Reichsfinanzministerium," October 22, 1936, in *Dokumente zur Kirchenpolitik des Dritten Reiches*, vol. 3: *1935–37*, ed. Gertraud Grünzinger and Carsten Nicolaisen (Gütersloh: Christian Kaiser Verlag, 1994), 3: 248.

82. Der Reichsminister des Auswärtigen Freiherr von Neurath an den Reichs- und preussischen Minister für Wissenschaft, Erziehung und Volksbildung Rust, February 18, 1937, in *Akten zur deutschen auswärtigen Politik 1918–1945: Aus dem Archiv des deutschen Auswärtigen Amtes*, ed. Hans Rothfels et al, Serie C: *1933–1937: Das Dritte Reich: Die ersten Jahre*, vol. 6, part 1: 1. *November 1936 bis 15. Mai 1937* (Göttingen: Vandenhoeck und Ruprecht, 1981), 481; Aufzeichnung des Gesandten von Bismarck, Auswärtiges Amt, August 27, 1937, in *Akten zur deutschen auswärtigen Politik 1918–1945: Aus dem Archiv des deutschen Auswärtigen Amtes*, ed. Raymond James Sontag, et al, Serie D: *1937–1945*, vol. 1: *Von Neurath zu Ribbentrop (September 1937–September 1938)* (Baden-Baden: Imprimerie Nationale, 1950), 811.

83. Der Reichsminister des Auswärtigen Freiherr von Neurath an den Apostolischen Nuntius in Berlin Monsignore Orsenigo, March 11, 1937, in *Akten zur deutschen auswärtigen Politik 1918–1945: Aus dem Archiv des deutschen Auswärtigen Amtes*, ed. Hans Rothfels et al, Serie C:

1933–1937: Das Dritte Reich: Die ersten Jahre, vol. 6, part 1: 1. *November 1936 bis 15. Mai 1937* (Göttingen: Vandenhoeck und Ruprecht, 1981), 561.

84. Martin Bormann, "Rundschreiben des Stabsleiters des Stellvertreters des Führers betr. Beseitigung konfessioneller Schuleinrichtungen," April 12, 1939, and "Rundschreiben des Stabsleiters des Stellvertreters des Führers betr. Beseitigung des kirchlichen Einflusses in der Jugenderziehung," June 9, 1939, in *Dokumente zur Kirchenpolitik des Dritten Reiches,* vol. 4: *1937–39,* ed. Gertraud Grünzinger and Carsten Nicolaisen (Gütersloh: Christian Kaiser/Gütersloher Verlagshaus, 2000), 4: 348–50, 363–64.

85. "Schreiben des Stellvertreters des Führers an den Reichserziehungsminister betr. Geistliche als Religionslehrer," February 28, 1937, in *Dokumente zur Kirchenpolitik des Dritten Reiches,* vol. 4: *1937–39,* ed. Gertraud Grünzinger and Carsten Nicolaisen (Gütersloh: Christian Kaiser/Gütersloher Verlagshaus, 2000), 4: 18.

86. Conway, *The Nazi Persecution of the Churches, 1933–45,*183.

87. Michael von Faulhaber, "Bericht Faulhabers über eine Unterredung mit Hitler," November 4–5, 1936, in *Akten Kardinal Michael von Faulhabers, 1917–1945,* vol. 2: *1935–1945,* ed. Ludwig Volk (Mainz: Matthias-Grünewald, 1978), 184–94.

88. Goebbels, diary entry for November 10, 1936, in *Die Tagebücher von Joseph Goebbels,* ed. Elke Fröhlich, part I: *Aufzeichnungen 1923–1941,* vol. 3/II: *März 1936–Februar 1937* (Munich: K. G. Saur, 2001), 245.

89. William Patch, "The Catholic Church, the Third Reich, and the Origins of the Cold War: On the Utility and Limitations of Historical Evidence," *Journal of Modern History* 82 (2010): 405.

90. Pius XI, "Mit brennender Sorge," accessed February 7, 2014, http://www.vatican.va/holy_father/pius_xi/encyclicals/documents/hf_p-xi_enc_14031937_mit-brennender-sorge_en.html.

91. Goebbels, diary entries for March 24, April 2, 7, 10, 14, May 26, 27, 28, 29, 1937, in *Die Tagebücher von Joseph Goebbels,* ed. Elke Fröhlich, part

I: *Aufzeichnungen 1923–1941*, vol. 4: *März–November 1937* (Munich: K. G. Saur, 2000), 65, 76, 83–84, 86, 94, 151, 153, 155, 157.

92. Goebbels, diary entry on May 12 and June 22, 1937, in *Die Tagebücher von Joseph Goebbels*, ed. Elke Fröhlich, part I: *Aufzeichnungen 1923– 1941*, vol. 4: *März–November 1937* (Munich: K. G. Saur, 2000), 135, 191.

93. "Vorschlag für eine Note an den Vatikan über die Hinfälligkeit des Reichskonkordats unter Verwendung der Stichworte, die am 11. Juni 1937 vom Auswärtigen Amt gegeben wurden," in *Akten zur deutschen auswärtigen Politik 1918–1945: Aus dem Archiv des deutschen Auswärtigen Amtes*, ed. Raymond James Sontag, et al, Serie D: *1937– 1945*, vol. 1: *Von Neurath zu Ribbentrop (September 1937–September 1938)* (Baden-Baden: Imprimerie Nationale, 1950), 835–37.

94. "Aufzeichnung des Staatssekretärs von Mackensen," September 29, 1937, in *Akten zur deutschen auswärtigen Politik 1918–1945: Aus dem Archiv des deutschen Auswärtigen Amtes*, ed. Raymond James Sontag, et al, Serie D: *1937–1945*, vol. 1: *Von Neurath zu Ribbentrop (September 1937– September 1938)* (Baden-Baden: Imprimerie Nationale, 1950), 814–15.

95. Joe Perry, *Christmas in Germany: A Cultural History* (University of North Carolina Press, 2010), 191–99, 224, 238; Joe Perry, "Nazifying Christmas: Political Culture and Popular Celebration in the Third Reich," *Central European History* 38 (2005): 572–605; and Corey Ross, "Celebrating Christmas in the Third Reich and the GDR: Political Instrumentalization and Cultural Continuity under the German Dictatorships," in Karin Friedrich, ed., *Festive Culture in Germany and Europe from the Sixteenth to the Twentieth Century* (Lewiston: Edwin Mellen Press, 2000), 323–42.

96. *Deutsche Kriegsweihnacht*, 3rd ed. (Munich: Zentralverlag der NSDAP, Franz Eher Verlag, 1943), 150.

97. Hitler, speech on January 30, 1939, in Christian Dube, "Religiöser Sprache in Reden Adolf Hitlers: Analysiert an Hand ausgewählter Reden aus den Jahren 1933–1945" (diss., University of Kiel, 2004), 312–14.

98. Goebbels, diary entries for November 9 and December 28, 1939, in *Die Tagebücher von Joseph Goebbels*, ed. Elke Fröhlich, part I: *Aufzeichnungen*

1923–1941, vol. 7: *Juli 1939–März 1940* (Munich: K. G. Saur, 1998), 188, 248.

99. Goebbels, diary entry for March 7, 1940, in *Die Tagebücher von Joseph Goebbels*, ed. Elke Fröhlich, part I: *Aufzeichnungen 1923–1941*, vol. 8: *April–November 1940* (Munich: K. G. Saur, 1998), 337.

100. "Schreiben des Reichsinnenministers an die Reichsstatthalter und Oberpräsidenten," July 24, 1940, in *Dokumente zur Kirchenpolitik des Dritten Reiches*, vol. 5: *1939–45*, ed. Gertraud Grünzinger and Carsten Nicolaisen (Gütersloh: Gütersloher Verlagshaus, 2008), 5: 177.

101. Goebbels, diary entry for August 5, 1941, in *Die Tagebücher von Joseph Goebbels*, ed. Elke Fröhlich, part II: *Diktate 1941–1945*, vol. 1: *Juli–September 1941* (Munich: K. G. Saur, 1996), 175.

102. Christa Schroeder, *Er War Mein Chef: Aus dem Nachlass der Sekretärin von Adolf Hitler*, ed. Anton Jaochimsthaler, 2nd ed. (Munich: Langen Müller, 1985), 125–26; Goebbels, diary entry for November 30, 1941, in *Die Tagebücher von Joseph Goebbels*, ed. Elke Fröhlich, part II: *Diktate 1941–1945*, vol. 2: *Oktober–Dezember 1941* (Munich: K. G. Saur, 1996), 397; Goebbels, diary entry for March 20, 1942, in *Die Tagebücher von Joseph Goebbels*, ed. Elke Fröhlich, part II: *Diktate 1941–1945*, vol. 3: *Januar–März 1942* (Munich: K. G. Saur, 1994), 513; Goebbels, diary entry for April 26, 1942, in *Die Tagebücher von Joseph Goebbels*, ed. Elke Fröhlich, part II: *Diktate 1941–1945*, vol. 4: *April–Juni 1942* (Munich: K. G. Saur, 1995), 177.

103. Goebbels, diary entry for December 13, 1941, in *Die Tagebücher von Joseph Goebbels*, ed. Elke Fröhlich, part II: *Diktate 1941–1945*, vol. 2: *Oktober–Dezember 1941* (Munich: K. G. Saur, 1996), 499–500.

104. Engel, diary entry on April 4, 1940, in Gerhard Engel, *Heeresadjutant bei Hitler 1938–1943: Aufzeichnugen des Majors Engel*, ed. Hildegard von Kotze (Stuttgart: Deutsche Verlags-Anstalt, 1974), 70, 78–79.

105. Rosenberg, diary entry for December 3, 1939, in Alfred Rosenberg Diary, 335, accessed January 22, 2014, http://collections.ushmm.org/view/2001.62.14; Lewy, *Catholic Church and Nazi Germany*, 236.

106. Doris Bergen, "Between God and Hitler: German Military Chaplains and the Crimes of the Third Reich," in *In God's Name: Genocide and Religion in the Twentieth Century*, ed. Omer Bartov and Phyllis Mack (New York: Berghahn Books, 2001), 123.

107. Engel, diary entry for January 20, 1940, in Gerhard Engel, *Heeresadjutant bei Hitler 1938–1943: Aufzeichnugen des Majors Engel*, ed. Hildegard von Kotze (Stuttgart: Deutsche Verlags-Anstalt, 1974), 71–72.

108. Martin Bormann, "Rundschreiben des Stabsleiters des Stellvertreters des Führers," March 15, 1941, in *Dokumente zur Kirchenpolitik des Dritten Reiches*, vol. 5: *1939–45*, ed. Gertraud Grünzinger and Carsten Nicolaisen (Gütersloh: Gütersloher Verlagshaus, 2008), 5: 263–64.

109. Martin Bormann, "Rundschreiben des Stabsleiters des Stellvertreters des Führers an alle Reichsleiter, Gauleiter und Verbändeführer," March 21, 1941, in *Dokumente zur Kirchenpolitik des Dritten Reiches*, vol. 5: *1939–45*, ed. Gertraud Grünzinger and Carsten Nicolaisen (Gütersloh: Gütersloher Verlagshaus, 2008), 5: 264.

110. Dietmar Süss, "Nationalsozialistische Religionspolitik," in *Die katholische Kirche im Dritten Reich: Eine Einführung, ed.* Christoph Kösters and Mark Edward Ruff (Freiburg im Breisgau: Herder Verlag, 2011), 60.

111. Max Domarus, *The Complete Hitler: A Digital Desktop Reference to His Speeches and Proclamations, 1932–1945* (Wauconda: Bolchazy-Carducci Publishers, 2007), 3:1880.

112. "Meldungen aus dem Reich (Nr. 93), Berlin, June 3, 1940," in Heinz Boberach, ed., *Berichte des SD und der Gestapo über Kirchen und Kirchenvolk in Deutschland, 1934–1944* (Mainz: Matthias-Grünewald-Verlag, 1971), 435.

113. "Meldung wichtiger staatspolizeilicher Ereignisse," in Heinz Boberach, ed., *Berichte des SD und der Gestapo über Kirchen und Kirchenvolk in Deutschland, 1934–1944* (Mainz: Matthias-Grünewald-Verlag, 1971), 554.

114. Kevin Spicer, *Resisting the Third Reich: The Catholic Clergy in Hitler's Berlin* (DeKalb: Northern Illinois University Press, 2004), 3, 178–81.

115. Hitler, monologue on October 25, 1941, in *Monologe im Führerhauptquartier 1941–1944: Die Aufzeichnungen Heinrich Heims*, ed. Werner Jochmann (Hamburg: Albrecht Knaus, 1980), 108; Rosenberg, diary entries for September 14 and December 14, 1941, in Alfred Rosenberg Diary, 617, 625–27, accessed January 22, 2014, http://collections.ushmm.org/view/2001.62.14; Goebbels, diary entry in late November 1941, in *Die Tagebücher von Joseph Goebbels*, ed. Elke Fröhlich, part II: *Diktate 1941–1945*, vol. 2: *Oktober–Dezember 1941* (Munich: K. G. Saur, 1996), 341; diary entry on December 14, 1941, in *Die Tagebücher von Joseph Goebbels*, ed. Elke Fröhlich, part II: *Diktate 1941–1945*, vol. 2: *Oktober–Dezember 1941* (Munich: K. G. Saur, 1996), 506; diary entry for December 2, 1944, in *Die Tagebücher von Joseph Goebbels*, ed. Elke Fröhlich, part II: *Diktate 1941–1945*, vol. 14: *Oktober bis Dezember 1944* (Munich: K. G. Saur, 1996), 327; Beth A. Griech-Polelle, *Bishop von Galen: German Catholicism and National Socialism* (New Haven: Yale University Press, 2002), 88.

116. Hitler, monologue on August 11, 1942, in *Monologe im Führerhauptquartier 1941–1944: Die Aufzeichnungen Heinrich Heims*, ed. Werner Jochmann (Hamburg: Albrecht Knaus, 1980), 337.

117. Hitler, monologue on April 7, 1942, in *Hitlers Tischgespräche im Führerhauptquartier*, ed. Henry Picker (Frankfurt: Ullstein, 1989), 201–3.

118. Hitler, monologue on July 4, 1942, in *Hitlers Tischgespräche im Führerhauptquartier*, ed. Henry Picker (Frankfurt: Ullstein, 1989), 415.

119. Rosenberg, diary entry for December 14, 1941, in Alfred Rosenberg Diary, 627–29, accessed January 22, 2014, http://collections.ushmm.org/view/2001.62.14.

120. John Conway, *The Nazi Persecution of the Churches, 1933–45* (New York: Basic Books, 1968), 224–25, 308–9.

121. Lammers, "Schreiben des Chefs der Reichskanzlei an den Reichskirchenminister," October 4, 1940, in *Dokumente zur Kirchenpolitik des Dritten Reiches*, vol. 5: *1939–45*, ed. Gertraud Grünzinger and Carsten Nicolaisen (Gütersloh: Gütersloher Verlagshaus, 2008), 5: 201–2.

122. Bormann, "Schreiben des Stabsleiters des Stellvertreters des Führers an den Chef der Reichskanzlei," November 1, 1940, in *Dokumente zur Kirchenpolitik des Dritten Reiches*, vol. 5: *1939–45*, ed. Gertraud Grünzinger and Carsten Nicolaisen (Gütersloh: Gütersloher Verlagshaus, 2008), 5: 202–3.

123. Rosenberg, diary entry for September 16, 1940, in Alfred Rosenberg Diary, 471, accessed January 22, 2014, http://collections.ushmm.org/view/2001.62.14.

124. Alexander Rossino, *Hitler Strikes Poland: Blitzkrieg, Ideology, and Atrocity* (Lawrence: University Press of Kansas, 2003), 14.

125. Hitler, meeting on October 2, 1940, in Max Domarus, *The Complete Hitler: A Digital Desktop Reference to His Speeches and Proclamations, 1932–1945* (Wauconda: Bolchazy-Carducci Publishers, 2007), 3:2100–1.

126. Hitler, monologue on December 13, 1941, in *Monologe im Führerhauptquartier 1941–1944: Die Aufzeichnungen Heinrich Heims*, ed. Werner Jochmann (Hamburg: Albrecht Knaus, 1980), 151–52.

127. Dan Kurzman, *A Special Mission: Hitler's Secret Plot to Seize the Vatican and Kidnap Pope Pius XII* (Cambridge: Da Capo Press, 2007), ix–xi, 11–15.

128. Robert A. Ventresca, *Soldier of Christ: The Life of Pope Pius XII* (Cambridge: Harvard University Press, 2013); William Patch, "The Catholic Church, the Third Reich, and the Origins of the Cold War: On the Utility and Limitations of Historical Evidence," *Journal of Modern History* 82 (2010): 410, 413; Michael Phayer, *Pius XII, the Holocaust, and the Cold War* (Bloomington: Indiana University Press, 2008), 28, 71.

129. Richard Steigmann-Gall, "Religion and the Churches," in *Nazi Germany: The Short Oxford History of Germany*, ed. Jane Caplan (Oxford: Oxford University Press, 2008), 166.

130. Rosenberg, diary entry on January 19, 1940, in Alfred Rosenberg Diary, 365, accessed January 22, 2014, http://collections.ushmm.org/view/2001.62.14.

131. Goebbels, diary entry for May 24, 1942, in *Die Tagebücher von Joseph Goebbels*, ed. Elke Fröhlich, part II: *Diktate 1941–1945*, vol. 4: *April–Juni 1942* (Munich: K. G. Saur, 1995), 360.

132. Goebbels, diary entry for August 20, 1942, *Die Tagebücher von Joseph Goebbels*, ed. Elke Fröhlich, part II: *Diktate 1941–1945*, vol. 5: *Juli–September 1942* (Munich: K. G. Saur, 1995), 359–60.

133. Christa Schroeder, *Er War Mein Chef: Aus dem Nachlass der Sekretärin von Adolf Hitler*, ed. Anton Jaochimsthaler, 2nd ed. (Munich: Langen Müller, 1985), 277.

134. Ernst von Weizsäcker, *Memoirs of Ernst von Weizsäcker*, trans. John Andrews (Chicago: Henry Regnery, 1951), 284.

135. Hitler, monologue on October 14, 1941, in *Monologe im Führerhauptquartier 1941–1944: Die Aufzeichnungen Heinrich Heims*, ed. Werner Jochmann (Hamburg: Albrecht Knaus, 1980), 82–83, 85.

136. Rosenberg, diary entry for December 14, 1941, in Alfred Rosenberg Diary, 625–27, accessed January 22, 2014, http://collections.ushmm.org/view/2001.62.14.

137. Martin Bormann, "Schreiben des Stellvertreters des Führers an den Reichsinnenminister betr. Kirchenneubauten," July 28, 1939, in *Dokumente zur Kirchenpolitik des Dritten Reiches*, vol. 5: *1939–45*, ed. Gertraud Grünzinger and Carsten Nicolaisen (Gütersloh: Gütersloher Verlagshaus, 2008), 4: 372.

138. Goebbels, diary entry for June 25, 1943, in *Die Tagebücher von Joseph Goebbels*, ed. Elke Fröhlich, part II: *Diktate 1941–1945*, vol. 8: *April–Juni 1943* (Munich: K. G. Saur, 1993), 528.

139. *Hitlers Städte: Baupolitik im Dritten Reich: Eine Dokumentation*, ed. Jost Dülffer, Jochen Thies, Josef Henke (Cologne: Böhlau Verlag, 1978), 20.

SIX: DID HITLER DERIVE HIS ANTI-SEMITISM FROM CHRISTIANITY?

1. Adolf Hitler, monologues on July 11–12, 1941 and February 17, 1942, in *Monologe im Führerhauptquartier 1941–1944: Die Aufzeichnungen Heinrich Heims*, ed. Werner Jochmann (Hamburg: Albrecht Knaus, 1980), 41, 279.

2. Hitler, *Mein Kampf*, 111, 113.

3. Robert Michael, *Holy Hatred: Christianity, Antisemitism, and the Holocaust* (New York: Palgrave Macmillan, 2006), 1, 154, 183; see also Robert Michael, *A History of Catholic Antisemitism: The Dark Side of the Church* (New York: Palgrave Macmillan, 2008).

4. Richard Steigmann-Gall, "Old Wine in New Bottles? Religion and Race in Nazi Antisemitism," in *Antisemitism, Christian Ambivalence, and the Holocaust*, ed. Kevin P. Spicer (Indianapolis: University Press, 2007), 285–308, quote at 304.

5. Alon Confino, *A World without Jews: The Nazi Imagination from Persecution to Genocide* (New Haven: Yale University Press, 2014); Joachim Riedl, "Der lange Schatten des Kreuzes: Von Golgotha zur Svastika," in *Der Nationalsozialismus als politische Religion*, ed. Michael Ley and Julius H. Schoeps (Bodenheim bei Mainz: Philo Verlagsgesellschaft, 1997), 53–73; Marvin Perry and Frederick Sweitzer, *Antisemitism: Myth and Hate from Antiquity to the Present* (New York: Palgrave Macmillan, 2002); Christine von Braun and Ludger Heid "Vorwort," and Christine von Braun, "Und der Feind ist Fleisch geworden: Der rassistische Antisemitismus," in *Der ewige Judenhass: Christlicher Antijudaismus, Deutschnationale Judenfeindlichkeit, Rassistischer Antisemitismus*, eds. Christine von Braun and Ludger Heid (Berlin: Philo Verlag, 2000), 8–9, 149–213; Susannah Heschel, *The Aryan Jesus: Christian Theologians and the Bible in Nazi Germany* (Princeton: Princeton University Press, 2008).

6. Paul Massing, *Rehearsal for Destruction: A Study of Political Antisemitism in Imperial Germany* (New York: Harper and Brothers, 1949), 75, 77, 82.

7. Arthur Hertzberg, *The French Enlightenment and the Jews* (New York: Columbia University Press, 1968).

8. Stephen Strehle, *The Dark Side of Church/State Separation: The French Revolution, Nazi Germany, and International Communism* (New Brunswick: Transaction Publishers, 2013), 250.

9. Karla Poewe, *New Religions and the Nazis* (New York: Routledge, 2006), 8.

10. Uriel Tal, *Christians and Jews in Germany: Religion, Politics, and Ideology in the Second Reich* (Ithaca: Cornell University Press, 1975), 16, 224–27, 301–5, quote at 226; see also Uriel Tal, "Religious and Anti-Religious Roots of Modern Anti-Semitism," in Uriel Tal, *Religion, Politics, and Ideology in the Third Reich* (London: Routledge, 2004), 171–90.

11. William I. Brustein, *Roots of Hate: Anti-Semitism in Europe before the Holocaust* (Cambridge: Cambridge University Press, 2003), xii–xiii, 44–46, 334–36, and passim.

12. Ibid., 52–54.

13. Olaf Blaschke, *Katholizismus und Antisemitismus im deutschen Kaiserreich* (Göttingen: Vandenhoeck und Ruprecht, 1997), quote at 282.

14. Robert Michael, *Holy Hatred: Christianity, Antisemitism, and the Holocaust* (New York: Palgrave Macmillan, 2006), 114; Wolfgang Gerlach, "Auf dass sie Christen werden: Siebzehnhundert Jahre christlicher Antijudaimus," in *Der ewige Judenhass: Christlicher Antijudaismus, Deutschnationale Judenfeindlichkeit, Rassistischer Antisemitismus*, eds. Christine von Braun and Ludger Heid (Berlin: Philo, 2000), 45–54.

15. Uriel Tal, *Christians and Jews in Germany: Religion, Politics, and Ideology in the Second Reich* (Ithaca: Cornell University Press, 1975), 250–59, quote at 258.

16. Christopher Probst, *Demonizing the Jews: Luther and the Protestant Church in Nazi Germany* (Bloomington: Indiana University Press, 2012); Doris Bergen, *Twisted Cross: The German Christian Movement in the Third Reich* (Chapel Hill: University of North Carolina Press, 1996), ch. 2.

17. Leon Poliakov, *The Aryan Myth: A History of Racist and Nationalist Ideas in Europe* (London: Sussex University Press, 1974), 326.

18. Ludwig Schemann, *Die Rasse in den Geisteswissenschaften: Studien zur Geschichte des Rassengedankens*, vol. 3: *Die Rassenfragen im Schrifttum der Neuzeit*, 2nd ed. (Munich: J. F. Lehmann, 1943 [the first edition was 1931]), 45–46.

19. Wilhelm Marr, *Der Sieg des Judentums über das Germanenthum*, 12th ed. (Bern: Rudolph Costenoble, 1879), 5, 13, quote at 38.

20. Brustein, *Roots of Hate: Anti-Semitism in Europe before the Holocaust*, 131.

21. Tal, *Christians and Jews in Germany: Religion, Politics, and Ideology in the Second Reich*, 246; see also Tal, *Religion, Politics, and Ideology in the Third Reich*, 173.

22. Alfred Rosenberg Diary, entry for September 17, 1936, p. 69, http://collections.ushmm.org/view/2001.62.14; accessed January 22, 2014. Lagarde is also listed as one of the *Wegbereiter und Vorkämpfer für das neue Deutschland*, ed. Wilhelm von Müffling (Munich: J. F. Lehmanns Verlag, 1933), 17.

23. Ulrich Sieg, *Germany's Prophet: Paul de Lagarde and the Origins of Modern Antisemitism*, trans. Linda Ann Marianiello (Waltham: Brandeis University Press, 2013), 267.

24. Paul de Lagarde, *Deutsche Schriften*, 4th ed. (Göttingen: Lüder Horstmann, 1903), 217–18, 228–34; Ulrich Sieg, *Germany's Prophet: Paul de Lagarde and the Origins of Modern Antisemitism*, trans. Linda Ann Marianiello (Waltham: Brandeis University Press, 2013), 61–63, 259, 269–71.

25. Fritz Stern, *The Politics of Cultural Despair: A Study in the Rise of the Germanic Ideology* (Garden City: Anchor Books, 1965), 91–95; Ulrich Sieg, *Germany's Prophet: Paul de Lagarde and the Origins of Modern Antisemitism*, trans. Linda Ann Marianiello (Waltham: Brandeis University Press, 2013), 6–9.

26. Timothy W. Ryback, *Hitler's Private Library: The Books that Shaped His Life* (New York: Alfred A. Knopf, 2008), 56.

27. Theodor Fritsch, *Mein Streit mit dem Hause Warburg: Eine Episode aus dem Kampfe gegen das Weltkapital* (Leipzig: Hammer-Verlag, 1925), Adolf Hitler's Personal Library, Third Reich Collection, United States Library of Congress; Hitler, "10 Jahre Kampf," *Illustrierter Beobachter*, August 3, 1929, in *Hitler: Reden, Schriften, Anordnungen, Februar 1925 bis Januar 1933*, vol. III: *Zwischen den Reichstsagswahlen, Juli 1928–September 1930*, part 2: *März 1929–Dezember 1929* (Munich: K. G. Saur, 1992–2003), 341–42.

28. Hitler to Theodor Fritsch, November 28, 1930, in *Hitler: Reden, Schriften, Anordnungen, Februar 1925 bis Januar 1933*, vol. IV: *Von der Reichstagswahl bis zur Reichspreäsidentenwahl Oktober 1930–März 1932*, part 1: *Oktober 1930–Juni 1931* (Munich: K. G. Saur, 1992–2003), 133.

29. Theodor Fritsch, *Handbuch der Judenfrage*, 27th ed. (Hamburg: Hanseatische Druck- und Verlags-Anstalt, 1910), 238–39; Theodor Fritsch, *Der falsche Gott: Beweismaterial gegen Jahwe*, 11th ed. (Leipzig: Hammer Verlag, 1935), 8, 181–85, 189–90, quote at 114.

30. Tal, *Religion, Politics, and Ideology in the Third Reich*, 175; Tal, *Christians and Jews in Germany: Religion, Politics, and Ideology in the Second Reich*, 226, 266.

31. Christa Schroeder, *Er War Mein Chef: Aus dem Nachlass der Sekretärin von Adolf Hitler*, ed. Anton Jaochimsthaler, 2nd ed. (Munich: Langen Müller, 1985), 65.

32. Dietrich, *The Hitler I Knew*, 163.

33. Rosenberg, diary entry for January 1938, in Alfred Rosenberg Diary, p. 193, http://collections.ushmm.org/view/2001.62.14; accessed January 22, 2014.

34. Hitler, monologue on January 16–17, 1942, in *Monologe im Führerhauptquartier 1941–1944: Die Aufzeichnungen Heinrich Heims*, ed. Werner Jochmann (Hamburg: Albrecht Knaus, 1980), 209.

35. Alfred Rosenberg, ed., *Dietrich Eckart: ein Vermächtnis*, 3rd ed. (Munich: F. Eher Nachf., 1935), 21–22; Raimund Lembert, *Dietrich Eckart: Ein Künder und Kämpfer des Dritten Reiches* (München: Zentralverlag der N.S.D.A.P., 1934), 42–46.

36. Dietrich Eckart, "Das Judentum in und ausser uns" (1919), in *Dietrich Eckart: ein Vermächtnis*, 3rd ed. (Munich: F. Eher Nachf., 1935), 203.

37. Reichspropaganda-Leitung der N.S.D.A.P., *Tatsachen und Lügen um Hitler*, 2nd ed. (Munich: Franz Eher Nachf., n.d. [1932]), 10–11.

38. Dietrich Eckart, *Der Bolschewismus von Moses bis Lenin. Zwiegespräch zwischen Adolf Hitler und mir* (Munich: Hoheneichen Verlag, 1924), 23–32.

39. Dietrich Eckart, "Das Judentum in und ausser uns" (1919), in *Dietrich Eckart: ein Vermächtnis*, 3rd ed. (Munich: F. Eher Nachf., 1935), 195–96.

40. Dietrich Eckart, *Der Bolschewismus von Moses bis Lenin. Zwiegespräch zwischen Adolf Hitler und mir* (Munich: Hoheneichen Verlag, 1924), 18–20. For further analysis of Eckart, see Claus-Ekkehard Bärsch, *Die politische Religion des Nationalsozialismus: die religiöse Dimension der NS-Ideologie in den Schriften von Dietrich Eckart, Joseph Goebbels, Alfred Rosenberg und Adolf Hitler* (Munich: W. Fink, 1998).

41. Dietrich Eckart, *Der Bolschewismus von Moses bis Lenin. Zwiegespräch zwischen Adolf Hitler und mir* (Munich: Hoheneichen Verlag, 1924), 45–49.

42. Michael Kellogg, *The Russian Roots of Nazism: White Émigrés and the Making of National Socialism, 1917–1945* (Cambridge: Cambridge University Press, 2005), 1–2.

43. Timothy W. Ryback, *Hitler's Private Library: The Books that Shaped His Life* (New York: Alfred A. Knopf, 2008), 56.

44. "Die Verleihung des ersten 'Deutschen Nationalpreises für Kunst und Wissenschaft,'" in *Der Parteitag der Arbeit vom 6. bis 13. September 1937: Offizieller Bericht über den Verlauf des Reichsparteitages mit sämtlichen Kongressreden* (Munich: Zentralverlag der NSDAP, Franz Eher Nachf., 1938), 50–51.

45. Alfred Rosenberg, *Letzte Aufzeichnungen: Nürnberg 1945/46*, 2nd ed. (Uelzen: Jomsburg-Verlag, 1996), 15, 29, 273–74.

46. Ibid., 275–77, 294, 297; Rosenberg, personal notes on "Über Religionsunterricht," July 2, 1918, in Alfred Rosenberg, *Schriften aus den Jahren 1917–1921* (Munich: Hoheneichen-Verlag, 1943), 83.

47. Rosenberg, personal notes on "Das Verbrechen der Freimaurerei," 1921, in Alfred Rosenberg, *Schriften aus den Jahren 1917–1921* (Munich: Hoheneichen-Verlag, 1943), 611–12.

48. Rosenberg, personal notes on "Über Religionsunterricht," in Alfred Rosenberg, *Schriften aus den Jahren 1917–1921* (Munich: Hoheneichen-Verlag, 1943), 86–87.

49. Alfred Rosenberg, *Letzte Aufzeichnungen: Nürnberg 1945/46*, 2nd ed. (Uelzen: Jomsburg-Verlag, 1996), 293.

50. Rosenberg, personal notes on "Der Jude," February 7, 1919, in Alfred Rosenberg, *Schriften aus den Jahren 1917–1921* (Munich: Hoheneichen-Verlag, 1943), 97.

51. Alfred Rosenberg, *Wesen, Grundsätze und Ziele der Nationalsozialistischen Deutschen Arbeiterpartei: Das Programm der Bewegung*, 15th ed. (Munich: Zentralverlag der NSDAP, Franz Eher Nachf., 1937) [originally published by Ernst Boepple's Deutsche Volksverlag in 1922], 7–8, 13–15, 20, 27, 56–57.

52. Adolf Hitler, *Mein Kampf*, trans. Ralph Manheim (Boston: Houghton Mifflin, 1943), 119–21.

53. Ibid., 122.

54. Hamann, *Hitler's Vienna: A Dictator's Apprenticeship*, ch. 10; Ian Kershaw, *Hitler, 1889–1936: Hubris* (New York: Norton, 1998), 60–69.

55. Hitler, *Mein Kampf*, 210.

56. Adolf Hitler, letter to Adolf Gemlich, September 16, 1919, in *Hitler: Sämtliche Aufzeichnungen, 1905–1924*, ed. Eberhard Jäckel (Stuttgart: Deutsche Verlags-Anstalt, 1980), 88–90.

57. Adolf Hitler, letter to Konstantin Hierl, July 3, 1920, in *Hitler: Sämtliche Aufzeichnungen, 1905–1924*, ed. Eberhard Jäckel (Stuttgart: Deutsche

Verlags-Anstalt, 1980), 156; Hitler hit on the same themes in his speech on August 7, 1920, in *Hitler: Sämtliche Aufzeichnungen, 1905–1924*, ed. Eberhard Jäckel (Stuttgart: Deutsche Verlags-Anstalt, 1980), 176–77.

58. Adolf Hitler, "Warum sind wir Antisemiten?" August 13, 1920, in *Hitler: Sämtliche Aufzeichnungen, 1905–1924*, ed. Eberhard Jäckel (Stuttgart: Deutsche Verlags-Anstalt, 1980), quote at 190.

59. Adolf Hitler, speech on May 1, 1923, in *Hitler: Sämtliche Aufzeichnungen, 1905–1924*, ed. Eberhard Jäckel (Stuttgart: Deutsche Verlags-Anstalt, 1980), 918.

60. Hitler, *Mein Kampf*, 290.

61. Ibid., 324.

62. Ibid., 52, 57–59, 63, 232, 301–9, 319–20, 325, 661; quotes at 306, 302.

63. Ibid., 311.

64. Ibid., 307.

65. Ibid., 305, 312.

66. Ibid., 58.

67. Adolf Hitler, monologue on December 1–2, 1941, in *Monologe im Führerhauptquartier 1941–1944: Die Aufzeichnungen Heinrich Heims*, ed. Werner Jochmann (Hamburg: Albrecht Knaus, 1980), 148.

68. Adolf Hitler, monologue on November 5, 1941, in *Monologe im Führerhauptquartier 1941–1944: Die Aufzeichnungen Heinrich Heims*, ed. Werner Jochmann (Hamburg: Albrecht Knaus, 1980), 130.

69. Adolf Hitler, monologue on December 1–2, 1941, in *Monologe im Führerhauptquartier 1941–1944: Die Aufzeichnungen Heinrich Heims*, ed. Werner Jochmann (Hamburg: Albrecht Knaus, 1980), 148.

70. Alon Confino, "Why Did the Nazis Burn the Hebrew Bible? Nazi Germany, Representations of the Past, and the Holocaust," *Journal of Modern History* 84 (2012): 369–400; quotes on 372, 387.

71. Richard Weikart, *Hitler's Ethic: The Nazi Pursuit of Evolutionary Progress* (New York: Palgrave Macmillan, 2009), 94–99, explains how Hitler saw the Jews as biologically immoral.

72. Hitler, Mein Kampf, 150.

73. Confino, *A World without Jews: The Nazi Imagination from Persecution to Genocide*, 8, 14.

74. Adolf Hitler, speech on January 30, 1939, in Max Domarus, *The Complete Hitler: A Digital Desktop Reference to His Speeches and Proclamations, 1932–1945* (Wauconda: Bolchazy-Carducci Publishers, 2007), 3:1447.

75. "Ansprache Hitlers vor Generalen und Offizieren am 26. Mai 1944 im Platterhof," in Hans-Heinrich Wilhelm, "Hitlers Ansprache vor Generalen und Offizieren am 26. Mai 1944," *Militärgeschichtliche Mitteilungen* 2 (1976): 141–61, esp. 149, 155–56.

76. Adolf Hitler speaking to Horthy, April 17, 1943, in Max Domarus, *The Complete Hitler: A Digital Desktop Reference to His Speeches and Proclamations, 1932–1945* (Wauconda: Bolchazy-Carducci Publishers, 2007), 4:2779.

77. Steigmann-Gall, "Old Wine in New Bottles? Religion and Race in Nazi Antisemitism," 299–300; Robert Michael, *Holy Hatred: Christianity, Antisemitism, and the Holocaust* (New York: Palgrave Macmillan, 2006), 180.

78. Kershaw, *Hitler, 1936–1945: Nemesis*, 1024–25, n. 121.

SEVEN: WAS HITLER AN OCCULTIST OR PAGANIST?

1. Wilfried Daim, *Der Mann, der Hitler die Ideen Gab: Jörg Lanz von Liebenfels*, 3rd ed. (Vienna: Ueberreuter, 1994).

2. Jackson Spielvogel and David Redles, "Hitler's Racial Ideology: Content and Occult Sources," Simon Wiesenthal Center Annual 3 (1986): 227–46; include other citations.

3. Michael Hesemann, *Hitlers Religion: Die fatale Heilslehre des Nationalsozialismus* (Munich: Pattloch, 2004), 16–21, 441.

4. George L. Mosse, *The Fascist Revolution: Toward a General Theory of Fascism* (New York: Howard Fertig, 1999), 117.

5. Timothy W. Ryback, *Hitler's Private Library: The Books that Shaped His Life* (New York: Alfred A. Knopf, 2008), 143.

6. Eric Kurlander, "Hitler's Monsters: The Occult Roots of Nazism and the Emergence of the Nazi 'Supernatural Imaginary,'" German History 30, 4 (2012): 528–49; see also Eric Kurlander, "The Orientalist Roots of National Socialism?: Nazism, Occultism, and South Asian Spirituality, 1919–1945," in *Transcultural Encounters Between Germany and India* (Routledge, forthcoming), 155–69.

7. Wilfried Daim, *Der Mann, der Hitler die Ideen Gab: Jörg Lanz von Liebenfels*, 3rd ed. (Vienna: Ueberreuter, 1994), 21–22, 27–29, and passim. Brigitte Hamann also expresses caution about believing Lanz's claim to have met Hitler in *Hitler's Vienna: A Dictator's Apprenticeship*, trans. Thomas Thornton (New York: Oxford University Press, 1999), 221.

8. The best scholarly treatment of Lanz is Nicholas Goodrick-Clarke, *The Occult Roots of Nazism: Secret Aryan Cults and Their Influence on Nazi Ideology* (New York: New York University Press, 1992).

9. Andrew G. Whiteside, *The Socialism of Fools: Georg Ritter von Schönerer and Austrian Pan-Germanism* (Berkeley: University of California Press, 1975), 253–54.

10. Helmut Zander, "Sozialdarwinistische Rassentheorien aus dem okkulten Untergrund," in *Handbuch zur "Völkischen Bewegung" 1871–1918*, ed. Uwe Puschner, Walter Schmitz, and Justus H. Ulbricht (Munich: K. G. Saur, 1996), 229–33.

11. Jörg Lanz-Liebenfels, "Politische Anthropologie," Das freie Wort 3 (1903–4): 778–82.

12. Ludwig Woltmann, *Politische Anthropologie: Eine Untersuchung über den Einfluss der Deszendenztheorie auf die Lehre von der politischen Entwicklung der Völker* (Jena: Eugen Diederichs, 1903), 254 and passim. See also my discussion of Woltmann in *From Darwin to Hitler*, 119–22; and *Hitler's Ethic*, 12–13.

13. Jörg Lanz von Liebenfels, "Adolf Harpf als Prediger der Rassenweisheit," Ostara 1. Gratisheft (March 1907): 38.

14. Wilfried Daim, *Der Mann, der Hitler die Ideen Gab: Jörg Lanz von Liebenfels*, 3rd ed. (Vienna: Ueberreuter, 1994), 100.

15. Jörg Lanz-Liebenfels, "Moses als Darwinist, eine Einführung in die anthropologische Religion," Ostara 2nd ed., no. 46 (1917 [the first edition was 1911]), 1, 3.

16. Jörg Lanz-Liebenfels, "Revolution oder Evolution? Ein freikonservative Osterpredigt für das Herrentum europäischer Rasse," Ostara 3 (April 1906), 8.

17. Jörg Lanz-Liebenfels, "Rasse und Wohlfahrtspflege, ein Anruf zum Streik der wahllosen Wohltätigkeit," Ostara Heft 18 (December 1907), 3 and passim.

18. Weikart, *Hitler's Ethic: The Nazi Pursuit of Evolutionary Progress*, for a discussion of all these themes in Hitler's worldview.

19. Jörg Lanz-Liebenfels, "Urheimat und Urgeschichte der Blonden heroischer Rasse," Ostara no. 50 (1911), 3–4.

20. Hitler, *Mein Kampf*, 402.

21. An excellent scholarly treatment of List is Nicholas Goodrick-Clarke, *The Occult Roots of Nazism: Secret Aryan Cults and Their Influence on Nazi Ideology* (New York: New York University Press, 1992).

22. Guido von List, *Die Armanenschaft der Ario-Germanen* (Vienna: Guido-von-List-Gesellschaft, 1908), 31.

23. Hamann, *Hitler's Vienna: A Dictator's Apprenticeship*, 206–21; George L. Mosse, *The Fascist Revolution: Toward a General Theory of Fascism* (New York: Howard Fertig, 1999), 131.

24. Nicholas Goodrick-Clarke, *The Occult Roots of Nazism: Secret Aryan Cults and Their Influence on Nazi Ideology* (New York: New York University Press, 1992), 49–50; see also George L. Mosse, *The Fascist Revolution: Toward a General Theory of Fascism* (New York: Howard Fertig, 1999), 121.

25. Weikart, *Hitler's Ethic: The Nazi Pursuit of Evolutionary Progress*.

26. Brigitte Nagel, "Die Welteislehre: Ihre Geschichte und ihre Bedeutung im Dritten Reich," in *Medizin, Naturwissenschaft, Technik und*

Nationalsozialismus, ed. Christoph Meinel and Peter Voswinckel (Stuttgart: Verlag für Geschichte der Naturwissenschaften und der Technik, 1994), 166–72; Michael Hesemann, *Hitlers Religion: Die fatale Heilslehre des Nationalsozialismus* (Munich: Pattloch, 2004), 277–80; Brigitte Hamann, *Hitler's Vienna: A Dictator's Apprenticeship*, trans. Thomas Thornton (New York: Oxford University Press, 1999), 225–26.

27. Peter Padfield, *Himmler: Reichsführer-SS* (New York: Henry Holt and Co., 1990), 171, 618, n. 13.

28. Hitler, monologue on January 25–26, 1942, in *Monologe im Führerhauptquartier 1941–1944: Die Aufzeichnungen Heinrich Heims*, ed. Werner Jochmann (Hamburg: Albrecht Knaus, 1980), 232–33.

29. Hitler, monologue on February 20–21, 1942, in *Monologe im Führerhauptquartier 1941–1944: Die Aufzeichnungen Heinrich Heims*, ed. Werner Jochmann (Hamburg: Albrecht Knaus, 1980), 285–86.

30. Michael Hesemann, *Hitlers Religion: Die fatale Heilslehre des Nationalsozialismus* (Munich: Pattloch, 2004), 281.

31. Rudolf von Sebottendorff, *Bevor Hitler kam: Urkundliches aus der Frühzeit der nationalsozialistischen Bewegung* (Munich: Deukula Verlag, 1933).

32. Rudolf von Sebottendorff, *Bevor Hitler kam: Urkundliches aus der Frühzeit der nationalsozialistischen Bewegung* (Munich: Deukula Verlag, 1933), 46–47.

33. Rudolf von Sebottendorff, *Bevor Hitler kam: Urkundliches aus der Frühzeit der nationalsozialistischen Bewegung* (Munich: Deukula Verlag, 1933), 22.

34. Rudolf von Sebottendorff, *Bevor Hitler kam: Urkundliches aus der Frühzeit der nationalsozialistischen Bewegung* (Munich: Deukula Verlag, 1933), 26.

35. Eduard Gugenberger, *Hitlers Visionäre: Die okkulten Wegbereiter des Dritten Reichs* (Vienna: Ueberreuter, 2001), 86.

36. Detlef Rose, *Die Thule Gesellschaft* (Tübingen: Grabert-Verlag, 1994), 124, 136, passim.

37. Richard Weikart, *Hitler's Ethic: The Nazi Pursuit of Evolutionary Progress* (New York: Palgrave Macmillan, 2009), 14–15, 150–52.

38. Hellmuth Auerbach, "Hitlers politische Lehrjahre und die Münchener Gesellschaft 1919–1923," Vierteljahrshefte für Zeitgeschichte 25 (1977): 8–9.

39. Michael Rissmann, *Hitlers Gott: Vorsehungsglaube und Sendungsbewusstsein des deutschen Diktators* (Zürich: Pendo, 2001), 123, 135, 196; Rainer Bucher, *Hitler's Theology: A Study in Political Religion*, trans. Rebecca Pohl (London: Continuum, 2011), 35–41.

40. Nicholas Goodrick-Clarke, *The Occult Roots of Nazism: Secret Aryan Cults and Their Influence on Nazi Ideology* (New York: New York University Press, 1992), 202.

41. Brigitte Hamann, *Hitler's Vienna: A Dictator's Apprenticeship*, trans. Thomas Thornton (New York: Oxford University Press, 1999), 203–4, 221.

42. For further discussion of these racial thinkers, see Richard Weikart, *From Darwin to Hitler: Evolutionary Ethics, Eugenics, and Racism in Germany* (New York: Palgrave Macmillan, 2004).

43. Peter Walkenhorst, *Nation – Volk – Rasse: Radikaler Nationalismus im Deutschen Kaiserreich 1890–1914* (Göttingen: Vandenhoeck & Ruprecht, 2007), 119–28.

44. Hitler, *Mein Kampf*, 35.

45. Ibid., 14.

46. See, for instance, J. Lanz-Liebenfels, "Urheimat und Urgeschichte der Blonden heroischer Rasse," Ostara no. 50 (1911).

47. Goodrick-Clarke, *The Occult Roots of Nazism: Secret Aryan Cults and Their Influence on Nazi Ideology*; Hamann, *Hitler's Vienna: A Dictator's Apprenticeship*; Ekkehard Hieronymus, "Jörg Lanz von Liebenfels," in *Handbuch zur "Völkischen Bewegung" 1871–1918*, ed. Uwe Puschner, Walter Schmitz, and Justus H. Ulbricht (Munich: K. G. Saur, 1996), 145; Michael Rissmann, *Hitlers Gott: Vorsehungsglaube und*

Sendungsbewusstsein des deutschen Diktators (Zürich: Pendo, 2001), 120–22.

48. Detlef Rose, *Die Thule Gesellschaft* (Tübingen: Grabert-Verlag, 1994), 150.

49. Rudolf von Sebottendorff, *Bevor Hitler kam: Urkundliches aus der Frühzeit der nationalsozialistischen Bewegung* (Munich: Deukula Verlag, 1933), 62–63.

50. Weikart, *Hitler's Ethic: The Nazi Pursuit of Evolutionary Progress*, 14–15, 150–52.

51. Derek Hastings, "How 'Catholic' Was the Early Nazi Movement? Religion, Race, and Culture in Munich, 1919–1924," Central European History 36 (2003): 394.

52. Jost Hermand, *Old Dreams of a New Reich: Volkish Utopias and National Socialism*, trans. Paul Levesque (Bloomington: Indiana University Press, 1992), 285; Hermand correctly argues that Hitler rejected mysticism.

53. Hitler, *Mein Kampf*, 361.

54. Adolf Hitler, speech on September 6, 1938, in *Der Parteitag Grossdeutschland* vom 5. bis 12. September 1938: *Offizieller Bericht über den Verlauf des Reichsparteitages mit sämtlichen Kongressreden* (Munich: Zentralverlag der NSDAP, Franz Eher Nachf., 1938), 76, 81–82; also in Max Domarus, *The Complete Hitler: A Digital Desktop Reference to His Speeches and Proclamations, 1932–1945* (Wauconda: Bolchazy-Carducci Publishers, 2007), 2:1145–47.

55. Ernst Hanfstaengl, *Unheard Witness* (Philadelphia: J. B. Lippincott, 1957), 88.

56. Joseph Goebbels, diary entry for August 21, 1935, in *Die Tagebücher von Joseph Goebbels*, ed. Elke Fröhlich, part I: Aufzeichnungen 1923–1941, vol. 3/I: April 1934–Februar 1936 (Munich K. G. Saur, 2005), 279.

57. Albert Speer, *Inside the Third Reich*, trans. Richard and Clara Winston (New York: Avon Books, 1970), 141, 143, 174.

58. Heinz Linge, *Bis zum Untergang: Als Chef des Persönlichen Dienstes bei Hitler*, 2nd ed. (Munich: Herbig, 1980), 131.

59. Adolf Hitler, monologue on October 14, 1941, in *Monologe im Führerhauptquartier 1941–1944: Die Aufzeichnungen Heinrich Heims*, ed. Werner Jochmann (Hamburg: Albrecht Knaus, 1980), 84.

60. Alfred Rosenberg, *Letzte Aufzeichnungen: Nürnberg 1945/46*, 2nd ed. (Uelzen: Jomsburg-Verlag, 1996), 96.

61. Joe J. Heydecker, *Das Hitler-Bild: Die Erinnerungen des Fotografen Heinrich Hoffmann* (St. Pölten-Salzburg: Residenz Verlag, 2008), 67.

62. Dietrich, *The Hitler I Knew*, 148.

63. Hans Frank, *Im Angesicht des Galgens: Deutung Hitlers und seiner Zeit auf Grund eigener Erlebnisse und Erkenntnisse* (Munich-Gräfelfing: Friedrich Alfred Beck Verlag, 1953), 411.

64. Peter Staudenmaier, *Between Occultism and Nazism: Anthroposophy and the Politics of Race in the Fascist Era* (Leiden: Brill, 2014), 234.

65. Corinna Treitel, *A Science for the Soul: Occultism and the Genesis of the German Modern* (Baltimore: Johns Hopkins University Press, 2004), 213–14, 224–25.

66. Joseph Goebbels, diary entry for June 13, 1941, in *Die Tagebücher von Joseph Goebbels*, ed. Elke Fröhlich, part I: Aufzeichnungen 1923–1941, vol. 9: Dezember 1940–Juli 1941 (Munich K. G. Saur, 1998), 370.

67. Treitel, *A Science for the Soul: Occultism and the Genesis of the German Modern*, 211–12, 216.

68. Eduard Gugenberger, *Hitlers Visionäre: Die okkulten Wegbereiter des Dritten Reichs* (Vienna: Ueberreuter, 2001), 90–91.

69. Treitel, *A Science for the Soul: Occultism and the Genesis of the German Modern*, 210–11, 220, 224, 242.

70. Ibid., 213.

71. Heather Wolffram, *The Stepchildren of Science: Psychical Research and Parapsychology in Germany, C. 1870–1939* (Amsterdam: Rodopi, 2009), 191, 219.

72. Treitel, *A Science for the Soul: Occultism and the Genesis of the German Modern*, 133.

73. Robert Proctor, *The Nazi War on Cancer* (Princeton: Princeton University Press, 1999), 256–57.

74. Adolf Hitler, "Staatsmänner oder Nationalverbrecher," (essay), in *Hitler: Sämtliche Aufzeichnungen, 1905–1924*, ed. Eberhard Jäckel (Stuttgart: Deutsche Verlags-Anstalt, 1980), 350.

75. Michael Rissmann, *Hitlers Gott: Vorsehungsglaube und Sendungsbewusstsein des deutschen Diktators* (Zürich: Pendo, 2001), 123.

EIGHT: WHO WAS HITLER'S LORD?

1. Hitler, *Mein Kampf*, 65.

2. As one example among many, see Alon Confino, *A World without Jews: The Nazi Imagination from Persecution to Genocide* (New Haven: Yale University Press, 2014), 31.

3. Hitler, *Mein Kampf*, 65.

4. Samuel Koehne, "Reassessing The Holy Reich: Leading Nazis' Views on Confession, Community and 'Jewish' Materialism," *Journal of Contemporary History* 48 (2013): 434.

5. Adolf Hitler, "Zum Parteitag 1923," January 27, 1923, in *Hitler: Sämtliche Aufzeichnungen, 1905–1924*, ed. Eberhard Jäckel (Stuttgart: Deutsche Verlags-Anstalt, 1980), 800.

6. Hitler, *Mein Kampf*, 244–45; for other examples, see 131–32, 289, 383.

7. Adolf Hitler, speech at the Nuremberg Party Congress, 1937, in Christian Dube, "Religiöser Sprache in Reden Adolf Hitlers: Analysiert an Hand ausgewählter Reden aus den Jahren 1933–1945" (diss., University of Kiel, 2004), 252.

8. Adolf Hitler, monologue on November 11, 1941, in *Monologe im Führerhauptquartier 1941–1944: Die Aufzeichnungen Heinrich Heims*, ed. Werner Jochmann (Hamburg: Albrecht Knaus, 1980), 135.

9. "Hitler vor Offizieren und Offiziersanwärtern am 15. Februar 1942," in *Hitler, "Es spricht der Führer": 7 exemplarische Hitler-Reden,* ed.

Hildegard von Kotze and Helmut Krausnick (Gütersloh: Sigbert Mohn Verlag, 1966), 307–8.

10. George Shuster, *Like a Mighty Army: Hitler versus Established Religion* (New York: D. Appleton-Century Company, 1935), 3–6, 279.

11. Pius XI, "Mit brennender Sorge," http://www.vatican.va/holy_father/pius_xi/encyclicals/documents/hf_p-xi_enc_14031937_mit-brennender-sorge_en.html; accessed February 7, 2014.

12. Walter Künneth, *Der große Abfall: Eine geschichtstheologische Untersuchung der Begegnung zwischen Nationalsozialismus und Christentum*, 2nd ed. (Hamburg: Friedrich Wittig Verlag, 1948), 120.

13. Robert Pois, *National Socialism and the Religion of Nature* (London: Croom Helm, 1986), 38–41 and passim.

14. André Mineau, *SS Thinking and the Holocaust* (Amsterdam: Rodopi, 2012), 35.

15. Michael Rissmann, *Hitlers Gott: Vorsehungsglaube und Sendungsbewusstsein des deutschen Diktators* (Zürich: Pendo, 2001), 65–67.

16. Michael Hesemann, *Hitlers Religion: Die fatale Heilslehre des Nationalsozialismus* (Munich: Pattloch, 2004), 277.

17. Friedrich Heer, *Der Glaube des Adolf Hitler: Anatomie einer politischen Religiosität* (Munich: Bechtle Verlag, 1968), 277, 287.

18. Dirk Bavendamm, *Der junge Hitler: Korrekturen einer Biographie, 1889–1914* (Graz: Ares Verlag, 2009), 457; Fritz Redlich, *Hitler: Diagnosis of a Destructive Prophet* (Oxford: Oxford University Press, 1998), 329; Paul Weindling, "Genetics, Eugenics, and the Holocaust," in *Biology and Ideology from Descartes to Dawkins*, ed. Denis R. Alexander and Ronald L. Numbers (Chicago: University of Chicago Press, 2010), 196; François Bédarida, "Nationalsozialistische Verkündigung und säkulare Religion," in *Der Nationalsozialismus als politische Religion*, ed. Michael Ley and Julius H. Schoeps (Bodenheim bei Mainz: Philo Verlagsgesellschaft, 1997), 162. See also Claudia Koonz, *The Nazi Conscience* (Cambridge: Belknap

Press of Harvard University Press, 2003), 158, on Nazi racial theorists and pantheism.

19. Richard Steigmann-Gall, *The Holy Reich: Nazi Conceptions of Christianity, 1919–1945* (Cambridge: Cambridge University Press, 2003), 36.

20. Thomas Schirrmacher, *Hitlers Kriegsreligion: Die Verankerung der Weltanschauung Hitlers in seiner religiösen Begrifflichkeit und seinem Gottesbild*, 2 vols. (Bonn: Verlag für Kultur und Wissenschaft, 2007), 1:122, 125–26, 137, 161, 489–90.

21. Todd Weir, "The Riddles of Monism: An Introductory Essay," in *Monism: Science, Philosophy, Religion, and the History of a Worldview*, ed. Todd Weir (New York: Palgrave Macmillan, 2012), 16.

22. Nicholas Riasanovsky, *The Emergence of Romanticism* (New York: Oxford University Press, 1992), 5, 47–48, 63, 71, 79–80.

23. Raymond Keith Williamson, *Introduction to Hegel's Philosophy of Religion* (Albany: State University of New York, 1984), 199–200, chs. 11–12.

24. George S. Williamson, *The Longing for Myth in Germany: Religion and Aesthetic Culture from Romanticism to Nietzsche* (Chicago: University of Chicago Press, 2004), 255–56.

25. Ernst Haeckel, *Der Monismus als Band zwischen Religion und Wissenschaft: Glaubensbekenntniss eines Naturforschers* (Bonn: Emil Strauss, 1892), 10. Todd Weir also interprets Haeckel's monism as naturalistic in "The Riddles of Monism: An Introductory Essay," in *Monism: Science, Philosophy, Religion, and the History of a Worldview*, ed. Todd Weir (New York: Palgrave Macmillan, 2012), 25.

26. Ernst Haeckel to Wilhelm Bölsche, July 1, 1898, in Wilhelm Bölsche papers, University of Wroclaw Library, Böl.Hae. 47.

27. Ernst Haeckel, *Die Welträthsel: Gemeinverständliche Studien über Monistische Philosophie* (Bonn: Emil Strauss, 1903), 116–17.

28. Todd Weir, "The Riddles of Monism: An Introductory Essay," in *Monism: Science, Philosophy, Religion, and the History of a Worldview*, ed. Todd Weir (New York: Palgrave Macmillan, 2012), 2.

29. Ernst Haeckel, "Monismus und Mystik," in *Der Düsseldorfer Monistentag: 7. Hauptversammlung des Deutschen Monistenbundes vom 5.-8. September 1913*, ed. Willy Blossfeldt, (Leipzig: Unesma, 1914), 93–98. This lecture by Haeckel (together with many passages in his books) completely refutes Daniel Gasman's claim that Haeckel's monism was mystical and even vitalistic; see Daniel Gasman, *The Scientific Origins of National Socialism: Social Darwinism in Ernst Haeckel and the German Monist League* (London: MacDonald, 1971), xiii–xiv, 64–69; Daniel Gasman, *Haeckel's Monism and the Birth of Fascist Ideology* (New York: Peter Lang, 1998), 43–44, 49, 60, 70.

30. Friedrich Lipsius, "Ernst Haeckel als Naturphilosoph," *Der Biologe: Monatsschrift zur Wahrung der Belange der Biologie und der deutschen Biologen* 3 (1934): 43–46, interprets Haeckel as a pantheist.

31. Eric Voegelin, *Hitler and the Germans*, in *The Collected Works of Eric Voegelin*, ed. and trans. Detlev Clemens and Brendan Purcell, vol. 31(Columbia: University of Missouri Press, 1999), 124.

32. Lawrence Sondhaus, *Franz Conrad von Hötzendorf: Architect of the Apocalypse* (Boston: Humanities Press, 2000), 8, see also 15–16.

33. Conrad von Hötzendorf, *Private Aufzeichnungen*, ed. Kurt Peball (Vienna: Amalthea, 1977), 148, 307.

34. Ibid., 307, 321.

35. *Der Parteitag der Freiheit vom 10.-16. September 1935: Offizieller Bericht über den Verlauf des Reichsparteitages mit sämtlichen Kongressreden*. 2nd ed. (Munich: Zentralverlag der NSDAP, Franz Eher Nachf., 1935), 54.

36. Hans F. K. Günther, *Frömmigkeit nordlicher Artung*, 3rd ed. (Jena, E. Diederichs, 1936), 14–16, 25, 27, 31–33, 41.

37. Ibid., 14–16, 25, 27, 31–33, 41.

38 Martin Bormann, "National Socialist and Christian Concepts are Incompatible," in *Nazi Culture: Intellectual, Cultural and Social Life in* *the Third Reich*, ed. George L. Mosse (New York: Schocken Books, 1966), 245; original German is Bormann, "Rundschreiben des Leiters der Parteikanzlei an alle Gauleiter betr. Verhältnis von Nationalsozialismus und Christentum," June 9, 1941, in *Dokumente zur Kirchenpolitik des Dritten Reiches*, vol. 5: *1939–45*, ed. Gertraud Grünzinger and Carsten Nicolaisen (Gütersloh: Gütersloher Verlagshaus, 2008), 307–8.

39. Rosenberg, diary entry on September 7, 1941, in Alfred Rosenberg Diaries, 603, http://collections.ushmm.org/view/2001.62.14; accessed January 22, 2014.

40. Martin Bormann to Alfred Rosenberg, February 22, 1940, in *Das politische Tagebuch Alfred Rosenbergs aus den Jahren 1934/35 und 1939/40*, ed. Hans-Günther Seraphim (Göttingen: Musterschmidt-Verlag, 1956), 171.

41. Martin Bormann to his mistress, February 21, 1944, in *The Bormann Letters: The Private Correspondence between Martin Bormann and His Wife from January 1943 to April 1945*, ed. H. R. Trevor-Roper (London: Weidenfeld and Nicolson, 1954), 54.

42. August Kubizek, *Adolf Hitler: Mein Jugendfreund* (Graz: Leopold Stocker Verlag, 1953), 37–38.

43. Hitler, *Mein Kampf*, trans. Ralph Manheim (Boston: Houghton Mifflin, 1943); Hitler, *Mein Kampf*, trans. Barrows Mussey (New York: Stackpole Sons, 1939); Hitler, *Mein Kampf*, trans. James Murphy (London: Hurst and Blackett, 1939); Hitler, *Mein Kampf*, trans. Michael Ford (n.p.: Elite Minds, 2009); Hitler, *Mein Kampf: The Official Nazi English Translation* (n.p.: Elite Minds, 2009).

44. Hitler, *Mein Kampf*, trans. Ralph Manheim (Boston: Houghton Mifflin, 1943), 131–32.

45. Othmar Plöckinger, *Geschichte eines Buches: Adolf Hitlers "Mein Kampf" 1922–1945* (Munich: R. Oldenbourg, 2006), 12.

46. Hitler, *Mein Kampf*, 285–87.

47. Ibid., 383.

48. Adolf Hitler, speech on September 8, 1934, in Domurus, 1:532. In this passage I have translated "Wunderbare" as "wonderful," rather than as "miraculous," which is misleading.

49. Adolf Hitler, speech on September 8, 1934, in Max Domarus, *The Complete Hitler: A Digital Desktop Reference to His Speeches and Proclamations, 1932–1945* (Wauconda: Bolchazy-Carducci Publishers, 2007), 1:533–34.

50. Adolf Hitler, speech on September 6, 1938, in *The Speeches of Adolf Hitler, April 1922–August 1939*, 2 vols., ed. Norman H. Baynes (Oxford: Oxford University Press, 1942), 1:396–97.

51. Otto Wagener, *Hitler—Memoirs of a Confidant*, ed. Henry Ashby Turner, trans. Ruth Hein (New Haven: Yale University Press, 1985), 224.

52. Ibid., 278–79.

53. Adolf Hitler, monologue on July 11–12, 1941, in *Monologe im Führerhauptquartier 1941–1944: Die Aufzeichnungen Heinrich Heims*, ed. Werner Jochmann (Hamburg: Albrecht Knaus, 1980), 40.

54. Adolf Hitler, monologue on November 20, 1941, in *Monologe im Führerhauptquartier 1941–1944: Die Aufzeichnungen Heinrich Heims*, ed. Werner Jochmann (Hamburg: Albrecht Knaus, 1980), 144.

55. Adolf Hitler, monologue on February 20–21, 1942, in *Monologe im Führerhauptquartier 1941–1944: Die Aufzeichnungen Heinrich Heims*, ed. Werner Jochmann (Hamburg: Albrecht Knaus, 1980), 285–86.

56. Brigitte Nagel, "Die Welteislehre: Ihre Geschichte und ihre Bedeutung im Dritten Reich," in *Medizin, Naturwissenschaft, Technik und Nationalsozialismus*, ed. Christoph Meinel and Peter Voswinckel (Stuttgart: Verlag für Geschichte der Naturwissenschaften und der Technik, 1994), 169, 172, n. 7.

57. Hitler, *Mein Kampf*, 244–45.

58. Adolf Hitler, speech to 1937 Nuremberg Party Congress, in Christian Dube, "Religiöser Sprache in Reden Adolf Hitlers: Analysiert an Hand ausgewählter Reden aus den Jahren 1933–1945" (diss., University of Kiel, 2004), 257.

59. Adolf Hitler, speech to 1937 Nuremberg Party Congress, in Christian Dube, "Religiöser Sprache in Reden Adolf Hitlers: Analysiert an Hand ausgewählter Reden aus den Jahren 1933–1945" (diss., University of Kiel, 2004), 257–58.

60. "Hitler vor Offizieren und Offiziersanwärtern am 15. Februar 1942," in Hitler, *"Es spricht der Führer": 7 exemplarische Hitler-Reden*, ed. Hildegard von Kotze and Helmut Krausnick (Gütersloh: Sigbert Mohn Verlag, 1966), 306–8.

61. Adolf Hitler, monologue on November 11, 1941, in *Monologe im Führerhauptquartier 1941–1944: Die Aufzeichnungen Heinrich Heims*, ed. Werner Jochmann (Hamburg: Albrecht Knaus, 1980), 135.

62. Adolf Hitler, monologue on December 1, 1941, in *Monologe im Führerhauptquartier 1941–1944: Die Aufzeichnungen Heinrich Heims*, ed. Werner Jochmann (Hamburg: Albrecht Knaus, 1980), 148–49.

63. Christa Schroeder, *Er War Mein Chef: Aus dem Nachlass der Sekretärin von Adolf Hitler*, ed. Anton Joachimsthaler, 2nd ed. (Munich: Langen Müller, 1985), 68.

64. Adolf Hitler, speech at Nuremberg Party Congress, September 1933, in *The Speeches of Adolf Hitler, April 1922–August 1939*, 2 vols., ed. Norman H. Baynes (Oxford: Oxford University Press, 1942), 1:463.

65. Adolf Hitler, speech on December 18, 1940, in Max Domarus, *The Complete Hitler: A Digital Desktop Reference to His Speeches and Proclamations, 1932–1945* (Wauconda: Bolchazy-Carducci Publishers, 2007), 3:2161.

66. Friedrich Tomberg, *Das Christentum in Hitlers Weltanschauung* (Munich: Wilhelm Fink, 2012), 158.

NINE: WAS HITLER A CREATIONIST?

1. Adolf Hitler, speech to the Nuremberg Party Congress, September 1935, in *The Speeches of Adolf Hitler, April 1922–August 1939*, 2 vols., ed. Norman H. Baynes (Oxford: Oxford University Press, 1942), 1:443–444.

2. Adolf Hitler, proclamation read by Goebbels, January 30, 1943, in Max Domarus, *The Complete Hitler: A Digital Desktop Reference to His Speeches and Proclamations, 1932–1945* (Wauconda: Bolchazy-Carducci Publishers, 2007), 4:2749–50.

3. Thomas Schirrmacher, *Hitlers Kriegsreligion: Die Verankerung der Weltanschauung Hitlers in seiner religiösen Begrifflichkeit und seinem Gottesbild*, 2 vols. (Bonn: Verlag für Kultur und Wissenschaft, 2007), 143–45.

4. Some examples are: Adolf Hitler, "Nationalkokarde und Pleitegeier" (essay), February 20, 1921, in *Hitler:Sämtliche Aufzeichnungen, 1905– 1924*, ed. Eberhard Jäckel (Stuttgart: Deutsche Verlags-Anstalt, 1980), 321; Adolf Hitler, monologues on November 5 and December 1–2, 1941, in *Monologe im Führerhauptquartier 1941–1944: Die Aufzeichnungen Heinrich Heims*, ed. Werner Jochmann (Hamburg: Albrecht Knaus, 1980), 128, 148.

5. Hitler, *Mein Kampf*, 288.

6. Wagener, *Hitler—Memoirs of a Confidant*, 312–13.

7. Adolf Hitler, October 24, 1941, in *Monologe im Führerhauptquartier 1941–1944: Die Aufzeichnungen Heinrich Heims*, ed. Werner Jochmann (Hamburg: Albrecht Knaus, 1980), 102–5.

8. Christa Schroeder, *Er War Mein Chef: Aus dem Nachlass der Sekretärin von Adolf Hitler*, ed. Anton Joachimsthaler, 2nd ed. (Munich: Langen Müller, 1985), 68.

9. Wagener, *Hitler—Memoirs of a Confidant*, 40.

10. Dietrich, *The Hitler I Knew*, 153.

11. Hitler, *Mein Kampf*, 131–37.

12. Robert J. Richards, *Was Hitler a Darwinian?: Disputed Question in the History of Evolutionary Theory* (Chicago: University of Chicago Press, 2013), 226.

13. Weikart, *From Darwin to Hitler: Evolutionary Ethics, Eugenics, and Racism in Germany*, 112–14, 192–94, 225.

14. Hitler, *Mein Kampf*, 285.

15. Robert J. Richards, *Was Hitler a Darwinian?: Disputed Question in the History of Evolutionary Theory* (Chicago: University of Chicago Press, 2013), 220.

16. *Erziehung und Unterricht in der Höheren Schule: Amtliche Ausgabe des Reichs- und Preussische Ministeriums für Wissenschaft, Erziehung und Volksbildung* (Berlin: Weidmannsche Verlagsbuchhandlung, 1938), 160; See also similar usages of *Entwicklung* on pp. 151–52, 157.

17. Paul Brohmer, *Der Unterricht in der Lebenskunde*, 4th ed. (Osterwieck-Harz: A. W. Zickfeldt, 1943), 3.

18. Adolf Hitler, *The Racial Conception of the World*, ed. Charles Grant Robertson (London: Friends of Europe, 1938), 8.

19. Adolf Hitler, *Mein Kampf*, trans. Barrows Mussey (New York: Stackpole Sons, 1939), 278.

20. Adolf Hitler, *Mein Kampf*, trans. James Murphy (London: Hurst and Blackett, 1939), 161–62.

21. One example among many is Hans Staudinger, *The Inner Nazi: A Critical Analysis of Mein Kampf* (Baton Rouge: LSU Press, 1981), 78.

22. Adolf Hitler, *Second Book*, ed. Gerhard Weinberg, trans. Krista Smith (New York: Enigma Books, 2003), 8–9. The word "evolution" is in Smith's translation.

23. Robert J. Richards, *Was Hitler a Darwinian?: Disputed Question in the History of Evolutionary Theory* (Chicago: University of Chicago Press, 2013), 227–29.

24. Hitler, *Second Book*, 7–8.

25. Ibid., 8. Again, the word "evolution" is in Smith's translation.

26. Adolf Hitler, speech on January 5, 1927, in *Hitler: Reden, Schriften, Anordnungen, Februar 1925 bis Januar 1933*, vol. II: *Vom Weimarer Parteitag bus zur Reichstagswahl Juli 1926–Mai 1928*, part 1: *Juli 1926–Juli 1927*, ed. BärbelDusik (Munich: K. G. Saur, 1992–2003), 112.

27. Adolf Hitler, "Was ist Nationalsozialismus?" August 6, 1927, in *Hitler: Reden, Schriften, Anordnungen, Februar 1925 bis Januar 1933*, vol. II: *Vom Weimarer Parteitag bus zur Reichstagswahl Juli 1926–Mai 1928*, part 2: *August 1927–May 1928*, ed. Bärbel Dusik (Munich: K. G. Saur, 1992–2003), 442.

28. Adolf Hitler, speech on April 26, 1928, in *Hitler: Reden, Schriften, Anordnungen, Febraur 1925 bis Januar 1933*, vol. II: *Vom Weimarer Parteitag bus zur Reichstagswahl Juli 1926–Mai 1928*, part 2: *August 1927–May 1928*, ed. Bärbel Dusik (Munich: K. G. Saur, 1992–2003), 796.

29. Adolf Hitler, "Ein Kampf um Deutschlands Zukunft," September 18, 1928, in *Hitler: Reden, Schriften, Anordnungen, Febraur 1925 bis Januar 1933*, vol. III: *Zwischen den Reichstsagswahlen, Juli 1928–September 1930*, Part 1: *Juli 1928–Februar 1929* (Munich: K. G. Saur, 1992–2003), 86–88.

30. Adolf Hitler, "Stellungnahme zu einem Ermittlungsverfahren wegen Hochverrats," n.d. [1929], in *Hitler: Reden, Schriften, Anordnungen, Febraur 1925 bis Januar 1933*, vol. III: *Zwischen den Reichstsagswahlen, Juli 1928–September 1930*, part 2: *März 1929–Dezember 1929* (Munich: K. G. Saur, 1992–2003), 76.

31. Adolf Hitler, speech on July 19, 1937, in J. Noakes and G. Pridham, *Nazism 1919–1945: A Documentary Reader*, 4 vols. (Exeter: University of Exeter Press, 2000), 2:205–6.

32. Adolf Hitler, "War der Zweite Weltkrieg für Deutschland vermeidbar?" May 30, 1942, in *Hitlers Tischgespräche im Führerhauptquartier*, ed. Henry Picker (Frankfurt: Ullstein, 1989), 492.

33. Adolf Hitler, "Ansprache des Führers vor Generalen und Offiziers am 22.6.1944 im Platterhof," p. 2, in Hoover Institution, NSDAP Hauptarchiv, Reel 2, Folder 51.

34. Adolf Hitler, "Ansprache des Führers vor Generalen und Offiziers am 22.6.1944 im Platterhof," pp. 3–4, in Hoover Institution, NSDAP Hauptarchiv, Reel 2, Folder 51.

35. Adolf Hitler, monologue on March 1, 1942, in *Monologe im Führerhauptquartier 1941–1944: Die Aufzeichnungen Heinrich Heims*, ed. Werner Jochmann (Hamburg: Albrecht Knaus, 1980), 310.

36. *Wofür kämpfen wir?* (Berlin: Heerespersonalamt, 1944), iv–vi, 67–72, 85, 87, 105, 109; quote at 67, 110.

37. See a thorough discussion of this in Richard Weikart, "The Role of Darwinism in Nazi Racial Thought," *German Studies Review* 36 (2013): 537–56; and "The Role of Evolutionary Ethics in Nazi Propaganda and Worldview Training," in *Nazi Ideology and Ethics*, eds. Wolfgang Bialas and Lothar Fritze (Cambridge: Cambridge Scholars Publishing, 2014), 193–208; a German translation of this essay is "Die Rolle der Evolutionsethik in der NS-Propaganda und imweltanschaulichen NS-Unterricht," in *Ideologie und Moral imNationalsozialismus*, eds. Wolfgang Bialasand Lothar Fritze (Göttingen: Vandenhoeck & Ruprecht, 2014), 193–207.

38. Adolf Hitler, monologue on January 25–26, 1942, in *Monologe im Führerhauptquartier 1941–1944: Die Aufzeichnungen Heinrich Heims*, ed. Werner Jochmann (Hamburg: Albrecht Knaus, 1980), 232–33.

39. Hanns Hörbiger, *Glazial-Kosmogonie: Eine neue Entwicklungsgeschichte des Weltalls und des Sonnensystems* (Leipzig: R. Voigtländers Verlag, 1925), 514–25.

40. Adolf Hitler, monologue on January 22, 1942, in *Monologe im Führerhauptquartier 1941–1944: Die Aufzeichnungen Heinrich Heims*, ed. Werner Jochmann (Hamburg: Albrecht Knaus, 1980), 218.

41. Adolf Hitler, October 24, 1941, in *Monologe im Führerhauptquartier 1941–1944: Die Aufzeichnungen Heinrich Heims*, ed. Werner Jochmann (Hamburg: Albrecht Knaus, 1980), 102–5.

42. Adolf Hitler, *The Speeches of Adolf Hitler, April 1922–August 1939*, 2 vols., ed. Norman H. Baynes (Oxford: Oxford University Press, 1942), 1:464.

43. Ernst Haeckel, *Die Lebenswunder: Gemeinverständliche Studien über Biologische Philosophie* (Stuttgart: Alfred Kröner, 1904), 327; Ernst Haeckel, *Generelle Morphologie*, 2 vols. (Berlin, 1866), II: 435. Emphasis in original. See also Ernst Haeckel, *Die Welträthsel: Gemeinverständliche Studien über Monistische Philosophie* (Bonn: Emil Strauss, 1903), 53.

44. Thomas Schirrmacher, *Hitlers Kriegsreligion: Die Verankerung der Weltanschauung Hitlers in seiner religiösen Begrifflichkeit und seinem*

Gottesbild, 2 vols. (Bonn: Verlag für Kultur und Wissenschaft, 2007), 1:145–46.

45. Hitler, *Mein Kampf*, 134.

46. Adolf Hitler, speech on December 18, 1940, in Max Domarus, *The Complete Hitler: A Digital Desktop Reference to His Speeches and Proclamations, 1932–1945* (Wauconda: Bolchazy-Carducci Publishers, 2007), 3:2161–62; See also Hitler, "20 Millionen Deutsche zuviel!" March 26, 1927, in *Hitler: Reden, Schriften, Anordnungen, Februar 1925 bis Januar 1933*, vol. II: *Vom Weimarer Parteitag bus zur Reichstagswahl Juli 1926–Mai 1928*, part 1: *Juli 1926–Juli 1927*, ed. Bärbel Dusik (Munich: K. G. Saur, 1992–2003), 196.

47. Charles Darwin, *Origin of Species* (London: Penguin, 1968), 458.

48. Charles Darwin, *Origin of Species*, 2nd ed. (1860), http://darwin-online.org.uk, p. 490.

TEN: WAS HITLER'S MORALITY BASED ON RELIGION?

1. Adolf Hitler, *Adolf Hitler spricht: Ein Lexikon des Nationalsozialismus* (Leipzig: R. Kittler Verlag, 1934), 23.

2. Adolf Hitler, speech on April 6, 1922, in *Hitler: Sämtliche Aufzeichnungen, 1905–1924*, ed. Eberhard Jäckel (Stuttgart: Deutsche Verlags-Anstalt, 1980), 599–600.

3. Herman Rauschning, "Preface," in *The Ten Commandments: Ten Short Novels of Hitler's War against the Moral Code*, ed. Armin Robinson (New York: Simon and Schuster, 1943), x, xiii. Hans Frank took a similar view; See Hans Frank, *Im Angesicht des Galgens: Deutung Hitlers und seiner Zeit auf Grund eigener Erlebnisse und Erkenntnisse* (Munich-Gräfelfing: Friedrich Alfred Beck Verlag, 1953), 205.

4. Hermann Rauschning, *Gespräche mit Hitler* (New York: Europa Verlag, 1940), 50.

5. Gunnar Heinsohn, *Warum Auschwitz? Hitlers Plan und die Ratlosigkeit der Nachwelt* (Reinbek bei Hamburg: Rowohlt, 1995), 18–20, 139.

6. In addition to Weikart, *Hitler's Ethic: The Nazi Pursuit of Evolutionary Progress*, see Weikart, "The Role of Evolutionary Ethics in Nazi Propaganda and Worldview Training," in *Nazi Ideology and Ethics*, eds. Wolfgang Bialas and Lothar Fritze (Cambridge: Cambridge Scholars Publishing, 2014), 193–208; this same essay is in German as "Die Rolle der Evolutionsethik in der NS-Propaganda und im weltanschaulichen NS-Unterricht," in *Ideologie und Moral im Nationalsozialismus*, eds. Wolfgang Bialas and Lothar Fritze (Göttingen: Vandenhoeck & Ruprecht, 2014), 193–207.

7. Wolfgang Bialas, "The Eternal Voice of the Blood: Racial Science and Nazi Ethics," in *Racial Science in Hitler's New Europe, 1938–1945*, eds. Anton Weiss-Wendt and Rory Yeomans (Lincoln: University of Nebraska Press, 2013), 351; see also Wolfgang Bialas, *Moralische Ordnungen des Nationalsozialismus* (Göttingen: Vandenhoeck & Ruprecht, 2014).

8. Richard J. Evans, *Third Reich in Power* (New York: Penguin, 2006), 259; and Hans-Walter Schmuhl, *Rassenhygiene, Nationalsozialismus, Euthanasie. Von der Verhütung zur Vernichtung 'lebensunwerten Lebens' 1890–1945* (Göttingen: Vandenhoek und Ruprecht, 1987), 151, and Peter J. Haas, "Science and the Determination of the Good," in *Ethics after the Holocaust: Perspectives, Critiques, and Responses*, ed. John Roth (St. Paul: Paragon House, 1999), 50–55, all mention the ethical thrust of social Darwinism. Joachim Fest, *Hitler*, trans. Richard and Clara Winston (New York: Helen and Kurf Wolff, 1974), 205–10, 37, 53–56, 201, 608, claims that Hitler based his ethics on nature and struggle. Many scholars have noted the importance of social Darwinism in Hitler's world view: Ian Kershaw, *Hitler*, 2 vols. (New York: Norton, 1998–2000), 2:xli; See also 1:290, 2:19, 208, 405, 780; Richard J. Evans, *The Coming of the Third Reich* (New York: Penguin, 2004), 34–35, and Richard J. Evans, *Third Reich in Power* (New York: Penguin, 2006), 4, 708; Eberhard Jäckel, *Hitler's World View: A Blueprint for Power* (Cambridge: Harvard

University Press, 1981), ch. 5; Mike Hawkins, *Social Darwinism in European and American Thought, 1860–1945: Nature as Model and Nature as Threat* (Cambridge: Cambridge University Press, 1997), 277–78; Rainer Zitelmann, *Hitler: Selbstverständnis eines Revolutionärs* (Hamburg: Berg, 1987), 15, 466; Karl Dietrich Bracher, *Die Deutsche Diktatur. Entstehung, Struktur, Folgen des Nationalsozialismus*, 7th ed. (Cologne: Kiepenheuer & Witsch, 1993) 13–15; Gerhard Weinberg, *The Foreign Policy of Hitler's Germany*, vol. 1: *Diplomatic Revolution in Europe, 1933–36* (Chicago: University of Chicago Press, 1970), 1–6; Wolfgang Wippermann, *Der consequente Wahn. Ideologie und Politik Adolf Hitlers* (Gütersloh: Bertelsmann, 1989), 179; Robert Gellately and Nathan Stolzfus, "Social Outsiders and the Construction of the Community of the People," in Robert Gellately and Nathan Stolzfus, eds. *Social Outsiders in Nazi Germany* (Princeton University Press, 2001), 4; Neil Gregor, *How to Read Hitler* (New York: Norton, 2005), 40; Alan Bullock, *Hitler and Stalin: Parallel Lives* (New York: Alfred Knopf, 1992), 23, 142; Stig Förster and Myriam Gessler, "The Ultimate Horror: Reflections on Total War and Genocide," in *A World at Total War: Global Conflict and the Politics of Destruction, 1937–1945*, eds. Roger Chickering, Stig Förster, and Bernd Greiner (Cambridge: Cambridge University Press, 2005), 67; Hans Staudinger, *The Inner Nazi: A Critical Analysis of Mein Kampf* (Baton Rouge: Louisiana State University Press, 1981), 78–79; Werner Maser, *Adolf Hitler: Legende, Mythos, Wirklichkeit* (Munich: Bechtle, 1971), 168, 236, 255–56, 283–84; Brigitte Hamann, *Hitler's Vienna: A Dictator's Apprenticeship*, trans. Thomas Thornton (New York: Oxford University Press, 1999), 102, 202–3; Jost Hermand, *Old Dreams of a New Reich: Volkish Utopias and National Socialism*, trans. Paul Levesque (Bloomington: Indiana University Press, 1992), 63; Gilmer Blackburn, *Education in the Third Reich: Race and History in Nazi Textbooks* (State University of New York Press, 1985), 21–22; Edward Westermann, *Hitler's Police Battalions: Enforcing Racial War in the East* (Lawrence: University Press of Kansas, 2005), 58; See also Hans-Günter Zmarzlik, "Der

Sozialdarwinismus in Deutschland als geschichtliches Problem," Vierteljahrshefte für Zeitgeschichte 11 (1963): 246–73. John Lukacs, *The Hitler of History* (New York: Vintage, 1997), 120–27, is one of only a few scholars to claim that social Darwinism was not very important in Hitler's ideology.

9. Alan Bullock, *Hitler: A Study in Tyranny*, revised ed. (New York: Harper and Row, 1964), 389.

10. Joachim Fest, *Hitler*, trans. Richard and Clara Winston (New York: Helen and Kurf Wolff, 1974), 210.

11. Claudia Koonz, *The Nazi Conscience* (Cambridge: Belknap Press of Harvard University Press, 2003), 2, 6, 79, 131, 254–55.

12. Robert S. Wistrich, *Hitler and the Holocaust* (New York: Modern Library, 2003), 132–34.

13. Ulf Schmidt, "Medical Ethics and Nazism," in *The Cambridge World History of Medical Ethics*, ed. Robert B. Baker and Laurence B. McCullough (Cambridge: Cambridge University Press, 2009), 596. Others stressing the anti-Christian character of Nazi ethics and morality include Richard J. Evans, *Third Reich in Power* (New York: Penguin, 2006), 515; Richard Overy, *The Dictators: Hitler's Germany and Stalin's Russia* (New York: W. W. Norton, 2004), 265–67; and Florian Bruns, *Medizinethik im Nationalsozialismus: Entwicklungen und Protagonisten in Berlin (1939–1945)* (Stuttgart: Franz Steiner Verlag, 2009), 44.

14. Wolfgang Bialas, *Moralische Ordnungen des Nationalsozialismus* (Göttingen: Vandenhoeck & Ruprecht, 2014); See also Wolfgang Bialas, "Nazi Ethics and Morality: Ideas, Problems and Unanswered Questions," in *Nazi Ideology and Ethics*, eds. Wolfgang Bialas and Lothar Fritze (Cambridge: Cambridge Scholars Publishing, 2014), 15–56. Another scholar largely agreeing with Bialas is André Mineau, *SS Thinking and the Holocaust* (Amsterdam: Rodopi, 2012).

15. Steigmann-Gall, *The Holy Reich: Nazi Conceptions of Christianity, 1919–1945*, 86; Steigmann-Gall argued this position even more forcefully at the 2004 German Studies Association Conference in a panel on "Nazi Ethics."

16. Hitler, "Gespräch mit Eduard August Scharrer," end of December 1922, in Hitler: Sämtliche Aufzeichnungen, 1905-1924, ed. Eberhard Jäckel (Stuttgart: Deutsche Verlags-Anstalt, 1980), 775.

17. Hitler, *Mein Kampf*, 266–68.

18. Adolf Hitler, speech on February 15, 1933, in *The Speeches of Adolf Hitler, April 1922–August 1939*, 2 vols., ed. Norman H. Baynes (Oxford: Oxford University Press, 1942), 1:240.

19. Adolf Hitler, monologue on October 24, 1941, in *Monologe im Führerhauptquartier 1941–1944: Die Aufzeichnungen Heinrich Heims*, ed. Werner Jochmann (Hamburg: Albrecht Knaus, 1980), 103–4.

20. Adolf Hitler, speech on January 30, 1939, in Christian Dube, "Religiöser Sprache in Reden Adolf Hitlers: Analysiert an Hand ausgewählter Reden aus den Jahren 1933–1945" (dissertation, University of Kiel, 2004), 288, 296.

21. Gilmer Blackburn, *Education in the Third Reich: Race and History in Nazi Textbooks* (State University of New York Press, 1985), 67.

22. Dietrich, *The Hitler I Knew*, 19, 153.

23. Hitler, *Mein Kampf*, 285–87.

24. Adolf Hitler, speech at the Nuremberg Party Congress, 1937, in Christian Dube, "Religiöser Sprache in Reden Adolf Hitlers: Analysiert an Hand ausgewählter Reden aus den Jahren 1933–1945" (dissertation, University of Kiel, 2004), 252, 257–58.

25. Adolf Hitler, speech on January 30, 1943, in Max Domarus, *The Complete Hitler: A Digital Desktop Reference to His Speeches and Proclamations, 1932–1945* (Wauconda: Bolchazy-Carducci Publishers, 2007), 4:2749.

26. Adolf Hitler, proclamation (read by Himmler), November 12, 1944, in Max Domarus, *The Complete Hitler: A Digital Desktop Reference to His Speeches and Proclamations, 1932–1945* (Wauconda: Bolchazy-Carducci Publishers, 2007), 4:2964.

27. Adolf Hitler, monologue on December 1–2, 1941, in *Monologe im Führerhauptquartier 1941–1944: Die Aufzeichnungen Heinrich Heims*, ed. Werner Jochmann (Hamburg: Albrecht Knaus, 1980), 148–49.

28. Cardinal Faulhaber, "Bericht Faulhabers über eine Unterredung mit Hitler," November 4–5, 1936, in *Akten Kardinal Michael von Faulhabers, 1917–1945*, vol. 2: 1935–1945, ed. Ludwig Volk (Mainz: Matthias-Grünewald, 1978), 194.

29. Hitler, *Mein Kampf*, 383.

30. Ibid., 132.

31. Adolf Hitler, "Tageskampf oder Schicksalskampf," March 3, 1928, in *Hitler: Reden, Schriften, Anordnungen, Febraur 1925 bis Januar 1933*, vol. II: Vom Weimarer Parteitag bus zur Reichstagswahl Juli 1926–Mai 1928, part 2: August 1927–May 1928, ed. Bärbel Dusik (Munich: K. G. Saur, 1992–2003), 722–27.

32. Adolf Hitler, speech on May 20, 1937, in "Es spricht der Führer": 7 exemplarische Hitler-Reden, ed. Hildegard von Kotze and Helmut Krausnick (Gütersloh: Sigbert Mohn Verlag, 1966), 220–21.

33. "Ansprache Hitlers vor Generalen und Offizieren am 26. Mai 1944 im Platterhof," in Hans-Heinrich Wilhelm, "Hitlers Ansprache vor Generalen und Offizieren am 26. Mai 1944," Militärgeschichtliche Mitteilungen 2 (1976): 146–47, 155–56. Thomas Schirrmacher, *Hitlers Kriegsreligion: Die Verankerung der Weltanschauung Hitlers in seiner religiösen Begrifflichkeit und seinem Gottesbild*, 2 vols. (Bonn: Verlag für Kultur und Wissenschaft, 2007), stresses the importance of social Darwinism in shaping Hitler's "war religion."

34. Adolf Hitler, "Appell an die deutsche Kraft," August 4, 1929, in *Hitler: Reden, Schriften, Anordnungen, Febraur 1925 bis Januar 1933*, vol. III: Zwischen den Reichstagswahlen, Juli 1928–September 1930, part 2: März 1929–Dezember 1929 (Munich: K. G. Saur, 1992–2003), 348–49.

35. Wagener, *Hitler—Memoirs of a Confidant*, 40, 315, 146–47.

36. Adolf Hitler, speech on May 1, 1923, in *Hitler: Sämtliche Aufzeichnungen, 1905–1924*, ed. Eberhard Jäckel (Stuttgart: Deutsche Verlags-Anstalt, 1980), 920.

37. Adolf Hitler, speech on October 8, 1935, in Max Domarus, *The Complete Hitler: A Digital Desktop Reference to His Speeches and Proclamations, 1932–1945* (Wauconda: Bolchazy-Carducci Publishers, 2007), 2:716.

38. Adolf Hitler, speech on October 6, 1935, in Max Domarus, *The Complete Hitler: A Digital Desktop Reference to His Speeches and Proclamations, 1932–1945* (Wauconda: Bolchazy-Carducci Publishers, 2007), 2:716.

39. Adolf Hitler, speech on March 16, 1936, in Max Domarus, *The Complete Hitler: A Digital Desktop Reference to His Speeches and Proclamations, 1932–1945* (Wauconda: Bolchazy-Carducci Publishers, 2007), 2:792.

40. Adolf Hitler, "Hitler zum 17. Jahrestag des Beginns der nationalen Erhebung am 24. Februar 1937," in "Es spricht der Führer": 7 exemplarische Hitler-Reden, ed. Hildegard von Kotze and Helmut Krausnick (Gütersloh: Sigbert Mohn Verlag, 1966), 96, 109.

41. Adolf Hitler, speech on February 28, 1926, in *Hitler: Reden, Schriften, Anordnungen, Februar 1925 bis Januar 1933*, vol. I: Die Widergründung der NSDAP Februar 1925–Juni 1926, ed. Clemens Vollnhals (Munich: K. G. Saur, 1992–2003), 330.

42. Hitler, *Mein Kampf*, 214.

43. Adolf Hitler, speech on February 10, 1933, in Max Domarus, *The Complete Hitler: A Digital Desktop Reference to His Speeches and Proclamations, 1932–1945* (Wauconda: Bolchazy-Carducci Publishers, 2007), 1:247.

44. Adolf Hitler, speech to Nuremberg Party Congress, 1935, in *The Speeches of Adolf Hitler, April 1922–August 1939*, 2 vols., ed. Norman H. Baynes (Oxford: Oxford University Press, 1942), 1:441.

45. "Adolf Hitlers Geheimrede vom 23. November 1937 auf der Ordensburg Sonthofen," in *Hitlers Tischgespräche im Führerhauptquartier*, ed. Henry Picker (Frankfurt: Ullstein, 1989), 485.

46. Adolf Hitler, speech on August 1, 1923, in *Adolf Hitler spricht: Ein Lexikon des Nationalsozialismus* (Leipzig: R. Kittler Verlag, 1934), 71.

47. Adolf Hitler, "Warum sind wir Antisemiten?" August 13, 1920, in *Hitler: Sämtliche Aufzeichnungen, 1905–1924*, ed. Eberhard Jäckel (Stuttgart: Deutsche Verlags-Anstalt, 1980), 190.

48. Dietrich Eckart, *Der Bolschewismus von Moses bis Lenin. Zwiegespräch zwischen Adolf Hitler und mir* (Munich: Hoheneichen Verlag, 1924), 33.

49. Adolf Hitler, "Warum sind wir Antisemiten?" August 13, 1920, in *Hitler: Sämtliche Aufzeichnungen, 1905–1924*, ed. Eberhard Jäckel (Stuttgart: Deutsche Verlags-Anstalt, 1980), 202.

50. Hans Frank, *Im Angesicht des Galgens: Deutung Hitlers und seiner Zeit auf Grund eigener Erlebnisse und Erkenntnisse* (Munich-Gräfelfing: Friedrich Alfred Beck Verlag, 1953), 46.

51. Goebbels, diary entry on December 14, 1941, in *Die Tagebücher von Joseph Goebbels, ed. Elke* Fröhlich, part II: Diktate 1941–1945, vol. 2: Oktober–Dezember 1941 (Munich: K. G. Saur, 1996), 506; Rosenberg recorded the same point in his entry for December 14, 1941, in Alfred Rosenberg Diaries, 625–27, http://collections.ushmm.org/view/2001.62.14; accessed January 22, 2014.

52. Adolf Hitler, speech at Nuremberg Party Congress, September 1933, in Christian Dube, "Religiöser Sprache in Reden Adolf Hitlers: Analysiert an Hand ausgewählter Reden aus den Jahren 1933-1945" (dissertation, University of Kiel, 2004), 200–2.

53. Adolf Hitler, monologue on October 17, 1941, in *Monologe im Führerhauptquartier 1941–1944: Die Aufzeichnungen Heinrich Heims*, ed. Werner Jochmann (Hamburg: Albrecht Knaus, 1980), 90–91.

54. Adolf Hitler, monologue on October 17, 1941, in *Monologe im Führerhauptquartier 1941–1944: Die Aufzeichnungen Heinrich Heims*, ed. Werner Jochmann (Hamburg: Albrecht Knaus, 1980), 90–91.

55. Adolf Hitler, *Second Book*, ed. Gerhard L. Weinberg (New York: Enigma Books, 2003), 18–19.

56. Adolf Hitler, speech on December 18, 1940, in Max Domarus, *The Complete Hitler: A Digital Desktop Reference to His Speeches and Proclamations, 1932–1945* (Wauconda: Bolchazy-Carducci Publishers, 2007), 3:2161.

57. Adolf Hitler, speech on December 18, 1940, Max Domarus, *The Complete Hitler: A Digital Desktop Reference to His Speeches and Proclamations, 1932–1945* (Wauconda: Bolchazy-Carducci Publishers, 2007), 3:2162.

58. See my discussion in chapter 9 of Adolf Hitler, "Ansprache des Führers vor Generalen und Offiziers am 22.6.1944 im Platterhof," in Hoover Institution, NSDAP Hauptarchiv, Reel 2, Folder 51; other examples are: "Adolf Hitlers Geheimrede vor dem 'Militärischen Führernachwuchs' vom 30. Mai 1942, 'War der Zweite Weltkrieg für Deutschland vermeidbar?'" in *Hitlers Tischgespräche im Führerhauptquartier*, ed. Henry Picker (Frankfurt: Ullstein, 1989), 491–502; Adolf Hitler, speech to officer cadets on May 3, 1940, in Max Domarus, *The Complete Hitler: A Digital Desktop Reference to His Speeches and Proclamations, 1932–1945* (Wauconda: Bolchazy-Carducci Publishers, 2007), 3:1981–82; "Hitler vor Offizieren und Offiziersanwärtern am 15. Februar 1942," in "Es spricht der Führer": 7 exemplarische Hitler-Reden, ed. Hildegard von Kotze and Helmut Krausnick (Gütersloh: Sigbert Mohn Verlag, 1966), 305–328.

59. "Hitler vor Offizieren und Offiziersanwärtern am 15. Februar 1942," in "Es spricht der Führer": 7 exemplarische Hitler-Reden, ed. Hildegard von Kotze and Helmut Krausnick (Gütersloh: Sigbert Mohn Verlag, 1966), 306–8.

60. Adolf Hitler, monologue on October 10, 1941, in *Monologe im Führerhauptquartier 1941–1944: Die Aufzeichnungen Heinrich Heims*, ed. Werner Jochmann (Hamburg: Albrecht Knaus, 1980), 76.

61. Goebbels, diary entry for December 11, 1940, in *Die Tagebücher von Joseph Goebbels*, ed. Elke Fröhlich, part I: Aufzeichnungen 1923–1941, vol. 9: Dezember 1940–Juli 1941 (Munich: K. G. Saur, 1998), 45–46.

62. Adolf Hitler, monologue on October 25, 1941, in *Monologe im Führerhauptquartier 1941–1944: Die Aufzeichnungen Heinrich Heims*, ed. Werner Jochmann (Hamburg: Albrecht Knaus, 1980), 109.

63. Adolf Hitler, monologue on May 12, 1942, in *Hitlers Tischgespräche im Führerhauptquartier*, ed. Henry Picker (Frankfurt: Ullstein, 1989), 288–89.

64. Adolf Hitler, monologue on March 1, 1942, in *Monologe im Führerhauptquartier 1941–1944: Die Aufzeichnungen Heinrich Heims*, ed. Werner Jochmann (Hamburg: Albrecht Knaus, 1980), 310–11.

CONCLUSION

1. Alfred Rosenberg, diary entry on January 19, 1940, in Alfred Rosenberg Diaries, 363, http://collections.ushmm.org/view/2001.62.14; accessed January 22, 2014.

2. Alfred Rosenberg, diary entry on January 19, 1940, in Alfred Rosenberg Diaries, 363, http://collections.ushmm.org/view/2001.62.14; accessed January 22, 2014.

3. Alfred Rosenberg, diary entry on September 11, 1940, in Alfred Rosenberg Diaries, 447, http://collections.ushmm.org/view/2001.62.14; accessed January 22, 2014.

4. See Richard Weikart, *Hitler's Ethic: The Nazi Pursuit of Evolutionary Progress* (New York: Palgrave Macmillan, 2009).

A NOTE ON SOURCES

1. Richard C. Carrier, *"Hitler's Table Talk*: Troubling Finds," *German Studies Review* 26 (2003): 561–76.

2. Theodor Schieder, *Hermann Rauschnings "Gespräche mit Hitler" als Geschichtsquelle* (Opladen: Westdeutscher Verlag, 1972).

3. Pia Nordblom, "Wider die These von der bewussten Fälschung. Bemerkungen zu den *Gesprächen mit Hitler*," in *Hermann Rauschning: Materialien und Beitrage zu einer politischen Biographie*, ed. Jürgen

Hensel and Pia Nordblom (Osnabrück: Fibre Verlag, 2003), 151–74. Christine von Braun also claims that Rauschning's portrayal of Hitler's religion is generally accurate in "Und der Feind ist Fleisch geworden: Der rassistische Antisemitismus," in *Der ewige Judenhass: Christlicher Antijudaismus Deutschnationale Judenfeindlichkeit Rassistischer Antisemitismus*, eds. Christine von Braun and Ludger Heid (Berlin: Philo, 2000), 149–50 and 211, n.1.

4. Hermann Rauschning, *Gespräche mit Hitler* (New York: Europa Verlag, 1940), 51.

5. Reichspropaganda-Leitung der N.S.D.A.P., *Tatsachen und Lügen um Hitler*, 2nd ed. (Munich: Franz Eher Nachf., n.d. [1932]), 10–11.

6. Christa Schroeder, *Er War Mein Chef: Aus dem Nachlass der Sekretärin von Adolf Hitler*, ed. Anton Jaochimsthaler, 2nd ed. (Munich: Langen Müller, 1985), 18–24.

7. Ian Kershaw, *Hitler,1936–1945: Nemesis* (New York: Norton, 2000), 1024–25, n. 121.

8. Richard Steigmann-Gall, "Old Wine in New Bottles? Religion and Race in Nazi Antisemitism," *Antisemitism Christian Ambivalence, and the Holocaust*, ed. Kevin P. Spicer (Indianapolis: Indiana University Press, 2007), 299–300; Robert Michael, *Holy Hatred: Christianity, Antisemitism, and the Holocaust* (New York: Palgrave Macmillan, 2006), 181.

INDEX